A-LEVEL
AND AS-LEVEL

ACCOUNTING

Geoff Black and Trevor Daff

Longman

LONGMAN A AND AS-LEVEL REVISE GUIDES

Series editors:
Geoff Black and Stuart Wall

Titles available:
Accounting
Art and Design
Biology
Business Studies
Chemistry
Computer Studies
Economics
English
French
Geography
Modern History
Mathematics
Physics
Sociology

Longman Group UK Limited,
Longman House, Burnt Mill, Harlow,
Essex CM20 2JE, England
and Associated Companies throughout the world.

© Longman Group UK Limited 1994

First published 1994

British Library Cataloguing-in-Publication Data

A catalogue record for this book is available from the
British Library

ISBN 0-582-22569-8 PPR

Set by 6QQ in 10/12pt Century Old Style

Printed in Great Britain by William Clowes Ltd.,
Beccles and London

CONTENTS

ACKNOWLEDGEMENTS

The authors and publishers are grateful to the following exam boards for permission to reproduce past examination questions:

Associated Examining Board (AEB)
Northern Examining and Assessment Board (Northern)
Oxford Delegacy of Local Examinations (Oxford)
University of Cambridge Local Examinations Syndicate (Cambridge)
University of London Examinations and Assessment Council (London)
Welsh Joint Education Committee (Wales)

The comments, outline answers and tutor's answers are entirely the responsibility of the authors and have neither been provided nor approved by the exam boards.

We are grateful to the BOC Group plc for granting permission to reproduce extracts from its published accounts, and to Atreus plc for permission to reproduce their offer for sale advertisement. The Financial Times has also kindly granted permission to reproduce an extract from its market prices section.

AUTHORS' PREFACE

Students of A-level Accounting come from a very wide range of ages and background. Many study the subject at night class over just one year, whilst overseas candidates are usually pupils at schools, with their courses lasting a full two years. Some students are already working in offices and want to know more about the finance function, others see the subject as providing a useful qualification for gaining employment.

The demands on all these students are high, as the subject requires not only numeracy, but also good communication and literacy. Indeed, the trend for several years has been away from questions requiring 'advanced book-keeping', to those which need higher skills such as interpretation and analysis.

We hope that you will enjoy your course, and gain success in the examinations. For those who have not studied accounting before, the guide starts with a thorough revision of basic double-entry principles. As well as providing an introduction to the newcomer, it serves as a useful refresher to those who have some knowledge.

The book itself has two main sections, Financial Accounting (Chapters 3 to 11) and Management Accounting (Chapters 12 to 20), which coincide with the way that most A-level syllabuses are structured. Any suggestions, from teachers or students, for improving the book will be gratefully received and possibly incorporated into future editions.

Geoff Black and Trevor Daff

SYLLABUSES AND THE EXAMINATION

STUDYING ACCOUNTING

THE SYLLABUSES

METHODS OF ASSESSMENT

GETTING STARTED

This Revise Guide is intended to be of use to students taking an examination course in Accounting at A-level, AS-level or Scottish Higher Grade. The book is also useful for students of the financial accounting or cost and management accounting examinations of the LCCI, RSA and Pitman. The book offers a systematic review of all the major areas covered in all the syllabuses, gives guidance on how to study Accounting for examinations and provides a large number of examination questions with answers. These questions have either *full answers* provided by the authors, *student answers* with examiner's comments or *outline answers*.

Review sheets at the end of the book are provided to reinforce the principles studied within the chapters. After completion, detach them from the book and add them to your own notes. They provide a useful overview of the topics.

A syllabus summary is given in this chapter which is cross referenced to chapter numbers. Be aware that individual questions may be drawn from several areas of the syllabus.

ESSENTIAL PRINCIPLES

STUDYING ACCOUNTING	A-level Accounting has become increasingly popular over the years, particularly for candidates returning to study who find it an interesting and relevant preparation for higher education, professional training or employment.

Those students who study at night class tend to join a one-year course, often following a pattern where Financial Accounting is studied in the first term, Management Accounting in the second term, with the third term devoted to revision. This is far from ideal, as the A-level syllabus is designed to be studied over a full two years. Consequently, there is often a high drop-out rate for night class students, who start with enthusiasm, but feel 'burned out' at the end of the first term. We hope that this study guide will give encouragement to such students to persevere with their course and to take the exams. Some Exam Groups (including London, Cambridge and AEB) offer their exams twice a year, so even if a candidate's result is poor, it is possible to do a retake after a short period of further study.

THE SYLLABUSES	Accounting is offered at A-level by nearly all UK examination boards, and at AS-level by AEB and Oxford. All boards assess by examination. There is no assessed coursework component.

Figure 1.1 shows an analysis of examination syllabuses by topic and chapter. If possible, try and obtain your own copy of the syllabus, by writing to the exam board.

METHODS OF ASSESSMENT (A-LEVEL)	All the A-level Accounting syllabuses are examined with two 3 hour papers, as follows:

ASSOCIATED EXAMINING BOARD (AEB)

(available in June and November)

Two papers carrying equal marks, each divided into two sections.
Section A contains three compulsory questions.
Sections B and C each contain two questions, and candidates must answer one from each section.

CAMBRIDGE (UCLES)

(available in June and November)

Two papers of equal weighting, containing six questions of which two are compulsory. Questions on managerial accounting are set in Paper 2 only.

LONDON (ULEAC)

(available in June and January)

Two papers of equal weighting, each split into three sections.
Section A contains three questions of 25 marks each of which two must be answered.
Section B contains three questions of 15 marks each of which two must be answered.
Section C contains two questions of 20 marks each of which one must be answered. These are usually essay-type questions.
Paper 1 contains mainly questions on financial accounting,
Paper 2 contains questions mainly on management accounting.

Chapter	AEB A	Cambridge A	London A	NEAB A**	Oxford A	N. Ireland A	Wales A	AEB AS	Oxford AS Financial Acc'ting	Oxford AS Management Acc'ting	Scottish Higher Grade (Accounting & Finance)
3 The double-entry system (1)	/	/	/	/	/	/	/	/*	/		/
4 The double-entry system (2)	/	/	/	/	/	/	/	/*	/		/
5 Control accounts and incomplete records	/	/	/	/	/	/	/	/	/		/
6 Accounting for partnerships	/	/	/	/	/	/	/	/	/		/
7 Accounting and financial reporting standards	/	/	/	/	/	/	/	/†	/		/
8 Accounting for limited liability companies (1)	/	/	/	/	/	/	/	/	/		/
9 Accounting for limited liability companies (2)	/	/	/	/	/	/	/	/	/		/
10 Cash flow statements	/	/	/	/	/	/	/	/	/		/
11 Interpretation of accounts	/	/	/	/	/	/	/	/	/		/
12 An introduction to management accounting	/	/	/	/	/	/	/	/		/	/
13 Material costs	/	/	/	/	/	/	/	/		/	/
14 Labour costs	/	/	/	/	/	/	/	/		/	/
15 Overhead apportionment	/	/	/	/	/	/	/			/	/
16 Product costing	/	/	/	/	/	/	/			/	/
17 Absorption and marginal costing	/	/	/	/	/	/	/			/	/
18 Budgets and budgetary control	/	/	/	/	/	/	/			/	/
19 Standard costing	/	/	/	/	/	/	/	/		/	/
20 Investment appraisal	/	/	/	/	/	/	/	/		/	/

* candidates are not expected to have a detailed knowledge of the double-entry system

† a broad knowledge of generally accepted accounting principles and major developments in accounting practice

** Subject title: Principles of Accounts

Fig. 1.1 Analysis of examination syllabuses by topic and chapter

NORTHERN (NEAB)

(available in June only)

Two papers of equal weighting, each split into two sections.
Section A contains two questions of which one must be answered (40% of total marks).
Section B contains five questions of which three must be answered (60% of total marks).
Paper 1 contains questions mainly on financial accounting,
Paper 2 contains questions mainly on management accounting.

OXFORD (ODLES)

(available in June only)

Two papers of equal weighting, each split into two sections.
Section A contains two questions of which one must be answered (31% of total marks).
Section B contains four questions of which three must be answered (69% of total marks).
Both sections will require calculations and the use of continuous prose.

NORTHERN IRELAND (NISEAC)

(available in June only)

Two papers of equal weighting, each split into two sections.
Section A contains three questions (max. 20 marks each) of which two must be answered (40% of total marks).
Section B contains four questions (max. 15 marks each) of which three must be answered (60% of total marks).

WALES (WJEC)

(available in June only)

Two papers of equal weighting. Each contains two compulsory questions (worth 30 marks and 15 marks respectively) and three further questions, one from each of the following pairs:

Question 3A or 3B
Question 4A or 4B
Question 5A or 5B

The mark allocation between the three pairs of questions will not be uniform.

METHODS OF ASSESSMENT (AS-LEVEL)

AEB (AS)

(available in June only)

Two papers with a total examination time of 3 hours.
Paper 1 (1 hour) worth 40% of total marks, requires candidates to answer compulsory questions based upon source material provided.
Paper 2 (2 hours) is in two sections:
Section A (30% of total marks) contains one compulsory structured question.
Section B (30% of total marks) contains three structured questions of which the candidate must answer two. Both papers may include computational questions and require the use of continuous prose.

OXFORD (AS)

(available in June only)

Two separate AS examinations are available, Financial Accounting and Management Accounting.

FINANCIAL ACCOUNTING

One 3-hour written paper, split into two parts,
   Section A contains two questions of which one must be answered (31% of total marks).
   Section B contains four questions of which three must be answered (69% of total marks).
   Both sections will require calculations and the use of continuous prose.

MANAGEMENT ACCOUNTING

One 3-hour written paper, split into two parts,
   Section A contains two questions of which one must be answered (31% of total marks).
   Section B contains four questions of which three must be answered (69% of total marks).
   Both sections will require calculations and the use of continuous prose.

METHODS OF ASSESSMENT (SCOTTISH HIGHER GRADE)

❝❞ The only exam with a computer based assignment ❝❞

Three papers, as follows:

Paper I, worth 80 marks, with an emphasis on Financial Accounting
Paper II, worth 80 marks, with an emphasis on Managerial Accounting
Paper III, worth 40 marks. This is a computer-based assignment.

Paper I ($2\frac{1}{4}$ hours) is in three sections:

Section A (computational question, 25 marks) contains one compulsory question which will involve the preparation of the final accounts and balance sheet of a limited company. Candidates will also be required to interpret financial information and/or prepare accounting statements.
   Section B contains three essay-type questions (15 marks each) of which one must be answered.
   Section C contains five questions, one of which will be an essay-style question (20 marks each). Two questions must be answered from this section.

Paper II ($2\frac{1}{4}$ hours) is in three sections:

Section A (computational question, 25 marks) contains one compulsory question which will involve making production decisions. Candidates will be required to interpret managerial information and/or prepare accounting statements.
   Section B contains three essay-type questions (15 marks each) of which one must be answered.
   Section C contains five questions, one of which will be an essay-style question (20 marks each). Two questions must be answered from this section.

Paper III

This is a computer-based assignment in which candidates are required to edit/amend and print a spreadsheet to show given accounting information. In response to defined extraneous factors, candidates will make appropriate adjustments to that information and report on the consequences.

CHAPTER 2

HOW TO STUDY, REVISE AND TAKE EXAMS

DURING THE COURSE

THE REVISION PERIOD

THE DAY OF THE EXAMINATION

THE EXAMINATION

TYPES OF QUESTIONS

AFTER THE EXAMINATION

GETTING STARTED

The golden rule concerning examination techniques is that there is no golden rule. Each examination candidate is an individual whose approach must allow for different circumstances and attitudes. What is certain, however, is that the candidates who pace their work at a steady rate throughout their course have a far better chance of gaining success than those who leave their efforts until the last moment. With this principle in mind, this chapter is designed to help you get organised during your course, in the pre-exam revision period, and for the exam itself.

Complete the work at a steady pace, and endeavour to hand work in on time. Explain to your teachers why you are unable to meet deadlines; they may be sympathetic! Be prepared to ask questions, either during the lecture or informally after the lecture. Don't 'suffer in silence' as this does you no good, and may lead the lecturer to believe that you do not need any help. If there are personal problems which are disrupting your study pattern, many schools and colleges have counselling services, or else discuss the problems with friends or relations.

Get into the habit of reading a quality newspaper. This will help you to keep abreast of current financial affairs and appreciate good literary styles, which will be useful when you need to write your own essays.

ESSENTIAL PRINCIPLES

DURING THE COURSE

Many students find it useful to make their own notes of each topic as they progress through the course. This serves to reinforce the learning process and provides excellent revision material when used in conjunction with this book. Try and get hold of a recent annual report of a major company. This will help you to appreciate the scope and complexity of published company financial statements. If you have difficulty in obtaining one, your nearest public library should be able to give you the address or phone number of a local Public Limited Company (plc). Usually such companies are very willing to send out copies. The Financial Times has an annual report service, where reports can be obtained by phoning 081 643 7181, quoting code FT OF1 and stating the name of the company whose report you want to receive. The service is free. For overseas students, try contacting a local office of a British multinational company.

>> Get an annual report <<

>> Find out what the examiners think <<

Examiner's reports are regularly produced by most Exam Boards, so ask your teacher if a copy is available. Some Boards are now publishing mark schemes and answers to A-level questions.

THE REVISION PERIOD

Revision is often undertaken in a haphazard way, when it should be approached in a logical and structured manner, particularly when several examinations are being taken. One way of achieving this is to prepare a revision planner, which sets out the work to be covered and the time available. This could be set out as shown in Figure 2.1.

Week	Date	Target	Done	Notes
8	3 April	Revise all of double-entry system	✓	Re-check control accounts
7				
6				
5				
4				
3				
2				
1				
Exams				

Fig. 2.1 Revision planner, with sample entry

The planner should allow time for some leisure activities, and be reasonably flexible. For example, there is no point in *forcing* yourself to work when you are over-tired. It is more beneficial to have a good night's sleep.

Use past examination papers and questions to help you to revise. Be strict over time allocations, and try and answer questions within the time allowed.

As the examination date draws near, establish the precise location of the exam hall, and make all necessary travel preparations. Check on writing materials, calculator, watch etc. Make an 'exam pack' to keep them all together. Include any official exam entry documents.

On the day before the examination, spend some time in reading through your notes. Get to bed early, and *set an alarm clock*!

THE DAY OF THE EXAMINATION

Have your usual breakfast, and choose clothes which are comfortable, and loose-fitting. Find your 'exam pack', and leave for the examination hall in good time, allowing for events such as traffic delays.

THE EXAMINATION

If you are allowed to choose your position in the hall, find a location which is well lit (but not in the full glare of the sun). Where possible, avoid desks which are next to radiators or the entrance doors.

Read the rubric carefully. You are not allowed any reading time before the exam, so you should commence by confirming the number of questions to be answered from each section. Read through the paper and identify a question on a topic on which you feel confident. Be careful to allocate the time available. In a three hour exam, a rough guide is 1.7 minutes per mark. This allows ten minutes for reading and checking your work.

Read *all* the questions. Make sure that you understand what is being asked, so that when you come to make your choice you are fully aware of the implications. Sometimes a question may be different from what it seems at first glance; make sure you read all the questions thoroughly.

Beware, too, of misinterpreting a question; a question asking how a system on budgetary control should be introduced does not require an answer on the advantages of budgetary control. If the question asks why it is important to control waste and scrap, you are not asked to state how these items might be controlled.

Sometimes, an essay question may contain within itself more than one part: *what are the functions of management accounting* and *how are these functions carried out?* It is essential to answer both the *what* and the *how*.

Having read the paper fully, and being aware of the choice available, you can choose your questions, and allocate the time for each based upon the marks they carry. Aim to attempt all the questions asked of you, even though you may be more confident of some than of others; and begin with what for you seems an easy question. In this way you begin by building on success, and your confidence increases once you have one good answer under your belt. It is not necessary to begin by answering any compulsory questions.

> **Answer the easiest question first**

Do not answer more questions than you are required: you will not receive additional credit, and you will have wasted time.

It is usually easier to earn the first half of the marks allocated for a question than for the second half, so it is essential that you do not exceed your time allocation for each question (see Figure 2.2). Be self-disciplined, and go on to the next question. Use the last ten minutes for tidying up.

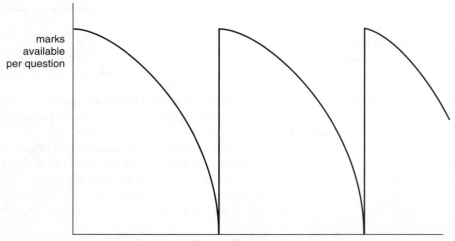

marks available per question

time for question 1.......   time for question 2......

Fig. 2.2 Time and marks per question

TYPES OF QUESTIONS

In A level Accounting examinations, there are three types of questions;

1.   those which require only a numerical response (for example, a question where an income and expenditure account has to be prepared)

2.   those which require both a numerical and a written response (for example, a question which not only requires an income and expenditure account to be drawn up, but also asks for an explanation of the weaknesses of a receipts and payments account)

3.   those which require only an essay response. Some exam papers (e.g. London and Wales) have separate sections with essay type questions. A typical question here might be in connection with the fundamental concepts of accounting, and why a receipts and payments account does not abide by the accruals concept.

NUMERICAL QUESTIONS

Examiners are often frustrated when candidates appear to know something about a topic, but do not show sufficient workings as to how they arrived at their figures. For example, in a question involving a trading account, a sales figure might have to be calculated as the balancing figure in a control account. Assume that the control account was as follows:

❝❝ Show your workings ❞❞

Sales Ledger Control Account

Debtors b/f	34,567	Cash received	98,850
Sales Invoices	99,677	Discount allowed	3,400
(balancing figure)		Bad Debts	4,800
		Debtors c/f	27,194
	134,244		134,244

Let us assume that 5 marks were allocated by the examiner for the correct calculation of 'Sales £99,677'. Three candidates attempted the question, all correctly calculated the sales figure, but one got 5 marks, another got 4 marks whilst the third got no marks at all. Here's why:

Candidate 1 got all the calculations correct, showed the correct Sales figure in the Trading Account, and also showed the control account as a working. This candidate was awarded the full 5 marks.

Candidate 2 got all the calculations correct, showed the control account as a working, but wrote the sales figure in the Trading Account as £98,677. This candidate would lose only one mark for the mistake, so scored 4 marks.

Candidate 3 got all the calculations correct on her calculator, but didn't show the control account as a working. She wrote the sales figure as £99,766 by mistake. As the examiner had no way of knowing where she got her figure from, no marks could be awarded.

THE 'ONE ERROR, ONE PENALTY' PRINCIPLE

Everybody makes some mistakes in an examination, and examiners are careful not to over-penalise candidates whose mistakes have a 'knock-on' effect causing other figures to be wrong.

For example, Candidates 2 and 3 mentioned above both got the sales figure wrong in their Trading Accounts. An incorrect sales figure also means an incorrect:

—gross profit
—net profit
—reserves (or capital account)

Although up to four figures will be wrong, the only penalty will be for the original mistake in recording the sales figure.

'OWN FIGURE' MARKS

Examiners are often instructed to allow marks for students 'own figures', where the principle behind an incorrect figure is sound. For example, if a gross profit percentage has been correctly calculated on the basis of an *incorrectly calculated* gross profit figure, the candidate will be awarded marks, even though the end result will not be correct. This follows on from the 'one error, one penalty' principle.

ROUGH WORK OR 'WORKINGS'?

66 'Workings' can also be called 'Calculations' 99

Rough work is that which is in draft or note form, which you *don't want to be marked*. It should be crossed through, but still submitted with the rest of your script. 'Workings' is another name for 'Explanation of Calculations', and the importance of these has already been stated.

UNCERTAINTIES AND ASSUMPTIONS

Sometimes candidates have to make their own assumptions when answering questions. This may be a deliberate part of the question, for example where a candidate has to report on a company's prospects. Occasionally, the candidate may wish to state an assumption so that an alternative answer can be presented to the question.

There should be no real problem here, provided that the assumptions are stated clearly as part of the answer. If the assumption is unrealistic, then the examiner is unlikely to award marks.

NOTES TO THE EXAMINER

Although it is alleged that examiners are human beings, they are totally unresponsive to emotional appeals and other pleas appended to exam scripts, so don't waste time in writing them. If there are any genuine causes for grievance or special consideration, then contact your exam centre or invigilator *as soon as possible*.

NUMERICAL AND WRITTEN RESPONSE QUESTIONS

Where there is a combination of both a numerical and written response required in a question, then make sure that *all parts* of the question are answered.

A long question may be broken down into three or more sections. For example, a London Board question in 1990 gave two company balance sheets, and asked the following questions:

(a) Calculate the following ratios for both of the companies;
    (i) the gearing ratio
    (ii) the working capital ratio
    (iii) return on capital employed

(7 marks)

(b) Comment briefly on the significance of the ratios which you have calculated in (a)

(6 marks)

(c) List SIX important financial matters (three for each company) which should be taken into consideration by a person who intends to invest in the ordinary shares of either company.

(12 marks)

Using the guide of 1.7 minutes per mark, this gave the time allocations (to the nearest minute) as (a) 12 minutes (b) 10 minutes and (c) 20 minutes.

Candidates who saw this as predominantly a numerical question spent perhaps 30 minutes on (a), and the balance of time split between the two other parts. Candidates aiming for high grades allocated their time wisely, and gave appropriate weighting to all three parts of the question.

SOLELY 'WRITTEN RESPONSE' QUESTIONS

Not all Exam Boards have questions which require exclusively non-numerical answers, but you can expect to use essay writing skills in some degree whichever Board sets your paper. When answering a question, use rough notes to marshal your facts, before drawing them together in your answer. Avoid 'waffle'; the best answers are those which are concise and relevant. If you are short of time, write your answer in note form.

Be as neat as possible; remember that an examiner has to read your answer, and is unlikely to be impressed with untidy work. Never waste time in writing out the question at the head of your answer, there are no marks to be gained by this. Keep the use of abbreviations to a minimum, and in any case only use those which are likely to be readily understood by the examiner, e.g. P&L, NPV, B/E Point.

When you set out most types of financial statements (e.g. Trial Balance, P&L a/c, Balance Sheet and Cash Flow Statement) don't forget to start with the '3W's';

●● Wt abbns cn be usd? ●●

●● The 3 W's ●●

- Who? — the name of the business
- What? — the type of statement (e.g. 'Cash Flow Statement')
- When? — the exact period it covers (e.g. 'for the year ended 31 December 1993)

Use the full time allocation allowed and don't be tempted to leave the exam hall early. If you have completed the required number of questions with time to spare, go back to the beginning of your answers, correcting errors and generally reviewing and neatening your work. Remember that even one extra mark gained in this way could mean the difference between success and failure.

AFTER THE EXAMINATION

Once the examination is over, it is better not to indulge in a 'post-mortem', as it may only serve to depress you when you compare your own answers with the textbook. Gain comfort from the fact that you do not need 100% to get a good grade. If you have given the examiner reasonably precise answers to the required number of questions, then success should be yours. If you have completed only the first paper make sure that you take the second one, even if you feel that you may have done badly. The examiner adds the marks from the two papers, and your grade is based on the *combined* mark. So, if you do better than expected on Paper 2, you can still get a reasonable grade.

THE DOUBLE-ENTRY SYSTEM (1)

THE BOOK-KEEPING SYSTEM

'FINAL' ACCOUNTS

CAPITAL EXPENDITURE OR REVENUE EXPENDITURE?

ACCRUALS AND PREPAYMENTS

DISPOSALS OF FIXED ASSETS

THE JOURNAL

GETTING STARTED

Students commencing their A-level Accounting course may previously have spent some time in a study of book-keeping, perhaps for GCSE. It is advisable, therefore, at the outset to establish the ways in which accounting differs from book-keeping, and the following definitions can be considered.

Book-keeping: The analysis, classification and recording of financial transactions in books of account.

Accounting: The analysis, classification and recording of financial transactions *and the ascertainment of how such transactions affect the performance and financial position of a business.*

Accounting, according to these definitions, takes over where book-keeping leaves off, and throughout this book it will be seen that the end use of the accounting information by 'non-accountants' is as important, if not of greater importance, as the provision by accountants of the 'means of production' via the book-keeping system. However, we must not lose sight of the fact that the accounting information will only be useful if the underlying book-keeping system can be relied upon to produce accurate and relevant data. Consequently, we shall use this chapter to revise some of the basic principles of book-keeping, and then look in detail at certain aspects which cause particular difficulties.

The study of accounting presupposes a good understanding of the double-entry system, and students who are in any doubt concerning the adequacy of their knowledge are advised to pay particular attention to the revision of basic principles which now follows.

ESSENTIAL PRINCIPLES

THE BOOK-KEEPING SYSTEM

The financial transactions of the business are methodically recorded in various books of account, collectively known as the 'double-entry book-keeping system'. This system has evolved over many centuries and has undergone comparatively few changes since the Middle Ages. The major change in recent years obviously concerns the word 'book', as the widespread use of computers by businesses of all sizes has meant a movement away from traditional pen and paper to the entries appearing on visual display units and computer print-outs. The underlying book-keeping system remains basically unaltered, but the speed with which the information can be processed and made available for interpretation has increased dramatically. In this Revise Guide (as in accounting examinations) the word 'book' is retained for convenience, but is used as a collective noun to include not only handwritten accounting records, but also mechanically and electronically processed systems.

BOOKS OF PRIME ENTRY

As the name implies, 'double-entry' book-keeping involves entering each financial transaction systematically in *two* locations within the records of the business. This is due to the recognition that there is a 'dual aspect' to each transaction; that the business both receives and gives value. For example, a business buying stock will

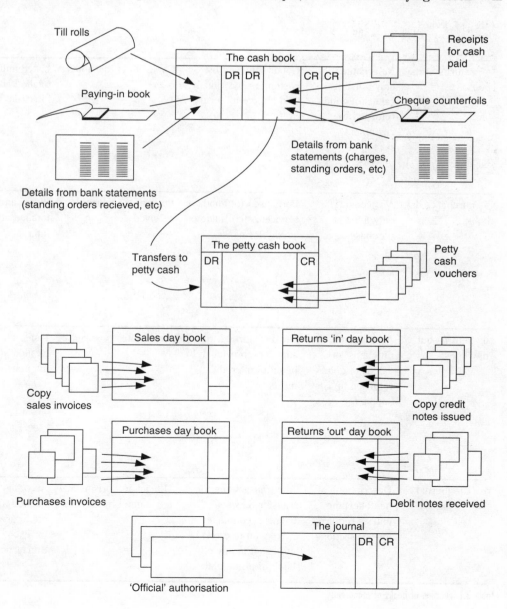

Fig. 3.1 The books of
prime entry

Name	Contents	Type of transactions	Source documents	How entered	Posted to:
1. Cash book	Cash account Bank account	Cash sales Cash from debtors Standing orders received Other cash receipts	Till rolls Sales summary sheets Bank statements Paying-in books	Debited	Credit of accounts in ledger
		Cheques paid Cash paid Standing orders paid	Cheque books Receipts for cash Bank statements	Credited	Debit of accounts in ledger
2. Petty cash book	Petty cash account	'Float' received from main cash account	Cashier's receipt	Debited	Credit of cash book
		Petty cash expenditure	Petty cash vouchers and accompanying receipts	Credited	Debit of ledger accounts
3. Sales day book	*No* accounts, only a list of sales	Sales made on 'credit' terms	Copies of sales invoices	Listed and totalled at intervals	Individual invoices to DR of customer's account in sales ledger, totals of invoices to CR of sales account in general ledger
4. Returns in day book	*No* accounts, only a list of values of goods returned by customers	Goods returned by customers (previously sold on 'credit' terms)	Copies of credit notes issued	Listed and totalled at intervals	Individual credit notes to CR of customer's account in sales ledger, totals of credit notes to DR of returns in account in general ledger
5. Purchases day book	*No* accounts, only a list of purchases	Purchases (of goods or services, etc.) made on 'credit' terms	Purchases invoices received	Listed and totalled at intervals	Individual invoices to CR of supplier's account in purchases ledger, total of invoices to DR of relevant accounts in general ledger
6. Returns out day book	*No* accounts, only a list of values of goods returned to suppliers	Goods returned to suppliers, previously bought on 'credit' terms	Debit notes received	Listed and totalled at intervals	Individual debit note to DR of supplier's account in purchases ledger, totals of debit notes to CR of returns out account in general ledger
7. The journal	Descriptions of book-keeping entries required for transactions	Any transactions (or transfer between ledger accounts, or correction of errors) not listed in any other book of prime entry	Official authorisation, e.g. signed by owner	Accounts to be debited and credit are shown for each transaction	DR and CR of ledger accounts as analysed in journal

Table 3.1 Function of books of prime entry

not only receive goods, but will also have to pay cash to the supplier. Similarly, when the business makes a sale, it not only receives cash from its customer, but also has to give goods or services in return.

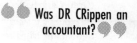

The record of 'receiving' and 'giving' is the essence of the double-entry system. As a general rule, entries on the debit (abbreviated DR) side of an account record value received, whilst entries on the credit (abbreviated CR) side record value given.

To be confident that all aspects of the business's financial life are fully recorded within the books, one must ensure that a system exists which is flexible enough to cope with the various types of transactions which occur. Figure 3.1 shows how information from various sources is processed at the first stage of the book-keeping system, by means of being entered in a 'book of prime entry', prior to being posted to the ultimate destination of a ledger account. Table 3.1 gives a detailed explanation of the function of each book.

In addition to providing the first link in the chain of accounting entries, books of prime entry are also used extensively by management as sources of reference, whether for purposes of day-to-day control, or for dealing with queries which may arise from customers or suppliers.

THE LEDGER

This is a collective title given to three separate books: the sales ledger, the purchases ledger and the general ledger. These act as 'books of secondary entry', taking information from the books of prime entry. Figure 3.2 illustrates the main routes of entries progressing from the books of prime entry into the ledger, and Table 3.2 is a summary of the contents of the three books which make up the ledger.

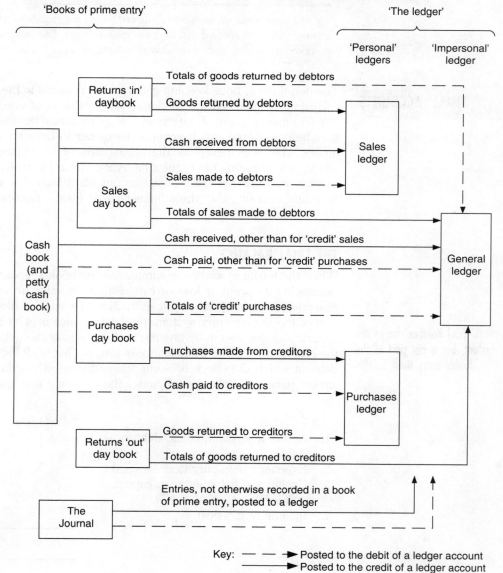

Fig. 3.2 The double-entry book-keeping system (showing Main 'routes' of entries)

Name	Contents	Entries posted from (Debit entries)	Entries posted from (Credit entries)
1. The sales ledger	The personal accounts of debtors, i.e. customers to whom the business sells on 'credit' terms	Sales invoices from sales day book	Returns in from returns in day book. Cash from cash book
2. The purchases ledger	The personal accounts of creditors, i.e. suppliers of goods and services from whom the business buys on 'credit' terms	Returns out from returns out day book. Cash paid, from cash book	Purchases invoices from purchases day book
3. The general ledger	'Impersonal' accounts of assets, liabilities, capital, income and expenditure*	Cash paid, from cash book. Purchase and expense invoice totals from purchases day book. Returns in totals from returns in day book	Cash received, from cash book. Sales invoice totals from sales day book. Returns out totals from returns out day book

* Three impersonal accounts are contained within the cash book and petty cash book: the cash account, the bank account and the petty cash account. The cash book and petty cash book are therefore technically part of the general ledger, as well as being 'books of prime entry'.

Table 3.2

'FINAL' ACCOUNTS

The definition of book-keeping given earlier referred to the 'analysis, classification and recording of financial transactions'. Whilst this is of course essential to ensure the efficient management of the day-to-day operations of the business, a further stage must now be considered which enables the owner to have an 'overview' of the business's affairs. This is achieved by the preparation of accounting summaries (often called simply 'the accounts') at regular intervals. These intervals, or 'financial periods', need not be of twelve months' duration, but each business will have to produce 'final accounts' covering the whole financial year for the purpose of taxation assessment.

THE TRIAL BALANCE

66 Trial Balance checks the system, but is not part of the double-entry itself 99

When the business wishes to summarise the book-keeping records for the purpose of calculating its profit or loss or establishing its value according to its books, then an essential preliminary step is the extraction of a 'trial balance'. Although not an integral part of the double-entry system, the trial balance acts as a check on the arithmetical accuracy of the system by proving that the total of the debit entries equals the total of the credit entries. The trial balance is simply a list of all the balances which exist at the date on which the check is being made, distinguishing between 'debit' balances and 'credit' balances. Balances fall under the following four major categories:

	Debit balances	Credit balances
1. Assets (e.g. plant, stock, debtors, cash)	X	
2. Expenses (e.g. purchases, wages)	X	
3. Capital and liabilities (e.g. capital, creditors)		X
4. Income (e.g. sales)		X
	X = equals =	X

Even though the trial balance agrees arithmetically, errors may still be present within the book-keeping system due to one or more of the following.

(a) Errors of commission, where the wrong person's account has been posted with the correct amount.
(b) Errors of omission, where a transaction has been completely omitted.
(c) Errors of principle, where the wrong type of account has been posted (e.g. rent posted to buildings account).
(d) Compensating errors, where two or more errors cancel each other.
(e) Errors of original entry, where the incorrect amount has been posted to the correct accounts.
(f) Reversed entries, where debit entries have been credited and vice-versa.

> ❛❛ COPCOR:
> Commission/Omission/
> Principle/
> Compensating/Original
> Entry/Reversals ❜❜

Despite the possibility of errors remaining, a 'balanced' trial balance still represents an invaluable check on the overall arithmetical accuracy of the entries, and previously undetected errors are often brought to light in the course of its preparation.

TRADING AND PROFIT AND LOSS ACCOUNTS AND THE BALANCE SHEET

The summary of the financial position of the business is divided into two distinct statements, the trading and profit and loss accounts, which show the 'income' or 'revenue' position over the entire financial period, and the balance sheet, which shows the 'capital' position (total net assets) of the business as at the last day of the financial period.

	'Income' or 'Revenue' Statement (Trading and Profit and Loss Account)			'Capital' Statement (the Balance Sheet)		
Trading Account	Sales	x		Fixed assets		x
	Less Cost of Sales	x		Current assets	x	
	Gross Profit	x		Less		
Profit and	Less Overheads	x		Current liabilities	x	x
						x
Loss Account	Net Profit	x		Capital		x

Note that the trading and profit and loss accounts are part of the double-entry system, but the balance sheet, like the trial balance, is merely a statement *extracted from the system*. Figure 3.3 illustrates the sources of entries in the 'final accounts'.

CAPITAL EXPENDITURE OR REVENUE EXPENDITURE?

We referred earlier to the trading and profit and loss accounts as the 'revenue' statement, and the balance sheet as the 'capital' statement. Expenditure can also be classified into 'capital' and 'revenue'. Why is this distinction so important? The answer lies in understanding the meaning of the two terms.

• *Revenue expenditure* is the cost incurred in the day-to-day running of the business, e.g. raw materials, wages, motor expenses, advertising.
• *Capital expenditure* relates to the purchase of fixed assets, i.e. those assets which are bought in order to be used by the business over several accounting periods, e.g. land and buildings, motor vehicles, computers.

All expenditure treated as 'revenue' has been debited (accountants often use the expression 'written off') either to the trading account or to the profit and loss account, thereby directly reducing the level of profit. If it had been incorrectly treated as 'capital' expenditure (e.g. petrol bills being added to the cost of a vehicle), then the effect is to both overstate the fixed assets on the balance sheet and also to overstate the net profit, due to expenses being understated. Not only is this misleading, but it may also lead to financial difficulties if the business believes that it is more profitable than it really is.

As the capital expenditure is used in the business, it usually loses value by reason of the increasing age of the fixed assets, or the gradual obsolescence caused by new technology. This loss of value is known as *depreciation*, and must be reflected in the revenue statement in the same way that other losses (expenses) are shown.

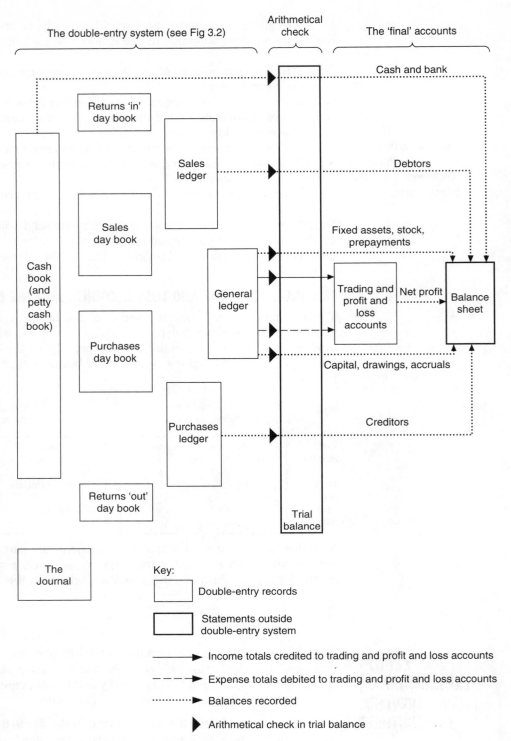

Fig. 3.3 The production of final accounts from the double-entry system

METHODS OF PROVIDING FOR DEPRECIATION

There are two main methods, the *straight line basis* and the *reducing balance basis*.

STRAIGHT LINE METHOD

This assumes that the loss in value of the fixed asset is spread evenly over the life of the asset. The annual depreciation is therefore calculated by using the following formula:

$$\frac{\text{Cost} - \text{'residual' value}}{\text{Estimated life in years}}$$

REDUCING BALANCE METHOD (ALSO CALLED 'DIMINISHING' BALANCE METHOD)

This method assumes that more depreciation is lost in the early years of the asset's life than in the later years. The calculation of the annual depreciation is made by applying a given percentage to the 'net book value' (cost less accumulated depreciation to the start of the year).

Note that depreciation does not necessarily set aside sufficient funds to provide for the eventual replacement of the asset. That is not the prime purpose of depreciation, as we are only reflecting the decline in value, rather than attempting to retain profits to buy new assets at the end of their useful lives.

OTHER PROVISIONS

The titles of the ledger accounts which record depreciation include the word 'provision', as the business is 'providing for' the loss in value of its fixed assets. Depreciation is an estimate, as no one really knows the true decline in value until the asset is sold. The business is being *prudent* (see Chapter 7) by reducing its profit to allow for the loss in value. Fixed assets are not however the only assets where a loss in value may take place. For example, losses (or reduced profits) may be incurred in one or more of the following circumstances.

- Customers failing to pay all or part of their sales ledger balances.
- Debtors taking advantage of discounts, thereby paying less into the business than the total of debtors disclosed on the balance sheet.
- Future unquantifiable expense, due to commitments under guarantees or warranties given by the business to customers.

In each of these cases, the most appropriate course of action is for the business to 'make provision' for the potential loss. Provisions can be either *specific* or *general*, the former being used where the source of the potential losses can be fairly accurately identified (e.g. 'doubtful' debtors, customers entitled to deduct discounts), the latter where this is not possible (e.g. future commitments under guarantees).

ACCRUALS AND PREPAYMENTS

The trading and profit and loss accounts summarise the revenue position over a particular period, usually a year. However, problems frequently arise due to the following:

1. Revenue expenditure 'consumed' in the financial period but not invoiced (or wages earned but not paid) until after the end of the period (e.g. an electricity account for the final three months of the financial year, not invoiced until six weeks after the year-end). Items falling within this category are referred to as 'accruals', and are current liabilities at the balance sheet date.

2. Payments made *during* the financial period, which relate to revenue expenditure either wholly or partly 'consumed' in the following financial period or periods (e.g. a payment for twelve months' insurance cover, only part of which relates to a period prior to the year-end, the remainder being related to the following financial year). These items are referred to as 'prepayments' and represent current assets at the balance sheet date.

3. Income received either in advance or in arrears (e.g. a tenant paying three months' rental prior to the financial year-end of the landlord, for a period following the financial year-end). Subscriptions paid to clubs and associations often 'overlap' the year-end and appropriate adjustments should be made to relate the receipts to the relevant years (See next chapter). Any income in advance is included as a current liability on the balance sheet, whilst income in arrears (i.e. due but not yet received) is shown as a current asset.

DISPOSALS OF FIXED ASSETS

The fixed assets and provision for depreciation accounts in the general ledger contain details of all fixed assets owned by the business, together with the depreciation charged over their lifetime. When a fixed asset is sold (or scrapped) we must ensure that the original cost and the total depreciation charged is removed from those accounts, and also make a calculation to show if the depreciation charged over its life was too much or too little when compared with the actual value when sold or scrapped. A transfer will be made to profit and loss account in the year of disposal to adjust for this 'over' or 'under' depreciation.

The book-keeping procedure to be adopted falls into two sections.

▶ *At the date of disposal*
Preliminary: Open a disposal of (named) fixed asset account

(a)   Enter the sale proceeds (DR cash a/c or debtor's a/c CR disposal a/c).

▶ *At the end of the financial period*

PCDB – Proceeds/ Cost/Depreciation/ Balance

(b)   Transfer the original cost (DR disposal a/c CR fixed asset a/c).
(c)   Transfer the *total* depreciation over the asset's life (DR provision for depreciation a/c CR disposal a/c).
(d)   Transfer the balance on the disposal account as follows:
(i)   A credit balance is transferred to the credit of profit and loss account, and represents an *overprovision* for depreciation in previous years (often referred to as a 'profit on sale').
(ii)   A debit balance is posted to the debit side of profit and loss account and represents an *underprovision* for depreciation in previous years (often referred to as a 'loss on sale').

The result of the above entries is to acknowledge that the asset no longer belongs to the business, and that both the fixed assets total and the provision for depreciation must be reduced accordingly. The amount of net profit is either increased or decreased dependent upon whether too much depreciation had been written off the asset (i.e. the 'book value' at the date of sale was lower than the 'real value') or too little depreciation had been written off (i.e. the 'book value' was greater than the 'real value').

THE JOURNAL

The day books referred to earlier in the chapter might also be called 'journals', but there is a separate book of prime entry, specifically called 'the journal' which has a very specialised function within the double-entry system.

Whilst the vast majority of a business's transactions follow one of the 'conventional' routes into the ledger, via the cash book or a day book (see Figure 3.2), there is a small number of transactions which cannot follow these routes. These include the following:

- Transfers between accounts.
- Correction of errors.
- Creation of, and alterations to, reserves and provisions.
- Adjustments for accruals and prepayments.
- Any other 'non-routine' transactions, e.g. the entries required on the disposal of fixed assets.

The journal simply provides a summary of the book-keeping entries required to record the transaction, together with a brief statement by way of explanation, known as a 'narration' or 'narrative'.

EXAMINATION QUESTIONS

1   The following trial balance as at 30 April 1992 has been extracted from the books of trader Boris Penfield by John Smith a very keen, but inexperienced, accounts clerk:

	£	£
Business premises: at cost	48 000	
provision for depreciation	13 000	
Motor vehicles: at cost	18 400	
provision for depreciation	6 300	
Fixtures and fittings: at cost	14 300	
provision for depreciation	3 100	
Stock at: 1 May 1991		22 400 16400
30 April 1992		23 660 17300
Creditors	8 400	
Debtors	9 300 -700	
Sales		141 640
Balance at bank (in hand)		8 900
Sales returns		2 000
Capital	40 000	
Drawings	14 000	
Purchases returns		1 800
Discounts allowed		310
Discounts received		470
Purchases	77 100	
Difference on trial balance		50 720
	251 900	251 900

Additional information:

(i)   It has now been discovered that the stock at 1 May 1991 and 30 April 1992 was valued at selling price on both occasions; the relevant cost of stock figures being:

    at 1 May 1991   £16 000
    at 30 April 1992   £17 300

(ii)   It has been decided to write off as bad the following debt at 30 April 1992:

    T White   £700

(iii)   A provision for doubtful debts of $2\frac{1}{2}$% of debtors as at 30 April 1992 is to be created.

REQUIRED

(a)   Journal entries for the accounting adjustments required for items (i), (ii) and (iii) above.
      Note: Narratives are required.   (10)
(b)   The corrected trial balance as at 30 April 1992 incorporating the adjustments covered in (a) above.   (10)
(c)   Explain the function of a provision for doubtful debts.   (5)

                                                                    (Cambridge 1992)

2   From the information given below, show:
    (a)   The provision for doubtful debts account for each of the three years ended 31 December 1991, 1992 and 1993.   (15)
    (b)   Extracts from the final accounts for each year, relating to debtors, bad debts and the provision for doubtful debts.   (10)

	Year to: 31 Dec 1991	31 Dec 1992	31 Dec 1993
	£	£	£
Debtors (before adjustments)	26,180	33,100	28,200
Bad debts to be written off	807	400	433
Doubtful debts at the year-end	670	2%*	500

Note: The balance on the provision for doubtful debts account at 1 Jan 1991 was £475.

* A general provision on debtors, less bad debts.

3   A property of a business was rented at £250 per month payable monthly. The rent was three months in arrears on 31 December 1991 and five months in arrears on 31 December 1992. The rates were £1,200 per annum payable half yearly in advance on 1 April and 1 October in each year. At 31 December 1991 the rates for the half year to 31 March 1992 had not been paid, but these arrears were cleared and rates for 1992 were paid when due.

Required:
From the information above prepare the combined rent and rates account for the year ended 31 December 1992 showing the figures that would appear for rent and rates in the profit and loss account and the figures in the balance sheet at 31 December 1992.   (20)

4   The balance sheet of Darn Ltd as at 30 April 1992 showed the following information concerning motor vehicles.

	£	£
Fixed assets		
Motor vehicles at cost	23,000	
Less: Provision for depreciation	14,000	9,000

It is company policy to depreciate motor vehicles at the rate of 15% on the cost of assets held at the end of each year.

The company purchased on 1 January 1993 a motor van for £4,000. A motor van purchased on 1 January 1991 for £3,000 was traded in for the new vehicle, and £1,800 cash was paid in full settlement.

In addition a motor car purchased on 1 January 1990 for £3,500 was involved in an accident during March 1993 and has been declared a write-off. The company's insurers have agreed to pay £1,800 as compensation for the loss.

Required:
(i)   The motor vehicles disposals account for the year ended 30 April 1993.   (7)
(ii) The provision for depreciation of motor vehicles account for the year ended 30 April 1993.   (7)
(iii) The appropriate figures relating to motor vehicles in the balance sheet at 30 April 1993.   (6)

5   The managing director of a medium-sized limited company has written to you as follows:

'In order to keep full financial control over the day-to-day operations of my company, I need up-to-date knowledge of the cash position, the debtors and the creditors. I can obtain this from the bank statements, my sales invoices and statements, and my suppliers' invoices and statements. Why then does my company need to incur the large expense of employing accountants to maintain a full double-entry book-keeping system?'

Prepare a reasoned answer to the managing director's question.   (20)
(London)

TUTOR'S ANSWER

Question 1
a) Journal

		£	£
i)	DR Capital	6,400	
	CR Stock		6,400
	— Stock at 1 May 1991 incorrectly valued at selling price		
ii)	DR Bad debts	700	
	CR T. White's account in Sales ledger		700
	— Bad debt written off		
iii)	DR Profit and loss account	215	
	CR Provision for bad debts		
	— Provision for doubtful debts ($2\frac{1}{2}$% of debtors)		215

TUTOR'S COMMENT

As the trading account has not been drawn up at the date of the trial balance, no adjustment is needed for the closing stock, which is shown as a note to the (corrected) trial balance.

b)

Boris Penfield

Trial balance as at
30 April 1992

	£	£
Business premises: at cost	48,000	
provision for depreciation		13,000
Motor vehicles: at cost	18,400	
provision for depreciation		6,300
Fixtures and fittings: at cost	14,300	
provision for depreciation		3,100
Stock at 1 May 1991	16,000	
Creditors		8,400
Debtors	8,600	
Sales		141,640
Balance at bank (in hand)	8,900	
Sales returns	2,000	
Capital (40,000 − 6,400 stock overvaluation)		33,600
Drawings	14,000	
Purchases returns		1,800
Discounts allowed	310	
Discounts received		470
Purchases	77,100	
Bad debts	700	
Provision for doubtful debts ($2\frac{1}{2}$% × [9300 − 700])		215
Profit and loss account	215	
	208,525	208,525

Note: Stock at 30 April 1992 was £17,300

TUTOR'S COMMENTS

1. The bad debts provision is $2\frac{1}{2}$% of the debtors *after* writing off the bad debt.
2. The overvaluation of opening stock meant that the previous year's profit was also overstated, requiring an adjustment to the owner's capital account.

c)   A provision for doubtful debts recognises that part of the debtors may be worthless due to customers being unable to pay their debts. The provision itself is built up from profits by debiting the profit and loss account, thus reducing net profit for the year. The provision is deducted from debtors in the balance sheet with the result that only 'good' debts are included in the total of assets. This is in line with the concept of *prudence* * whereby potential losses should be recognised in the financial statements as soon as they are known with certainty or can be estimated in the light of information available.

* See Chapter 7.

STUDENT'S ANSWER WITH EXAMINER'S COMMENTS

Question 4

(i)   *Motor Vehicles Disposal Account*

	£				£
4/93 Transfer cost of van and car	6,500	1/93	Proceeds on sale of van		2,200
		3/93	Compensation for car		1,800
		4/93	Transfer depreciation (900 + 1,575)		2,475
			P&L a/c		25
	6,500				6,500

Show workings

(ii)   *Motor Vehicles Depreciation Account*

	£			£
4/93 Transfer disposals	2,475	5/92	Balance b/f	14,000
Balance c/f	14,600	4/93	P&L a/c (15% × 20,500)	3,075
	17,075			17,075

When?

(iii)   *Balance sheet extract*

Fixed Assets

	£	£
Motor Vehicles		
Cost brought forward	23,000	
Additions	4,000	
	27,000	
Sales	6,500	20,500
Depreciation brought forward	14,000	
Provision for year	3,075	
	17,075	
Depreciation on sales	2,475	14,600
Net book value		£ 5,900

'Disposals' would have been better

Examiner's Comments

All the entries are correct, though workings should have been shown for the depreciation transfer. The balance sheet extract could have been shown as 'Motor Vehicles £5,900' with all the detail shown in a separate note. A good answer, though, worth 17/20.

OUTLINE ANSWERS

Question 2

(a) 1-1-91 B/F 475 + 31-12-91 P + L 195 = 670 − 31-12-92 P + L
16 = 654 − 31-12-93 P + L 154 = 500 CR balance at 31-12-93

(b) P + L: y/e 31-12-91 Bad debts 807 Increase in prov. 195
y/e 31-12-92 Bad debts 400 Decrease in prov. (16)
y/e 31-12-93 Bad debts 433 Decrease in prov. (154)
Balance sheets (1991) Debtors 25,373 − Provis 670 = 24,703
(1992) Debtors 32,700 − Provis 654 = 32,046
(1993) Debtors 27,767 − Provis 500 = 27,267

Question 3

Rent and rates a/c
DR 1-4-92 Cheque (Rates) 1,200; 1-10-92 Cheque (Rates) 600, Jan—July
Cheques (Rent) (10 × 250) = 2,500; 31-12-92 Rent in arrears (5 × 250) c/f
1,250.
CR 1-1-92 Rent in arrears b/f (3 × 250) 750, Rates accrual b/f ($\frac{1}{2}$ × 600)300;
31-12-92 P + L Rent 3,000, Rates 1,200; Prepayments (Rates) ($\frac{1}{2}$ × 600) = 300

Question 5

'Full financial control' extends much further than simply knowledge of cash, debtors and creditors, and the answer must indicate such matters as control of assets (fixed and current), complying with legislation (e.g. taxation and company reporting) and responsibility to shareholders. The answer should attempt to define 'full double-entry book-keeping'. Mention should also be made of the legal requirement to keep proper books of account, and the role of the auditor in relation to company accounts.

The 'value for money' argument could be explored, and the possibility of fraud occurring if accountants are *not* employed.

Now attempt the review questions on page 303. Answers are given on page 321.

THE DOUBLE-ENTRY SYSTEM (2)

OTHER FORMS OF FINAL ACCOUNTS

'SERVICE ONLY' BUSINESSES

'MANUFACTURING' BUSINESSES

'NON-TRADING' ORGANISATIONS, INCLUDING CLUBS

GETTING STARTED

In this chapter we take a first look at the final accounts of partnerships and limited companies (these are covered in detail in Chapters 6, 8 and 9) and also the variation to the normal layout when we are dealing with manufacturing, service, and non-trading organisations.

There are estimated to be over 3 million firms in the UK, of which over 2 million are sole traders or small partnerships. Most of the other firms are limited companies, of which 13,000 are public limited companies (p.l.c.'s). In Chapter 8 we shall see that the final accounts of limited companies must be prepared in accordance with the requirements of Companies Acts, but in this chapter we are complying only with accounting, rather than statutory, rules.

ESSENTIAL PRINCIPLES

OTHER FORMS OF FINAL ACCOUNTS

As outlined in Chapter 3, the final accounts of a sole trader will normally consist of the statements shown in Figure 4.1.

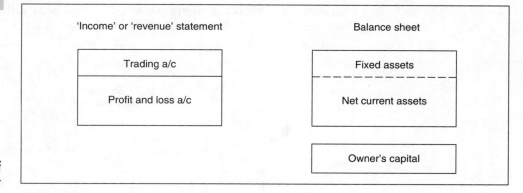

Fig. 4.1 The final accounts of a sole trader

THE APPROPRIATION ACCOUNT

If the business organisation is either a partnership or a limited company, the ownership is, by definition, in the hands of more than one person. Consequently, the revenue statement must be extended to include an 'appropriation account' which shows the ways in which the profits of the business are divided between the partners or, in the case of a limited company, divided between the company and shareholders. In later chapters both partnerships and limited companies will be described in detail, but it is necessary to know at this stage the basic form which the appropriation account takes (see Figure 4.2).

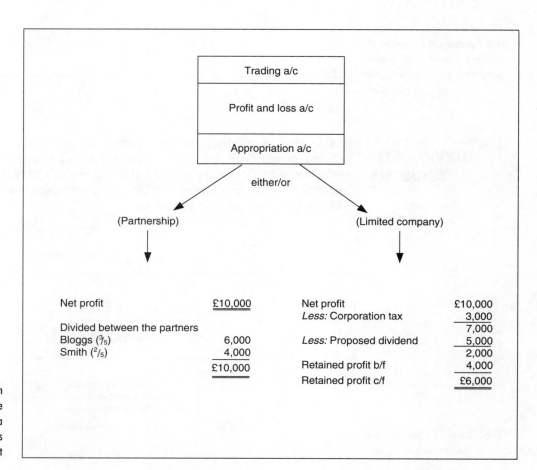

Fig. 4.2 The appropriation account—its place in the revenue statement and simple examples of a partnership and limited company's appropriation account

BALANCE SHEETS OF PARTNERSHIPS AND LIMITED COMPANIES CONTRASTED WITH THOSE OF A SOLE TRADER

The appropriation account is the main difference to be noticed when contrasting the revenue statement of a sole trader with that of a partnership or a limited company. The balance sheet will also contain certain different items dependent on the type of business organisation, and these are summarised in Figure 4.3. As with appropriation accounts, it is important to grasp the basic differences at this stage, although a more detailed study of these topics is made in Chapters 6 and 8.

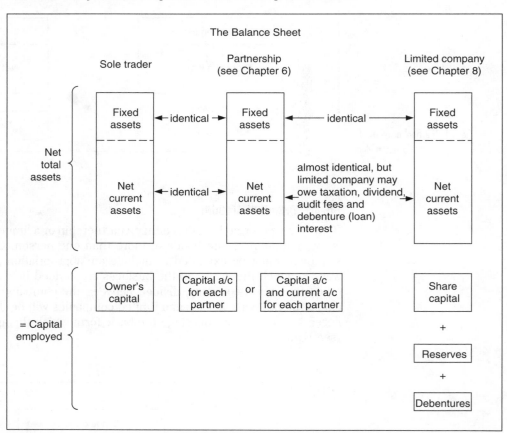

Fig. 4.3 Comparison of the contents of the balance sheets of sole traders, partnerships and limited companies (simplified)

'SERVICE ONLY' BUSINESSES

A sole proprietor who provides a service as opposed to trading (i.e. 'buying and selling') goods does not need a 'trading' account, and consequently the revenue statement will only contain a profit and loss account. The balance sheet will be virtually identical with that of a trading business, although there will be no 'stock of goods on hand' at the year-end (see Figure 4.4).

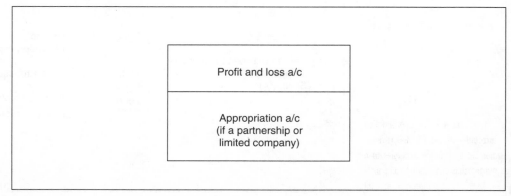

Fig. 4.4 The revenue statement of a 'service only' business

<table>
<tr><td>

'MANUFACTURING' BUSINESSES

</td><td>

Any business which *makes* the products which it sells will need to show more information in its final accounts than one which merely *buys in* products from other manufacturers. Consequently, a 'manufacturing account' is provided at the start of the revenue statement, which itemises all the factory costs associated with the production process. This 'factory production cost' is divided into 'direct' and 'indirect' expenses, the former (also known as 'variable' expenses) being those which can be specifically related to the product being made, e.g. raw materials, wages of 'production' workers, the latter (indirect) being other costs incurred within the factory, but of a more general nature, e.g. a supervisor's wages, factory insurance.

</td></tr>
</table>

The collective term for all direct expenditure is the 'prime cost' of production, and this is clearly shown in the manufacturing account. Marginal costing is dealt with in Chapter 17. It explains in detail the importance of identifying direct (variable) expenses. Here, it is sufficient to recognise that as production increases, so do the direct expenses. For example, if a bakery producing wrapped loaves bakes 1,000 loaves in a week, then it is reasonable to assume that 1,000 plastic bags will be needed to put them in. If production increases to 10,000, then 10,000 plastic bags will be needed. However, the rent of the bakery will remain the same, regardless of whether the production level is 1,000 or 10,000. The plastic bags therefore represent a direct cost, and are part of the prime cost of production, whilst the rent is an indirect expense.

STOCKS IN A MANUFACTURING BUSINESS

There are usually three separate types of stock:

1. Stocks of raw materials, i.e. quantities of 'ingredients' as yet unused in the production process. The opening and closing stocks of raw materials are incorporated within the 'prime cost' section of the manufacturing account.

> WIP is usually valued inclusive of indirect costs

2. Stocks of work-in-progress, i.e. quantities of products which have not completed all stages of the production process. The opening and closing stocks of work-in-progress are usually shown after all the factory costs have been listed. The only (rare) exception is when the information is given that the work-in-progress has been valued at *prime cost*, in which case the adjustment is made within the prime cost section of the manufacturing account.

3. Stocks of finished goods, i.e. goods which have completed the production process but have not yet been sold. These are adjusted in exactly the same way as the stocks of a non-manufacturing business, being incorporated within the 'cost of goods sold' section of the trading account.

Note that all three closing stock figures must be shown on the balance sheet.

<table>
<tr><td>

'NON-TRADING' ORGANISATIONS, INCLUDING CLUBS

> Receipts & Payments Account = Summary of Cash Book

</td><td>

Clubs, societies and associations require a different form of 'final accounts' compared with a trading concern, as their main function is neither trading nor profitmaking, but the provision of, for example, social, sporting or cultural activities for their members. One of the main handicaps from which such organisations suffer is the lack of accounting expertise amongst its members. Because of this, the financial statements are often very rudimentary, perhaps consisting of a 'receipts and payments account' which is merely a summary of the cash and bank transactions of the period. Whilst this is better than nothing, it has very limited value as it does not show the club's liabilities, and only shows assets bought during the period, without disclosing those assets bought in previous years. It fails to show whether the club had 'broken even' or whether expenditure was running at a higher level than income. The absence of a balance sheet could result in assets being sold without the club's knowledge, or liabilities being amassed without proper financial provision being made to meet them.

</td></tr>
</table>

Whilst a 'receipts and payments account' might suffice where there are only a handful of members and very few financial complications, more sophisticated control must be exercised in other circumstances. This is achieved by producing an 'income and expenditure account' and a balance sheet, which conforms with all usual book-keeping principles in order to give a true picture of the affairs of the organisation.

Particular features relating to income and expenditure accounts are as follows.

1. If the club has a bar, it is usual to show its finances in a separate 'bar account' within the income and expenditure account. This enables the members to see what surplus the bar has contributed to the overall finances of the club.

2. Membership subscriptions are subject to adjustments for amounts in arrear or paid in advance at the start and end of the period. These calculations can be relatively complex (particularly in examination questions) and the use of an 'account' format is recommended for your workings.

3. An 'honorarium' (a 'gift' of cash) is sometimes paid to the secretary or treasurer of the club in recognition of the time they spend engaged in club activities.

The balance sheet of the club follows the familiar pattern, with the only exception being that 'capital' is replaced by an 'accumulated fund', to which surpluses of income over expenditure are added (or excesses of expenditure over income deducted). The calculation of the opening balance on the fund is a simple matter of adding together all the opening assets of the club, and deducting the opening liabilities.

EXAMINATION QUESTIONS

1   Phillipa Lee is the treasurer of the Utopia Sports Club. The following is the receipts and payments account for 1992 which she presented to the members at the club's annual general meeting on 3 March 1993:

	£	£
Opening bank balance 1 January 1992		800
Add Receipts		
Subscriptions re 1991	600	
re 1992	8,400	
Competition fees	1,050	
Proceeds from sale of sports equipment	700	
Sales of dance tickets	820	
	———	11,570
		12,370
Less Payments		
Refund of 1991 subscription overpaid	20	
Wages of sports assistants	9,900	
Printing and publicity costs	750	
Repairs to duplicating machine	500	
Competition prizes	600	
Dance expenses	450	
Sports equipment purchased	3,600	
Sundry expenses	820	
	———	16,640
Closing bank overdraft 31 December 1992		4,270

At the meeting, a member of the club who possessed a knowledge of accountancy criticised the treasurer for failing to provide adequate financial information to the members, and volunteered to redraft the statement into what he regarded as an acceptable form.

He established the following additional information.

(i) The assets and liabilities at the start and end of 1992 were:

	1 Jan £	31 Dec £
Subscriptions due from members	600	520
Subscriptions received in advance	280	—
Stock of competition prizes	350	200
Value of duplicating machines (cost £2,000)	1,400	1,200
Sports equipment (at net book value)	4,000	5,000
Sports equipment (cost)	15,000	8,600

(ii) Sports equipment with a net book value of £2,000 on 1 January 1992 was sold during the year. The equipment had been owned for exactly four years prior to its sale, and had been depreciated on the straight line method with an estimated life of five years.

(iii) At the annual general meeting, members agreed to an increase in subscription rates for 1993 of 15%. The 1992 subscription was £40 per annum.

    (a) Prepare revised statements for the club which reveal 'adequate financial information' to the members as to the income and expenditure for the year ended 31 December 1992 and the overall position of the club as at that date. (20)

    (b) Calculate the cash due to be received from subscriptions during 1993 on the assumption that 10% of the existing membership resign during the year without paying their subscriptions, but forty new members are enrolled. Assume that all members enrolled at 31 December 1993 pay their subscriptions by that date, and that all subscriptions owing by members at 31 December 1992 were paid during 1993. (5)

(London)

2 Outlaws plc, a company which manufacturers bottled drinks, arrived at a draft net profit before taxation of £327,000 for the year ended 31 October 1992. In January 1993, on reviewing the accounts, the auditors queried the following items:

1. An amount of £10,000 paid to the company's legal advisors as a fee for negotiating the sale of leasehold property during the year has been shown as part of 'Professional Fees' in the Profit and Loss Account. The property, which had an amortised value of £400,000 at the date of sale, was sold for £435,000. The 'profit' of £35,000 has been credited to a suspense account, which has been included in the balance sheet at 31 October 1992.

2. A motor lorry which cost £40,000 during the year has been written off in the profit and loss account, although the normal depreciation policy is to write off such assets over four years.

3. Stock valued at £7,000 at 31 October 1992 has been included at its retail price, which is 40% higher than its cost.

4. A customer, whose debt of £20,000 was considered bad and was written off in the year to 31 October 1992, paid the debt in full in December 1992.

    (a) Re-calculate the company's net profit before taxation after making any adjustments necessary for items 1—4 above. (7)

    (b) Explain your treatment of each of the items 1—4 above. (8)

(London)

3 Complex Limited was formed as a company on 1 January 1993. It manufactures several different products from the same raw materials and also provides design services to other companies. The company has not yet appointed an accountant, but has enlisted the services of an inexperienced friend of the managing director. The

friend has drawn up the following 'finance statement' for the year ended 31 December 1993.

	£	£
Fees from design services		23,980
Sales of product A		34,900
Sales of product B		6,980
Sales of product C		30,662
		96,522
Raw Materials purchased	26,000	
Administration Expenses	9,000	
Selling and distribution	13,000	
		48,000
Gross Profit		48,522
Less Closing Stock of raw materials		5,900
		42,622
Production Labour	15,000	
Factory Expenses	10,000	
		25,000
		17,622
Closing Stock of finished Goods		12,300
Net Profit		29,922

You have been appointed to advise the managing director on accounting matters, and soon realise that, whilst the figures used by the inexperienced friend are accurate, the 'finance statement' is not in accordance with normal accounting practice. You establish the following additional information:

(1) There was no work in progress at the year-end.
(2) Raw materials consumed, production labour, factory expenses and closing stocks of finished goods are divided between products as follows:

     A   30%   B   10%   C   60%

(3) Other overheads are divided

     Products: A   20%   B   8%   C   32%

     Design services department   40%

Prepare an accounting statement in columnar form for Complex Limited for the year ended 31 December 1993, showing the net profit for each product and the overall performance for the year in as much detail as is possible from the information given above.
(15)
(London)

£10,000 has already been shown in the P&L. The correct figure should be £35,000

To eliminate the profit element, £7,000 should be multiplied by 40/140 = £2,000

Correct figure should be £410,000

Good

STUDENT'S ANSWER TO QUESTION 2

(a)

	£	
Net profit before tax	327,000	✓
(1) *Add* profit on property	25,000	✗
(2) *Add* depreciation	30,000	✓
(3) *Less* stock adjustment	(2,800)	✗
(4) *Add* bad debt recovered	20,000	✓
New net profit	£399,200	

(b) (1) There shouldn't be a suspense account in the balance sheet, so I have shown the profit in the profit and loss account, less the legal fee.
     (2) The concept of consistency applies here, so I have adjusted the depreciation back to the normal amount.

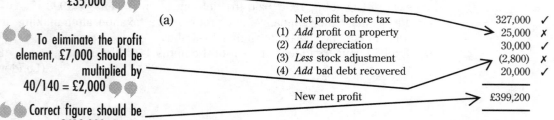

66 'or net realisable value', to be precise (see Chapter 7) **99**

(3) Stock must be valued at cost, so I have taken out the profit which was included.

(4) The bad debt has now been paid, so it can be added to this year's profit.

TUTOR'S COMMENT

A reasonable answer which could have been improved by more detail in part (b). It was a good idea to mention relevant concepts, but in (b) part (3) the prudence concept could have been referred to. No workings for the stock adjustment were given, therefore no marks could have been awarded for the £2,800.

OUTLINE ANSWERS

Question 1

(a) Income and expenditure account:

Income: Subscriptions £9,180*; competitions (1050–750) £300; dance (820–450) £370 (Total £9,850)

Expenditure: Wages £9,900; printing etc £750; repairs £500; sundries £820; loss on sale of equipment £1,300; depreciation of equipment £600; depreciation of duplicator £200 (Total £14,070)

Excess of expenditure over income £4,220

*

Subscription Account

1.1.92	b/f	600	1.1.92	b/f		280
31.12.92	Refund	20	31.12.92	Cash (1991)		600
	Int. + Exp. A/C	9,180		Cash (1992)		8,400
				c/f		520
		9,800				9,800

Balance Sheet:

Fixed Assets: Duplicator £1,200; sports equipment £5,000

Current Assets: prizes £200; subs due £520

Current liability: overdraft £4,270

Balance sheet total = £2,650

Accumulated fund; opening balance

(800 + 600 − 280 + 350 + 1,400 + 4,000) = £6,870

Less Excess of expenditure over income £4,220 = £2,650

(b) Total cash due to be received = £11,882*

*No. of members = £9200 £40 =	230
less withdrawn	23
	207
New members	40
	247 @ £46 = £11,362

Add cash due in 1993 re 1992 subscription   520

£11,882

Question 3

Factory Production Cost: A £13,530   B £4,510   C £27,060   Total £45,100

Sales: A £34,900   B £6,980   C £30,662   Design Fees £23,980

Cost of Sales: A £9,840   B £3,280   C £19,680
Gross Profit A £25,060   B £3,700   C £10,982   Total £39,742
Admin. expenses: A £1,800   B £720   C £2,880   Design £3,600
Selling: A £2,600   B £1,040   C £4,160   Design £5,200
Net Profit A £20,660   B £1,940   C £3,942   Design £15,180   Total £41,722

Now attempt the review questions on page 303. Answers are given on page 321.

CHAPTER

5

GETTING STARTED

The financial statements should show a 'true and fair' view both of the state of the business during the financial period, and of the net asset position on the final day of that period. This will only be possible when the underlying accounting system can be relied upon to produce consistently accurate data which fully reflect all aspects of the business's financial affairs. One way of ensuring this is by means of 'controls' over certain key areas, especially the personal ledgers. In this chapter we see how the entries in the ledgers can be summarised in control accounts, and how these accounts are used not only to check the accuracy of the ledger entries but also to help find missing information where records are incomplete.

CONTROL ACCOUNTS AND INCOMPLETE RECORDS

CONTROL ACCOUNTS

INCOMPLETE RECORDS

CONTROL ACCOUNTS

❝❝ Control accounts are the same as Total accounts ❞❞

ESSENTIAL PRINCIPLES

The personal ledgers of even a relatively small business are likely to contain many hundreds of individual accounts for customers and suppliers. For large businesses, the number of accounts may total tens or even hundreds of thousands, the vast majority being contained within the sales ledger.

To be able to confirm the overall accuracy of the book-keeping entries within these ledgers, 'control accounts' (also called 'total accounts') can be drawn up. These accounts work on a simple principle: that if you can produce an account which contains summarised totals of all the thousands of individual entries posted to a ledger's accounts, then the closing balance on that one account should equal the total of the individual account balances within the ledger (see Fig. 5.1).

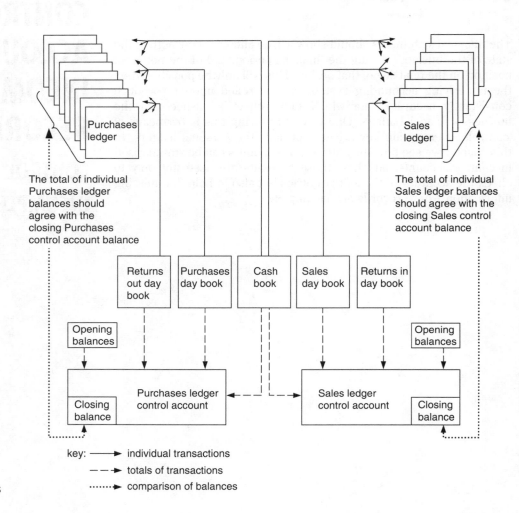

Fig. 5.1 Control accounts

The check on the 'double-entry' comes about due to the fact that the 'summarised totals' mentioned in the previous paragraph do not come from the personal ledger itself, but from the appropriate 'book of prime entry'. As these totals are used within the book-keeping system to complete the double-entry transactions (e.g. by the totals of the purchase day book being debited to the purchases account in the general ledger), the satisfactory 'balancing' of the control account proves the arithmetical accuracy of that part of the accounting system.

SALES LEDGER CONTROL ACCOUNT

Table 5.1 on page 37 lists the types of entries which might appear within customers' accounts in the sales ledger, divided between debited entries and credited entries. The 'source' of the entries is also given.

Debited entries	'Source'	Credited entries	'Source'
Opening debtors broungt forward	Previous closing balance	Opening credit balances brought forward*	Previous closing balance
Sales on credit terms	Sales day book	Returns inwards	Returns in day book
Cheques dishonoured	Cash book		
Interest charged on overdue accounts†	Sales day book	Cash and cheques received	Cash book
		Discount allowed	General ledger
Cash refunded to customers	Cash book	Bad debts written off	Journal
		Contra purchases ledger‡	Journal
Closing credit balances carried forward*	—	Closing debtors carried forward	—

* These may occur owing to debtor having mistakenly overpaid an invoice, duplicated a payment, or returned goods after having paid for them.
† A sales contract may include a clause which allows for interest to be charged if the account is not settled by a given date.
‡ If the customer also *sells* goods to the business then the balance on his sales ledger accounts can be 'contra d' (i.e. set-off) against the balance due to him on his purchase ledger account. This has an advantage for both parties in that by transferring one of the two ledger balances, only one amount is then to be paid or received, thus saving unnecessary paperwork.

Table 5.1 Where sales ledger entries come from

The sales ledger control account will be very similar in form to the summary of entries in Table 5.1. The closing balances on the account are compared with the total of the list of individual balances within the sales ledger. If they agree, then the arithmetical accuracy of the book-keeping system for this ledger is proved. If there is a disagreement, then one or more of the following errors may have occurred:

1. *Errors within the control account*
   (a) Addition error within the control account.
   (b) Incorrect total posted from a book of prime entry to the control account owing to arithmetical error or transposition of figures.
   (c) A total which, despite appearing in a book of prime entry, was not posted to the control account.
   (d) A total being understated owing to an item being posted to the ledger, but omitted from the book of prime entry.
2. *Errors within the ledger*
   (a) An arithmetical error within one or more individual accounts.
   (b) An item which, although shown in a book of prime entry, has been omitted from the individual ledger account.
3. *Other possible errors*
   (a) The list of ledger balances being incorrectly totalled.
   (b) One or more balances being excluded from the list of balances.
   (c) Debit balances being listed as credit balances, or vice versa.

EXAMPLE 1

The following figures relating to debtors were extracted from the books of Boz Ltd at 31 March 1993.

	£
Debtor balances 1 April 1992	22,093
Credit balances 1 April 1992	286
Receipts from debtors	157,708
Sales	168,212
Bad debts written off	763
Discounts allowed	1,549
Contras: Purchases ledger	274
Sales returns	3,468
Cash refunded to debtors	638
Credit balances 31 March 1993	197

A control account was prepared from the above figures but the balance of debtors at 31 March 1993 did not agree with the total of the balances extracted from the sales ledger.

Further examination revealed the following errors.

1. Cash discounts allowed for one month, of £148, had been posted to debtors' accounts but not to the discount allowed account.
2. The debtor balance on a debtor's account had been included in the list of debtors extracted from the sales ledger as £239 instead of £329.
3. Goods returned by a customer to the value of £56 had been correctly posted to the customer's account but entered in the sales returns account as £156.
4. A sales invoice for £95 had been recorded in the customer's account but had not been entered in the sales day book.
5. The contra item transferred from the purchases ledger had been incorrectly shown in the control account, the correct figure being £247.

Required:
Draw up the sales ledger control account as at 31 March 1993, incorporating the necessary corrections to the above errors.

Solution:

Boz Ltd
Sales Ledger Control Account as at 31 March 1993

	£		£
Debtor balances 1 April 1992	22,093	Credit balances 1 April 1992	286
Sales	168,307	Receipts from debtors	157,708
Cash refunded to debtors	638	Bad debts written off	763
Credit balances 31 March 1993	197	Discounts allowed	1,697
		Contras: Purchases ledger	247
		Sales returns	3,368
		Debtor balances 31 March 1993*	27,166
	191,235		191,235

*Balancing figure.

Workings:

Four of the original figures needed adjustment, as follows:

	£	re: paragraph
Sales	+ 95	(4)
Discounts allowed	+148	(1)
Contras: Purchases ledger	- 27	(5)
Sales returns	-100	(3)

Tutor's comments

Of the five 'errors' which were revealed, four caused adjustments to be made to the control account figures. The reasons for the adjustments are given below.

Error (1)   The total discount allowed is obtained from the discount allowed account in the general ledger. The £148 was omitted from this account, and therefore the control account must be amended.

Error (2)   Any error in compiling the list of balances has no effect on the figures in the control account. The list of debtors is only used to confirm the accuracy of the control account balance.

Error (3)   As the sales returns total had been overstated by £100, a deduction of that amount must be made within the control account.

Error (4)   The omitted invoice must be included in the sales total.

Error (5)   The total of contra items had been overstated in the control account by £27.

PURCHASES LEDGER CONTROL ACCOUNT

This follows a similar pattern to the sales ledger control account.

The summarised entries which might be found in the purchases ledger are given in Table 5.2.

The purchases ledger control account will take a similar form to the summary given in Table 5.2. The closing balances on the account are compared with the total of the list of individual balances within the purchases ledger. If the figures agree, then the arithmetical accuracy of the book-keeping entries is proved. If there is a difference then similar errors to those relating to the sales ledger control account (see previous section) might be present.

Debited entries	'Source'	Credited entries	'Source'
Opening debit balances brought f/wd*	Previous closing balance	Opening creditors brought f/wd	Previous closing balance
Returns outwards	Returns out day book	Purchases on credit terms	Purchases day book
Cash and cheques paid	Cash book	Interest charged on overdue accounts‡	Purchases day book
Discount received	General ledger		
Contra sales ledger†	Journal	Cash refunded by suppliers	Cash book
Closing creditors carried f/wd	—	Closing debit balances carried f/wd	—

* The business may have overpaid an invoice, duplicated a payment, or returned goods after having paid for them, thereby giving rise to a debit balance appearing in a supplier's account.
† This is the 'mirror image' of the contra item which is shown in the sales ledger control account. It records the transfer of a debtor's balance to offset the same person's creditor's balance.
‡ The purchase contract may allow for interest to be charged if an amount is overdue for payment.

Table 5.2 Where purchases ledger entries come from

EXAMPLE 2

J. Dunkley prepared a purchases ledger control account for April 1993 from the totals in his subsidiary books. The closing credit balance of the control account, which was £7,210, failed to agree with the total of the balances in the purchases ledger.

The following errors were discovered.

1. A debit balance of £367 from M. Taylor's account in the sales ledger had been transferred to M. Taylor's account in the purchases ledger, and the transfer had not been entered in the control account.
2. The total of the purchases day book for April 1993 had been undercast by £228.
3. A credit purchase of £788 from R. Summer had been omitted from the books of account.
4. A cash payment to a supplier, F. Grant, of £870 had been correctly entered in the cash book but posted to his account as £830.

Required:

(a) Show the purchases ledger control account after the errors have been corrected.
(b) Calculate the total of the balances in the purchases ledger before the errors were discovered.

Solution:

(a)

J. Dunkley

Purchases Ledger Control Account – April 1993

	£		£
Contra item omitted	367	Closing creditors per original control account	7,210
Closing creditors after correction of errors, carried forward	7,859	Purchases day book total undercast	228
		Invoice omitted	788
	8,226		8,226

(b) Errors which affect individual balances are numbers (3) and (4).

	£
(3) Creditors are increased by	788
(4) Creditors are decreased by	(40)
Net increase	748

	£
Total revised creditors per control account	7,859
Original list of balances understated by	748
Total of balances prior to discovery of errors	7,111

TUTOR'S COMMENTS

In part (a) the *detailed* control account cannot be shown, as we are given only the closing credit balance. This figure therefore becomes the starting point to enable the errors to be corrected, as follows:

(Detailed original control account)			
	X		X
	X		X
	X		X
Closing creditors c/d	7,210		
	X		X
		Closing creditors b/d	7,210

In part (b), we can ignore errors (1) and (2) as they have no effect whatsoever on the total of the individual balances. Errors (3) and (4), however, require a revision to be made of the original list. The 'proof' of the figures is shown below.

	£
Original list of balances as in (b) above	7,111
Increase in balances due to errors	748
	£7,859
Balance as per control account	£7,859

SUSPENSE ACCOUNTS

Suspense accounts are temporary

If the control accounts reveal that there are one or more errors within the ledgers, then a suspense account can be opened, pending their discovery. The suspense account, when used in this way, acts as a temporary 'holding' account whilst the work of checking is carried out. Once the mistakes have been rectified, the suspense account is dispensed with.

EXAMPLE 3

After the extraction of the balances from the books of Phiz, the totals of the trial balance failed to agree. In addition, the credit balance of £2,450 on the purchases ledger control account, included in the trial balance, did not agree with the total of balances extracted from the purchases ledger. The following items have subsequently been discovered.

1. The payment of £265 for office supplies has been entered correctly in the cash book but has been credited to the office expenses account in the nominal ledger as £256.
2. The payment of £290 for the maintenance of an item of machinery has been correctly entered in the cash book but has been debited to the machinery account.
3. The total of the discount received column in the cash book has been undercast by £27.
4. No entry has been made in the accounts relating to the return to a supplier of goods to the value of £175 which had been purchased on credit.
5. The purchase on credit of goods for £110 from Smith, who is a customer and a supplier, has been correctly entered in the accounts. It has now been decided to set off the amount owing against the balance on Smith's account in the sales ledger.

Required:
(a) A purchases ledger control account showing clearly the amendments to the original balance.
(b) A suspense account showing clearly the original discrepancy on the trial balance.

Solution:

(a)

Phiz
Purchases Ledger Control Account

	£		£
Discount received understated	27	Closing creditors per original	
Returns out omitted	175	control account	2,450
Contra item: Smith	110		
Closing creditors after amendments carried f/wd	2,138		
	2,450		2,450

(b)

Suspense Account

	£		£
Original trial balance discrepancy	521	Office expenses; errors in posting	521
	521		521

TUTOR'S COMMENTS

In part (a), the control account is affected by items (3), (4) and (5) for the following reasons:

Item (3): If the total of the discount received column in the cash book was undercast then the corresponding total in the control account must also be incorrect.

Item (4): Once corrected, the omitted entry has the effect of increasing the total of returns outwards in the general ledger, and of decreasing the total creditors.

Item (5): The setting off of a debtor's account against a creditor's account, whilst having no overall effect on the trial balance, does reduce the totals of both the debtors and creditors.

In part (b), the only entry to be shown in the suspense account is that relating to item (1). The amount of £521 shown in the account consists of two distinct halves; the one being the amount required to cancel the original, incorrect posting (£256), the other being the corrected entry (£265). Note that there were *two* errors present in this item; not only was the incorrect amount posted but also the account had been credited instead of being debited.

The only item which had no effect on the arithmetical accuracy of either the trial balance or the control account was (2), which was an error of principle, requiring a simple transfer between accounts.

USE OF CONTROL ACCOUNTS IN A COMPUTERISED ACCOUNTING SYSTEM

Data to be input into a computerised ledger system is usually sorted into batches of items. The batch totals are ascertained and ultimately checked against the difference between the balance outstanding on the relevant control account, before and after the batch is posted.

ADVANTAGES OF MAINTAINING CONTROL ACCOUNTS

1. The closing balances on the control accounts should represent, at any date, the summarised totals of the individual sales ledger or purchases ledger balances. This ready access to debtors and creditors totals is of great importance to management when determining the current strengths or weaknesses of the business. For smaller business with relatively unsophisticated accounting systems, control accounts enable owners quickly to asertain debtors and creditors figures, without the necessity of calculating individual personal ledger balances.
2. As control accounts can prove the arithmetical accuracy of individual ledgers, they can be used to locate differences occurring within the book-keeping system. For example, if a trial balance failed to balance, but the sales ledger and purchase ledger control accounts were agreed, then the difference would lie within the general ledger or the cash book.

    A further aid to the location of errors in larger companies is the division of the control accounts into several sub-sections, divided usually by letters of the alphabet, e.g. A–J, K–M, etc. This requires a similar analysis to be made within the books of prime entry, but the advantage is that if errors have been made, only small sections of the ledger need be checked.
3. If the control accounts are maintained by persons unconnected with the day-to-day book-keeping procedures, then this will provide an independent check on the quality of the accounting work being performed by the ledger clerks.
4. If the staff maintaining the control accounts are independent of the ledger clerks, then the chance of fraud is minimised, as a considerable degree of collusion would be needed for sales or purchases ledger records to be manipulated.

INCOMPLETE RECORDS

Any method of recording the financial transactions of a business which does not use a full double-entry system is described as 'incomplete'. There are varying levels of incompleteness, ranging from a total absence of written records through to the maintenance of an efficient 'single-entry' system, providing the owner of a small 'cash' business with all his day-to-day accounting needs. The following represents some of the 'incomplete' methods in use:

1. No written records; all transactions on a 'cash only' basis; invoices not issued by the trader nor retained from suppliers. There may be a deliberate attempt to conceal true earnings in order to evade the payment of taxation.
2. A bank account is operated and copy sales invoices and purchases invoices are retained. Cheque book counterfoils and bank paying-in receipts are available.
3. 'Single-entry' records are maintained, perhaps by using a pre-printed commercially available record book (e.g. 'Simplex'). A cash book and day books are written up, but personal ledgers may not be in use.

4. Conventional accounting records are in use, but no 'final accounts' are prepared by the trader.

The necessity for many businesses in the United Kingdom to be registered for Value Added Tax (VAT) purposes has seen a decline in the number of traders who fall within categories (1) and (2) above, as businesses are regularly visited by VAT inspectors to ensure that VAT-registered traders have an accounting system capable of providing accurate records.

Although a fully double-entry system might be inappropriate for very small traders owing to the time and expense involved in its maintenance, there are genuine disadvantages in having incomplete records:

(a) Control over expenses is made difficult, and comparisons between periods may not be possible.

(b) It is harder to trace errors or deal with queries from customers or suppliers on accounting matters.

(c) There is a greater risk of running foul of legislation, particularly in relation to taxation matters.

(d) No continual record is kept of assets, liabilities and capital.

(e) The owner may not know if a profit is being made.

(f) The owner may find that the cost of employing professional accountants to unravel the records far outweighs any savings which he believes he is making by having an incomplete accounting system.

 **A Companies Act requirement** Note that limited companies are bound by legislation to keep proper books of account, and it is therefore the responsibility of company directors to ensure that an adequate book-keeping system is in operation.

PREPARATION OF ACCOUNTS FROM INCOMPLETE RECORDS

If no written records have been maintained or where records have been destroyed, then a 'statement of affairs' needs to be assembled from such information as is available.

The statement resembles a balance sheet in that it lists all assets and liabilities, with the net assets total equalling the capital balance. To establish whether a profit or loss has been made during a period, a closing statement of affairs is produced, and the closing capital is then compared with the opening capital. The difference when adjusted for drawings and any capital introduced or withdrawn during the period will be either a profit or a loss.

EXAMPLE 4

Carl, a sole trader dealing in motor vehicles since 1988, has been trading for the past year without keeping full accounting records. The last statement of affairs which is available for the business is set out below:

Statement of Affairs as at 31 December 1992

	£	£	£
Fixed assets: Premises at cost			31,400
Fixtures at net book value			4,200
Vehicles at net book value			12,700
			48,300
Current assets: Stock in trade		29,000	
Debtors		4,000	
Cash		1,200	
		34,200	
Current liabilities: Creditors	14,500		
Bank	3,400	17,900	
			16,300
			64,600
Capital			64,600

The following information is available for the year to 31 December 1992:

1. Carl drew a total of £7,000 cash for his personal use during the year, but paid a legacy of £4,000 into the business bank account.
2. An extension to the premises had been built in the year, costing £12,600.
3. The fixtures and vehicles were depreciated at 20% on the reducing balance basis.
4. Stock in trade at the year-end was valued at £25,000 and creditors totalled £16,000. Debtors were valued at £6,000 of which £1,200 was thought to be doubtful.
5. The bank statement at the year-end showed a credit balance of £2,600, but a cheque for £400 in payment for a newspaper advertisement had not been presented.
6. Cash in hand at the year-end was £800.
7. Carl has refused an offer of £20,000 for the goodwill of the business, but believes that this should be shown as an asset of the business.

Required:

Carl's statement of affairs as at 31 December 1992, together with a calculation of his net profit or loss for the year ending on that date.

Solution:

Carl
Statement of Affairs as at 31 December 1992

		£	£
Fixed assets:	Premises		44,000
	Fixtures at net book value		3,360
	Vehicles at net book value		10,160
			57,520
Current assets:	Stock in trade	25,000	
	Debtors	4,800	
	Bank	2,200	
	Cash	800	
		32,800	
Current liabilities:	Creditors	16,000	16,800
			74,320
Capital			74,320

Calculation of trading result for the year to 31 December 1992

	£
Opening capital	64,600
Add: Cash introduced	4,000
	68,600
Less: Drawings	7,000
	61,600
Closing capital per statement of affairs	74,320
Profit	12,720

TUTOR'S COMMENTS

It is evident that the statement of affairs is a balance sheet by a different name. All usual accounting principles are followed, hence the depreciation of the fixed assets and the exclusion of doubtful debts.

The 'goodwill' in item (7) represents a value placed on the reputation of the business. It may be real or imagined, but from an accounting point of view it can only be included as an asset if the trader purchased the business at an earlier date and paid an amount for goodwill as part of the overall price paid. Even in such cases, the goodwill is usually 'written off' in as short a time as is practicable. This recognises the transitory nature of the asset, as its value depends entirely on the state of the business at *the time of its disposal*, not at the date of the capital statement (see Chapter 6).

USE OF CONTROL ACCOUNTS WHERE RECORDS ARE INCOMPLETE

The 'statement of affiars' will only be used when the trader's accounting records are very limited. However, if sufficient information is available, there is no reason why a full set of final accounts should not be prepared. The minimum required information relates to debtors and creditors, cash paid and received, accruals and prepayments, and asset valuations.

When producing the trading account, the key lies in the preparation of control accounts, where balancing figures are used to give the total sales and purchases figures.

EXAMPLE 5

From the following figures relating to a sole trader, calculate the total sales and purchases for the year to 31 March 1993:

	£
Opening debtors balances 1 April 1992	13,400
Opening creditors balances 1 April 1992	20,600
Cash and cheques paid to suppliers	89,650
Cash and cheques received from customers	126,430
Total discount allowed in year	2,050
Total discount received in year	1,800
Closing debtors balances 31 March 1993	14,700
Closing creditors balances 31 March 1993	18,450

Solution:

$$\text{Sales} = \pounds129{,}780, \ \text{Purchases} = \pounds89{,}300$$

Workings:

Sales Control Account

	£		£
Opening debtors b/f	13,400	Cash and cheques received	126,430
		Discount allowed	2,050
Sales			
(balancing figure)	129,780	Closing debtors c/f	14,700
	143,180		143,180

Purchases Control Account

	£		£
Cash and cheques paid	89,650	Opening creditors b/f	20,600
Discount received	1,800		
		Purchases	
Closing creditors c/f	18,450	(balancing figure)	89,300
	109,900		109,900

TUTOR'S COMMENTS

By the simple means of preparing control accounts we are able to calculate the total sales and purchases for the year. Both of these figures will be shown in the trading account of the business. Many students fall into the trap of completely ignoring normal accounting procedures, and assume that 'sales' equals cash received and 'purchases' equals cash paid. A fundamental basis of accounting is the 'accruals concept', which states simply that accounting statements should reflect all the business's transactions of the financial period, regardless of whether or not the cash relating to those transactions has been received or paid.

EXAMINATION QUESTIONS

1   Helen Highwater runs a retail clothing business and makes up her accounts to 31 October in each year. At 31 October 1992 her accountant had difficulty balancing the books but eventually the following list of balances was produced:

	£
Fixed assets at cost (1 November 1991)	240 000
Provision for depreciation (1 November 1991)	75 000
Capital account (1 November 1991)	130 000
Sales	612 000
Sales returns	4 500
Debtors	107 300
Creditors – stock purchases	67 200
– expenses and accruals	8 200
Wages	58 000
Other operating expenses	32 000
Drawings	37 000
Bank overdraft	104 100
Loan from grandfather (interest payable at 12%)	30 000
Purchases	470 300
Discounts received	7 500
Provision for bad debts (1 November 1991)	4 400
Stock at 1 November 1991	88 500
Suspense account	to be calculated

In the course of preparing the accounts the following information was ascertained:

1. The sales returns account had been undercast by £200.
2. A contra entry between a supplier and a customer of £600 had been entered only in the debtors' ledger.
3. A purchase invoice for £3 000 had been entered in the purchases account as £300.
4. Debtor balances totalling £1 400 had been included twice.
5. A fully depreciated fixed asset, original cost £4 000, was sold during the year. The proceeds of sale, £1 500, were entered in the bank account only. New fixed assets which cost £6 000 and which were purchased during the year had been included in purchases (of stock).
6. All fixed assets in use on 31 October 1992 are to be depreciated at the rate of 10% on cost.
7. The provision for bad debts is to be reduced to £3 500.
8. The closing stock on hand at 31 October 1992 was £115 000 valued at cost. This figure does not include stock which cost £3 700 and which had been sent out to certain regular customers on approval, nor does it include stock which cost £2 200 which was stolen from one of the firm's vehicles during the year. The company is not insured for stock losses of this kind.
9. No entries have been made in respect of goods costing £1 800 and taken by Helen during the year for her own use.
10. The loan from Helen's grandfather was obtained several years ago and interest has been paid on the loan on the due dates of 31 March and 30 September by cheques drawn on Helen's personal bank account.
11. The remaining balance on the Suspense account cannot be traced and it is to be treated in the most suitable manner.

Required

(a)   Calculate the balance on the Suspense account at the time the list of balances was drawn up and incorporate the necessary entries to eliminate the balance on the Suspense account.   (5)

(b)   Prepare a profit statement for the year ended 31 October 1992 giving as much detail as possible for Helen's business.   (11)

(c)   Prepare a balance sheet at 31 October 1992.   (9)

(Cambridge 1992)

2 John Bryant, a retailer, does not keep proper books of account, but he was able to provide his accountant with the following information for the year ended 31 December 1991:

Balances as at 1 January 1991	£	Balances as at 31 December 1991	£
Freehold premises at cost	60 000		
Wages and salaries in arrears	1 900	Trade debtors	28 600
Trade creditors	21 400	Trade creditors	19 400
Trade debtors	36 700	Stock at cost	31 700
Stock at cost	24 500	Long term loan as from 1 September 1991	30 000
Motor vehicles at net book value	15 900	Lighting and heating in arrears	850
Fixtures and fittings at net book value	21 000	Wages and salaries in arrears	2 470

	Cash £	Bank £		Cash £	Bank £
Balance 1 January 1991	4 050		Balance 1 January 1991	—	7 200
Receipts from trade debtors	73 000		Bank	73 000	
Cash		73 000	Bank	15 000	
Cash sales	21 000		Payments to trade creditors	850	54 500
Loan receipt		30 000	Cash purchases	3 500	
Cash		15 000	Rates		6 000
Sale of surplus fixtures and fittings	1 850		Wages and salaries		14 700
			Lighting and heating		3 400
			Drawings	500	8 000
			Motor vehicle expenses	50	1 450
			Purchase of new motor vehicle		16 500
			Payment for private holiday		3 500

Additional information.

(1) A cheque for £1500 received from R. Jones a trade debtor was dishonoured by the bank. No adjustment had been made for this in any of the above figures, including the closing trade debtors.

(2) The net book value of the fixtures and fittings sold was £3000.
The remaining fixtures and fittings and all the motor vehicles are to be depreciated at 25% per annum on a reducing balance basis.

(3) Of the stock held at 31 December 1991, £5000 of stock at cost is shop soiled. Its estimated market value is £2900.

(4) During the year Bryant took goods worth £1500 at cost from stock for his own personal use.

(5) A provision has not been made for interest on the long term loan. The rate being charged is 14% per annum.

(6) The following discounts had occurred during the year:

	£
Discounts received	5 500
Discounts allowed	3 850

Required

(a) A trading and profit and loss account for the year ended 1991. (15)
(b) A balance sheet as at 31 December 1991. (10)

(AEB 1992)

3 Ahmed Rashid, retailer, whose accounting year end is 31 October, suffered a burglary on 23 October 1991 when a large quantity of stock was stolen along with most of the stock records.

However, the following information has been obtained from the accounting records:

	£
As at 31 October 1990—	
Trading stock, at cost	32 100
Sales ledger—debit balances	24 300
credit balances	710
Purchases ledger—debit balances	1 100
credit balances	33 900
Year ended 31 October 1991–	
Purchases, at list prices	384 000
Purchases returns, at list prices	26 000
Sales	312 000
Sales returns	14 600
Bad debts written off (sales ledger)	970
Discounts allowed	1 090
Cash paid to suppliers	343 200
Discounts received	2 910
Cash received from customers	287 090
General administrative overheads	45 100
As at 31 October 1991–	
Trading stock, at cost	38 200
Sales ledger—debit balances	to be determined
credit balances	530
Purchases ledger—debit balances	390
credit balances	to be determined

Additional information:

(i) All purchases are obtained at 10% off list prices.
(ii) Normally all sales produce a gross profit of 25% of turnover. However, during the year ended 31 October 1991, goods costing Ahmed Rashid £9 000 were sold at half normal retail price.
(iii) It can be assumed that Ahmed Rashid will receive from his insurers the cost price of the goods stolen.
(iv) All purchases and sales are on a credit basis.

Required

The following accounts for the year ended 31 October 1991:
(a) The sales ledger control account; (8)
(b) The purchases ledger control account; (8)
(c) The trading and profit and loss account. (9)

(Cambridge 1991)

4   Stephen Delplace was in the process of balancing his accounts. The total of the sales ledger balances did not agree with the debit balance of £140 800 on his sales ledger control account. The following items were discovered in attempting to reconcile the sales ledger and the sales ledger control account:

(1) The total of the sales returns book had been overcast by £1500.
(2) Goods sold on credit to H. Irwin for £6890 had been entered in the sales day book as £6980.
(3) (i) Cash of £600 received from V. Spivey a customer, had been correctly recorded in the cash book, but posted to Spivey's account as £60.
     (ii) On the same day D. Spencer returned £540 worth of goods as unsatisfactory, and he wished to close his account: debit balance of £540. The account was correctly closed but no entry was made in the sales returns book.
(4) A sale of goods on credit for £10 000 to B. Taylor was correctly entered in the sales day book but incorrectly debited to B. Tayler's account.
(5) The discounts allowed column in the cash book had been overcast by £450.

After making appropriate adjustments for the above items the sales ledger and the sales ledger control account were agreed.

Required

(a) The sales ledger control account showing the amendments to the original balance. (7)

(b) A reconciliation statement of the original incorrect total of the sales ledger balances with the amended sales ledger control account balance. (5)

(AEB 1991)

TUTOR'S ANSWER TO QUESTION 2

(a)

John Bryant
Trading and Profit and Loss Account
for the year ended 31 December 1991

	£	£	£
Sales (W.1.)			89,750
Cost of Goods Sold			
Opening Stock		24,500	
Purchases (W.2.)	62,350		
Drawings	1,500	60,850	
		85,350	
Less Closing Stock		29,600	
			55,750
Gross Profit			34,000
Discount Received			5,500
			39,500
Expenses			
Wages and salaries (W.3.)		15,270	
Rates		6,000	
Light and heat (W.4.)		4,250	
Motor expenses		1,500	
Loss on sale of fixtures		1,150	
Depreciation of fixtures		4,500	
Depreciation of motor vehicles		8,100	
Loan interest		1,400	
Discount allowed		3,850	
			46,020
Net Loss			(6,520)

(b)

Balance sheet as at
31 December 1991

	£	£	£
Fixed Assets			
Freehold Premises, at cost			60,000
Fixtures and fittings, at net book value			13,500
Motor vehicles, at net book value			24,300
			97,800
Current Assets			
Stock		29,600	
Trade debtors		30,100	
Bank		1,250	
Cash		7,000	
		67,950	
Current liabilities			
Trade creditors	19,400		
Accruals	3,320		
Loan interest owing	1,400		
		24,120	
Net current assets			43,830
			141,630
Capital Account			
Opening balance (W.5.)		131,650	
Less Net loss		6,520	
		125,130	
Less Drawings (W.6.)		13,500	
			111,630
Long-term loan			30,000
			141,630

Workings:

(1) *Calculation of sales*

		£
Receipt from trade drs		71 500
+Closing debtors	28 600	
	+1 500	30 100
+Discounts allowed		3 850
		105 450
−Opening debtors		36 700
		68 750
+Cash sales		21 000
		89 750

(2) *Calculation of purchases*

	£
Payments to trade crs	54 500
+Payments to trade crs	850
+Discounts received	5 500
+Closing crs	19 400
	80 250
−Opening crs	21 400
	58 850
+Cash purchases	3 500
	62 350

(3) $14,700 + 2,470 - 1.900 = 15,270$

(4) $3,400 + 850 = 4,250$

(5)   Opening capital

	£		£
Premises	60 000	Wages owing	1 900
Trade drs	36 700	Trade crs	21 400
Stock	24 500	Bank o/d	7 200
Motor vehicles	15 900	Opening	
Fixtures & Fits	21 000	Capital (=)	131 650
Cash	4 050		
	162 150		162 150

(6) $500 + 8,000 + 3,500 + 1,500 = 13,500$

OUTLINE ANSWERS

Question 1

(a) Suspense Account
DR   Balance per t.b. £800, duplicated debtors £1,400, profit on sale of asset £1,500
CR   Sales returns £200, contra creditors £600, purchases £2,700, difference (=drawings) £200

(b) P + L a/c year to 31 October 1992
Sales (612 − 4.7 returns) £607,300
Cost of Goods Sold £432,800
(op. stock £88,500, Purchases (£470,300 + £2,700 − £6,000) £467,000, less Goods for own use £1,800, Closing stock £118,700, stock stolen £2,200
Expenses: Wages £58,000; operating expenses £32,000; Loan interest £3,600; Depreciation (24.0 + .6 − .4) £24,200; stock stolen £2,200
Income: Discount received £7,500; Doubtful debts written back £900; Profit on sale of asset £1,500
Gross Profit £174,500, Net Profit £64,400

(c) Balance sheet
Fixed Assets (242 − 71 − 24.2) £146,800
Stocks £118,700; Debtors (105,900 − 3,500) £102,400
Creditors £66,600; Accruals £8,200; Overdraft 104,100
Loan £30,000
Capital £130,000 + Profit £64,400 − Drawings (37,000 + 1,800 + 200 − 3,600) £35,400 = £159,000

Question 4

(a) Sales ledger control account
Dr   Balances b/f £140,800; sales returns £1,500; Discount allowed £450
CR   H. Irwin £90; sales returns (D. Spencer) £540; Balance c/f £142,120

(b) Original total of sales ledger balances   £142,750

Less H. Irwin	£90	
Less V. Spivey	£540	630
		£142,120

STUDENT'S ANSWER TO QUESTION 3

(a) *Sales Ledger Control*

	£		£
B/F	24,300	B/F	710
Sales	312,000	Sales returns	14,600
		Bad debt written off	970
C/F	530	Discount allowed	1,090
		Cash received	287,090
		Debtors C/F	32,370
	336,830		336,830

No! These should be less 10% (see note i of the question)

(b) *Purchases Ledger Control*

	£		£
B/F	1,100	B/F	33,900
Purchases returns	26,000	Purchases	384,000
Cash to suppliers	343,200		
Discount received	2,910		
Creditors C/F	45,080	C/F	390
	418,290		418,290

●● Date? ●●

●● The wrong figures, but no more marks lost on the 'one error, one penalty' principle ●●

(c) *Trading and Profit and Loss Account*

	£	£	£
Sales			312,000
Less returns			14,600
			297,400
Opening Stock		32,100	
Purchases	384,000		
Less returns	26,000		
		358,000	
		390,100	
Stock stolen (balancing figure)		(124,350)	
Closing stock		(38,200)	
Gross Profit (see workings)			227,550
			69,850
Add Discount Received			2,910
			72,760
Less Admin overheads		45,100	
Bad debts written off		970	
Discount allowed		1,090	47,160
Net Profit			25,600

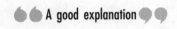

Workings

●● A good explanation ●●

(1) The special sale of goods which cost £9,000 would normally have sold for £12,000 (£9,000 × $\frac{100}{75}$), but in fact sold for only £6,000, making a gross loss of £3,000.

(2) The gross profit on normal sales was

		£
£297,400 − £6,000 (special sale)	=	291,400
× 25%	=	72,850
less the gross loss on the special sale		3,000
	=	69,850

TUTOR'S COMMENTS

This was answered well, despite the incorrect figures in the purchases control account. The workings are clear, and cross-referenced in the trading account. The stock stolen is shown to be a balancing figure in the trading account, and care has been taken to get the figure right (careful use of the calculator!). It would have been easy to have omitted the 'bad debts written off' from the P + L account. For information, the amount due from the insurance company would be shown as a current asset on the balance sheet. If the sum had *not* been insured, then the full amount would be debited in the profit and loss account.

Now attempt the review questions on page 304. Answers are given on page 322.

CHAPTER 6

ACCOUNTING FOR PARTNERSHIPS

THE PARTNERSHIP AGREEMENT

THE PARTNERSHIP APPROPRIATION ACCOUNT

GOODWILL AND CHANGES IN THE STRUCTURE OF A PARTNERSHIP

THE DISSOLUTION OF A PARTNERSHIP

PARTNERSHIP AMALGAMATIONS

CONVERSION OF A PARTNERSHIP INTO A LIMITED COMPANY

GETTING STARTED

The simplest form of business organisation—that of a sole trader—is ideal for the type of person who wishes to retain absolute control over the way in which the business develops. The advantages of sole trading include:

- the business can be established with a minimum of legal formalities;
- the owner is totally in control of the fortunes of the business;
- personal supervision by the owner usually results in a better service to customers;
- the owner does not have to reveal the financial results of the business to the general public

However, there are significant disadvantages, including:

- the personal liability of the owner for all the debts of the business, without limitation;
- total control and personal supervision normally require long hours and very hard work;
- there is no one with whom to share the problems and anxieties associated with running the business;
- if the owner is absent from the business due to sickness or other reasons, this may have a serious effect on the state of the business;
- exclusive reliance on the owner's ability to raise finance may hamper prospects of expansion.

Although many people prefer to remain independent and continue as sole traders with varying degrees of success, it is extremely difficult to enlarge a business without also increasing the number of people who own it. The main choice for those who wish to form or convert to a multi-owner enterprise is between a partnership and a limited liability company. Limited companies are dealt with in Chapters 8 and 9.

The definition of a partnership, as contained in the Partnership Act of 1890 is as follows:

'The relation which subsists between persons carrying on a business in common with a view of profit.'

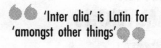

ESSENTIAL PRINCIPLES

The qualities which a sole proprietor will look for when deciding whether or not to take a partner will include:

▶ The amount of capital the prospective partner can introduce into the business.
▶ The business skill and existing contacts which the potential partner may have.

In addition, and perhaps most vital of all, the sole proprietor must judge whether he/she will be able to work happily with the partner. Many partnerships do not survive because of clashes of personality between the partners.

Once the decision has been taken to form the partnership, the partners will agree upon various matters which affect their financial relationship, such as the way in which profits or losses are to be shared, the amount of capital to be contributed by each partner, and the amount of drawings which are to be allowed. In addition, some partnerships allow interest to be credited on capital accounts, and charge interest on drawings; the former to reward partners for allowing the partnership to use their money, the latter to deter partners from withdrawing sums from the partnership.

In order to avoid misunderstandings at some future date, it is advisable that the partners draw up a partnership agreement which covers not only the matters mentioned in the previous paragraph but also the following:

- basic matters concerning the business, e.g. trading name, type of business, place or places of business;
- the rights and duties of partners, e.g. who shall be the book-keeper, who shall be the salesman;
- circumstances which may cause the partnership to be dissolved, e.g. a partner setting up a rival business;
- the duration of the partnership, e.g. for a fixed term, for the length of a particular contract, or undefined;
- rules for admitting new partners to the firm.

THE PARTNERSHIP ACT, 1890

'Inter alia' is Latin for 'amongst other things'

In the perhaps unlikely event of the partners failing to reach agreement over such matters as the proportions in which profits and losses are to be shared, section 24 of the Partnership Act of 1890 helps to solve the problem. It states, *inter alia*, that subject to any agreement, express or implied, between the partners:

i   profits and losses should be shared equally
ii   no interest on capital is to be allowed
iii   no partners shall be entitled to a salary
iv   interest at 5% per annum is allowed to partners on advances in excess of the agreed amount of capital to be contributed by them.

PARTNERSHIP BOOKS

The same section further states:

'The partnership books are to be kept at the place of business of the partnership ... and every partner may, when he thinks fit, have access to and inspect and copy any of them.'

The Act does not define 'the partnership books', but there is little difference between the records required to be kept by a partnership and those needed by a sole trader. Certainly the day-to-day book-keeping will operate on identical lines; it is only the financial relationship of the partners that requires special accounts to be maintained.

During the course of the partnership's financial year, individual partners might, depending upon the partnership agreement:

(a)   draw a salary;
(b)   make occasional or regular cash drawings;
(c)   contribute more capital or withdraw part of their existing capital.

In addition, at the year-end, they may be charged interest on the drawings that they have made, or be credited with interest on their capital account balances. Finally, they will be either credited or debited with their shares of profit or loss. In the general ledger, accounts will be opened, for convenience, in a columnar format with columns for each partner on debit and credit sides. In addition to a partners' salaries account, a drawings account, interest on drawings account and interest on capital account, the partnership has the choice of keeping either (a) capital accounts (known as 'variable') which record all the corresponding entries from the previously mentioned accounts, or, (b) capital accounts (known as 'fixed') which record *only* the capital contributed by each partner and subsequent additions or withdrawals of capital, *and* current accounts which serve to record all financial matters affecting partners, other than capital.

The latter arrangement is more common, as most partnerships wish to maintain a permanent record of the amounts of capital contributed by each partner, which is not possible with variable capital accounts.

Summary:
The general ledger of a partnership may have:

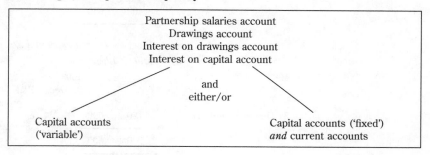

Partnership salaries account
Drawings account
Interest on drawings account
Interest on capital account

and
either/or

Capital accounts ('variable')

Capital accounts ('fixed') *and* current accounts

EXAMPLE 1

Mills and Bloggs are in partnership, sharing profits and losses in the ratio of 3:2. Their partnership agreement provides for the following:

Bloggs to be credited with a salary of £7,000 p.a.
Interest to be charged on drawings at 8% p.a.
Interested to be allowed on capital at 6% p.a.

During the year ended 31 December 1993, the partnership made a profit of £30,000 *after* adjusting for the above items. Capital and drawings were as follows:

	Capital £	Drawings £
Mills	12,000	8,000
Bloggs	10,000	13,000

The capital remained unchanged throughout the year. The drawings were made in two equal instalments, on 1 March and 1 August. Current accounts are maintained, the balances on 1 January 1993 being:

	£	
Mills	1,250	DR
Bloggs	600	CR

Show the general ledger accounts in the books of the partnership recording the above information.

Solution:

Mills and Bloggs
General Ledger

Partnership salaries a/c

		Mills	Bloggs				Mills	Bloggs
1993				1993				
31 Dec	Current a/c	—	7,000	31 Dec	P&L Appropriation a/c		—	7,000
		—	7,000				—	7,000

Drawings a/c

		Mills	Bloggs				Mills	Bloggs
1993				1993				
1 Mar	Cash	4,000	6,500	31 Dec	Current a/c		8,000	13,000
1 Aug	Cash	4,000	6,500					
		8,000	13,000				8,000	13,000

Interest on drawings a/c

		Mills	Bloggs				Mills	Bloggs
1993				1993				
31 Dec	P&L Appropriation a/c	400	650	31 Dec	Current a/c		400	650
		400	650				400	650

Interest on capital a/c

		Mills	Bloggs				Mills	Bloggs
1993				1993				
				31 Dec	P&L Appropriation a/c			
31 Dec	Current a/c	720	600				720	600
		720	600				720	600

Capital accounts

		Mills	Bloggs				Mills	Bloggs
1993				1993				
31 Dec	Balances c/f	12,000	10,000	1 Jan	Balances b/f		12,000	10,000
		12,000	10,000				12,000	10,000

Current accounts

		Mills	Bloggs				Mills	Bloggs
1993				1993				
1 Jan	Balance b/f	1,250	—	1 Jan	Balance b/f		—	600
31 Dec	Drawings	8,000	13,000	31 Dec	Salary		—	7,000
	Interest on drawings	400	650		Interest on capital		720	600
	Balances c/f	9,070	6,550		Shares of profit		18,000	12,000
		18,720	20,200				18,720	20,200

Workings:

		£
Mills	$8\% \times \frac{10}{12} \times £4,000 =$	267
	$8\% \times \frac{5}{12} \times £4,000 =$	133
		400

Bloggs	$8\% \times \frac{10}{12} \times £6,500 =$	433
	$8\% \times \frac{5}{12} \times £6,500 =$	217
		650

TUTOR'S COMMENTS

Whilst the capital accounts have remained unchanged, the current accounts have taken all the other relevant information relating to the partners. The columnar format has helped to save time and space in drawing up the accounts.

It is interesting to speculate as to why Bloggs gets a salary; perhaps it is because he is the more active partner of the two: Mills might be elderly and, although contributing both capital and expertise to the firm, plays a less demanding role than his junior partner.

THE PARTNERSHIP APPROPRIATION ACCOUNT

When drawing up the final accounts of the partnership, we must be aware that they should fully reflect the financial relationship between the partners. Section 28 of the Partnership Act 1890 declares: 'Partners are bound to render true accounts and full information of all things affecting the partnership to any partner or his legal representative.'

Partners have a joint responsibility for meeting the debts of their business, and so 'full information' is vital if the partners are to be aware of the financial standing of the partnership. For this reason, an 'appropriation account' is shown following the profit and loss account in the financial statements, and a breakdown of the capital and current account position is given on the face of the balance sheet (or in a note attached to it).

EXAMPLE 2

Show the profit and loss appropriation account and balance sheet extracts for the partnership of Mills and Bloggs (see Example 1).

Solution:

Mills and Bloggs

Profit and Loss Appropriation Account
for the year ended 31 December 1993

	£	£
Net profit (from P&L a/c) – see workings		30,270
Interest on drawings:		
Mills	400	
Bloggs	650	1,050
		31,320
Interest on capital:		
Mills	720	
Bloggs	600	1,320
		30,000
Profit divisible:		
Mills	18,000	
Bloggs	12,000	30,000

Workings:

The net profit is calculated as follows:

	£
Profit before adjustments (given)	30,000
Add Interest on capital	1,320
	31,320
Less Interest on drawings	1,050
	30,270

TUTOR'S COMMENTS

The other parts of the revenue statement and balance sheet follow a similar pattern to that of a sole trader.

Summary:

The 'final' accounts of a partnership are shown in Figure 6.1.

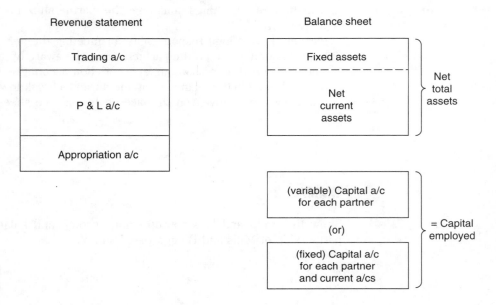

Fig. 6.1 Component parts of the final accounts of a partnership

GOODWILL AND CHANGES IN THE STRUCTURE OF A PARTNERSHIP

Although a balance sheet has been described as a 'snapshot of the business at one moment in time' this description fails to state that the camera is fitted with a very narrow lens! Although invaluable as a record of the book value of assets and liabilities, the balance sheet is not able to show such things as:

(a) the prospects of the business;
(b) the reputation of the business;
(c) the price someone might be prepared to pay for the business.

For example, the balance sheet of a practising accountant may appear as follows:

Fixed assets (net of depreciation)	£	£
Computer	1,300	
Office furniture (desk, etc.)	1,600	
		2,900
Current assets		
Debtors (fees owing)	2.000	
Bank	500	
	2,500	
Current liabilities	600	1,900
Creditors (rent, etc.)		
		4,800
Capital		4,800

The accountant might have annual fees of over £50,000 but as he rents his office and does not have any stocks, his business has a 'book value' of less than £5,000. If he wanted to sell his practice to another accountant, he would ask for rather more than £5,000; the normal method for valuing such a business is based on a multiple (e.g. one and a half times) of the annual 'recurring' fees. He would therefore seek

$$1\frac{1}{2} \times £50,000 = £75,000$$

Assuming he was able to sell the business for this sum, he is charging £70,200 (£75,000 − £4,800) for *goodwill*, i.e. the right for the purchaser to take over his profitable, well-run business. Attempts have been made for centuries to give a precise legal definition to goodwill, but, as Lord Macnaghten said in 1910:

'It is a thing very easy to describe, very difficult to define'.

However, an Australian judge (Gowans, J.) made this attempt in 1970:

'The goodwill of a business is the advantage, whatever it may be, which a person gets by continuing to carry on and being entitled to represent to the outside world that he is carrying on a business which has been carried on for some time previously.'

Goodwill might appear in the books of a sole trader, partnership or limited company: in the case of a sole trader it will only appear if it has been *purchased* when taking over another business (e.g. the accountant quoted previously who took over the practice would show £70,200 as goodwill). It is normal practice to *write off* such goodwill in the year of acquisition, as its continued inclusion on the balance sheet (as an intangible asset) may be misleading owing to the fact that the precise value of goodwill is only known when the business is sold.

In the books of a partnership, goodwill takes on a particularly important role. This is because, even though the business is not to be sold, its value must be assessed whenever:

i   a partner dies or retires,
ii   a new partner joins the partnership,
iii   the existing partners decide to alter their profit-sharing ratios.

The actual method of valuation will be left to the partners to decide upon, and the partnership agreement itself may lay down a precise formula for its calculation. Alternatively, especially where a new partner is to be admitted, negotiations will take place so that the value can be reached by mutual agreement. The partners may also take the opportunity to revalue other partnership assets, such as property. A 'revaluation account' will be opened in the general ledger to record the alterations being made to book values. It is closed by transferring the profit or loss to the partners' accounts.

Once the value of goodwill has been established, the partners have the choice of either recording it in the books, or omitting it entirely. If the former alternative is taken, the balance sheet will contain a goodwill valuation, and a goodwill a/c will be opened in the general ledger. In the latter case, goodwill does not appear in the books, any adjusting entries of value between partners being made within the capital accounts.

ADVANTAGES AND DISADVANTAGES OF RECORDING GOODWILL

Advantages

> **Intangible means it cannot be touched**

Goodwill is recognised as an intangible asset of the business. The valuation may form the basis for any future negotiations which might arise or for an adjustment to the composition of the partnership.

Disadvantages

Goodwill valuations are notoriously unreliable, and its inclusion may seriously overstate (or understate) the true value. If goodwill has been included at a low valuation, any attempt at a future date to negotiate a higher value with a prospective purchaser may be difficult.

THE EFFECT OF CHANGES TO THE PARTNERSHIP COMPOSITION

In the following, assume that the composition of the partnership prior to the change (the 'old' partnership), was that of three partners, A, B and C sharing profits equally.

1. A partner dies or retires (profits shared equally)

'Old' partnership	$A(\frac{1}{3})$	$B(\frac{1}{3})$	$C(\frac{1}{3})$

'New' partnership (C dies or retires)	$A(\frac{1}{2})$	$B(\frac{1}{2})$

Because A and B now own a greater proportion of the business than previously, they owe C or his executors an amount equivalent to his share of the old partnership (i.e. one-third of the agreed value).

2. A new partner joins the partnership (profits shared equally)

'Old' partnership	$A(\frac{1}{3})$	$B(\frac{1}{3})$	$C(\frac{1}{3})$

'New' partnership (D joins, profits to be shared equally)	$A(\frac{1}{4})$	$B(\frac{1}{4})$	$C(\frac{1}{4})$	$D(\frac{1}{4})$

D is taking part of the value of the business from A, B and C. He must therefore compensate the three 'old' partners (i.e. by paying for one-quarter of the agreed value).

3. A change in profit-sharing ratios

'Old' partnership	$A(\frac{1}{3})$	$B(\frac{1}{3})$	$C(\frac{1}{3})$

'New' partnership (new proportions 4:3:3)	$A(\frac{2}{5})$	$B(\frac{3}{10})$	$C(\frac{3}{10})$

As A has increased his profit-sharing entitlement, he must compensate B and C for the value that they have given up.

In each of the above cases, the book-keeping entries required to make the adjustments between the partners will depend upon whether a goodwill account exists in the partnership books.

(a) Where there is a goodwill account:
DR Goodwill   CR 'Old' partners in 'old' profit-sharing ratios – with any increase in valuation of the goodwill (vice-versa for a decrease) at the date of change

(b) Where there is no goodwill account, but an account is to be opened at the date of change:

DR Goodwill CR 'Old' partners in 'old' profit-sharing ratios – with the full value of goodwill at the date of change

(c) Where goodwill is not to be recorded in the partnership books:

DR 'New' partners in 'new' profit-sharing ratios CR 'Old' partners in 'old' profit-sharing ratios – with the full value of goodwill at the date of change.

> **DR the new, CR the old**

The following three examples show how to cope with questions involving the three main changes to a partnership.

Example 3 shows a partner retiring.

Example 4 reflects the situation when a new partner is admitted.

Example 5 shows a change in a profit-sharing ratio.

Example 3 (where a partner retires)

A. Wright, B. Bloor and C. Cornes were partners in a light engineering firm and they shared profits and losses in the ratio 2:2:1. The firm's balance sheet as at 31 December 1992 was as set out below:

	£	£
Fixed assets		
Freehold property		30,000
Equipment		14,500
		44,500
Current assets		
Stock of goods	5,750	
Debtors	4,750	
Bank	3,000	
	13,500	
Less Current liabilities		
Creditors	6,750	
		6,750
		51,250
Capital accounts		
A. Wright	20,000	
B. Bloor	15,000	
C. Cornes	10,000	
		45,000
Current accounts		
A. Wright	2,000	
B. Bloor	3,000	
C. Cornes	1,250	6,250
		51,250

Bloor decided to retire at 31 December 1992, whereupon the partners (including Bloor) revalued the assets as follows:

Freehold property £42,500; equipment £13,250; goodwill £15,000.

Wright and Cornes decided to form a limited company to take over the partnership business and they agreed to retain the revised values for the assets except goodwill which was to be reduced to nil on an equal basis. On 31 December 1992 Wright and Cornes both paid £7,500 into the partnership cash account. The partners' current accounts were transferred to their capital accounts and £12,500 was paid to Bloor on account of the money due to him. The balance was left on loan to the company. The other two partners received from the new company £1 ordinary shares in place of their capital account balances on a £ for £ basis.

Note: The company had an authorised capital of £60,000 in ordinary shares of £1 each.

Required:

Prepare:

(a) A partnership revaluation account.

(b) The partnership capital accounts of Wright, Bloor and Cornes.

(c) The balance sheet of the new company Wright and Cornes Ltd as at 31 December 1992.

See Chapter 8 for limited company balance sheets

Solution:

(a)

Partnership Revaluation Account

1992		£	1992		£
31 Dec	Equipment	1,250	31 Dec	Freehold property	12,500
				Goodwill	15,000
	Surplus on revaluation:				
	Wright	10,500			
	Bloor	10,500			
	Cornes	5,250			
		26,250			
		27,500			27,500

(b)

Partnership Capital Accounts

	Wright	Bloor	Cornes		Wright	Bloor	Cornes
1992				1992			
31 Dec				31 Dec			
Cash	—	12,500	—	Balance b/f	20,000	15,000	10,000
Goodwill	7,500	—	7,500	Current a/cs	2,000	3,000	1,250
Loan a/c	—	16,000	—	Cash	7,500	—	7,500
Balances to				Revaluation			
Wright and				a/c	10,500	10,500	5,250
Cornes Ltd	32,500	—	16,500				
	40,000	28,500	24,000		40,000	28,500	24,000

(c)

Wright and Cornes Ltd

Balance Sheet as at 31 December 1992

Fixed assets:	Freehold property		42,500	
	Equipment		13,250	
			55,750	
Current assets:	Stock of goods	5,750		
	Debtors	4,750		
	Bank	5,500		
		16,000		
Current liabilities:	Creditors	6,750		
			9,250	
			65,000	

Issued share capital (Authorised: 60,000 ordinary shares of £1 each) 49,000 ordinary shares of £1 each, fully paid	49,000
Loan: B. Bloor	16,000
	65,000

TUTOR'S COMMENTS

Because Bloor is retiring, Wright and Cornes have to compensate him for the share of the partnership which they are acquiring from him. This is achieved by the entries in the revaluation account, where the increase in the value of the 'old' partnership of £26,250 is being credited to all three partners, whilst the value of goodwill is debited only to the two remaining partners in their capital accounts. This automatically compensates Bloor for the value that he is passing to Wright and Cornes.

The goodwill account would appear as follows.

1992				1992		
31 Dec	Revaluation account	15,000	31 Dec	Transfer: Wright		7,500
				Cornes		7,500
		15,000				15,000

If the partners had decided *not* to open a goodwill account in the books, then the revaluation account would have been shown as follows.

1992				1992		
31 Dec	Equipment		1,250	31 Dec	Freehold property	12,500
	Surplus on					
	revaluation:					
	Wright	4,500				
	Bloor	4,500				
	Cornes	2,250	11,250			
			12,500			12,500

The changes in the distribution of goodwill between the partners would be shown as an 'adjustment' in the capital accounts, using the journal entry:

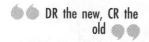

DR the new, CR the old

DR 'New' partners	Wright	7,500	
	Cornes	7,500	
CR 'Old' partners	Wright		6,000
	Bloor		6,000
	Cornes		3,000

The net effect being:

DR	Wright	1,500	
	Cornes	4,500	
CR	Bloor		6,000

The capital accounts would be shown in the following way:

	Wright	Bloor	Cornes		Wright	Bloor	Cornes
1992				1992			
31 Dec				31 Dec			
Cash	—	12,500	—	Balance b/f	20,000	15,000	10,000
Loan a/c	—	16.000	—	Current a/cs	2,000	3,000	1,250
Adjustment	1,500	—	4,500	Cash	7,500	—	7,500
Balances to				Revaluation a/c	4,500	4,500	2,250
W&C Ltd	32,500	—	16,500	Adjustment	—	6,000	
	34,000	28,500	21,000		34,000	28,500	21,000

The overall effect is the same, regardless of whether or not the goodwill account is used.

Example 4 (where a new partner joins the partnership)

A and B are in partnership sharing profits and losses equally after allowing A a salary of £3,000 per annum. The following trial balance has been extracted from the accounts after the net profit, which accrued evenly throughout the year, has been calculated for the year ended 30 September 1993

	DR £	CR £
Net profit		12,000
Fixed assets	11,000	
Debtors	3,700	
Stock	3,100	
Bank	11,200	
Creditors		2,400
Capital account A at 1 October 1992		4,000
Capital account B at 1 October 1992		6,000
Prepayments and accruals	700	400
Current account A at 1 October 1992		800
Current account B at 1 October 1992		1,200
Drawings A	3,700	
Drawings B	3,400	
Suspense account		10,000
	36,800	36,800

It has been decided to admit C, a part-time adviser to the business, as a partner with effect from 1 January 1993, and to share profits on the following basis.

1. Interest at the rate of 12% per annum is to be paid on partners' fixed capital.
2. A is to be credited with a salary of £5,000 per annum and C with £4,000 per annum.
3. The balance of profits and losses are to be shared equally between the partners.

C paid £10,000 cash into the partnership on 1 January 1993 and the double entry made to record this transaction was to debit the bank account and credit a suspense account. The partners have agreed that C's share of goodwill should be valued at £2,000 but that no goodwill account should appear in the books of the partnership.

It has been discovered that A's salary for the year ended 30 September 1992 had not been entered in the accounts and it has been agreed to make the appropriate adjustments by entries in the partners' current accounts.

Required:

(a) The profit and loss appropriation account for the year ended 30 September 1993.
(b) The balance sheet as at 30 September 1993 after the admission of C.

Solution:

(a)

A, B and C
Profit and Loss Appropriation Account
for the year to 30 September 1993

	£	£		£	£
Net profit for the year					12,000

	3 months to 31 Dec 1992			9 months to 30 Sep 1993	
Net profit	3,000				9,000
Less Salaries to partners					
A ($\frac{3}{12}$ × 3,000)	750		($\frac{9}{12}$ × 5,000)	3,750	
C	—	750	($\frac{9}{12}$ × 4,000)	3,000	6,750
		2,250			2,250
Less interest on partners' capital					
A	—		(12% × $\frac{9}{12}$ × 5,000)	450	
B	—		(12% × $\frac{9}{12}$ × 7,000)	630	
C	—		(12% × $\frac{9}{12}$ × 8,000)	720	1,800
Net profit to be divided between partners		2,250			450
Divided as follows					
A ($\frac{1}{2}$)	1,125		($\frac{1}{3}$)	150	
B ($\frac{1}{2}$)	1,125		($\frac{1}{3}$)	150	
C —	—	2,250	($\frac{1}{3}$)	150	450

(b)

Balance Sheet as at 30 September 1993

	£	£	£
Fixed assets			11,000
Current assets			
Stock		3,100	
Debtors		3,700	
Prepayments		700	
Bank		11,200	
		18,700	
Current liabilities			
Creditors	2,400		
Accruals	400	2,800	15,900
			26,900

			£	£
Capital accounts (see workings)	A		5,000	
	B		7,000	
	C		8,000	20,000
Current accounts (see workings)	A		4,825	
	B		(1,795) DR	
	C		3,870	6,900
				26,900

Workings:

Capital accounts

	A	B	C		A	B	C
				1-10-92 b/f	4,000	6,000	—
1-1-93 Journal	—	—	2,000	1-1-93 Cash	—	—	10,000
30-9-93 c/f	5,000	7,000	8,000	Journal	1,000	1,000	—
	5,000	7,000	10,000		5,000	7,000	10,000

Current accounts

	A	B	C		A	B	C
30-9-93 Drawings	3,700	3,400	—	1-10-92 b/f	800	1,200	—
Omitted 1992							
Salary	1,500	1,500	—	31-12-92 Salary	750	—	—
c/f	4,825	—	3,870	Net profit	1,125	1,125	—
				30-9-93 Salaries	3,750	—	3,000
				Interest on capital	450	630	720
				Net profit	150	150	150
				Omitted 1992 salary	3,000	—	—
				c/f	—	1,795	—
	10,025	4,900	3,870		10,025	4,900	3,870

Journal

1-1-93	DR	A's Capital account	2,000		Net
		B's Capital account	2,000		A 1,000 CR
		C's Capital account	2,000		B 1,000 CR
	CR	A's Capital account		3,000	C 2,000 DR
		B's Capital account		3,000	

Adjustment in respect of the share of goodwill being purchased by C from the existing partners (Goodwill = £2,000 × $\frac{3}{1}$, as the three partners share profits equally).

TUTOR'S COMMENTS

Although this appeared to be a relatively straightforward question, there were several points of difficulty which were included. These were:
(a) the division of the appropriation account into two time periods;
(b) the calculation of salaries and interest;
(c) the treatment of goodwill.

By working through the answer, you will see a full explanation of the way in which individual figures were arrived at. It is a good examination technique to explain how figures have been calculated, and some marks are often awarded by examiners to students who have shown a reasonably correct breakdown of a calculation, even if the final total is inaccurate.

Example 5 (where partners alter their profit-sharing ratios)

James, Harry and Bert are partners sharing profits 3:2:1. The following summarised trial balance has been prepared at the end of 1993:

	£	£
Fixed capital accounts (1 January 1993)		
James		12,000
Harry		15,000
Bert		10,000
Current accounts:		
James		800
Harry		2,000
Bert	400	
Fixed assets at cost	29,060	
Accumulated depreciation on fixed assets to 31 Dec 1993		4,700
Fees invoiced for services rendered during the year		28,600
Business expenses for the year excluding depreciation	8,700	
Expenses owing		280
Depreciation on fixed assets for 1993	1,760	
Stocks (31 December 1993)	275	
Fees owing from clients	2,280	
Goodwill	12,000	
Bank	2,860	
Creditors		95
Drawings:		
James	6,060	
Harry	7,100	
Bert	2,980	
	73,475	73,475

Under the partnership agreement, interest on fixed capital balances at the commencement of each year is allowed at 8% per annum.

As from 1 January 1994, James intends to play a less active part in the business, and from that date profits will be shared 1:2:1. Goodwill is now valued at £15,000.

Required:

i Prepare the profit and loss account (including the appropriation account) of the partnership for the year ended 31 December 1993.
ii Prepare the partnership balance sheet as at 1 January 1994, effecting any adjustment(s) through the fixed capital accounts.

Solution:

(i)

James, Harry and Bert
Profit and Loss Account for the year to 31 December 1993

	£	£
Fees invoiced for services rendered		28,600
Business expenses excluding depreciation	8,700	
Depreciation	1,760	10,460
		18,140
Net profit		
Less: Interest on capital		
James	960	
Harry	1,200	
Bert	800	2,960
Net profit available for division		15,180
Divided as follows:		
James ($\frac{1}{2}$)	7,590	
Harry ($\frac{1}{3}$)	5,060	
Bert ($\frac{1}{6}$)	2,530	15,180

(ii)

Balance Sheet as at 1 January 1994

Fixed assets:	Cost	29,060	
	Depreciation	4,700	24,360
	Goodwill		15,000
			39,360
Current assets:	Stock	275	
	Fees owing	2,280	
	Bank	2,860	
		5,415	
Current liabilities:	Creditors	95	
	Expenses owing	280	375	5,040
			44,400
Capital accounts (see Workings)			
	James	13,500	
	Harry	16,000	
	Bert	10,500	40,000
Current accounts (see Workings)			
	James	3,290	
	Harry	1,160	
	Bert	(50)DR	4,400
			44,400

Workings:

(a) Goodwill has increased by £3,000 (£15,000–£12,000). As there is a goodwill account in the books, this will be credited to the partners in their 'old' profit-sharing ratios, as shown by the following journal entry:

DR	Goodwill	3,000	
CR	James ($\frac{1}{2}$)		1,500
	Harry ($\frac{1}{3}$)		1,000
	Bert ($\frac{1}{6}$)		500

∴   New capital balances are:

James $12,000 + 1,500 = 13,500$

Harry $15,000 + 1,000 = 16,000$

Bert $10,000 +\ \ 500 = 10,500$

(b)

		James	Harry	Bert			James	Harry	Bert
1-1-93	b/f	—	—	400	1-1-93	b/f	800	2,000	—
31-12-93	Drawings	6,060	7,100	2,980	31-12-93	Interest	960	1,200	800
	c/f	3,290	1,160	—		Profit	7,590	5,060	2,530
						c/f	—	—	50
		9,350	8,260	3,380			9,350	8,260	3,380

The partners' shares of profits change from:

James ($\frac{1}{2}$)	Harry ($\frac{1}{3}$)	Bert ($\frac{1}{6}$)

to:

James ($\frac{1}{4}$)	Harry ($\frac{1}{2}$)	Bert ($\frac{1}{4}$)

It can be seen that only James' share has decreased, and therefore Harry and Bert must compensate him for the extra value that they are acquiring. This is achieved by distributing the increase in goodwill in the 'old' profit-sharing ratios, which results in James being credited with the full one-half of the updated goodwill valuation at the date of change.

THE DISSOLUTION OF A PARTNERSHIP

A partnership might be dissolved for many reasons, including:

* The death of a partner.
* The bankruptcy of a partner.
* Agreement by the partners to cease trading.
* Expiration of a fixed-term or a particular contract, if the partnership had been entered into only for a set period or for a specific purpose.

Once the decision has been taken to end the partnership, the partners must ensure that assets are realised and liabilities settled. In addition, the individual partners may have to contribute cash if there is an overall deficiency of assets compared with liabilities, or will receive cash if there is a surplus after all liabilities have been paid. Some of the partnership assets may be taken over at a valuation by one or more partners. In such a case a 'fair price' will be agreed upon by the partnership.

The book-keeping mechanism to record the closing off of the partnership's books revolves around a *realisation account*, which serves as a 'clearing house' for the partnership's assets. The account comprises some or all of the entries shown in Table 6.1.

Transfer assets (other than cash) at book values	X	Transfer liabilities taken over at book values	X
		Transfer to capital accounts the agreed valuation of assets taken over by partners	X
Cash paid for expenses of realisation	X	Cash received from debtors	X
		Cash received from the sale of assets	X
Profit on realisation transferred to partners' capital accounts	(or) X	Loss on realisation transferred to partners' capital accounts	X
	X		X

Table 6.1 The Realisation Account

In addition to the entries in the realisation account, the financial relationship of the partners with the partnership must also be settled. If current accounts have been maintained, their balances must be transferred to the capital accounts. Under normal circumstances the balances then remaining on the capital accounts will represent the amounts due to be paid (a) by the partners to the partnership (debit balances) or (b) by the partnership to the partners (credit balances). However, it sometimes happens that a partner who owes money to the partnership is unable to pay his debt owing to bankruptcy or other reasons. In such a case, the 'solvent' partners must bear the loss, *not in their normal profit/loss sharing ratios, but in proportion to their capital balances*. This is known as the 'Garner v. Murray' rule, named after a celebrated court case in 1904 which determined this principle. The court took the decision because it held that a loss caused by a partner's insolvency should be distinguished from a normal trading loss: the former thus being a 'capital' loss, to be divided in proportion to partners' capitals.

PARTNERSHIP AMALGAMATIONS

Where two or more partnerships combine to form a larger enterprise, the entries required will be similar to those for a partnership dissolution with realisation accounts being opened in each firm's books. A 'new partnership' account will be opened which is debited with the agreed valuations of the assets to be taken over by the new business, the realisation account being credited.

CONVERSION OF A PARTNERSHIP INTO A LIMITED COMPANY

At the beginning of this chapter it was seen how a sole trader might take the decision to share the ownership of his business with one or more persons by establishing a partnership. For reasons discussed in Chapter 8, there may come a time when the partnership decides to change its form of business organisation into that of a limited company. The partners will receive shares in the company in return for transferring their portion of the partnership value.

A simple illustration of such a conversion was given in Example 3 above. Although not required in that question, a realisation account would be opened, with asset values being debited in the normal way, and the 'purchase consideration' (shares in the new company and possibly cash or debentures) being credited ('new company' account debited). The profit/loss on realisation is then transferred to the partners' capital accounts. The capital accounts are closed by firstly transferring each partner's portion of the value of shares, etc. to the debit of his account, with the 'new company' account being credited. Secondly, each partner pays in or withdraws cash to clear the capital account balance remaining.

Example 6

Thomas Ward and Edwina Grant are in partnership, and at 1 January 1994 they agreed to sell their business to Low Ltd. The partnership balance sheet was as follows:

Balance Sheet as at 31 December 1993

	£	£		£	£
Capital accounts			*Fixed assets*		
Thomas Ward	12,000		Freehold premises		6,000
Edwina Grant	8,000		Plant and machinery		4,500
		20,000	Fixtures and fittings		1,200
					11,700
Current accounts			*Current assets*		
Thomas Ward	200		Stock	5,000	
Edwina Grant	350		Sundry debtors	6,000	
		550	Balance at bank	1,250	
					12,250
Current liabilities					
Sundry creditors		3,400			
		£23,950			£23,950

Low Ltd was a new company formed to purchase the above partnership business. Its authorised share capital was £150,000 made up of 50,000 8% preference shares of £1 each, and 100,000 ordinary shares of £1 each.

The company agreed to take over all the assets except the bank account, and also agreed to take over the responsibility for payment of the creditors. The company valued the acquired assets as follows:

	£
Freehold premises	10,000
Plant and machinery	3,500
Fixtures and fittings	600
Stock	4,600

The company also agreed to pay £5,850, included in the purchase price, for the total debtors taken over. The purchase price was to be £25,000, and the company proposed to settle this amount by the issue at par of 18,000 £1 ordinary shares, issued as fully paid to the partners, the balance of the purchase price to be settled in cash on 15 January 1994.

Required:
In the books of the partnership, show the entries necessary, in the following accounts, to close the business:

1. Realisation account.
2. Bank account.
3. Partners' capital accounts.
4. Business purchase account (Low Ltd account).

Note: Assume that the share distribution was made in the capital ratio of the partners at 31 December 1993.

Solution:

Realisation Account (T. Ward and E. Grant)

(1)

1994			£	1994		£
1.1	Freehold premises		6,000	1.1	Creditors	3,400
	Plant and machinery		4,500		Low Ltd (business	
	Fixtures and fittings		1,200		purchases a/c)	25,000
	Stock		5,000			
	Debtors		6,000			
	Profit on realisation					
	to					
	Capital a/cs					
	T. Ward	2,850				
	E. Grant	2,850				
			5,700			
			28,400			28,400

(2)

Bank Account

1994		£	1994		£
1.1	Balance b/d	1,250	15.1	Capital a/cs T. Ward	4,250
15.1	Low Ltd (business			E. Grant	4,000
	purchase a/c)	7,000			
		8,250			8,250

(3)

Capital Accounts

1994		Ward £	Grant £	1994			Ward £	Grant £
1.1	Low Ltd (shares)	10,800	7,200	1.1	Balances b/d		12,000	8,000
				1.1	Current a/cs		200	350
15.1	Bank	4,250	4,000	1.1	Realisation a/c		2,850	2,850
		15,050	11,200				15,050	11,200

(4)

Business Purchase Account (Low Ltd)

1994		£	1994			£	£
1.1	Realisation account	25,000	15.1	Capital a/cs (shares)			
				T. Ward	10,800		
				E. Grant	7,200	18,000	
			15.1	Bank			7,000
		25,000					25,000

Workings:

Division of shares between the partners:

$$18,000 \times \frac{12,000}{20,000} = 10,800 \text{ for T. Ward}$$

$$18,000 \times \frac{8,000}{20,000} = 7,200 \text{ for E. Grant}$$

TUTOR'S COMMENTS

As the company is taking over responsibility for the payment of creditors, the realisation account is credited with £3,600. Often the partnership itself will pay creditors, as in the previous example, in which case the creditors are *not* transferred to the realisation account.

EXAMINATION QUESTIONS

1. At the close of business on 31 May 1992, Mixers, a partnership, had the following balances on its capital and current accounts.

Capital Accounts	£
Mark Solo	21,000
Lara Todd	10,000
Norma Unison	6,000

Current Accounts	£	
Mark Solo	14,000	
Lara Todd	6,000	
Norma Unison	3,000	(Debit)

At 31 May 1992, the goodwill of the partnership was agreed at £28,000, but no goodwill account existed in the partnership books. Mark, Lara and Norma shared partnership profits and losses in the ratio 5:5:4 respectively.

On 1 June 1992, the partners decided to convert their partnership into a limited company, Shakers Limited, and the following decisions were made.

1. The company should have an issued and fully paid up share capital of 90 000 ordinary shares of £1 each, to be issued amongst the partners of Mixers in *equal* proportions.
2. Norma should acquire a computer owned by the partnership at a valuation of £750, which was £140 less than its book value. All other assets and liabilities will be transferred to the company.
3. Any balances remaining on partners' current accounts after the above decisions have been implemented should be transferred to partners' capital accounts. The balances on the capital accounts should then be settled by the partners paying in cash to or drawing out cash from the partnership bank account. Assume that there is sufficient cash available for this purpose.

    (a)   Show the entries in the partners' capital and current accounts required to close off the partnership books.   *(8)*
    (b)   Show the opening balance sheet of Shakers Limited as at 1 June 1992.   *(3)*
    (c)   Explain why a limited company must make public certain information about its financial affairs, whereas a partnership is not required to publish accounting information.   *(4)*

                                                                                                        (London 1993)

2. Swift, Rook and Dove are designers who operate in a partnership. Their written agreement states that they share the profits or losses of the business in the ratio 2:2:1. The day to day management of the business is under the control of Crowe with a salary of £15 000 per annum, together with a commission of 6% of the net profit after charging such commission.

    On 1 January 1991 Swift, Rook and Dove invited Crowe to join them in partnership. At that date the partnership's goodwill was valued at £41 600 and it was agreed that the value of the fixed assets should be raised by £8400 and that a goodwill account should not be retained in the new partnership.
    Crowe brought into the partnership £50 000 as his capital and no other payments took place.
    The four partners agreed that the new arrangement for sharing profits or losses would be in the following ratio:

                    Swift 4: Rook 3: Dove 2: Crowe 1.

    As it was realised that Crowe's share of any profits would only be modest, it was decided to make a special arrangement to cover this situation. This stated that if in any year Crowe's share of the profit fell below what he would have received from salary and commission when he managed the business, then Swift would contribute the difference to Crowe from his own share of the profit.
    The net profit for the year ended 31 December 1991 amounted to £190 000; the partners agreed that £16 000 of this excellent result should be paid to the staff as a bonus.

    Required

    (a)   The journal entries, including those relating to cash, to give effect to the introduction of Crowe's capital, the arrangements relating to the goodwill and the revaluation of the fixed assets. Narratives are required.   *(8)*
    (b)   A statement to show how the profit for 1991 is distributed among the partners before and after the special arrangement is taken into consideration.   *(7)*
    (c)   A list of provisions of the Partnership Act 1890 regarding profit sharing that apply when no agreement exists between the partners.   *(3)*

                                                                                                        (AEB 1992)

3. Penny and Victor are in partnership, sharing profits and losses in the ratio 3:2. On 31 May 1990, the balance sheet of the partnership was as follows:

Fixed Assets:

	£
Freehold Land and Buildings	52,000
Machinery	60,000
Fixtures	9,000
Motor Vehicles	22,000
Computers	13,000
	156,000

Current Assets:

Stock	9,000	
Debtors	12,000	
Bank and Cash	3,000	
	24,000	

Current Liabilities:

Creditors	7,000		
Loan from Connie	4,000	11,000	13,000
			169,000

Capital Accounts:

Penny	102,000	
Victor	67,000	
		169,000

On 1 June 1990, the partnership was dissolved, and a Company, PVC Limited was formed to take over the business. The following values were agreed:

	£
Goodwill	20,000
Freehold Land and Buildings	70,000
Machinery	40,000
Fixtures	6,000
Motor Vehicles (see note 1)	7,000
Computers	12,000
Stock	9,000
Debtors	10,000
Bank and Cash	3,000
Creditors	7,000
Loan from Connie (see note 2)	4,000

Notes:

1. Penny acquired one of the vehicles, which had a book value of £11,000, for her private use, at an agreed valuation of £10,000.

2. Connie's loan was not taken over by the new company. Instead, the debt to Connie was settled by an issue of shares shown below.

The authorised capital of the company was in the form of ordinary shares of £1 each, and they were issued at a premium of 70p each. The shares were allocated as follows:

(i) To Connie: the exact number of shares necessary for her to own $\frac{1}{40}$th of the new company.

(ii) To the partners: in the same proportion as the closing balances on their capital accounts.

3. No current accounts are maintained.

Required:

(a) The capital ccounts of Penny and Victor, showing the entries required to close off the books of the partnership.

(12)

(b) The balance sheet of PVC Limited on 1 June 1990. *(4)*

(c) A breakdown on the shareholdings of Penny, Victor and Connie. *(4)*

(d) An explanation of the permissible treatments of goodwill in the limited company's accounts, according to standard accounting practice. *(5)*

(London 1991)

TUTOR'S ANSWER TO QUESTION 1

(a)

Capital Accounts

	S	T	U		S	T	U
31.5.92 Shares in Shakers Ltd	30,000	30,000	30,000	31.5.92 b/f	21,000	10,000	6,000
				Tfr current a/c	23,950	15,950	4,210
Cash	14,950	—	—	Cash	—	4,050	19,790
	44,950	30,000	30,000		44,950	30,000	30,000

Current Accounts

	S	T	U		S	T	U
31.5.92 b/f	—	—	3,000	31.5.92 b/f	14,000	6,000	—
Transfer Computer	—	—	750	Goodwill (5:5:4)	10,000	10,000	8,000
Loss on Computer	50	50	40				
To Capital a/c	23,950	15,950	4,210				
	24,000	16,000	8,000		24,000	16,000	8,000

(b)

Shakers Ltd

Balance Sheet at 1 June 1992

	£
Goodwill	28,000
Net Assets	62,000
	90,000

	£
Ordinary Share Capital 90,000 Ordinary Shares of £1	90,000

(c) A limited company is bound by the Companies Acts to publish information, whereas there is no such requirement either for sole traders or partnerships.

The reason lies in the fact that as the potential loss to creditors/investors is far greater with a limited company than with the other two forms of business, then full disclosure should be made. Also, the fact that the creditors act in a stewarding capacity on behalf of the shareholders requires disclosure of the company's financial results to the shareholders.

STUDENT'S ANSWER TO QUESTION 3

(a)

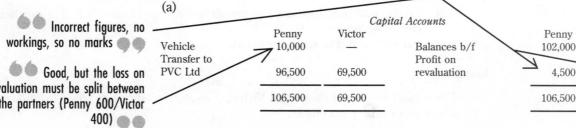

Capital Accounts

	Penny	Victor		Penny	Victor
Vehicle	10,000	—	Balances b/f	102,000	67,000
Transfer to PVC Ltd	96,500	69,500	Profit on revaluation	4,500	2,500
	106,500	69,500		106,500	69,500

Incorrect figures, no workings, so no marks

Good, but the loss on valuation must be split between the partners (Penny 600/Victor 400)

(b)

Balance Sheet of PVC Ltd, 1 June 1990

Assets	177,000
— Liabilities	7,000
	170,000
Share Capital	170,000

66 **Correct figures, but poor presentation** 99

66 **In fact, the figures should be 'Share capital 100,000, Share Premium Account £70,000 (see Chapter 8)** 99

66 **1/40 × 100,000, but 'one error, one penalty' principle applies** 99

66 **These are shares, not pounds!** 99

66 **Good, though could make some reference to 'purchased' and 'non-purchased' goodwill (see next chapter)** 99

(c) Connie gets $\frac{1}{40}$th of 170,000 shares = 4,250
Balance 165,750
Split in the ratio of the capital accounts
Penny 96,500, Victor 69,500
= Penny £96,355, Victor £69,395

(d) The preferred treatment is to write off goodwill in the first year, but it can also be written off over several years.

TUTOR'S COMMENT

The lack of workings resulted in an avoidable loss of marks in part (a). The correct profit on revaluation was £8,000, split between Penny (£4,800) and Victor (£3,200). This was calculated by comparing the book values (less the vehicle, £158,000), with the agreed value of £166,000.

OUTLINE ANSWERS

Question 2

(a)

Partnership Journal

(i) Goodwill a/c	41,600	
Swift Capital a/c 2/5		16,640
Rook Capital a/c 2/5		16,640
Dove Capital a/c 1/5		8,320
Goodwill created and shared by the original partners		
(ii) Fixed assets a/c	8,400	
Swift Capital a/c 2/5		3,360
Rook Capital a/c 2/5		3,360
Dove Capital a/c 1/5		1,680
Revalued assets shared by the partners		
(iii) Swift Capital a/c 4/10	16,640	
Rook Capital a/c 3/10	12,480	
Dove Capital a/c 2/10	8,320	
Crowe Capital a/c 1/10	4,160	
Goodwill a/c		41,600
Goodwill written off among the new partners		
(iv) Bank a/c	50,000	
Crowe Capital a/c		50,000
(New) capital introduced		

(b)

Statement of profit distribution for the year ended 31 December 1991

	Without special clause
Profit for 1991	190,000
Less staff bonus	16,000
	174,000
Profit shared	
Swift 4/10	69,600
Rook 3/10	52,200
Dove 2/10	34,800
Crowe 1/10	17,400

	With special clause
Crowe's salary	15,000
Commission 6/106 (£174,000 less £15,000)	9,000
	24,000
Less share of profits	17,400
Amount due from Swift	6,600
Revised share of profits	
Swift	63,000
Rook	52,200
Dove	34,800
Crowe	24,000

(c)   (i)   Partners are not entitled to interest on capital.

      (ii)   Partners are not allowed salaries.

     (iii)   Partners are not charged interest on drawings.

     (iv)   5% interest only to be allowed on partners loans in excess of agreed capital.

      (v)   Profits and losses are shared equally.

Now attempt the review questions on page 305. Answers are given on page 322.

CHAPTER 7

ACCOUNTING AND FINANCIAL REPORTING STANDARDS

GETTING STARTED

If you buy a map to enable you to find your way to a certain destination, or to explore a particular locality, you naturally assume that the map-maker has followed the usual conventions relating to his profession: that the top edge of the map represents 'north'; that the scale of the map has been applied consistently over the entire area covered; and that the symbols used accurately reflect the physical nature of the landscape which is represented.

The accountant, as with the map-maker, must also follow 'usual conventions' when drawing up a set of accounts. The reason for this is simply so that the user of the accounting information can be assured that the statements have been drawn up according to best practice as recognised by the accountacy profession as a whole, and not merely according to the whim of the individual accountant. The interpretation of 'best practice' has been evolving since the early days of accounting, although it is only in comparatively recent times that Statements of Standard Accounting Practice (SSAPs) and Financial Reporting Standards (FRSs) have been issued. They describe the recommended procedures and practices to be adopted by professional accountants when faced with particular accounting problems or circumstances.

Although some standards cover relatively routine matters such as how to account for value added tax, or the treatment of government grants, there are many standards which are very complex. In this chapter, the reader will find a summary of only those standards which are relevant to A-level examinations.

ESSENTIAL PRINCIPLES

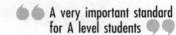

Only the standards examinable at A-level are referred to in this chapter.

SSAP 1   ACCOUNTING FOR THE RESULTS OF ASSOCIATED COMPANIES

This topic is covered in Chapter 9.

SSAP 2   DISCLOSURE OF ACCOUNTING POLICIES

> ❝❝ It is not essential to memorise the numbers of the standards ❞❞

The standard identifies and defines three terms which are used when attempting to describe the assumptions upon which financial statements are based: *fundamental accounting concepts, accounting bases* and *accounting policies.*

1. Fundamental accounting concepts (sometimes referred to as conventions or postulates) are defined as 'broad basic assumptions which underlie the periodic financial accounts of business enterprises'. It goes on to mention four specific concepts: the 'going concern' concept, the 'accruals' concept, the 'consistency' concept and the 'prudence' concept. These are dealt with in detail below.
2. Accounting bases are defined as 'the methods which have been developed for expressing or applying fundamental accounting concepts to financial transactions and items.' Examples of accounting bases include the procedure of charging depreciation on the fixed assets of the business, and the valuation methods for stocks and work-in-progress.

> ❝❝ A very important standard for A level students ❞❞

3. Accounting policies are defined as 'the specific accounting bases judged by business enterprises to be most appropriate to their circumstances and adopted by them for the purpose of preparing their financial accounts'. Examples of accounting policies include the choice of the 'straight line' basis for charging depreciation, and the 'first in, first out' method of valuing stocks.

The standard requires that, if accounts are prepared on the basis of assumptions which differ in material respects from any of the four fundamental accounting concepts stated in paragraph (1) above, the facts should be explained. It further states 'In the absence of a clear statement to the contrary, there is a presumption that the four fundamental concepts have been observed.'

Finally, it states that 'The accounting policies followed for dealing with items ... should be disclosed by way of note to the accounts.'

THE CONCEPTS IN DETAIL

(a)   *The 'going concern' concept*

Under this concept it is assumed, unless stated otherwise, that the business enterprise will continue in operational existence for the foreseeable future.

The significance of the concept is perhaps best understood by looking at the situation if a business can *not* be regarded as a 'going concern'. In such a case the balance sheet is likely to contain several totally unrealistic valuations, particularly for fixed assets and stock. This is because the forced termination of a company's business almost invariably leads to the disposal of fixed assets and stock at minimal prices, often by way of auction. Estimates of these lower valuations must be made and incorporated within the balance sheet of a company which is no longer a 'going concern'.

(b)   *The 'accruals' concept*

This is also known as the 'matching' concept, whereby revenue and costs are accounted for as they are earned or incurred, *not* as money is received or paid, and they should be matched with one another so that, for example, the cost of goods should not be charged against profit until those goods have been sold. Other implications of this concept include the following:

(i)   The cost of fixed assets should be matched with the period of their usage, by apportioning the diminution in value over the asset's life by means of depreciation.

(ii) An adjustment will be made in the accounts for expenses incurred within the accounting period but not paid for until after the end of the period (e.g. an accrual for electricity).

(iii) An adjustment will be made in the accounts for payments made within the accounting period for expenses which have not been fully utilised within the period (e.g. a prepayment of insurance).

(c)   *The 'consistency' concept*

This concept is that the same accounting treatment of items should be adopted from one period to the next.

Note that this is not a rigid requirement, for if a better way of treating an item becomes apparent then this revised treatment should be adopted. The company's accounts will contain a note explaining the nature of, and the reasons for, the revised treatment.

(d)   *The 'prudence' concept*

Also known as 'conservatism', this concept states that revenue and profits should not be anticipated but should only be included in the profit and loss account when *realised* in the form of cash or other asset (e.g. as a debtor). In addition, provision is made for all known liabilities (expenses and losses) either where the amount is known with certainty, or a reasonable estimate can be made.

The prudence concept is of paramount importance to the users of accounting information, as it ensures that the accounting statements have not been drawn up on the basis of over-optimistic or speculative forecasts, and that due consideration has been taken of the likely impact of all foreseeable expenses and losses. If there is a conflict between any of the concepts when determining the treatment of a particular item, the prudence concept takes precedence.

SSSAP 2 AND THE COMPANIES ACT

The four accounting concepts listed in SSAP 2 have statutory backing, being included in the 1985 Companies Act. The Act refers to these concepts as 'fundamental principles', and adds two other principles of its own:

(i)   It is not permissible to set off amounts representing assets or income against amounts representing liabilities or expenditure. For example if a business has both a bank overdraft and cash at the bank in a separate account, they should be shown separately on the balance sheet, not combined into one net balance.

(ii) In determining the aggregate amount of any item in the accounts, the amount of each component item must be calculated separately. This is explained in Example 1 below.

The Companies Act also contains a provision which has a direct influence over the way in which the concepts are applied. Its effect is that the requirement to show a 'true and fair view' shall *override* the fundamental principles and all other requirements of the Act as to the matters to be included in a company's accounts or in notes to those accounts. In circumstances where a fundamental concept is abandoned, full details must be given in the accounts to comply with SSAP 2.

Example 1

A company has stocks of five separate products, A, B, C, D and E. At its year-end, the value of the stocks was recorded as follows.

	Cost	Net realisable value
	£	£
A	18,000	24,000
B	15,000	9,000
C	34,000	37,000
D	10,000	15,000
E	4,000	5,000
	81,000	90,000

At what value should stock be shown in the balance sheet?

Solution:

Due to the principle that the value of assets should be determined separately, the value of each stock item must be calculated.

The basic rule for stock valuation (see SSAP9) is that stock should be valued at the *lower of cost and net realisable value*. Consequently, the valuations must be:

	£
A	18,000
B	9,000
C	34,000
D	10,000
E	4,000
Total valuation	75,000

This contrasts with the 'combined' lower figure of £81,000, which cannot be used.

SSAP3   EARNINGS PER SHARE

This standard only applies to listed companies (i.e. those public companies whose shares are traded on the stock market). The earnings per share (eps) is calculated by the following (simplified) formula, the result being stated in price per share:

$$eps = \frac{\text{Net profit} - (\text{tax} + \text{preference dividends})}{\text{Number of ordinary shares in issue}}$$

The reason for the inclusion of an eps figure in published accounts is to provide a simple measure of comparison between the results of companies. It is of particular importance to potential investors in companies, as one of the most commonly used indicators of a company's standing in the eyes of the stock market is the *price/earnings* (p/e) *ratio* which is calculated in the following way:

$$p/e = \frac{\text{stock market price}}{\text{eps}}$$

The higher the p/e ratio (e.g. over 15) then the higher the market expectations of future profits. A low p/e ratio (e.g. under 10) indicates a depressed share price due (usually) to continually poor company performance.

SSAP 4 THE ACCOUNTING TREATMENT OF GOVERNMENT GRANTS

If a company receives a government grant towards meeting an expense, e.g. rent or rates, then the grant is simply credited against that expense in the same period.

If the grant relates to capital expenditure (i.e. fixed assets) then two treatments are suggested by the standard. However, *only the second one is allowed by the Companies Act.*

1. Reduce the cost of the fixed asset by the amount of the grant, e.g. a machine costs £10,000 and the grant received is £2,000. The asset will appear at a cost of £8,000, which is then depreciated in the normal way.
2. Treat the grant as a 'deferred credit' which is written back to profit and loss account over the life of the asset. E.g. facts as in (1) above: The asset will appear at a cost of £10,000 in the balance sheet which is then depreciated in the normal way. The grant is credited to a separate account (disclosed as 'deferred income' on the balance sheet) and then transferred to profit and loss account over the depreciation period.

SSAP 5 ACCOUNTING FOR VALUE ADDED TAX

Value Added Tax (VAT) is a system of taxation in the United Kingdom whereby businesses with an annual turnover in excess of a certain prescribed limit must be 'registered' with HM Customs and Excise. The tax is payable whenever goods or services pass from one registered business to another or to a private consumer. In the case of registered businesses, a VAT return (usually covering a three-month period) will be prepared, showing whether the business paid more VAT than it received, or vice-versa. The business will then either have to pay 'excess collections' to the Customs and Excise, or will have 'excess payments' refunded by the Customs and Excise. Those who bear the tax are the private consumer and unregistered businesses, who have no means of recouping the VAT paid.

The technical name for VAT charged on sales is 'Output' tax, whilst VAT paid on purchases and expenses is known as 'Input' tax.

When a business becomes registered it must maintain an accounting system which can identify both output and input tax, as well as provide the other information required in the VAT return.

The Standard does not refer to the ways in which VAT should be recorded in the book-keeping system, but states how VAT information should be disclosed in the financial statements of a registered business, as follows: turnover as shown in the revenue statement should *exclude* VAT; on certain assets, e.g. motor cars, VAT input tax cannot be offset against output VAT. In such cases, the 'irrecoverable' VAT should be included as part of the cost of the asset.

In the case of an unregistered business, VAT is included as part of the cost of goods, services and fixed assets.

SSAP 8 THE TREATMENT OF TAXATION UNDER THE IMPUTATION SYSTEM IN THE ACCOUNTS OF COMPANIES

Although a detailed knowledge of company taxation is outside your A-level syllabus, students should be aware of the way in which companies show taxation in their accounts. Tax on the year's profit is deducted to arrive at the profit which is available for dividends. On the company's balance sheet, the tax due is shown as part of creditors due for payment within one year.

The taxable profit is unlikely to be the same as the profit as recorded in the profit and loss account, owing to a number of factors, including: (a) certain expenses deducted in arriving at the net profit are 'not allowable' when determining the taxable profit (e.g. depreciation, entertainment); (b) the company may receive capital allowances on fixed asset expenditure, which serve to reduce the amount of profit upon which corporation tax is levied.

SSAP 9 STOCKS AND LONG-TERM CONTRACTS

Stock is to be stated at the total of the lower of cost and net realisable value of the separable items of stock or of groups of similar items.

The standard gives the following definitions:

Cost
'... that expenditure which has been incurred in the normal course of business in bringing the product or service to its present location and condition ...'

Net realisable value
'... the estimated proceeds from the sale of items of stock less all further costs to completion and less all costs to be incurred in marketing, selling and distributing directly related to the items in question.'

The principal situations in which net realisable value is likely to be less than cost are where there has been:

(a)   an increase in costs or a fall in selling price;
(b)   physical deterioration of stocks;
(c)   obsolescence of products;
(d)   a decision as part of a company's marketing strategy to manufacture and sell products at a loss;
(e)   errors in production or purchasing.

What is cost?

Although *net realisable value* is a relatively simple concept to grasp, the *cost* of stock is rather more complicated. The price paid for the asset *might* be easily ascertained, e.g. from a purchase invoice. However, in many cases the price paid cannot be matched to actual goods, due, perhaps, to the physical nature of the stock. For example, petrol might be delivered to a garage on fifty separate occasions and at fifty separate prices during an accounting year. The stock of petrol at the end of the year may be 'cheap' petrol, 'expensive' petrol, or, more likely, a mixture of prices. No amount of expertise could determine this by a physical stock inspection, so various pricing methods have been created for this purpose.

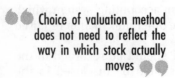 **Choice of valuation method does not need to reflect the way in which stock actually moves**

Three such methods are LIFO (last in, first out), FIFO (first in, first out) and AVCO (average cost). Each of these is a *theoretical* basis of valuation and does not necessarily reflect the way in which the stock physically moves through the business. Once a particular valuation method is chosen, it should be used in future years owing to the *consistency* concept. See Chapter 13 for worked examples.

In periods of rising prices the LIFO method will result in a lower stock valuation and consequently a lower profit figure than either of the other two methods. (Note however that SSAP 9 does *not* regard LIFO as an acceptable method of stock valuation.)

The principle to be adopted is that the methods used in allocating costs to stock need to be selected with a view to providing the *fairest possible approximation to the expenditure actually incurred in bringing the product to its present location and condition.*

Some companies value stock on the basis of 'selling price less gross profit margin'. This is only acceptable in cases where it can be proved that this results in a close approximation of cost.

LONG-TERM CONTRACTS

The definition of a long-term contract given in the standard is:

A contract entered into for the design, manufacture or construction of a single substantial asset or the provision of a service (or of a combination of assets or services which together constitute a single project) where the time taken substantially to complete the contract is such that the contract activity falls into different accounting periods. A contract that is required to be accounted for as long-term by this accounting standard will usually extend for a period exceeding one year ...

Where a company has contracts which come under the definition given above, and their outcome can be assessed with 'reasonable certainty before their conclusion', the standard allows it to record a proportion of turnover and profit arising whilst the contracts are in progress. Otherwise, the profit and loss account is likely to reflect the results of only those contracts *completed* in the year, rather than those on which the company has been actively working during the period.

The profit, to be calculated on a prudent basis, needs to reflect the proportion of the work carried out at the accounting date and to take into account any known inequalities of profitability in the various stages of the contract.

If the outcome of the contract is uncertain, then no profit should be taken to profit and loss account, though if no loss is expected it may be appropriate to show as turnover a proportion of the total contract value, using a zero estimate of profit.

If a *loss* is expected, then all the loss should be recognised *as soon as it is foreseen*, in line with the prudence concept, by being written off to P&L account.

SSAP 12 ACCOUNTING FOR DEPRECIATION

Specific methods for depreciating assets have been explained in Chapters 3 and 4, but it is useful to note the definition of depreciation as given in the standard:

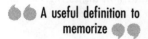 A useful definition to memorize

Depreciation is the measure of the wearing out, consumption or other reduction in the useful economic life of a fixed asset whether arising from use, effluxion of time or obsolescence through technological or market changes.

SSAP 13 ACCOUNTING FOR RESEARCH AND DEVELOPMENT

Many companies can only maintain their profitability and market leadership by investing large sums in researching and developing new products, techniques and designs.

Prior to the inception of this standard, companies were able to decide for themselves how such expenditure should be disclosed in the accounts. Some took the prudent view of 'writing off' all such expenditure as it was incurred, whilst others 'capitalised' the expenditure by including it on the balance sheet as an asset.

This divergence of treatment led to some companies overstating their profits (or understating their losses) as well as overstating balance sheet values, by virtue of capitalising massive sums spent on futile or non-commercial ventures.

The standard distinguishes between 'research' and 'development' costs as follows:

1. *Research* can be either 'pure' or 'applied'; both are undertaken in order to gain new scientific or technical knowledge and understanding, but the former is not primarily directed towards any practical aim or application, whereas the latter is.
2. *Development* is the use of scientific or technical knowledge in order to produce new or substantially improved materials, devices, products, processes, systems or services prior to the commencement of commercial production.

The accounting treatment is as follows.

(a) *Fixed assets* bought for research and development activities (e.g. laboratory equipment) should be *capitalised* and written off over their useful lives.
(b) Expenditure on *research* (pure and applied) should be *written off* in the year of expenditure.
(c) *Development expenditure* should also be *written off* in the year of expenditure, *except in the following circumstances*, when it may be shown as a 'deferred asset' on the balance sheet:

    a) there is a clearly defined project, *and*
    b) the related expenditure is separately identifiable, *and*
    c) the outcome of such a project has been assessed with reasonable certainty as to
        i) its technical feasibility, and
        ii) its ultimate commercial viability considered in the light of factors such as likely market conditions (including competing products), public opinion, consumer and environmental legislation, *and*

d) the aggregate of the deferred development costs, any further development costs and related production, selling and administration costs is reasonably expected to be expected by related future sales or other revenues, *and*

e) adequate resources exist, or are reasonably expected to be available, to enable the project to be completed and to provide any consequential increases in working capital.

SSAP 17 ACCOUNTING FOR POST BALANCE SHEET EVENTS

Although the financial statements are dated 'for the year ended ...' and 'as at ...', it is wrong to assume that events taking place after the date quoted have no bearing on their contents. It should be recognised that several months may elapse between the end of the accounting year and the date on which the directors are expected to approve those accounts for publication to the shareholders, and many things might happen in that period which could cause either a revision to be made to the figures, or the necessity for an explanatory note to be given.

The standard defines a 'post balance sheet event' as *an event which occurs between the balance sheet date and the date on which the financial statements are approved by the board of directors*, and classifies them into *adjusting events* and *non-adjusting events*, as follows.

1. *Adjusting events,* if material, *require changes to be made* in the financial statements. Such events provide additional evidence relating to conditions existing at the balance sheet date, examples being;

   (a) The determination of the purchase price or sales proceeds of fixed assets bought or sold before the year-end (e.g. where a sale contract had been signed before the year-end, but the price agreed after the year-end).

   (b) Evidence that the valuation of stocks was inaccurate (e.g. where the sale proceeds of the stock were substantially lower than the year-end value placed on that stock).

   (c) A valuation of property which provides evidence of a permanent diminution of value.

   (d) The insolvency of a debtor in the post-balance sheet period, causing the provision for bad debts to be revised as at the balance sheet date.

   It is important to appreciate that the occurrence of some post-balance sheet events, such as a critical deterioration in operating results and in the financial position, may indicate a need to reconsider the appropriateness of the going concern for the preparation of the financial statements.

2. *Non-adjusting events* are events which arise after the balance sheet date and concern conditions which did not exist at the time. *They do not require changes to be made to amounts in the financial statements*, but must, if material, be disclosed by way of notes. Examples include: (a) issues of shares; (b) purchases and sales of fixed assets; (c) opening new trading activities; (d) strikes and other labour disputes.

SSAP 18 ACCOUNTING FOR CONTINGENCIES

A contingency is a condition which exists at the balance sheet date, where the outcome will be confirmed only on the occurrence or non-occurrence of one or more uncertain future events. This definition is not intended to apply to the routine estimates which have to be made regarding such matters as the anticipated lives of fixed assets, the likely amount of bad debts or the net realisable values of stocks.

Thus, a contingency is something which *may* happen, and it can be either good or bad for the company if it does! For example, a company may have been the subject of a legal action by a customer relating to faulty goods, and has in turn sued the customer for a breach of the contract relating to payment for those goods. The legal cases might be won or lost: in the former case the company may have to pay legal costs, but may be awarded damages. In the latter case, the company may have to pay both costs and damages.

The standard reminds us of the prudence concept in SSAP 2 when it says that:

1. A material contingent *loss* should be accrued in the financial statements where it is *probable* that a future event will confirm a loss which can be estimated with reasonable accuracy at the date on which the financial statements are approved by the board of directors. Any material contingent loss not accrued, should be disclosed by way of note, except where the possibility of loss is remote.
2. Contingent *gains* should *not* be accrued in financial statements, and should only be noted in the financial statements if it is probable that the gain will be realised.

So what about the court cases? It depends entirely upon their progress in the courts in the post-balance sheet period: if it is apparent that the cases are likely to be lost, then full provision for costs and damages should be made in the accounts. If the outcome is uncertain, the prudence concept would indicate that provision be made for the likely legal costs involved, and that the contingent loss regarding damages be noted in the accounts.

If the cases have gone well, but the court ruling is still awaited, prudence dictates that legal costs should still be provided for. A note regarding a contingent gain should not be made under those circumstances, not least for the risk that if the judge happens to read it he may well regard the company as both arrogant and presumptive!

Figure 7.1 shows an extract from the accounts of BOC plc giving details of that company's contingent liabilities.

Contingent liabilities and bank guarantees	Group £ million	Parent £ million
Guarantees of related undertakings' borrowings	19.3	19.0
Guarantees of wholly owned subsidiaries' borrowings	—	584.3
Other guarantees and contingent liabilities	20.6	—

Additional consideration may be payable to the vendors of acquired businesses contingent on future performance. The maximum aggregate amount of contingent payments is £84.2 million, the majority payable in stages over a minimum period of five years after 1997.

Various Group undertakings are parties to legal actions and claims which arise in the ordinary course of business, some of which are for substantial amounts. While the outcome of some of these matters cannot readily be foreseen, the directors believe that they will be disposed of without material effect on the net asset position as shown in these accounts.

Fig. 7.1 BOC plc: contingent liabilities

SSAP 19 ACCOUNTING FOR INVESTMENT PROPERTIES

Investment properties are fixed assets held not for use by a business for the purposes of manufacturing or trading, but purely for their investment potential. Examples are buildings owned by a property company to be let to tenants.

The standard exempts such properties from the depreciation requirements of SSAP 12, except for properties held on leases of less than twenty years' duration, which would be amortised in the usual way. In addition, investment properties should be included in the balance sheet at their open market value rather than the price originally paid for them. Details of the value and the basis of the valuation must be given.

SSAP 21 ACCOUNTING FOR LEASES AND HIRE PURCHASE CONTRACTS

The accounting treatment depends on whether the leasing contract is categorised as a 'finance lease' or an 'operating lease'. As the treatment of both hire purchase and lease contracts is virtually identical, the term 'lease' is used to cover both types of transaction.

An *operating lease* involves the lessee paying a rental for the hire of an asset for a period of time which is normally substantially less than its useful economic life (e.g. a builder hiring a concrete mixer for a period of two months).

A *finance lease* usually involves payment by a lessee to a lessor of the full cost of the asset together with a return on the finance provided by the lessor (i.e. the company which initially purchases the asset). Finance leases are likely to be relatively long term, covering the full useful economic life of the asset (e.g. a company leasing a computer for a five-year period).

The Standard recognises that many companies regularly use assets which they do not (and may never) own. It is felt to be misleading to exclude from the balance sheet those assets where the lessee has both rights and responsibilities extending over virtually their entire useful lives. The standard 'turns a blind eye' to the fact that the company does not have legal ownership, but instead recognises that 'substance over form' demands that the assets be included in the balance sheet total.

A simple summary of the accounting treatment recommended by SSAP 21 is as follows:

		Finance lease	*Operating lease*
(a)	**Lessor's books**		
	P + L a/c	Earnings from leases allocated to relevant accounting periods	Rentals treated as income, using a straight line basis over the lease term
	Balance sheet	(Assets subject to finance leases are excluded from 'fixed assets')	Assets subject to operating leases are included in 'fixed assets'
		Debtors include the appropriate amount due from the lessee	Debtors include the appropriate amount due from the lessee
(b)	**Lessee's books**		
	P + L a/c	Expenditure includes a proportion of the total finance charge payable under the lease	Expenditure includes rental payments, using a straight line basis over the lease term.
	Balance sheet	Assets subject to finance leases are included in 'fixed assets'	(Assets subject to operating leases are excluded from 'fixed assets')
		Creditors include the appropriate amount due to the lessor for future rentals	Creditors include the appropriate amount due to the lessor for future rentals.

SSAP22 ACCOUNTING FOR GOODWILL

Goodwill is the difference (positive or negative) between the value of a business as a whole and the aggregate of the fair values of its separable net assets.

The standard makes an important contrast between 'purchased' and 'non-purchased' goodwill:

Purchased goodwill is goodwill which is established as a result of the *purchase* of a business. (E.g. a company paying £150,000 for a business with net assets of £100,000 is purchasing £50,000 goodwill)

Non-purchased goodwill is any goodwill other than purchased goodwill. (E.g. A company might value its own goodwill at £50,000, but this has not been proved by a commercial transaction)

It is not an accepted practice to recognise non-purchased goodwill in the financial statements, because the value has not been proved. Purchased goodwill should be written off against reserves immediately on purchase, but the standard allows companies with insufficient reserves to write off the goodwill over a longer period.

FRS 1   CASH FLOW STATEMENTS
This topic is covered in Chapter 10.

FRS 2   ACCOUNTING FOR SUBSIDIARY UNDERTAKINGS
This topic is covered in Chapter 9.

FRS 3   REPORTING FINANCIAL PERFORMANCE
This topic is covered in Chapter 8.

Because new standards are issued each year, it is worth checking your examination syllabus to make sure which are examinable.

EXAMINATION QUESTIONS

1 Prado PLC has prepared accounts for the year to 31 December 1991 showing a profit before tax of £3,700,000. On reviewing the accounts, the directors have decided to seek advice on the following matters.

(i) During 1991 a government grant of £220,000 was received and credited to the profit and loss account. This grant was made as a contribution to the cost of purchasing a machine for £1,100,000. The machine is being depreciated by the straight line method over a period of five years.

(ii) On 1 January 1991 a business was acquired by the company. Goodwill of £300,000 arising on the acquisition was written off immediately in the profit and loss account, on the grounds that the goodwill has an estimated economic life of only three years.

(iii) Plant costing £360,000 on 1 January 1990 was initially estimated to have a five year life with no residual value, and was depreciated accordingly. During 1991 experience has shown that an estimate of a total ten year life would be more appropriate, so that £36,000 depreciation has been charged on this item.

(iv) On 1 January 1991 an item of plant with a fair value of £55,404 was leased from a finance company. During the year payments on the lease have been £18,616. In practice the company expects to have the use of the asset for a total of four years, and the implicit finance charge for 1991 is £5,283. The company has accounted for this as an operating lease, but now accepts that finance lease treatment would be more appropriate.

You are required to advise on the best treatment of **each** of the above items, quoting relevant Statements of Standard Accounting Practice (SSAPs) and computing any necessary adjustments to the profit figure. *(20)*

(Northern 1992)

2 The Directors of Morrison Hill plc have been sent a letter by their auditors concerning a number of items which are relevant to the published accounts of the company for the financial year ended 30 April 1990, which are in the course of preparation. The following paragraphs are extracted from the directors' reply.

(a) You asked for details of the development expenditure of £45,000 shown as a deferred asset (not depreciated) in the balance sheet. It represents the cost of laboratory buildings and equipment for the development of our new wonder drug 'Aspracetamol', which will definitely be on sale in four years' time.

(b) The fire in the stock warehouse which destroyed the entire month's production of the soft toys division (£35,000) occurred on 2 May 1990. It is irrelevant to the year being dealt with.

(c) The buildings bought on 1 May 1987 are being depreciated for the first time this year, so we have charged P&L account with three years' depreciation (£15,000).

(d) The earnings per share figure (17p) is irrelevant; nobody is interested in it, so we haven't bothered to show it.

(e) The asset replacement reserve (£5,000) shown in the balance sheet is based on the difference between the current cost of the fixed assets and the historic cost.

For each of the five items listed above, explain whether the auditors are likely to accept or reject the accounting treatment adopted by the directors. *(25)*

(London 1990)

3 Shadbolt plc provides you with the following draft statement of accounting policies as a note to its published financial statements for the year ended 31 December 1990

1. Accounting Convention
The accounts have been prepared using the historical cost convention as modified by the revaluations of certain fixed assets.

2. Turnover
Sales turnover includes the amount of value added tax (VAT) charged on sales to customers.

3. Stocks
Stocks are valued at selling price, less gross profit margin.

4. Research and Development
All research expenditure is capitalised, whilst all development expenditure is written off against profits in the year in which it is incurred.

5. Fixed Assets
The cost of fixed assets is shown, where applicable, after the deduction of government grants. No depreciation is provided on freehold land and buildings.

Comment on the acceptability of each of the five accounting policies listed, having regard to recognised accounting concepts, conventions and relevant Statements of Standard Accounting Practice. *(15)*

(London)

TUTOR'S ANSWER TO QUESTION 1

a) i) SSAP4, Accounting for Government Grants, requires that grants should be credited to profit and loss as the related expenditure is charged. Since depreciation is being charged evenly over a five year period the grant should be credited in the same way:

	£
Credited in the accounts	220,000
Correct credit (220,000/5) =	44,000
Deduct from profit	176,000

ii) SSAP 22, Accounting for Goodwill, allows either immediate write off of goodwill against reserves or an amortisation policy which, in this case, would be over three years. Thus, depending on the policy chosen:

a) A write off policy would add £300,000 back to profit, this being taken directly against reserves
or
b) An amortisation policy would add £200,000 back to profit, the other £100,000 representing one year's amortisation.

iii) The rules laid down in SSAP 12 'Accounting for Depreciation' provide that when an estimate of asset life is changed then the written down value should be amortised over the revised useful life. Thus the charge for 1991 should be:

		£
Cost		360,000
Less 1990 depreciation @ 20%		72,000
		288,000
Revised life—9 years	divide by	9
	=	£32,000
Charged in P & L		36,000
Credit in P & L		£4,000

iv)   SSAP 21 requires that under a finance lease the charge to the profit and loss account will consist of two elements, the depreciation charge and the finance charge. These are:

			£
Depreciation	$\dfrac{55,404}{4}$	=	13,851
Finance charge as given			5,283
			19,134
Less—operating lease rental			18,616
Extra charge to P & L			518

b)   Revised profit—two possibilities

		Goodwill written off £	Goodwill amortised £
As given		3,700,000	3,700,000
Adjustment:	1	(176,000)	(176,000)
	2	300,000	200,000
	3	4,000	4,000
	4	(518)	(518)
		3,827,482	3,727,482

STUDENT'S ANSWER TO QUESTION 2

(a)   The £45,000 was spent on fixed assets, and so should be depreciated in the usual way. ✓

(b)   This is an adjusting post balance sheet event, so the May figures must be adjusted. ✗

(c)   This is a change of accounting policy, so the previous two years' depreciation (£10,000) should be a prior-year adjustment to be deducted from the opening reserves. The current year's depreciation (£5,000) will be debited to P] L a/c in the normal way. ✓

(d)   It's not for the directors to decide if the earnings per share figure is shown. It is required by an accounting standard. ✓

(e)   This is not acceptable. ✗

> Mention SSAP 13 here: fixed assets can't be deferred assets!
>
> No: it's a non-adjusting event, as it's after the year-end. A note about the fire should be given in the 1990 accounts
>
> Yes: SSAP3 only refers to plc's
>
> This is acceptable, unless the amount is immaterial

TUTOR'S COMMENT

Some good points, but some explanation should have been given for the answer in (d). Some marks might have been awarded if the decision had been based on some logical train of thought. Incidentally, it is not essential to memorise the *numbers* of the accounting standards, but the names should be known.

OUTLINE ANSWER

Question 3

1. Acceptable (cost concept, adapted)
2. Unacceptable according to SSAP 5. Turnover to be shown exclusive of VAT
3. Acceptable only if it gives a reasonable approximation of cost price
4. Unacceptable according to SSAP 13. All research expenditure is written off. Development expenditure can only be capitalised in certain defined circumstances.
5. The grants should be shown in a separate account, and then written back over the life of the related assets. Freehold *buildings* should be depreciated.

Now attempt the review questions on page 306. Answers are given on page 323.

ACCOUNTING FOR LIMITED LIABILITY COMPANIES (1)

THE PRICE TO PAY FOR LIMITED LIABILITY

TYPES OF LIMITED COMPANY

TYPES OF SHARE CAPITAL

OTHER MEANS OF FUNDING

RESERVES AND DIVIDEND POLICY

GEARING

THE CONVERSION OF AN UNINCORPORATED BUSINESS INTO A LIMITED COMPANY

THE UNPUBLISHED FINANCIAL STATEMENTS OF LIMITED COMPANIES

THE PUBLISHED ACCOUNTS OF LIMITED COMPANIES

FRS 3 REPORTING FINANCIAL PERFORMANCE

GETTING STARTED

Although sole traders and partnerships are the most common form of business organisation in the United Kingdom, their advantages of simplicity and informality are often heavily outweighed by the fact that the owner or partners have personal responsibility for all the debts of their business. Whilst this may be of little concern to the proprietors of a healthy and profitable business, it can have a devastating effect on the fortunes of owners of failing and loss-making enterprises, as it means that they must meet the claims of their creditors from their personal assets (possibly by selling their house and its contents) if the assets of the business are insufficient. Another major disadvantage of operating as a sole trader or partnership is the restricted opportunity to raise money in order to expand and develop the business.

These disadvantages have long been recognised and consequently a third type of business organisation, that of the limited liability company, has become well established. The main feature of limited companies is that they are treated as a separate legal entity, able to own assets and owe money in their own right. The owners (the shareholders or 'members') of the company have the satisfaction of knowing that, even if the company amassed considerable debts, their own loss is limited to the amount of share capital (and possibly any loans) which they have subscribed. In small companies, the shareholders are often the managers of the business with one or more of them taking an official capacity as a director. In larger companies, the directors may own only a tiny proportion of the shares in issue.

ESSENTIAL PRINCIPLES

THE PRICE TO PAY FOR LIMITED LIABILITY

Although limited liability status gives shareholders a greater degree of protection from personal indebtedness, there is a price to pay in terms of compliance with legal requirements and lack of privacy regarding the company's financial position. Specifically:

1. The annual accounts must be audited

An audit is an examination of the final accounts by a professionally qualified accountant to see whether or not they show a 'true and fair view' of the state of affairs of the business and of its profit or loss. There is no equivalent requirement for sole traders and partnerships, although at the time of writing there is considerable discussion as to whether 'small' limited companies should be exempt from the audit requirements.

2. Companies must publish their audited annual accounts

❝❝ Anyone can get copies of this information ❞❞

This is done by sending a copy of the accounts to the Registrar of Companies, where they are made available for public inspection on the payment of a small fee. This lack of privacy is justified by the legitimate interest of creditors and lenders, who should satisfy themselves that the business is financially sound before entering into a credit or loan agreement with the company. The fact that the name of every limited company must contain the word 'limited' or 'public limited company' or their abbreviations is a warning to potential creditors and others that they have no recourse to the personal assets of the owners if the business fails. Consequently, any research on the Company's financial stability should be done *prior to* entering into the transaction.

3. A copy of the audited annual accounts must be sent to shareholders and debenture holders

Whilst this may not appear to be too onerous for a small limited company with perhaps a handful of shareholders, the cost of production and distribution may be significant in the case of larger companies (e.g. British Telecom plc has over a million individual shareholders). Again, the cost must be seen as essential to satisfy the legitimate interests of the owners of the business. The Companies Acts do allow companies to send summarised versions of their accounts to shareholders, but must supply full accounts on request.

4. There are greater legal complexities and bureaucratic requirements

The 1985 and 1989 Companies Acts impose a mass of statutory regulations concerning the running of a limited liability company, and the company's directors frequently have to consult professional advisers to ensure correct compliance with the Acts. Such matters as the appointment or resignation of directors or auditors must be notified to the Registrar of Companies and an annual return giving particulars of share capital and shareholders must also be completed.

Although the cost of forming a limited company may be as little as £100, the costs of complying with the various rules and regulations are far greater.

TYPES OF LIMITED COMPANY

One disadvantage of the lack of limited liability status the restricted ability to raise funds for business development. Not every limited company can, however, raise funds from the general public, as this is restricted to those companies which are designated *public* limited companies (plcs) as defined by the Companies Acts.

The definition of a plc is a company:

(a) limited by shares;

(b) whose memorandum of association (i.e. 'rule book') states that the company is to be a public company;

(c) which is registered under the Companies Acts as a plc.

In addition, it must have a minimum value of allotted (i.e. distributed to shareholders) share capital – currently £50,000.

Any limited company which is not a plc is referred to as a *private* limited company. Both plcs and private limited companies must have a minimum of two shareholders, with no maximum being specified.

The only advantage for a plc over a private company is the former's right to offer shares or debentures (see below) to the public. In return for this benefit, plcs are subject to far more stringent controls than private companies. On 1 February 1993 there were only 13,000 plcs out of over 900,000 registered companies. In terms of size and influence, however, they far outweigh all the private companies.

> **Only plc's can offer their shares to the public**

TYPES OF SHARE CAPITAL

The two major types of share capital are those of ordinary shares and preference shares.

ORDINARY SHARES

Every company has ordinary shares. They give the holder the right to vote at general meetings of the company (e.g. to vote in an election of directors), rights to share in any dividends which are declared, and, if the company ceases to exist by being put into liquidation, the right to share in any surplus which remains after the claims of creditors and preference shareholders have been met. Each share has a normal or 'par' value, e.g. 25p, which may or may not be the same as any market value.

Although they carry the risk of loss in the event of the company failing, their attraction is the potential dividend which can be earned if the company is profitable, and also the increase in their intrinsic value.

PREFERENCE SHARES

These are shares which confer a preference to the holder as to income or capital, or both, over the ordinary share capital of the company. The dividend paid to preference shareholders is expressed as a fixed percentage of the nominal value and is presumed to be cumulative (a dividend not paid in one year being carried forward to be paid in a future year) unless stated to be non-cumulative. Preference shareholders do *not* normally have the right to vote at company general meetings.

Preference shares are a safer form of investment than ordinary shares owing to their prior claims to dividend and capital repayment in the event of a liquidation. The drawback is that the dividend will remain static, regardless of any growth in company profits.

Both ordinary and preference shares can be classified as 'redeemable', a topic which is covered in detail in Chapter 9.

The only other type of share worth noting is that of deferred or founders' shares which are occasionally issued to the initial promoters of a company. They may carry disproportionately high voting rights, whilst leaving the bulk of the capital to be subscribed by the ordinary shareholders.

A company's balance sheet will contain details of both its *authorised* share capital and its *issued* share capital. The former is simply the maximum amount of share capital which the company is allowed to issue, as stated in its memorandum of association, whereas the latter is the actual amount issued to shareholders at the balance sheet date.

> **The memorandum of association is part of the company's rule-book.**

OTHER MEANS OF FUNDING

Nearly all limited companies have the implied power to borrow money for the purposes of their business. Many businesses use this power to raise overdrafts or loans from banks, whilst others, being plcs, seek to raise finance from the general public by means of issuing loan capital as distinct from share capital.

Whichever form the borrowing takes, the company will be committed to paying interest on the amount advanced, and may well have to offer some or all of its assets to provide security to the lender by means either of a 'fixed' charge over specific assets, or a 'floating' charge over all the company's assets. The most common form of contract which the company enters into in relation to the borrowing is known as a *debenture* deed, and the loan capital is usually referred to either as debenture stock (if secured) or loan stock (if unsecured), preceded by the interest percentage which the stock carries. If the stock is repayable at a certain date then the year of repayment, or earliest and latest years for repayment, will also be stated, e.g. 8% debenture stock 1995–1998.

If the debenture deed has been entered into with one or only a small number of persons, then the word 'stock' is usually omitted from the title.

It must be emphasised that debenture or loan stock is *not* part of the company's share capital, and payments made to the stockholders represent interest and not dividends. Interest is an overhead of the company (shown in the profit and loss account) and is treated as an 'allowable' expense which serves to reduce the company's taxation charge. A dividend is an appropriation of the company's profits (shown in the company's appropriation account) and is not allowable for taxation purposes. In the event of the company's liquidation, the debenture holders will be able to utilise their security to gain repayment of their loans.

RESERVES AND DIVIDEND POLICY

If a sole trader's business makes a profit it is simply transferred to his/her capital account, and treated as his/her private income which is subject to income tax. A company which makes a profit will find that there is a certain amount of choice available to the directors regarding the amount of profit which finds its way back to the owners in the form of dividends.

There are four stages to this process, which can best be explained by showing a simplified profit and loss appropriation account of a company. (The figures in brackets represent deductions.)

1.	Net profit for year		X
	Less: Corporation tax		(X)
	Net profit after tax		X
2.	Transfer to or (from) reserves		(X) or X
			X
3.	Dividends:		
	on preference shares	(X)	
	on ordinary shares	(X)	(X)
	Retained profit for the year		X
4.	Retained profit brought forward		X
	Retained profit carried forward		X

A detailed explanation of these stages is as follows.

1. As the company is a separate legal entity, it is liable to pay corporation tax on its profits.
2. The company can transfer part of its profit into general or specific *reserves*, which can be brought back into the appropriation account at some future date as the need arises. These reserves are not necessarily matched by equivalent amounts of cash, but are represented by value in various assets, including fixed assets, debtors or stock. They are known as 'distributable' or 'revenue' reserves (i.e. available for dividend payments if required) if they have been built up out of 'earned' profits.
3. After providing for its corporation tax liability and deciding whether or not to transfer profits to or from reserves, the company will then turn its corporate mind to the question of dividends. Unfortunately, profit does not equal cash, as much of

the profit may be 'tied up' in the form of stocks, debtors, machinery, etc. Consequently, the company must perform a balancing act between the needs of the shareholders for an income from their investment, and the necessity for the company to retain a reasonable cash balance (or to limit the size of its overdraft). Assuming that the company has both profit and cash available, then it will firstly propose the payment of the fixed dividend on its preference shares, and then decide upon the amount to be proposed for the ordinary dividend. An increasing number of companies are declaring 'scrip dividends', which reward shareholders with shares rather than cash. They might also give shareholders the choice between receiving cash or shares. The advantage to the shareholders in opting for extra shares is that they are increasing their shareholdings without having to pay charges to a stockbroker, and they are not paying any income tax on a cash dividend.

4. Any profit which remains is known as 'retained profit' and is added to the balance of retained profits which was brought forward at the start of the year. The combined total is another 'distributable reserve'.

A company may have other types of reserves, known as 'non-distributable' or 'capital' reserves. These have been built up, not out of 'earned' profits, but from various adjustments to the capital structure of the company or from the revaluation of fixed assets. As their name suggests, they are *not* available for the payment of dividends.

The three main non-distributable reserves are as follows.

1.   SHARE PREMIUM ACCOUNT

When a company sells its shares, it may ask a price in excess of the nominal value of those shares (e.g. £2 for a share with a 25p nominal value). The excess over the nominal value (£1.75) is known as the share premium, and must be transferred to a separate account. Whilst the balance on the share premium account cannot be used for the payment of dividends, it can be used, *inter alia*, for the purpose of issuing bonus shares to existing shareholders. (Bonus shares are shares issued free of charge to existing shareholders—see next chapter.)

2.   CAPITAL REDEMPTION RESERVE

The topic of redemption of share capital is dealt with in detail in the next chapter, but at this stage it is sufficient to appreciate that if shares are redeemed otherwise than out of the proceeds of a new issue of shares (i.e. part or all of the redemption comes from 'profits') a sum equal to the shares so redeemed must be transferred to a non-distributable capital redemption reserve. This reserve can be used for the issue of bonus shares.

3.   REVALUATION RESERVE

Many companies decide to revalue fixed assets at intervals to ensure that balance sheet values reflect material and permanent changes. Any increase arising on a revaluation is not available for the payment of dividends, which is a prudent policy considering that the mere fact of revaluing assets has no beneficial effect whatsoever on the company's bank balance! On the contrary, the expenses of employing a professional valuer and subsequent increases in insurance premiums related to the property values may substantially decrease the company's cash resources.

Why then do companies revalue assets? Apart from the need to update balance sheet values as mentioned above, a company with significantly undervalued assets may become the target for a takeover bid, with the price offered being based on the historic values rather than current ones. This tactic is known as 'asset stripping' and was prevalent in the late 1960s and early 1970s, before companies became wise to its dangers.

As with the other capital reserves, the revaluation reserves can be used for the issue of bonus shares.

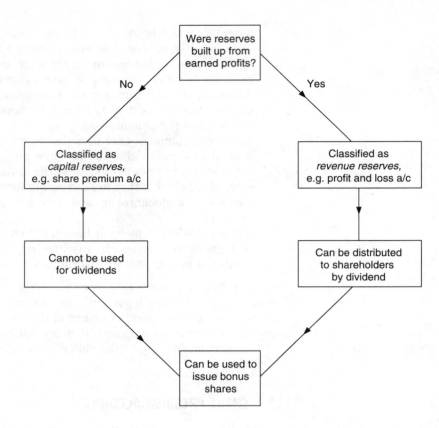

Fig. 8.1 Capital and revenue reserves

GEARING

It has already been stated that every company will have ordinary shares, and in many cases they will be the business's only form of capital. Whether or not a company seeks 'fixed return' funding in the form, primarily, of preference shares and debentures is a decision which may have far-reaching consequences for both the company and its existing and future shareholders.

The relationship between 'risk' capital (i.e. ordinary shares) and fixed return funding is known as the company's *gearing*, and is of major importance because of the varying priorities of interest and dividend payments, as follows:

First priority: Debenture interest—must be paid.
Second priority: Preference dividend—only paid if profits are available after paying debenture interest.
Third priority: Ordinary dividend—only paid of profits are available after both debenture interest and preference dividend have been paid.

It can be seen that the ordinary shareholders will do well in a profitable year when there is 'plenty for everybody', but a poor year may result in no dividend being paid to the providers of the risk capital after the fixed charges have been paid. This danger increases in direct proportion to the level of the company's gearing.

Gearing can be either high or low, and is calculated by using either of the following formulae:

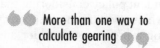 More than one way to calculate gearing

$$\frac{\text{Fixed return funding}}{\text{Total long-term capital} + \text{Reserves*}} \quad or \quad \frac{\text{Fixed return funding}}{\text{Equity capital} + \text{Reserves*}}$$

*In both cases the value of goodwill, if any, is deducted from this total owing to the intangible nature of the asset and the basic unreliability of its valuation.

These formulae will produce a gearing *ratio*, but a gearing *percentage* can be obtained simply by multiplying by 100/1. 'High' gearing is said to exist where the proportion of fixed return funding is relatively high (over 50%) in relation to total funding. 'Low' gearing is where the risk capital is dominant.

The effect that different gearing levels have on a company's ability to pay dividends can be seen in the following illustration.

Example 1

Two companies, H and L, each have total long-term capital and reserves of £150,000, divided as follows:

	H £	L £
Fixed return funding (8% preference shares)	100,000	10,000
Equity capital (£1 shares)	30,000	120,000
Reserves	20,000	20,000

The net profit before appropriations of each company for the three years ended 31 December 1993 were:

	£
1991	8,000
1992	25,000
1993	50,000

Calculate: (a) the gearing ratio of each company; (b) the maximum percentage dividend which each company could pay to its ordinary shareholders in each of the three years ended 31 December 1993, assuming that the company had sufficient cash resources.

Solution:

(a) Using the formula $\dfrac{\text{Fixed return funding}}{\text{Total long-term capital} + \text{Reserves}}$

The ratio for H is $\dfrac{£100,000}{£150,000}$ or 0.67:1 (67%)

The ratio for L is $\dfrac{£10,000}{£150,000}$ or 0.07:1 (7%)

Company H is said to be high geared; company L is low geared.

(b)

	H 1991	H 1992	H 1993	L 1991	L 1992	L 1993
Profits before appropriations	8,000	25,000	50,000	8,000	25,000	50,000
Preference dividend	8,000	8,000	8,000	800	800	800
Available for ordinary dividend	NIL	17,000	42,000	7,200	24,200	49,200
Maximum percentage dividend*	NIL	56.7	140	6	20.2	41

*$\dfrac{\text{Profits available}}{\text{Equity capital}} \times \dfrac{100}{1}$

TUTOR'S COMMENTS

Shareholders in L are able to receive a dividend in each of the three years due to the low gearing ratio of their company. Only a relatively small proportion of profits is committed to paying the fixed percentage dividend, and consequently the holders of the 120,000 ordinary shares can expect a 6% dividend in 1991 when profits are at their lowest point.

H's ordinary shareholders will not receive a penny in 1991, as the prior commitment to the holders of the 100,000 preference shares has meant that there are no surplus profits available.

Once the profit level goes beyond the level of the fixed dividend, the holders of the 30,000 ordinary shares enjoy significantly greater dividends than their counterparts in the low-geared company. This is best illustrated by means of a graph as shown in Figure 8.2.

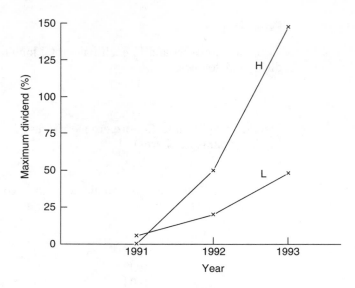

Fig. 8.2 The effect of gearing on dividend levels

The importance of gearing

A company may decide to increase its gearing ratio for a number of reasons, as follows:

(a) Debenture interest (but not preference dividends) is an allowable charge against profits for the purposes of taxation assessment, and so the real rate of interest payable is reduced.

(b) If the company can earn a greater return on its capital than the cost of that capital, then the company will benefit by using borrowed money to expand its business.

(c) A high gearing ratio will attract 'risk' investors in a period of high profits as they are likely to receive much higher dividends than would be the case in a low-geared company.

(d) In periods of inflation, companies which borrowed money at fixed percentage rates are at a distinct advantage over companies whose cost of capital is directly linked to prevailing interest rates.

The major disadvantages which gearing carries for a company are:

(a) The loss of flexibility enjoyed by directors concerning the way in which the profit might be appropriated, as a large proportion is already committed for the fixed interest payments.

(b) The possibility that potential investors would prefer low geared companies at a time when an economy is depressed and profits are stagnant, as only a small amount of such profits are attributed to fixed rate borrowing.

THE CONVERSION OF AN UNINCORPORATED BUSINESS INTO A LIMITED COMPANY

When a sole trader or a partnership takes the decision to become a limited company, one form of business organisation ends its life whilst another is born. This 'death and birth' is reflected in the accounting records by closing off the sole trader's or partnership's books and the making of opening entries in the books of the company.

The closing entries are made via a *realisation account*, which contains the following transfers from asset and liability accounts, as well as the purchase consideration for the business.

Debit	*Credit*
Transfer asset balances	Transfer liability balances
	Purchase consideration (e.g. shares, cash, debentures)

Occasionally certain balances, notably trade creditors, are not to be transferred to the new company, but are to be paid off prior to the transfer. In such cases, there is no necessity to post the creditors' balances to the realisation account, as they will be paid out of the business's bank account.

A number of assets and/or liabilities might be revalued prior to the transfer, and the purchase price of the business might be greater or less than the book value of its net assets.

Where the purchase price is greater than the agreed value of the net assets, the company is paying for goodwill. This represents a profit for the owners of the business being taken over, and is transferred from the realisation account to the capital account(s) of the owner or owners. If the purchase consideration is less than the agreed value of the business's net assets, then this represents *negative* goodwill, and is a loss to the owners which is debited to their capital accounts.

Note that the capital account balances are not posted to the realisation account, but are closed by transferring the appropriate amount of cash, shares, etc. (See Chapter 6 pp 68–69.)

THE UNPUBLISHED FINANCIAL STATEMENTS OF LIMITED COMPANIES

It has already been stated that all limited companies must *publish* their annual financial statements. These published accounts must be in a format prescribed by the 1985 Companies Act, as described later in this chapter. Prior to preparing accounts for publication, the company will prepare 'unpublished' accounts which are more detailed than those required by statute. In addition to being the basis for the published accounts, they will be used by the Inland Revenue for the purposes of taxation assessment and, in all probability, a copy will be sent to the company's bank manager in order to give him or her a detailed insight into the company's performance.

The preparation of a limited company's final accounts in their unpublished form follows the usual book-keeping conventions, but there are a number of items which are unique to companies when contrasted with the final accounts of sole traders and partnerships, as can be seen in Table 8.1.

Revenue statement	Sole trader	Partnership	Limited company
Manufacturing account (if applicable)	√	√	√
Trading account (if applicable)	√	√	√
Profit and loss account	√	√	√ includes' salaries, auditors fees and possibly debenture interest
Appropriation account	No	√ showing financial implications of partnership agreement (see Chapter 6)	√ showing the ways in which profit is appropriated
Balance sheet			
Fixed assets	√	√	√
Current assets	√	√	√
Current liabilities	√	√	√ may include liabilities for corporation tax, dividends and debenture interest
Capital account	√	√ for each partner	No
Current account	No	√ for each partner if 'fixed capital method' used	
Share capital	No	No	√
Reserves	No	No	√
Debentures	No	No	√ (if any)

Table 8.1 Comparison between the financial statements (unpublished) of limited companies and those of sole traders and partnerships.

THE PUBLISHED ACCOUNTS OF LIMITED COMPANIES

With over 900,000 registered companies in the United Kingdom, it is of obvious benefit to have a degree of uniformity in the form of presentation adopted for the published accounts. Prior to 1981, individual companies were given relative freedom as to the way in which information was given, provided that the disclosure requirements of company law were observed. The 1981 Companies Act (later consolidated in the 1985 Act) brought an end to such individuality by requiring companies to use the formats given in the Act when presenting profit and loss accounts and balance sheets for publication.

There are several formats (four for the profit and loss account and two for the balance sheet). The choice of format is even more restricted than appears at first sight, as the balance sheet format 2 is merely the 'horizontal' version of format 1, whilst profit and loss account formats 3 and 4 are the 'horizontal' versions of formats 1 and 2 respectively. The most popular formats are shown in Table 8.2.

Once a company has chosen between the various formats, the same format must be used each year unless, in the opinion of the directors, there are special reasons for a change. Items may be shown in *greater* detail than required by the formats, and headings or subheadings in the formats may be omitted if there is no amount to be shown in respect of the financial year in question and the previous year.

WHICH FORMAT TO CHOOSE?

1. Balance sheet – there is no real choice, as format 2 contains the same information as format 1, but in a horizontal as opposed to a vertical layout. In practice most companies use the vertical style of format (see Table 8.2(a)).
2. Profit and loss account (see Table 8.2(b)) – ignoring the 'horizontal' options of formats 3 and 4, the choice is between:
   (a) Format 1, which discloses gross profit, and presents the information in a way which should be reasonably familiar to students. Most companies use this format.

Balance Sheet
FORMAT 1

A Called-up share capital not paid

B Fixed assets
  I Intangible assets
    1. Goodwill
    2. Other intangible assets
  II Tangible assets
    1. Land and buildings
    2. Plant and machinery etc
  III Investments
    1. Shares in group undertakings and participating interests
    2. Loans to group undertakings and undertakings in which the company has a participating interest
    3. Other investments other than loans
    4. Others

C Current Assets
  I Stocks
    1.Stocks
    2. Payments on account
  II Debtors
    1. Trade debtors
    2. Amounts owed by group undertakings and Undertakings in which the company has a participating interest
    3. Others
  III Investments
    1. Shares in group undertakings
    2. Other investments
  IV Cash at bank and in hand

D Prepayments and accrued income

E Creditors: amounts falling due within one year
  1. Bank loans and overdrafts
  2. trade creditors
  3. Amounts owed to group undertakings and undertakings in which the company has a participating interest
  4. Other creditors

F Net current assets (liabilities)

G Total assets less current liabilities

H Creditors: amounts falling due after more than one year
  1. Bank loans and overdrafts
  2. Trade creditors
  3. Amounts owed to group undertakings and undertakings in which the company has a participating interest
  4. Other creditors

I Provisions for liabilities and charges

J Accruals and deferred income

K Capital and reserves
  I Called-up share capital
  II Share premium account
  III Revaluation reserve
  IV Other reserves
  V Profit and loss account

Table 8.2a Balance sheet Format 1

Profit and loss account

FORMAT 1

1. Turnover
2. Cost of sales
3. Gross profit or loss
4. Distribution costs
5. Administration expenses
6. Other operating income
7. Income from shares in group companies
8. Income from shares in related companies
9. Income from other fixed asset investments
10. Other interest receivable and similar income
11. Amounts written off investments
12. Interest payable and similar charges
13. Tax on profit or loss on ordinary activities
14. Profit or loss on ordinary activities after taxation
15. Extraordinary income
16. Extraordinary charges
17. Extraordinary profit or loss
18. Tax on extraordinary profit or loss
19. Other taxes not shown under the above items
20. Profit or loss for the financial year

FORMAT 2

1. Turnover
2. Change in stocks of finished goods and work-in-progress
3. Own work capitalised
4. Other operating income
5. (a) Raw materials and consumables
   (b) Other external charges
6. Staff costs:
   (a) wages and salaries
   (b) social security costs
   (c) other pension costs
7. (a) Depreciation and other amounts written off tangible and intangible fixed assets
   (b) Exceptional amounts written off current assets
8. Other operating charges
9. Income from shares in group companies
10. Income from shares in related companies
11. Income from other fixed asset investments
12. Other interest receivable and similar income
13. Amounts written off investments
14. Interest payable and similar charges
15. Tax on profit or loss on ordinary activities
16. Profit or loss on ordinary activities after taxation
17. Extraordinary income
18. Extraordinary charges
19. Extraordinary profit or loss
20. Tax on extraordinary profit or loss
21. Other taxes not shown under the above items
22. Profit or loss for the financial year

Table 8.2b Profit and Loss Account Formats 1 and 2

(b) Format 2, which is more suited to a manufacturing business, does not disclose the company's gross profit, but requires more detail than format 1 concerning such matters as 'own work capitalised' (e.g. wages paid to the company's own workers for the construction of fixed assets) and staff costs.

Note that items 7–20 in format 1 are identical to items 9–22 in format 2. Students do not require a comprehensive knowledge of this topic, but should be aware of the main features of the formats.

FRS 3 *REPORTING FINANCIAL PERFORMANCE*

This important standard, issued in October 1992, replaced an earlier SSAP (SSAP 6 *Extraordinary items and prior year adjustments*). SSAP 6 allowed companies to show 'extraordinary items' as a separate item in the profit and loss account, after the 'profit on ordinary activities' had been calculated. As the earnings per share figure (see p. 80) had, prior to the introduction of FRS 3, been calculated on profits *excluding* extraordinary items, it was easy for companies to present much higher than warranted eps figures by reclassifying 'ordinary' expenditure as extraordinary. This meant that costs such as those associated with reorganisation and redundancies were excluded in arriving at the eps. This resulted in SSAP 6 being discredited, and the Accounting Standards Board issued FRS 3 to replace it. This introduced:

—the virtual abolition of 'extraordinary' items;
—changes to the format of the profit and loss account;
—changes to the calculation of earnings per share, so that it reflects the true results for a period;
—a requirement for companies to provide:
   a statement of total recognised gains and losses;
   a note of historical cost profits and losses;
   a reconciliation of movements in shareholders' funds.

The main requirements of FRS 3 are dealt with on p. 103.

CONSOLIDATED PROFIT AND LOSS ACCOUNT
YEARS ENDED 30TH SEPTEMBER

		NOTES	1992 £ million		1991 £ million	
TURNOVER	Continuing operations		2 787.6		2 733.9	
	Acquisitions		3.7			
			2 791.3			
	Discontinued operations		71.4		110.4	
	Turnover, including share of related undertakings	1		2 862.7		2 844.3
	Less related undertakings' turnover			131.5		125.8
	Turnover			2 731.2		2 718.5
	Cost of sales	2		(1 464.0)		(1 462.3)
	Gross profit			1 267.2		1 256.2
	Net operating expenses	2		(856.3)		(855.9)
OPERATING PROFIT	Continuing operations		415.3		411.3	
	Acquisitions		(7.2)			
			408.1			
	Discontinued operations		2.8		(11.0)	
	Operating profit	1		410.9		400.3
Exceptional items	Goodwill write-off on disposal of operations	12		(117.1)		–
	Reorganisation & disposal of Glasrock	12		14.0		(19.6)
	Loss on disposal of operations	12		–		(5.4)
	Reorganisation of Health Care			(25.4)		–
	Profit on disposal of fixed assets on continuing operations			1.6		13.9
	Profit on ordinary activities before interest			284.0		389.2
	Interest (net)	3		(69.0)		(79.1)
	Profit on ordinary activities before taxation			215.0		310.1
	Tax on profit on ordinary activities	4		(109.6)		(95.8)
	Profit on ordinary activities after taxation			105.4		214.3
	Minority interests			(14.0)		(20.8)
	Profit for the financial year			91.4		193.5
	Dividends			(104.1)		(96.0)
	Surplus/(deficit) for the financial year			(12.7)		97.5
EARNINGS PER SHARE per 25p ordinary share net basis, undiluted	– on published earnings	2		19.34p		41.12p
	– adjustment for goodwill write-off			24.81p		–
	– before goodwill write-off			44.15p		41.12p

Fig. 8.3 BOC plc: profit and loss account

Profit and Loss Account

A layered format is to be used for the P&L account to highlight:

  i)   results of continuing operations (including the results of acquisitions);
 ii)   results of discontinued operations;
iii)   profits or losses on the sale or termination of an operation, costs of a fundamental reorganisation or restructuring and profits or losses on the disposal of fixed assets;
iv)   extraordinary items (very rare).

Notes:

1. If businesses had been acquired during the period, the results from these acquisitions are shown separately under 'Continuing Operations'.
2. The whole of the profit and loss account, to the level of 'operating profit', should be split between continuing and discontinued operations.
3. Exceptional items (other than those listed in 4 below) should be included under the statutory format headings to which they relate. These are material items which are of exceptional size in relation to the business as a whole. They should be separately disclosed by way of note, or where it is necessary in order that the financial statements give a true and fair view, on the face of the P&L account.
4. Profits or losses on the sale or termination of an operation, costs of a fundamental reorganisation or restructuring and profits or losses on the disposal of fixed assets should be shown separately on the face of the P&L account after 'operating profit' and before 'interest'.

There are also a number of other statements required to be presented with the profit and loss account, but these are outside the A-level syllabus.

Figure 8.3 shows the profit and loss account of BOC plc. The profit and loss account has been prepared in accordance with FRS 3, showing separately the proportions of turnover and profit contributed by continuing operations, acquisitions (i.e. business bought during the period) and discontinued properties (i.e. business sold or closed down during the period). It is a 'format 1' profit and loss account.

EXAMINATION QUESTIONS

1   The following trial balance was extracted from the books of Togo Ltd. on 31 December 1991.

	£	£
Share capital (ordinary shares of £1)		800,000
Share premium		400,000
Revenue reserve		92,800
Freehold premises cost	650,000	
Plant—cost	600,000	
Plant—depreciation		208,000
Purchases	2,017,000	
Sales		3,178,900
Wages	312,000	
Salaries	231,200	
Rent and rates	43,000	
Light and heat	15,500	
General expenses	316,900	
Bad debts	7,500	
Bad debt provision		8,600
Debtors	217,800	
Stock	256,900	
Creditors		175,200
Bank	173,700	
Suspense	22,000	
	4,863,500	4,863,500

You are given the following additional information.

(i) In preparing the trial balance two errors were made:

debtor balances were undercast by £20,000;
an item of plant purchased for £1,000 had been correctly credited to the bank account but had been credited instead of debited to the plant account.

(ii) A review of debtors has revealed balances of £5,300 that are irrecoverable and £7,900 that are doubtful.

(iii) Closing stock amounted to £313,200.

(iv) Plant costing £20,000 with accumulated depreciation of £18,000 at 1 January 1991 was sold for £3,000. The only accounting entry made so far for this transaction has been to debit bank and credit the sale proceeds to the sales account.

(v) The company's policy is to depreciate plant by the straight line method at 10%. The company provides a full year's depreciation in the year of acquisition and no depreciation in the year of disposal.

(vi) Payments due at the end of the year were:

	£
Wages	5,800
Light and heat	1,900

(vii) Rates paid in advance at the end of the year were £3,200.

(viii) A final dividend of £100,000 is proposed for the year.

(a) You are required to prepare a profit and loss account for the year ended 31 December 1991 and a balance sheet as at 31 December 1991.   (24)

(b) The Chairman of Togo Ltd. says "I have read that a company's most important asset is the skill and dedication of its employees. Why is this not shown in the balance sheet?" Discuss this question.   (8)

(c) Discuss the extent to which company accounts do, and can, report the full costs of pollution.   (8)

(Northern 1992)

2 The trial balance of Oscar Limited at 31 December 1992 appeared as follows:

	£	£
Ordinary shares of £1 each, fully paid		100,000
Purchases	440,000	
Retained profit		60,000
Freehold land at cost	160,000	
Fixtures, at cost	30,000	
Depreciation on fixtures		18,000
Business rates	6,000	
Motor vehicles, cost	56,000	
Depreciation on vehicles		28,000
Insurance	4,000	
Stock at 1 January 1992	80,000	
Debtors	60,000	
Trade creditors		48,000
Sales		620,000
Bank	24,200	
12% Debentures (issued in 1989)		80,000
Debenture interest	4,800	
Wages and salaries	68,000	
Heat and light	8,200	
Professional fees	7,800	
General expenses	2,400	
Motor expenses	4,000	
Provision for bad debts		2,000
Bad debts	600	
	956,000	956,000

Notes:

1. Stock at 31 December 1992 was £90,000.

2. Depreciation for 1992 has yet to be provided on the following bases:

Fixtures	10% straight line
Motor vehicles	20% straight line

3. Account was to be taken of an adjusting post balance sheet event on 21 January 1993, when a customer, who owed £15,000 to Oscar Limited on 31 December 1992, was declared bankrupt. The debt had been considered as good at the year end. The provision for bad debts (a general provision of 3% of debtors), was to be adjusted and carried forward.
4. Insurance of £600 had been prepaid at the year end, and wages of £6,000 were to be accrued.
5. The directors propose a dividend of £15,000 for the year.
6. Taxation of £5,450 is to be provided.

(a) Prepare a profit and loss account and balance sheet based on the above information (not necessarily in a form suitable for publication).   (18)

(b) Explain why the company has retained profits carried forward at the end of its financial year, and why it does not distribute all these profits to its shareholders.   (7)

(London 1993)

TUTOR'S ANSWER TO QUESTION 1

a)   Togo Ltd—Profit and loss account for the year ended 31 December 1991.

	£	£
Sales (3,178,900 − 3,000)		3,175,900
less:		
Opening Stock	256,900	
Purchases	2,017,000	
	2,273,900	
Closing stock	313,200	
Cost of Sales		1,960,700
Gross Profit		1,215,200
Wages (312,000 + 5,800)	317,800	
Salaries	231,200	
Rent & Rates (43,000 − 3,200)	39,800	
Light & Heat (15,500 + 1,900)	17,400	
General expenses	316,900	
Bad debts (7,500 + 5,300 − 700)	12,100	
Depreciation	58,200	
Profit on plant disposal	(1,000)	992,400
Net Profit		222,800
Dividend		100,000
Retained profit for the year		122,800
Retained profit b/fwd		92,800
Retained profit c/fwd		215,600

Togo Ltd—Balance Sheet as at 31st December 1991.

Fixed Assets	£ Cost	£ Depreciation	£ NBV
Freehold Property	650,000	—	650,000
Plant (see Workings)	582,000	248,200	333,800
	1,232,000	248,200	983,800

Current Assets		
Stock	313,200	
Debtors		
(217,800 + 20,000 − 5300 − 7,900)	224600	
Prepayments	3,200	
Bank	173,700	
	714,700	
Current Liabilities		
Creditors	175,200	
Accruals (5,800 + 1,900)	7,700	
Proposed dividend	100,000	
	282,900	
Net current assets		431,800
		1,415,600
Share capital—ordinary shares of £1		800,000
Share Premium		400,000
Retained Profit		215,600
		1,415,600

b)   Under normal accounting conventions the only assets recorded in the balance sheet are those to which the company has firm legal title and which have been paid for. Employees are free to leave the company after giving due notice, and in practice the costs of developing their training and skills cannot be easily identified and allocated across a number of accounting periods. Thus it is not appropriate to record investment in employees as an asset except in the rare circumstances, such as transfer fees for footballers, where an explicit payment has secured a firm legal entitlement to services for a substantial contract period.

Where another business is acquired then the price paid may cover, in addition to identifiable specific assets, an element of 'goodwill'. Goodwill covers the whole range of benefits of acquiring a business as a whole, including the accumulated expertise of employees.

c)   The 'full' costs of pollution fall on a range of parties, including individuals who may suffer personal injury or loss of amenity, other enterprises that may be denied facilities to which they are entitled, and the community as a whole that may have to bear costs of restoring the environment.

To some extent these costs fall, in turn, on the polluter. Injured parties may have a legal claim on the polluter, while legislation may provide for penalties to be imposed. Since these costs will ultimately fall on the business causing the pollution it is a failure in the accounting system if provision is not made for them in the period when pollution occurs rather than in later periods when claims are actually made. In practice accounts do frequently fail to make adequate provision for such a problem, partly because of technical difficulties in making such predictions and partly because of a failure by accountants to show an adequate awareness of such risks.

Some authors have argued the case for some form of 'social accounting' including provision of company accounts to report not just the impact of pollution costs on the company itself but to identify the cost to society as a whole.

Workings

Plant	Cost	Depr
Per T.B.	600,000	208,000
Correction of error	2,000	
Disposal	(20,000)	(18,000)
Depr Charge		58,200
	582,000	248,200

Provision for bad debts

c/fwd	7900	b/fwd	8600
P & L	700		
	8600		8600

STUDENT'S ANSWER TO QUESTION 2

(a)

66 No! For the year ended **99**

OSCAR LIMITED
TRADING ACCOUNT AT
31 DECEMBER 1992

Sales		620,000
Less Cost of Goods Sold		
Opening Stock	80,000	
Purchases	440,000	
	520,000	
Less Stock at 31 Dec 1992	90,000	430,000
Gross Profit carried forward		190,000

66 A very odd way of showing a vertical account. Why split it like this? **99**

OSCAR LIMITED
PROFIT AND LOSS ACCOUNT
31 DECEMBER 1992

Gross Profit brought forward		190,000
Provision for bad debts		2,000
		192,000
Less expenses:		
Business rates	6,000	
Insurance	3,400	
Debenture interest	4,800	
Wages and salaries	74,000	
Heat and light	8,200	
Professional fees	7,800	
General expenses	2,400	
Motor expenses	4,000	
Bad debts	600	
Provision for doubtful debts	1,800	
Depreciation on fixtures	3,000	
Depreciation on motor vehicles	11,200	127,200
Net Profit carried forward		64,800

66 The new provision is $3\% \times (60{,}000 - 15{,}000) = £1{,}350$, so write-back is £650. **99**

66 The full year's interest is £9,600, so accrue £4,800 **99**

66 The post balance sheet event was 'adjusting', so an extra £15,000 here **99**

66 Wrong **99**

66 Again, no need for splitting the account like this **99**

OSCAR LIMITED
APPROPRIATION ACCOUNT
31 DECEMBER 1992

Net Profit brought forward		64,800
Less Proposed dividend	15,000	
Taxation	5,450	20,450
		44,350
Reserves b/f		60,000
Reserves c/f		104,350

66 Correct heading, at last! 99

OSCAR LIMITED
BALANCE SHEET AT
31 DECEMBER 1992

	Cost	Depreciation	Net
Fixed Assets	£	£	£
Freehold land	160,000	—	160,000
Fixtures	30,000	21,000	9,000
Motor vehicles	56,000	39,200	16,800
	246,000	60,200	185,800
Current Assets			
Stock		90,000	
Debtors	60,000		
Less provision	1,800	58,200	
Prepayments		600	
Bank		24,200	
		173,000	
Less Current Liabilities			
Creditors	48,000		
Wages accrued	6,000		
Proposed dividend	15,000		
Corporation tax	5,450	74,450	
			98,550
			284,350
Ordinary shares of £1 each, fully paid			100,000
Reserves			
Profit for the year		104,350	
12% Debentures		80,000	184,350
			284,350

66 Correct fixed assets, but debtors should be £43,650, net of provision 99

66 Correct, apart from missing debenture interest accrual 99

66 All profit, not just this year 99

66 A fundamental error. Debentures are not part of reserves, they should be shown separately as long term loans 99

66 Not well expressed, only worth perhaps one or, at most, two marks 99

(b)   The company has retained profits carried forward at the end of its financial year because after they had calculated their proposed dividend and corporation tax the profit is liable for the payments or the purchase of new machinery, motor vehicles and fixtures. Since the business is a limited company the shareholders' profits remain in the business for capital expenditure.

TUTOR'S COMMENTS

Part (a) showed that the candidate had a good general knowledge of accounting, but had trouble with the more complicated items such as the bad debts provision and debenture interest. The balance sheet was well drafted apart from the inexcusable error in showing debentures as part of reserves Part (b) was totally inadequate. A good answer would have included the following points

— the company has retained profits as it is a separate legal entity which is under no obligation to distribute all its profits to its members
— the fact that there are profits in reserves does not also mean that there is cash available to pay a large dividend
— profits are used to build up the strength of the company, by being re-invested rather than being paid as dividends.

Now attempt the review questions on page 307. Answers are given on page 323.

ACCOUNTING FOR LIMITED LIABILITY COMPANIES (2)

GETTING STARTED

The life cycle of a limited company might range from a matter of months to several hundred years: indeed there are companies in existence which can trace their roots to the seventeenth century. Once formed, the company can grow by virtue of its profitability, its ability to raise funds, and the use of those profits and funds to expand the business, perhaps by taking over other profitable companies.

This chapter looks at the ways in which a company's share capital might change over time, and also gives a brief introduction to the topic of *consolidated* accounts. These have to be prepared for groups of companies whereby the results of parent (holding) companies and subsidiaries have to be combined to form a meaningful financial summary of the entire group. A detailed knowledge of consolidated accounts is outside A-level syllabuses, but you are expected to have a basic understanding of the subject for most boards, except Cambridge.

ESSENTIAL PRINCIPLES

ISSUES OF SHARES

The issued share capital of a limited company can increase in a number of ways, including:

1. By a sale of shares, usually for cash: only plcs are allowed to sell their shares *to the general public*, by means of a prospectus issue or an offer for sale. Private limited companies are not allowed to offer their shares to the public.
2. By a rights issue, whereby shares are sold to existing shareholders, usually at a discounted price.
3. By a bonus issue, whereby shares are given to existing shareholders without any cash being payable to the company.

SALE OF SHARES

As mentioned in the previous chapter, the overwhelming majority of companies in the United Kingdom are private ones and as such are not allowed to offer their shares or debentures to the general public. However, they *are* able to sell their shares, but the persons buying are likely to be friends, relatives or business acquaintances of existing shareholders.

A plc wishing to raise capital by means of a share issue will usually do so by means of an *offer for sale*, whereby the shares are sold by the company to a merchant bank, which in turn offers the shares for sale to the general public by placing advertisements (known as prospectuses) in national newspapers (see Fig. 9.1). The prospectus

---

This Notice is issued in compliance with the requirements of The International Stock Exchange of the United Kingdom and Republic of Ireland Limited ('London Stock Exchange')

A T R E U S
P L C

Incorporated and registered in England and Wales under the Companies Act 1985 under number 2650119

Placing and Public Offer
by Sheppards

of 27,500,000 Ordinary Shares of 1p each at 20p per share
payable in full on application
of which 11,250,000 Ordinary Shares are being placed and
16,250,000 are being offered to the public

The business of Atreus, which will principally comprise that of the DB (UK) Group, will be the designing, manufacturing, marketing and selling of a range of shower screens, shower enclosures and mirrors, mainly in the bathroom market

Share capital following the merger, Offer and Acquisition

Authorised			Issued and fully paid	
Number	Amount		Number	Amount
50,000,000	£500,000	in ordinary shares of 1p each	36,051,123	£360,511

The Ordinary Shares now being issued will rank pari passu in all respects with the existing issued ordinary shares of Atreus PLC and will rank in full for all dividends and other distributions hereafter declared, made or paid in respect of the ordinary share capital of the Company.

Listing Particulars have been published which alone contain full details of the history and business of Atreus PLC.

Copies of the Listing Particulars relating to the above may be obtained during normal business hours on any workday, Saturdays and public holidays excepted, up to and including 18 March 1993 from the Company Announcements Office at the London Stock Exchange, London Stock Exchange Tower, Capel Court entrance, off Bartholomew Lane, London EC2 (for collection only) and up to 30 March 1993 from

Sheppards	The Royal Bank of Scotland plc	The Royal Bank of Scotland plc	Atreus PLC
No. 1 London Bridge	Registrar's Department	Registrar's Department	10 Newhall Street
London SE1 9QU	PO Box 451 Owen House	67 Lombard Street	Birmingham B3 3LX
	8 Bankhead Crossways North	London EC3P 3DL	
	Edinburgh EH11 ONU		

A MINI-PROSPECTUS AND APPLICATION FORM WILL BE PUBLISHED IN
THE FINANCIAL TIMES ON 16 MARCH 1993
15 March 1993

Fig. 9.1 Atreus plc: notice of offer for sale of shares (*not a full prospectus*)

contains very detailed information concerning the background of the company, its past financial performance and profit forecasts. Persons wishing to buy shares simply return an application form to the merchant bank, together with a cheque for the appropriate amount.

The price at which shares are offered will be set at the point which, in the opinion of the company, demand for the shares will match the supply. In practice, however, share issues are either *oversubscribed* or *undersubscribed*, the former resulting from a high demand for shares due to such factors as favourable price and good press comment, the latter resulting from weak demand caused perhaps by adverse newspaper reports or over-pricing. The share price, whether considered high or low, will invariably be set at a premium to the nominal value, and the company may require the purchase price to be paid at intervals, rather than in one lump sum. Example 1 shows how the company accounts for a share issue where part of the purchase price is paid when the shares are applied for, part when the shares are allotted (i.e. issued to shareholders) and the final part (known as a 'call') four months after the application date.

Example 1

Corker plc (which has issued share capital of £4 million) wishes to raise additional capital by the issue of shares.

On 1 April 1993, 400,000 ordinary shares of £1 each were issued at £2.25 per share, payable as to £1.50 on application, including the premium, 30p on allotment due by 30 June 1993 and 45p on the first and only call to be made on 1 August 1993. By the closing date, applications for 450,000 shares were received, and all applications were scaled down on a pro rata basis. All surplus cash received on applications was used as part payment of the amount due on allotment.

Write up the ledger accounts necessary to record the above transactions and prepare an extract from the company's balance sheet at 1 August 1993. Assume that all sums due were paid in full by the appropriate dates.

> 'Scaled down' means that applications for 450,000 shares are reduced to the number of shares being sold (400,000)

> £75,000 = 50,000 excess applications @ £1.50 each

Solution: (numbers in brackets represent the sequence of entries)

Corker plc

Bank account

1993			£
1 April	Application monies	(2)	675,000
30 June	Allotment monies	(8)	45,000
1 Aug	Call money	(12)	180,000

Application and allotment account

1993			£	1993			£
1 April	Share capital (400,000 × £0.25)	(4)	100,000	1 April	Cash on application (450,000 × £1.50)	(3)	675,000
	Share premium (400,000 × £1.25)	(6)	500,000	30 June	Cash on allotment (400,000 × £0.30 less £75,000)	(9)	45,000
30 June	Share capital (400,000 × £0.30)	(10)	120,000				
			720,000				720,000

Call account

1993			£	1993			£
1 Aug	Share capital	(14)	180,000	1 Aug	Cash (400,000 × £0.45)	(13)	180,000

Share capital account

		1993				£
		1 April	b/f		(1)	4,000,000
			Application and allotment a/c		(5)	100,000
		30 June	Application and allotment a/c		(11)	120,000
		1 Aug	Call account		(15)	180,000
						4,400,000

Share premium account

1993				£
1 Apr	Application and Allotment a/c		(7)	500,000

Balance Sheet as at 1 August 1993 (extract)

Share capital			£
Authorised:	? ordinary shares of £1 each		?
Issued:	4,400,000 ordinary shares of £1 each, fully paid		4,400,000
Reserves:	Share premium account		500,000

Tutor's comments

The sequence of entries is very straightforward, and can best be followed by referring to the entry order shown in brackets. (These numbers would *not* be included in the actual ledger.) The net effect of the entries is to increase the bank account by £900,000, the share capital account by £400,000 and the share premium account by £500,000. It has been assumed that there was no opening balance on the share premium account.

FORFEITED SHARES

Most share issues are paid in full at the time of application, but the offer for sale particulars will make it quite clear whether calls are to be made at intervals after the shares have been allotted. Occasionally, shareholders may have difficulty paying these calls, in which case they run the risk of having their shares forfeited, and the loss of the monies paid on application and allotment. The company may, if it wishes, re-issue these shares at some future date.

RIGHTS ISSUES

If a plc decides to sell shares by means of an offer for sale, it will have to pay a considerable sum by way of advertising costs, and fees to professional advisers. An alternative method of raising money by an established company is to make a *rights issue* whereby existing shareholders are given the right to buy more shares from the company at a price which is usually lower than the current market value. The company will, at the time it announces the rights issue, send a document to the shareholders explaining why it has decided to raise more capital. Reasons most often cited include the expansion of the business by takovers, the reduction in the level of borrowings, and the need to fund research and development. Shareholders have the following choices when the company makes a rights issue:

(a) Take up the rights issue by buying the additional shares.
(b) Sell the rights to another person, who will then take up the rights in place of the original shareholder. This course of action is taken by shareholders who either do not have the money available to pay for the rights, or do not wish to invest further sums in the company owing to there being better investment opportunities elsewhere.

BONUS ISSUES

Also called a *capitalisation issue* or *scrip issue*, a bonus issue is an issue of shares to existing shareholders without any cash being required by the company. The shares are 'paid up' by utilising the reserves (both capital and revenue) of the company. This distribution of the reserves is an effective way of transferring value to shareholders without the need for cash to be paid to them. There are many reasons why the reserves increase in value over a period, including the upward revision of fixed asset values, particularly land and buildings, and the accumulation of retained earnings from profit and loss account over several years. Capital reserves will increase by virtue of a share issue at a premium over nominal value, or the transfer of profits into a capital redemption reserve (see p. 95) when shares are redeemed other than from the proceeds of a new share issue.

EFFECTS OF BONUS ISSUE

A bonus issue has the following effects on the company:

1. The company's balance sheet becomes more realistic following the issue, as the shareholders are then likely to be shown as holding the major part of the company's value, rather than such value being left within the company as reserves.
2. As value is being distributed, but not cash, there is no drain on the company's liquid resources, as would be the case if a dividend were to be paid.
3. The increase in share capital might spur the company to make higher profits if the dividend per share is to be maintained.
4. Although companies often regard bonus issues as worthwhile in terms of good 'public relations' *vis-à-vis* its shareholders, the administration costs of the issue might be high when contrasted with the benefits to be gained.

From the shareholder's viewpoint:

(a) The bonus issue will result in each shareholder owing proportionately more shares in the company. The overall value of the shares does not change as a direct result of the issue, however, as the market price of each share will be reduced in consequence of the issue. The possession of a greater number of shares does lead to an increase in their marketability as it becomes easier for shareholders to dispose of part-holdings.
(b) If the company is able to maintain its dividend per share, then shareholders will receive a greater total dividend than enjoyed prior to the bonus issue. However, if revenue reserves have been used for the bonus issue, the company has less funds available to distribute.

Note that a bonus issue should be distinguished from a *share split*, whereby the marketability of shares with a very high market value (e.g. £20) is improved by splitting the nominal value (e.g. by a '10 for 1' share split). All that results is a share with a lower nominal value (10p if previously £1) and a corresponding reduction in its market value (£2).

Example 2 includes a bonus issue, a share split and also a redemption of debentures.

Example 2

After the trading and profit and loss accounts had been drawn up for Goring plc for the year ended 31 March 1993, the following balances remained in the accounts:

	DR £	CR £
Issued share capital (£1 shares)		200,000
General reserve		160,000
Profit and loss account balance		70,000
Debentures		87,500
Debtors and creditors	87,500	61,250
Goodwill	5,000	
Plant and machinery	231,250	
Stock	115,000	
Cash at bank	140,000	
	578,750	578,750

It was decided:

i   To capitalise £100,000 of the general reserve by issuing 25p bonus shares in proportion to the number of shares already held by shareholders.
ii To convert the existing £1 ordinary shares to ordinary shares of 25p each.
iii To pay a dividend of 20% on the existing ordinary shares. No dividend was to be paid on the bonus shares.
iv To write £3,000 off goodwill by a transfer from profit and loss account.
v   To redeem £35,000 of the debentures.

Required:

Give the ledger entries necessary to record the above transactions and show the (unpublished) balance sheet as it would appear after the transactions were completed.

Solution:

Goring plc

General Ledger

Issued share capital a/c

1993				1993			
31 Mar	c/f		300,000	31 Mar	b/f		200,000
					Transfer general reserve		100,000
			300,000				300,000

General reserve a/c

1993				1993			
31 Mar	Transfer share capital		100,000	31 Mar	b/f		160,000
	c/f		60,000				
			160,000				160,000

Profit and loss a/c

1993				1993			
31 Mar	Goodwill written off		3,000	31 Mar	b/f		70,000
	Proposed dividend (20% × £200,000)		40,000				
	c/f		27,000				
			70,000				70,000

Debentures a/c

1993				1993			
31 Mar	Redemption of debentures		35,000	31 Mar	b/f		87,500
	c/f		52,500				
			87,500				87,500

Redemption of debentures a/c

1993				1993			
31 Mar	Cash		35,000	31 Mar	Debentures		35,000

Goodwill a/c

1993				1993			
31 Mar	b/f		5,000	31 Mar	Profit and loss		3,000
					c/f		2,000
			5,000				5,000

Cash a/c

1993				1993			
31 Mar	b/f		140,000	31 Mar	Redemption of debentures		35,000
					c/f		105,000
			140,000				140,000

Proposed dividend a/c

1993				1993			
31 Mar	c/f		40,000	31 Mar	Profit and loss a/c		40,000

Balance Sheet as at 31 March 1993

		£	£
Fixed assets:	Plant and machinery		231,250
Intangible asset:	Goodwill		2,000
Current assets:	Stock	115,000	
	Debtors	87,500	
	Cash at bank	105,000	
		307,500	
Current liabilities:	Creditors	61,250	
	Proposed dividend	40,000	
		101,250	
			206,250
			439,500
Share capital:			
Authorised and issued			
1,200,000 ordinary shares of 25p each, fully paid			300,000
Reserves:	General	60,000	
	Profit and loss account	27,000	
			87,000
			387,000
Long-term liabilities: Debentures			52,500
			439,500

Tutor's comments

There are no book-keeping entries for a share split, the only effect being a revision of the number of shares and their nominal value as shown on the balance sheet. The bonus (capitalisation) issue is accounted for in this question by simple transfer from the general reserve account to the share capital account. Note that some questions state that it is the policy of the directors to main the *maximum flexibility* regarding the company's reserves. This is merely another way of saying that if there is a choice of using reserves which are available for dividend distribution (i.e. revenue reserves) and those which may not be distributed (i.e. capital reserves), then the latter should be used for the purpose of the bonus issue in preference to the former.

> ❝❝ More flexibility if capital reserves used before revenue reserves ❞❞

In some cases the redemption of debentures is accompanied by a transfer from profits into a debenture redemption reserve of a sum equal to the amount redeemed. Although not a statutory requirement (cf. capital redemption reserve) it is considered prudent to reduce the profit and loss account by the cash repaid to debenture holders, since the liquid funds available for future dividend payments have been depleted. By making the transfer, the balance of distributable reserves will not be overstated to the detriment of the company.

If the question had required such a transfer, the journal entry would have been:

		£	£
DR	Profit and loss account	35,000	
CR	Debenture redemption reserve		35,000
—	Transfer of an amount equal to the cost of debentures redeemed.		

CAPITAL REORGANISATION

After having studied the previous sections of the chapter, it should be apparent that share capital need not be a static feature of a company, but can be subject to certain changes. To summarise the position, we have seen that share capital can be:

(a) Increased by means of (i) a fresh issue of shares; (ii) a rights issue to existing share-holders; (iii) a bonus issue to existing shareholders.

(b) Decreased by means of (i) the redemption of capital; (ii) the purchase of the company's own shares.
(c) Made more 'marketable' by means of a share split.

In addition to (b) above, there could be a situation where a company may seek to decrease its share capital, without the necessity of compensating for the decrease by a transfer from revenue to capital reserves. This is known as a capital reduction scheme, and is generally undertaken by companies which have suffered substantial losses, causing 'negative reserves' to appear on the balance sheet, i.e. there is a debit balance on the profit and loss account.

By reducing the nominal value of its share capital, the company is acknowledging that there has been a decline in the value of its shares. However, the shareholders may well agree to such a reduction if it is felt that the company is 'getting back on its feet', and would be able to pay dividends out of future profits. Any capital reorganisation scheme which results in a reduction in the company's share capital must be within the company's powers as stated in its articles, and must also be approved by the court. The company's shareholders must also approve the scheme at a general meeting.

GROUPS OF COMPANIES

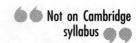

Not on Cambridge syllabus

When a business reaches a certain size, it may find that opportunities for further increasing its profits are restricted by a number of factors, including:

(a) difficulty in developing new products due to the costs involved;
(b) the emergence of strong competitors;
(c) restrictions on the geographical area which the business can satisfactorily cover;
(d) limitations to the expertise of existing employees;
(e) insufficient funding resulting in under-utilisation of assets;
(f) over-dependence on suppliers of raw materials and/or services resulting in events such as stoppages caused by stock shortages or machine breakdowns.

There are a number of ways to circumvent these problems, the most obvious being to 'take over' competing companies, supplier companies or, so as to diversity the range of activities, companies which make products or provide services which are dissimilar from those presently being made or offered.

Parent companies

Most large business organisations are comprised of a *parent* company and numerous *subsidiaries*. The simplified FRS 2 definition of a parent company is one which:

▶ holds a majority of the voting rights in another undertaking, or
▶ is a member of the undertaking and has the right to appoint or remove directors holding a majority of the voting rights, or
▶ has the right to exercise a *dominant influence* over the undertaking.

As can be seen from the above, a company does not necessarily require a 51% shareholding in another company to be classed as its parent. The fact that the company is a member (i.e. shareholder) and controls the way in which the other company's directors are selected would also create a parent-subsidiary relationship.

There is no limitation on the number of subsidiaries that a holding company might have. For example, Tate and Lyle plc had fifty eight subsidiaries on 26 September 1992 whilst the BOC group plc had seventy five.

Associated companies

In addition to subsidiaries, many companies also have associated companies. The definition of an associated company, as contained in SSAP 1, is as follows:

'An *associated company* is a company not being a subsidiary of the investing group or company in which the interest of the investing group or company is for the long term and is substantial and, having regard to the dispostion of the other shareholdings, the investing group or company is in a position to exercise a *significant influence* over the company in which the investment is made'.

The term 'investing group or company' simply means the business entity which is considering whether another company is an associated company. A 'significant influence' is presumed to be in existence where the investing group or company holds in excess of 20% of the equity voting rights (i.e. shares which give an entitlement to vote at company general meetings).

Basis of accounting for associated companies

If a company has one or more 'associated companies' then any income received from investments in those companies should be accounted for as follows:

(a) in the investing company's own profit and loss account: dividends received and receivable are credited;
(b) in the investing company's own balance sheet: the cost of the investment is shown, less any amounts written off.

The major part of the standard deals with the way in which the results of associated companies are included in the *consolidated* accounts of a group of companies (i.e. the 'combined' financial statements of a parent company and its subsidiaries). A simplified summary of the provisions are:

(a) in the consolidated profit and loss account: the investing group's *share of the profits or losses* (not just dividends received) of the associated company is included;
(b) in the consolidated balance sheet: the investing group's *share of the net assets* of the associated company is included.

THE CONSOLIDATED BALANCE SHEET

When a company has a subsidiary, it is obliged by law to present *consolidated* accounts to its members, i.e. financial statements showing the combined position of all the group companies. These comprise mainly a consolidated balance sheet and a consolidated profit and loss account.

The consolidated balance sheet is compiled from the individual company balance sheets, with adjustments for the following:

'UNREALISED' PROFIT ON STOCK MUST BE ELIMINATED

Where a group company has sold goods to another group company at a price above cost, and some or all of those goods remain in stock at the end of the financial year, then the 'profit' arising from those goods left in stock must be eliminated when consolidating the balance sheet. For example, H plc sells goods which cost £7,000 to S Ltd (its subsidiary) for £10,000. At the date of the consolidated balance sheet, the 'profit' of £3,000 must be eliminated if S Ltd has not sold the goods to a purchaser who is 'outside' the group of companies. This is achieved by reducing H plc's profit and loss account balance by £3,000 and similarly reducing the value of S Ltd's stock.

> **Real profit is only earned by selling outside the group**

The purpose of this adjustment is to eliminate the risk of over-stating profit by means of artificial inter-group transactions. If no such adjustment were needed, then there would, in theory, be no limit to the amount of profit which could be recorded, despite the fact that sales might never have been made to 'real' customers outside the group!

INTER-COMPANY INDEBTEDNESS MUST BE ELIMINATED

As the consolidated balance sheet shows the combined position of the group, it would be misleading to show assets and liabilities which have arisen solely by virtue of the creation of loans between companies within the group. If this adjustment were not made, both consolidated asset and liability totals would be overstated because of the existence of purely internal financing arrangements. For example, H plc is owed £12,000 by S A Ltd and owes £7,000 to S B Ltd, both being subsidiaries of H plc. Although the loans would appear either as assets or liabilities in the individual balance sheets of the three companies, they would be cancelled out when the figures were consolidated. Any loans shown on the consolidated balance sheet will thus represent monies owed or owing by persons or companies who are *outside* the group.

Dividends owed by one group company to another must similarly be cancelled, unless there is a 'minority interest' (see below) in the subsidiary company, in which case that proportion of the dividend belonging to the minority is included in the consolidated balance sheet as part of the minority interest.

'INVESTMENT IN SUBSIDIARIES' IS ELIMINATED

Although the balance sheet of the parent company includes 'investment in subsidiary' as a fixed asset, when preparing the consolidated balance sheet this is cancelled against the share capital and reserves of the subsidiary as shown in the subsidiary's balance sheet. However, it often happens that the amount paid for the investment differs from the combined total of the subsidiary's share capital and reserves. The reasons for this might be:

1. The price paid for the shares was greater than the balance sheet value of those shares at the time of purchase. The surplus price represents *goodwill*, and should be written off or amortised in accordance with SSAP 22.
2. The price paid for the shares was less than the balance sheet value of those shares at the time of purchase. This difference is treated as a *capital reserve*, and is included as such in the consolidated balance sheet.
3. The reserves of the subsidiary have changed since the date of acquisition by the holding company. Increases are known as 'post-acquisition' profits and decreases are referred to as 'post-acquisition' losses. Such changes are added to or deducted from the group reserves on the consolidated balance sheet, after which such reserves are available for distribution. This position should be contrasted with that of '*pre*-acquisition' profits, which represent part of the net assets in existence at the time of the purchase by the holding company. Such profits are *not* available for distribution to the holding company's shareholders, as it would be prejudicial to the interests of creditors and financiers if part of the price paid for the subsidiary were to be used for the purpose of paying dividends.

> 〝〝 Profits earned before acquisition are not available for group dividends 〞〞

'MINORITY INTERESTS' MUST BE COMPUTED

In many cases, a holding company does not own the entire share capital of its subsidiary. The proportion of shares which it does not own is referred to as 'the minority', and a calculation must be made of the value of the minority's stake in the subsidiary. This calculation is made as follows:

Minority % of subsidiary capital and reserves at date of consolidated balance sheet	x
Minority % of subsidiary's proposed dividend	x
Total minority interest	x

EXAMINATION QUESTIONS

1. Expansion p.l.c. is to issue shares to the public at the same time as a rights issue is made to its existing members. Bonus shares will also be issued.

The company's most recent balance sheet provides the following information:

Paid up share capital–	£
100,000 preference shares at £1	100,000
500,000 ordinary shares at 50p	250,000
Reserves–	
Share premium account	100,000
Capital redemption reserve	75,000
Revaluation reserve	100,000
General reserve	200,000
Asset replacement reserve	50,000
Profit and loss account	75,000
	£950,000

Authority to increase the company's capital has been obtained.
An extraordinary meeting of members has resolved the following:

(i)   One bonus share is to be issued for each five ordinary shares held.
(ii) Both preference and ordinary shareholders will be allowed to subscribe for ten ordinary shares for every ten shares (excluding bonus shares) of either class held: 10p per share is payable on application and 80p on allotment.
(iii) Additional shares may be applied for both by existing shareholders and the public. Applications from existing shareholders are to be accepted in full before any allotments are made to the public: 25p per share is payable on application and £1.50 on allotment.

When the application lists closed it was found that:

(i)   The rights issue was entirely taken up and no shareholder at the time held less than 10 shares. No shareholders held any fraction of 5 shares.
(ii) Existing shareholders applied for and were allotted 50,000 shares.
(iii) Members of the public sent in application monies for a further 75,000 shares, of which only 50,000 were allotted. The directors allotted two shares for every three applied for. No fractional adjustments were required.

REQUIRED:

(a) An extract from the company's balance sheet showing the shares and reserves after the allotments have taken place but before amounts due on allotment have been paid.   (10)
(b) A statement of the entries to be included in the bank account.   (4)
(c) An explanation of why shares are sometimes issued at a premium.   (4)

(Wales 1991)

2.   The following is the draft Balance Sheet and an extract from the Profit and Loss Account of Wood plc:

Balance sheet as at 31 March 1992:

	£	£
Fixed Assets		570,000
Current Assets		
Stock	99,000	
Debtors	170,000	
Bank	3,000	
	272,000	
Current Liabilities		
Creditors	160,000	112,000
		682,000

Capital and Reserves

Ordinary shares	400,000
Share premium	50,000
Revaluation reserve	80,000
Capital redemption reserve	50,000
General reserve	100,000
Profit and loss account	2,000
	682,000

Profit and Loss Account extract for the year ended 31 March 1992

Net loss	(5,000)
Retained profit brought forward	7,000
Retained profit carried forward	2,000

The Chairman is concerned that no ordinary share dividend has been recommended, and suggests that part of the various reserves should be utilised to provide a dividend to the ordinary shareholders.

He also suggests the following as a means of financing the acquisition of additional fixed assets:

(i)   Bonus shares of £50,000 to be issued.

(ii)   Stock valued at £30,000 can be sold at a profit of £15,000 in August 1992. The profit should be taken into account immediately.

(iii) The company has a prime location together with a skilled workforce. These are very valuable assets and therefore Goodwill of £40,000 should be introduced into the accounts.

(iv)   Research costs incurred during the year have been charged to the Profit and Loss Account. These should be treated under intangible assets in the Balance Sheet thereby increasing profit.

REQUIRED

A.   Explain to the Chairman how each of the various reserves in the draft Balance Sheet may have been created, and advise him on his suggestion that they be used for ordinary share dividend.   *(15)*

B.   *Comment briefly on each of the suggestions* (i) to (iv) as a means of providing finance for the acquisition of additional fixed assets.   *(8)*

(Oxford 1992)

3.   The accounts of Richmal plc included the following balances on 31 December 1992:

	£	£
Issued Share Capital:		
2m ordinary shares of 25p each, fully paid		500,000
300,000 12% redeemable preference shares of £1 each, fully paid		300,000
		800,000
Share Premium	20,000	
Retained Earnings	243,000	
		263,000
		1,063,000

In January 1993, the company made a bonus issue of 300,000 ordinary shares of 25p each, by utilising part of the balance of retained earnings. It also redeemed 100,000 redeemable preference shares at a premium of 10p each. When issued, the redeemable preference shares had been sold at £1.06 each.

(a)   Prepare the appropriate ledger accounts (excluding the bank account) necessary to record the above transactions.   *(12)*

(b) Show the shareholders' funds section of the balance sheet immediately after the bonus issue of ordinary shares and the redemption of preference shares.   *(5)*

(c) Explain why a company might choose to issue *redeemable* preference shares.   *(4)*

(d) State the circumstances where a *capital redemption reserve* is created, and explain why such a reserve is needed.   *(4)*

(London 1993)

4. The balance sheet of De Vere Carter plc included the following information at 31 May 1992:

	£
Issued Share Capital:	
Ordinary shares of £1 each, fully paid	240,000
10% Preference shares of £1 each, fully paid	90,000
Reserves:	
Share premium account	65,000
Capital redemption reserve	40,000
Revaluation reserve	120,000
Profit and loss account	56,000

On 1 June 1992, the company is planning to increase its ordinary share capital in the following ways:

(i) An issue of bonus shares to existing members, with one bonus share being issued for every three ordinary shares held. The directors wished to retain the maximum flexibility regarding future dividend payments, so an appropriate choice of reserves was to be made for the purpose of the bonus issue.

(ii) A rights issue, whereby existing shareholders (both of ordinary and preference shares) may subscribe for five ordinary shares at £1.90 each for every three shares of either class held (excluding bonus shares). £1 is payable on application (by 30 June 1992), and 90p on allotment (by 31 July 1992).

(iii) A public issue of 100,000 ordinary shares to be made at £2.50 each, with £1.10 payable on application (by 30 June 1992) and the balance on allotment (by 31 July 1992). Existing shareholders are to be given priority, as their applications will be accepted before those of the general public.

Applications were received as follows:

1. 90% of the rights issue was taken up, and paid for by the due dates.

2. Existing shareholders applied for, and were allotted, 60 000 of the share issue. Other applications totalled 90 000 shares, and these were scaled down on a pro-rata basis, with excess application money being refunded on 10 July 1992. All application and allotment monies were paid by the due date, with the exception of £3,000 allotment money due from existing shareholders.

(a) Show the company's application and allotment account, and ordinary share capital account for the period 1 June 1992 to 31 July 1992.   *(12)*

(b) Calculate the final number of shares held by a shareholder with an initial holding of 900 ordinary shares, who applied for the rights issue and 500 shares in the new share issue.   *(3)*

(c) Explain two advantages and two disadvantages to a company of raising funds by a share issue, and suggest three alternative ways of raising funds that the company could have considered.   *(10)*

(London 1992)

TUTOR'S ANSWER TO QUESTION 4

a)   *Application and Allotment Account*

		£			£
10.7.92	Excess Application Money		30.6.92	Right issue –Application	
	refunded (50,000 × £1.10)	55,000		$(330,000 \times \frac{5}{3} \times \frac{90}{100} \times £1)$	495,000
31.7.92	Transfer Share Capital	1,190,500		Share issue (application)	
				–(existing shareholders)	
				(60,000 × £1.10)	66,000
				–(general public)	
				(90,000 × £1.10)	99,000

	31.7.92	Rights issue	
		–Allotment	
		$(330{,}000 \times \frac{5}{3} \times \frac{90}{100} \times 90p)$	445,500
		Share Issue (allotment)	
		–existing shareholders	
		$[(60{,}000 \times £1.40) - £3000]$	81,000
		–general public	
		$(40{,}000 \times £1.40$	56,000
		Allotment money c/d	3,000

		£1,245,500			£1,245,500

1.8.92	Allotment money b/d	3,000	

Ordinary Share Capital Account

31.7.92	Balance c/d	1,510,500	1.6.92	Balance b/f		240,000
				Transfer		
				Cap. Red. Reserve		40,000
				Revaluation Reserve		40,000
			31.7.92	Applic. + Allot. a/c		1,190,500
		1,510,500				1,510,000
			1.8.92	Balance b/d		1,510,500

b)

Original holding	900 shares
Add Bonus Issue	300 shares
	1,200
Add Rights Issue 900 × $\frac{5}{3}$	1,500 shares
	2,700 shares
Add Share Issue	500 shares
Final holding	3,200 shares

c)   Advantages
   1)   Not part of gearing–no fixed interest
   2)   Flexibility over dividend payments
   3)   Proceeds can be used to strengthen business by e.g. buying fixed assets, or reducing debt.
   4)   No need to give assets as security
Disadvantages
   1)   risk of dilution of original shareholders' stake
   2)   Effect on eps figure
   3)   Risk of failure of share issue
   4)   Cost of issue
Other sources
     Bank lending
     Sales of assets
     Debentures

STUDENT'S ANSWER TO QUESTION 3

a)

🌑🌑 Correct 🌑🌑

Ordinary Share Capital

1.1.93	Balance c/d	575,000	1.1.93	Balance b/f	500,000
				Retained earnings	75,000
		575,000			575,000
			1.1.93	Balance b/d	575,000

🌑🌑 Correct 🌑🌑

12% Redeemable Preference Shares

1.1.93	Preference Share Redemption	100,000	1.1.93	Balance b/f	300,000
	Balance c/d	200,000			
		300,000			300,000

	1.1.93	Balance b/d	200,000

Transfer should be £100,000 (nominal value redeemed)

See Tutor's comments

CRR account

1.1.93	Retained earnings	110,000

Retained earnings (P + L a/c)

CRR	110,000	Balance b/f	243,000
Balance c/d	137,000	Preference Share redemption	4,000
	247,000		247,000
		Balance b/d	137,000

Almost right except that only £4,000 can be taken from Share Premium Account (100,000 × [10p − 6p]), the balance comes from P&L

Preference share redemption a/c

1.1.93	Bank	110,000	1.1.93	Preference share capital	100,000
				Share Premium account	10,000
		110,000			110,000

Balance c/d should be £16,000, but 'one error, one penalty' applies

Share Premium a/c

1.1.93	Preference share redemption a/c	10,000	1.1.93	Balance b/f	20,000
	Balance c/d	10,000			
		20,000			20,000
			1.9.93	Balance b/d	10,000

No heading, no share premium account, capital redemption reserve or P&L shown so very few marks gained here

(b)

Issued share capital

2,300,000 ordinary shares of 25p each fully paid	575,000
200,000 12% redeemable preference shares of £1 each fully paid	200,000
	775,000

(c) ?

Good, concise answer

(d) A capital redemption reserve is created when the value of the shares being redeemed is greater than the proceeds from the issue of shares made for redemption. Such a reserve is needed so that a reserve is created in order not to endanger the position of third parties, i.e. creditors, debenture holders etc.

Tutor's comments

This was in some ways a strange answer, as the candidate had a good knowledge of the accounting procedures and scored full marks on part (d), but didn't answer part (c) and set out an inadequate and incomplete balance sheet.

The retained earnings account should appear as follows:

1.1.93	Share capital (Bonus issue)	75,000	1.1.93	Balance b/f	243,000
	Redemption of preference shares (Part of premium on redemption)	6,000			
	Capital redemption reserve	100,000			
	Balance c/f	62,000			
		243,000			243,000

An answer to part (c) could be as shown below.

The company may wish to raise capital for a relatively short term project, with the option of repaying the capital to shareholders once the project is completed. If the company believes that prevailing interest rates are set to fall in the long term, then by issuing redeemable shares, it can replace them with shares bearing a lower % dividend rate in due course.

OUTLINE ANSWERS

Question 1

(a)

	Preference shares	100,000	
	Ordinary shares (1)	650,000	750,000
	Reserves:		
	Share Premium (2)	465,000	
	CRR (3)	25,000	
	Revaluation reserve	100,000	
	Gen reserve	200,000	
	Asset replacement	50,000	
	Profit and loss	75,000	915,000
			1,665,000
	Less Allotment monies due (4)		623,750
			1,041,250

Workings:

(1) Ordinary shares b/f (500,000) £250,000 + Bonus issue (100,000) £50,000 + Rights to existing shareholders (600,000) £300,000 + New issue (100,000) £50,000 = £650,000 (No. of shares shown in brackets)

(2) Share premium b/f £100,000 + Rights issue (600,000 @ 40p) £240,000 + New issue to existing shareholders (50,000 @ £1.25) £62,500 + New issue to new shareholders (50,000 @ £1.25) £62,500 = £465,000

(3) Capital redemption reserve b/f £75,000 − utilised for bonus issue £50,000 = £25,000

(4) Allotment monies due

600,000 @ 80p =		£480,000
100,000 @ £1.50 = £150,000		
less overpaid		
application money		
25,000 @ 25p = £6,250		143,750
		623,750

(b) Entries in bank account

Application money:	rights issue 600,000 @ 10p		60,000
	new issue 125,000 @ 25p		31,250
Allotment money:	rights issue 600,000 @ 80p		480,000
	new issue (see W4 above)		143,750
			£715,000

(Proof: 600,000 shares @ 90p = £540,000 plus 100,000 shares @ 1.75 = £175,000, total £715,000)

(c) Share premium is an extra amount added to the nominal value of the shares to reflect the *market* value which can be obtained by selling the shares.

Question 2

(a) See text

(b)   (i) bonus shares do not bring in any cash, so cannot be seen as a means of providing finance.

    (ii) prudence concept states that profit should not be anticipated, therefore a future, uncertain, profit cannot be brought in to the 1991/2 accounts.

    (iii) 'non-purchased' goodwill cannot be included in a balance sheet, regardless of the justification. Furthermore, there is no financial benefit of considering such a measure even if it were allowed. (See SSAP 22)

    (iv) under SSAP 13, research costs must be written off against profits and cannot be carried forward. In any case, it would have no relevance to the provision of finance for acquiring additional fixed assets.

Now attempt the review questions on page 307. Answers are given on page 323.

CASH AND FUNDS FLOW STATEMENTS

FRS 1 CASH FLOW STATEMENTS

THE FIVE FORMAT HEADINGS

FURTHER REQUIRED ANALYSIS

SOURCE AND APPLICATION OF FUNDS STATEMENTS

GETTING STARTED

SSAP 10 *Source and Application of Funds Statements* was withdrawn in 1991, being replaced by FRS 1 *Cash Flow Statements*. SSAP 10 had been a mainstay of A-level examiners for many years, providing interesting computational questions which usually gave two years' profit and loss accounts and balance sheets in order for the candidate to prepare a Source and Application of Funds ('Funds Flow') Statement. This showed where a company derived its 'funds' (usually from profits, sales of assets, sales of shares and the receipt of loans) and how those funds were applied (including the purchase of fixed assets, the redemption of loans and the repayment of taxation and dividends). The net source or net application of funds was then reconciled with either an increase or decrease in working capital during the year, showing changes to the individual current assets and liabilities from one balance sheet date to the next.

A prime weakness of the Funds Flow Statement was that its emphasis on *working capital* meant that a significant decrease in cash could be obscured by an increase in stock or debtors. SSAP 10 had come in for heavy criticism due to much publicised cases where apparently solvent companies had collapsed due to lack of liquidity. In particular, the demise of the Polly Peck group (an international group trading in various goods and commodities ranging from fruit to electronics) was highlighted. In its Source and Application of Funds Statement, the group recorded a healthy funds *inflow* of £172m in 1989. Had the figures been restated as a *cash flow statement,* a cash *outflow* of £129m would have been shown.

Because FRS 1 is a relatively recent standard, some A-level syllabuses are still testing candidates on the old SSAP 10, and so the principles of both new and old standards are given in this chapter. Although their layouts are different, there is some similarity in the calculations needed.

SSAP 10 applied to all businesses with a turnover of more than £25,000 p.a., whereas FRS 1 exempts small* companies. Consequently, the vast majority of businesses will *not* need to disclose cash flow information with their annual accounts, but shareholders in plc's will expect to see it as a matter of course.

*Defined as a company (not a plc) which meets two out of the following three size criteria: Turnover < £2.8 m, Asset total < £1.4 m, Ave. employees < 50

ESSENTIAL PRINCIPLES

FRS 1 *Cash Flow Statements* was introduced in 1991, replacing SSAP 10 *Source and Application of Funds Statements*. Its emphasis is on *cash,* rather than *funds*, as it was felt that cash is a term universally understood, whereas 'funds' is open to different interpretations. Unlike SSAP 10, it includes a standard layout for the statement. This helps comparability between companies and limits the scope for 'creative' presentation by individual companies. As SSAP 10 is still examinable under some A-level syllabuses, Funds Flow statements are covered later in this chapter.

Cash flow statements can be complex to prepare, particularly for international groups (thankfully outside A-level syllabuses!), though FRS 1 has introduced wide exemptions for smaller companies (SSAP 10 required *all* companies with a turnover greater than £25,000 p.a. to present a funds flow statement). Although acknowledged as a significant improvement on SSAP 10, Cash Flow statements are still based on historical data and should not be seen as an infallible guide to a company's future financial performance.

OBJECTIVE

The objective of the FRS is for companies to report on a standard basis their cash generation and cash absorption for a period. This is achieved by them providing a primary financial statement analysing cash flows under the standard headings of:

ORTIF

- Operating activities;
- Returns on investments and servicing of finance;
- Taxation;
- Investing activities;
- Financing.

These five headings are looked at in detail below, and are summarised in Fig. 10.2. Their objective is to highlight the significant components of cash flow and also aid comparison between companies. Additionally, users of the financial statements will be helped in their assessment of the company's liquidity, viability and financial adaptability.

Small Company Exemptions

Small companies (see p. 124) do not have to present cash flow statements. The rationale behind this exemption is that 'the costs ... for small entities, which are often owner managed, of producing historical cash flow information in a highly standardised form are likely to be disproportionate to the benefits.' However, if the benefits outweigh the costs, then small companies are encouraged to publish a statement.

❝❝ Very useful for smaller companies to look at cash flow, even though not compulsory to produce statement under FRS 1 ❞❞

FORMAT

Cash flow statements have to be presented in a defined format, as shown in Figure 10.1.

XYZ Limited
Cash flow statement for year ended 31 March 1993

	£000	£000
Operating activities: net cash inflow (note 1)		6,889
Returns on investments and servicing of finance:		
Interest received	3,011	
Interest paid	(12)	
Dividends paid	(2,417)	
Net cash inflow from returns on investments and servicing of finance		582
Taxation		
Corporation tax paid	2,922	
Tax Paid		(2,922)
Investing activities		
Payments to acquire intangible fixed assets	(71)	
Payments to acquire tangible fixed assets	(1,496)	
Receipts from sales of tangible fixed assets	42	
Net cash outflow from investing activities		(1,525)
Net cash inflow before financing		3,024
Financing		
Issue of ordinary share capital	211	
Repurchase of debenture loan	(149)	
Expenses paid in connection with share issues	(5)	
Net cash inflow from financing		57
Increase in cash and cash equivalents		3,081

Notes to the cash flow statement

1. Reconciliation of operating profit to net inflow from operating activities

	£000
Operating profit	6,022
Depreciation charges	893
Loss on sale of tangible fixed assets	6
Increase in stocks	(194)
Increase in debtors	(72)
Increase in creditors	234
Net cash inflow from operating activities	6,889

2. Analysis of changes in cash and cash equivalents in the year

	£000
Balance at 1 April 1992	21,373
Net cash flow	3,081
Balance at 31 March 1993	24,454

3. Analysis of the balances of cash and cash equivalents as shown in the balance sheet

	1993	1992	Change in year
	£000	£000	£000
Cash at bank and in hand	529	681	(152)
Short-term investment	23,936	20,700	3,236
Bank overdraft	(11)	(8)	(3)
	24,454	21,373	3,081

4. Analysis of changes in financing during the year

	Share capital	Debenture loan
	£000	£000
Balance at 1 April 1992	27,411	156
Cash inflow/(outflow) from financing	211	(149)
Profit on repurchase of debenture loan for less than its book value		(7)
Balance at 31 March 1993	27,622	–

Fig. 10.1 Cash Flow Statement for a single company

The headings within the format can be explained more simply as follows:

	Heading	Explanation
A	Operating Activities: Net cash inflow[1]	Profit[2] for the year, adjusted for non-cash items and changes in working capital items
B	Returns on investment and servicing of finance	Interest received less interest paid; dividends received less dividends paid (not accrued/proposed: PAID!!)
C	Taxation	Taxation PAID in year (not what has been provided for)
D	Investing activities	Payments to buy fixed assets, receipts from selling fixed assets
	Net cash inflow[1] before financing	(A+B) - (C+D)
E	Financing	Cash In/Out due to share issues, loan repayments etc.
	Increase[3] in cash and cash equivalents	(A+B) - (C+D+E)

Notes:
1 or outflow for some companies
2 or loss for some companies
3 or decrease for some companies

Fig. 10.2 Explanation of Headings in Cash Flow Statement

DEFINITIONS

The format includes the terms *cash* and *cash equivalents*. These are defined as follows:

Cash

Cash in hand and deposits repayable on demand with any bank or other financial institution.

Cash equivalents

Short-term, highly liquid investments which are readily convertible into known amounts of cash without notice and which were within three months of maturity when acquired; less advances from banks repayable within three months from the date of the advance.

THE FIVE FORMAT HEADINGS

1. OPERATING ACTIVITIES

Net cash flow from operating activities represents the net increase or decrease in cash and cash equivalents resulting from the operations shown in the profit and loss account in arriving at operating profit.

There are two methods, 'indirect' and 'direct' which can be used for reporting net cash flows generated from operating activities.

Indirect Method

The *indirect method* (as shown in note 1 in Figure 10.1) starts with operating profit (as stated in the P&L account) and adjusts it for non-cash charges and credits to arrive at the net cash flow from operating activities.

The principal advantage claimed for this method is that it highlights the differences between operating profit and net cash flow from operating activities. As some investors and creditors assess future cash flows by estimating future income and then allowing for accruals adjustments, knowledge of past accruals adjustments may be useful for this purpose.

Direct Method

Optional under FRS 1

The *direct method* shows operating cash receipts and payments, aggregating to the net cash flow from operating activities. For example, if Figure 10.1 had been presented using the direct method, the amounts in the first part of the statement may have appeared as follows (using assumed figures):

Operating activities	£000	£000
Cash received from customers	132,876	
Cash payments to suppliers	(65,432)	
Cash paid to and on behalf of employees	(47,709)	
Other cash payments	(12,846)	
Net cash inflow from operating activities		6,889

This information would be *in addition to* the reconciliation provided in note 1 in Figure 10.1. This reconciliation must show separately:

—movements in stocks
—movements in debtors
—movements in creditors
—other differences between cash flows and profits (e.g. depreciation, profits/losses on sales of assets)

The principal advantage of the direct method is that it shows the specific sources of operating cash receipts and payments, which may be useful in assessing future cash flows. The standard does not insist on this information being presented, but encourages companies to do so where it is perceived that the benefits outweigh the costs.

Summary

Companies *must* give the information required by the Indirect method (as in Fig. 10.1), but *may* also give the additional information required by the Direct method. In an A-level question, show the statement in the form as shown in Fig. 10.1, unless you are given enough information, and the instruction, to use the Direct method as explained above. Either way, there should be no difference in the overall result obtained.

2. RETURNS ON INVESTMENTS AND SERVICING OF FINANCE

In general terms, these are receipts resulting from the ownership of an investment (e.g. dividends and interest received), and payments to providers of finance (e.g. dividends and interest paid).

3. TAXATION

This heading includes corporation tax paid during the year, less any tax which may have been refunded.

4. INVESTING ACTIVITIES

Cash flows under this heading relate to the acquisition or disposal of a fixed asset.

5. FINANCING

Financing cash *inflows* include receipts from issuing shares, debentures and loans. Financing cash *outflows* include repayments of amounts borrowed, purchase or redemption of share capital, and expenses paid in connection with share issues etc.

In addition to the reconciliation between operating profit and the net cash flow from operating activities, the standard requires a number of analyses and notes, as follows:

ANALYSIS OF CHANGES IN CASH AND CASH EQUIVALENTS DURING THE YEAR

This summary (see Note 2 in Figure 10.1) shows the opening balance of cash and cash equivalents and then adds or deducts the net cash inflow or outflow.

Where several balance sheet amounts are combined to effect the reconciliation, sufficient detail should be shown to allow the movements to be understood. This may take the form of the following reconciliations:

▶ *Analysis of the balances of cash and cash equivalents as shown in the balance sheet*, as shown in Note 3 in Figure 10.1;
▶ *Analysis of changes in financing during the year*, as shown in Note 4 in Figure 10.1.

An explanation of the notes to the cash flow statement is given in Figure 10.3.

	Note	Explanation
1	Reconciliation of operating profit to net cash inflow from operating activities	Converts 'profit' figure into a 'net cash flow' by adjusting for non-cash items such as depreciation. The effect of the accruals concept is cancelled by adjusting for changes in stock, debtors and creditors in the year
2	Analysis of the balances of cash and cash equivalents during the year	Shows the overall effect on cash and cash equivalent balances during the year. (opening balance ± change in year = Closing balance)
3	Analysis of the balances of cash and cash equivalents as shown in the balance sheet	Only required if there are several separate items making up the 'cash and cash equivalents' item
4	Analysis of changes in financing during the year	Only required if several balance sheet items have been combined to make the reconciliation.

Fig. 10.3 Explanation of Notes to Cash Flow Statement

Example 1

The balance sheets of Wenyon plc as at 31 October 1992 and 1993 are as follows:

	£000	31.10.92 £000	£000	31.10.93 £000
Fixed Assets (net book value)		6,277		6,814
Current Assets:				
Stock	735		922	
Debtors	1,055		1,125	
Bank	3,071		3,362	
	4,861		5,409	
Creditors: amounts due for payment within one year:				
Creditors	847		1,035	
Taxation	2,812		2,282	
Proposed dividends	2,327		2,800	
Bank overdraft	80		120	
	6,066		6,237	
Net current liabilities		(1,205)		(828)
		5,072		5,986
Share Capital:				
Ordinary Shares of 25p each		910		1,085
Share Premium Account		70		92
Retained Earnings		4,092		4,809
		5,072		5,986

The summarised profit and loss accounts for the two years ended 31 October 1993 are as follows:

	1992 £000	1993 3000
Net Operating Profit (note 1)	6,006	5,767
Interest Received	52	42
Interest Paid	(10)	(10)
Net Profit	6,048	5,799
Taxation	2,812	2,282
Net Profit after tax	3,236	3,517
Dividends:	2,327	2,800
Retained Earnings	909	717
Retained Earnings b/f	3,183	4,092
Retained Earnings c/f	4,092	4,809

Notes:

1. Net Operating Profit for 1993 is calculated after charging:

	£000
Provision for Depreciation	857
Profit on sale of assets	5

2. The assets which were sold realised £40,000, resulting in a profit on disposal of £5,000 when compared with their book value.

You are required to produce a cash flow statement for Wenyon plc for the year ended 31 October 1993, in accordance with Financial Reporting Standard (FRS) 1: Cash Flow Statements.

Solution

Wenyon plc

Cash flow statement

for the year ended 31 October 1993

	£000	£000	'step'
Operating activities: net cash inflow (note 1)		6,550	2
Returns on investments and servicing of finance:			
Interest received	42		
Interest paid	(10)		
Dividends paid	(2,327)		
Net cash outflow from returns on investments and servicing of capital		(2,295)	3
Taxation			
Corporation tax paid		(2,812)	4
Investing activities			
Payments to acquire tangible fixed assets*	(1,429)		
Receipts from sales of tangible fixed assets	40		
Net cash outflow from investing activities		(1,389)	5
Net cash inflow before financing		54	
Financing			
Issue of ordinary share capital**	197		
Net cash inflow from financing		197	6
Increase in cash and cash equivalents		251	

Notes to the cash flow statement

1. Reconciliation of operating profit to net cash inflow from operating activities

	£000
Operating profit	5,767
Depreciation	857
Profit on sale of tangible fixed assets	(5)
Increase in stocks	(187)
Increase in debtors	(70)
Increase in creditors	188
Net cash inflow from operating activities	6,550 1

2. Analysis of changes in cash and cash equivalents in the year

	£000
Balance at 1 November 1992	2,991
Net cash inflow	251
Balance at 31 October 1993	3,242 7

3. Analysis of the balances of cash and cash equivalents as shown in the balance sheet.

	1993	1992	Change in year	
	£000	£000	£000	
Cash at bank	3,362	3,071	291	
Bank overdraft	(120)	(80)	(40)	
	3,242	2,991	251	8

4. Analysis of changes in financing during the year.

	Share capital (including premium)	
	£000	
Balance at 1 November 1992	980	
Cash inflow from financing	197	
Balance at 31 October 1993	1,177	9

(Note that the 'Step' column is not shown as part of the answer—see Tutor's Comments below.)

*Workings

Fixed Assets (at net book value)

	£000		£000
b/f	6,277	Disposals (40-5)	35
Additions (=)	1,429	Depreciation	857
		c/f	6,814
	7,706		7,706

**Workings

Increase in Share Capital (1085 – 910)	=	175
Increase in Share Premium (92 – 70)	=	22
		197

Tutor's Comments

3W's –
Who/What/When?

The following procedure was used to draw up the cash flow statement.

Preliminary: Taking a new sheet, write in the '3 W's' and then draw up a skeleton statement, using the five main headings as in Figure 10.2. Leave at least four lines between the headings. On a second page, write in the headings to the notes, leaving at least five lines between headings. There should also be enough space for your workings. If not, go on to a third page.

Steps:

1   Identify the operating profit from the 1993 profit and loss account (£5,767,000), and enter in Note 1. Look for any 'non-cash' items (primarily depreciation) which may have been deducted in arriving at the profit figure, and add back in the note. Calculate the differences between opening and closing stocks, debtors and creditors, and adjust in the note. These adjustments serve to cancel out the effect of the accrual concept, by adjusting figures to the cash paid or received in the financial year. For information, increases and decreases in these figures have the following effect on the profit figure:

Item	Increase	Decrease
Stock	Decrease in profit	Increase in profit
Debtors	Decrease in profit	Increase in profit
Creditors	Increase in profit	Decrease in profit

2   Enter the net cash inflow (or outflow) from note 1 on to the statement.
3   Enter interest PAID or RECEIVED, adjusting for any accrued interest if necessary.

Enter dividends PAID or RECEIVED, adjusting for proposed dividends where necessary. The dividend account in this example would be as follows:

Dividends (£000s)

Dec (?) 1992 Bank	2,327	1 Nov 1992 Proposed dividend b/f	2,327
31 Oct 1993 Proposed div c/f	2,800	31 Oct 1993 P & L a/c	2,800
	5,127		5,127

As you can see, it is the dividend from the 1992 balance sheet which has been paid in 1993, and so is entered in the cash flow statement. If you have time in an examination, you could show this (and the taxation account – see below) as part of your workings.

4   As with the dividends, it is the taxation PAID in the year which is entered in the statement. The taxation account in the company's ledger would be as follows:

Corporation Tax (£000s)

Dec (?) 1992 Bank	2,812	1 Nov 1992 Tax provision b/f	2,812
31 Oct 1993 Tax provision c/f	2,282	31 Oct 1993 P & L a/c	2,282
	5,094		5,094

The amount entered in the cash flow statement is the tax *paid* of £2,812,000.

5   The fixed assets are a particular problem, as the question only gives the balance sheet values at the start and end of the year together with details of asset sales. What is needed is the construction of a fixed assets account, at *net book values*. This is shown in the first Working to the solution. The 'additions' is a balancing figure, representing the cost of fixed assets bought in the year. This, and the cash received from selling assets, is entered on the cash flow statement.

6   Changes in the financing of the company are calculated in the second Working to the solution, with the net total being entered on the statement.

7, 8 & 9   To conclude, the notes are completed. If your calculations have been performed correctly, then the final figures in each of the notes should correspond to the figures in the company's closing balance sheet.

In some questions, there might be 'internal' transfers between reserves, for example an amount of profit switched to a general reserve from profit and loss account, or an asset revaluation reserve created after a revision of fixed asset values. As these have no effect on cash flows, they are ignored when preparing the cash flow statement. Bonus issues of shares are also ignored, as no cash is being received for them.

INTERPRETATION OF THE CASH FLOW STATEMENT

If we look at the cash flow statement of Wenyon plc, we can see that £6,550,000 of cash has been generated from the company's operating activities in the year. Of this, £2,295,000 has been used to pay dividends, and includes a relatively small net inflow from interest. Taxation accounts for £2,812,000 whilst the net outflow on the purchase of fixed assets amounts to £1,389,000.

This leaves just £54,000 as the net cash inflow before financing. Shares have been sold at a premium during the year, so the overall increase in cash rises to a seemingly respectable £251,000.

It is difficult to assess a cash flow statement without knowing more about the company, its competitors and trading environment. It would also be very useful to have comparative statements for previous years. However, in the case of Wenyon plc, the following questions are relevant:

(i)   The net cash outflow from returns on investments and servicing of finance represents over 35% of the operating activities: net cash inflow. How does this compare with competitors, and previous years?

(ii)   The taxation seems high, though it does relate to a previous year's profit figure. Check the accuracy of the amount paid.

(iii)   What is the trend of fixed asset investment by the company. Is this year's figure particularly high or low?

(iv)   Why are stocks increasing? Is the rise matched by an increase in sales volume; if not, what is the point of keeping excess stock?

(v)   The final cash increase seems reasonable in the absence of any contrary information, but it should be borne in mind that shareholders may not be willing to buy new shares every year. As the new share capital represented 78% of the final cash increase, this may give some cause for concern.

SOURCE AND APPLICATION OF FUNDS STATEMENTS

Until the introduction of FRS 1, all businesses with a turnover exceeding £25,000 p.a. had to present a funds flow statement as part of their annual accounts. The main differences when compared to cash flow statements are as follows:

(i) there is no defined format for a funds flow statement, although the majority of companies presented the statement in a similar form to that shown in Figure 10.4. Cash flow statements *must* follow the format prescribed in the Standard.

(ii) the emphasis in funds flow statements is on the change in working capital whereas the cash flow statement emphasises cash inflows and outflows. It will be much more difficult to disguise liquidity problems when using cash flow statements.

(iii) Many more businesses are exempted from the requirements of FRS 1 than were compelled to provide funds flow statements under SSAP 10.

Nickleby plc

Statement of Source and Application of Funds
for year ended 30 June 1994

	£000	£000
Profit before tax		33,470
Adjustments for items not involving movement of funds		
Depreciation	6,750	
Loss on disposal of equipment	360	
Profit on disposal of vehicles	(780)	
		6,330
Total funds generated from operations		39,800
Funds from other sources		
Issue of ordinary shares for cash	2,000	
Issue of 8% debentures	5,000	
Proceeds of sale of assets:		
equipment	1,440	
vehicles	1,980	
		10,420
		50,220
Application of funds		
Cost of acquisitions of		
premises	30,000	
equipment	6,000	
vehicles	11,000	
Tax paid	2,205	
Dividends paid	540	
		49,745
		475
Increase/(decrease) in working capital		
Increase in stocks	1,167	
Increase in debtors/prepayments	273	
Increase in creditors and accruals	(551)	
Movement in net liquid funds		
Decrease in bank balance	(448)	
Increase in cash	34	
		475

Fig. 10.4 Usual layout for funds flow statement

PREPARATION OF FUNDS FLOW STATEMENT

As with cash flow questions, opening and closing profit and loss accounts and balance sheets will be given. Similar calculations will be needed to establish dividends and taxation paid in the year, and if full details of fixed asset movements have not been given, then a reconstruction of a fixed assets account is needed. Sometimes the operating profit is not given, so the candidate has to work back to the figure by preparing an appropriation account. This will contain all relevant details such as opening and closing balance on profit and loss account, proposed dividends and taxation. The operating profit will then be the balancing figure on the account.

Example 2

Prepare a source and application of funds statement from the final accounts of Wenyon plc shown on p. 131 in Example 1.

Solution

Wenyon plc
Source and Application of Funds Statement
for the year ended 31 October 1993

	£000	£000
Source of funds		
Profit before taxation		5,799
Adjustment for items not involving the movement of funds:		
Depreciation	857	
Profit on sale of fixed assets	(5)	852
Total generated from operations		6,651
Funds from other sources		
Issue of ordinary share capital	197	
Proceeds on sale of fixed assets	40	237
		6,888
Application of funds		
Purchase of fixed assets	1,429	
Taxation paid	2,812	
Dividends paid	2,327	
		6,568
Net source of funds		320
Increase in working capital		
Increase in stocks	187	
Increase in debtors	70	
Increase in creditors	(188)	
Movement in net liquid funds:		
Increase in cash at bank	291	
Increase in bank overdraft	(40)	251
		320

Tutor's Comments

All the figures should be easily identifiable from the cash flow statement in Example 1. As can be seen, the emphasis is on 'funds', which, at £320,000, are £69,000 higher than the *net* cash inflow recorded in the cash flow statement.

EXAMINATION QUESTIONS

1 The balance sheets of Parsnip plc at 31 December 1992 and 1993 are as follows.

	31.12.92 £	31.12.93 £
Fixed assets (net book value)	167,000	178,000
Current assets:		
stock	32,000	48,000
debtors	19,000	27,500
bank		6,800
Total assets	218,000	260,300
Share Capital:		
Ordinary shares of £1 each	100,000	125,000
Share premium account	—	12,500
Retained earnings	80,300	93,300
Current liabilities:		
creditors	13,000	14,500
taxation	9,000	7,000
proposed dividends	7,000	8,000
bank	8,700	—
	218,000	260,300

The summarised profit and loss accounts for the two years ended 31 December 1992 and 1993 are as follows.

	31.12.92 £	31.12.93 £
Gross profit	137,892	123,700
Less expenses	76,392	108,300
	61,500	15,400
Profit on sale of fixed assets	—	12,600
Net profit	61,500	28,000
Less taxation	9,000	7,000
Net profit after tax	52,500	21,000
Dividends	7,000	8,000
Retained earnings	45,500	13,000
Retained earnings b/f	34,800	80,300
Retained earnings c/f	80,300	93,300

The following additional information is available.

(1) A summary of the company's disposal of fixed assets account in the general ledger for the year ended 31 December 1993 is shown below.

	£		£
31 Dec 1993 Fixed Assets a/c	34,000	31 Dec 1993 Proceeds of sale	13,800
31 Dec 1993 Profit & Loss a/c	12,600	31 Dec 1993 Depreciation a/c	32,800
	46,600		46,600

The company bought fixed assets at a cost of £54 000 during the year.

(2) The increase in share capital was due to a rights issue.

Prepare a cash flow statement of Parsnip plc for the year ended 31 December 1993.

(25)

2 The balance sheets of Midge PLC as at 31 December 1992 and 1993 are as follows:

	31.12.92 £	31.12.93 £
Fixed Assets (net book value)	150,000	190,000
Current Assets:		
Stock	79,000	63,000
Debtors	15,000	23,000
Bank	22,900	—
Creditors due for payment within one year:		
Trade creditors	(49,800)	(42,800)
Taxation	(11,000)	(9,000)
Proposed dividends	(8,000)	(12,000)
bank	—	(26,700)
	198,100	185,500
Creditors due for payment after one year:		
16% Debentures 1989–94	(100,000)	—
	98,100	185,500
Share Capital:		
Ordinary shares of £1 each	40,000	100,000
Share premium account	10,000	14,000
Retained earnings	48,100	71,500
	98,100	185,500

The summarised profit and loss accounts for the two years ended 31 December 1993 are as follows:

	1992 £	1993	£
Gross profit	90,600		80,700
Less expenses	35,700		30,300
	54,900		50,400
Loss on sale of fixed assets	—		3,000
Net profit	54,900		47,400
Less taxation	11,000		9,000
Net profit after tax	43,900		38,400
Dividends:			
interim	—	3,000	
final	8,000	12,000	
			15,000
Retained earnings	35,900		23,400
Retained earnings b/f	12,200		48,100
Retained earnings c/f	48,100		71,500

Notes:

1. A summary of the company's fixed assets account for the year ended 31 December 1993 is shown below:

	£		£
1 Jan 1993 Cost b/f	270,000	31 Dec 1993 Disposals	20,000
31 Dec 1993 Additions	60,000	Cost c/f	310,000
	330,000		330,000

The assets which were disposed of realised £700, resulting in a loss on disposal of £3,000 when compared with their book value.

2. A bonus issue of 10,000 shares of £1 each was made during the year ended 31 December 1993, paid up from the share premium account.

   (a) Draw up a cash flow statement for the year ended 31 December 1993.

(21)

(b) Give two possible reasons why the debentures were redeemed in the year ended 31 December 1993 despite the company's lack of liquidity at the year end.

(4)

3 Prepare a source and application of funds statement from the data contained in question 1.

TUTOR'S ANSWER TO QUESTION 1

Parsnip plc
Cash Flow Statement
for the year ended 31 December 1993

	£	£
Net cash inflow from operating activities (note 1)		34,200
Returns on investments and servicing of finance		
Dividends paid	(7,000)	
Net cash outflow from returns in investments and servicing of finance		(7,000)
Taxation		
Corporation tax paid		(9,000)
Investing activities		
Payments to acquire intangible fixed assets	(54,000)	
Receipts from sales of intangible fixed assets	13,800	
Net cash outflow from investing activities		(40,200)
Net cash outflow before financing		(22,000)
Financing		
Issue of ordinary share capital	37,500	
Net cash inflow from financing		37,500
Increase in cash and cash equivalents		£15,500

Notes to the cash flow statement

1. Reconciliation of operating profit to net cash inflow from operating activities.

	£
Operating profit	28,000
Depreciation charges	41,800
Profit on sale of tangible fixed assets	(12,600)
Increase in stocks	(16,000)
Increase in debtors	(8,500)
Increase in creditors	1,500
Net cash inflow from operating activities	£34,200

2. Analysis of changes in cash and cash equivalents during the year.

	£
Balance at 1 January 1993	(8,700)
Net cash inflow	15,500
Balance at 31 December 1993	6,800

Workings

Fixed Assets (at net book value)

		£			£
1.1.93	b/f	167,000	31.12.93	Disposals a/c (cost)	34,000
	Disposals a/c (Depn)	32,800		P + L a/c depreciation (=)	41,800
	Additions	54,000	31.12.93	c/f	178,000
		253,800			253,800

TUTOR'S COMMENTS

The year's depreciation can only be found by constructing a fixed asset account, at net book values, as shown in the workings.

OUTLINE ANSWERS

Question 2

Net Cash inflow from operating activities £67,700*; Dividend paid (£11,000); Taxation paid (£11,000); Investing activities: purchase of assets (£60,000); receipts from sales of assets £700; Financing: Share issue £64,000; repayment of debentures (£100,000). Net cash decrease (£49,600).

*Profit £47,400 + Dep'n £16,300[†] + Loss on disposal £3,000 + Decrease in stock £16,000 − Increase in debtors (£8,000) − Decrease in creditors (£7,000) = £67,700

†Depreciation calculated by drawing up an account as follows:

31.12.93	Disposals a/c	16,300	1.12.93	Dep'n b/f (270–150)	120,000
	(20,000–[3000 + 700])		31.12.93	P + L a/c, depreciation for	
	(cost − book value)			year (balancing figure)	16,300
	Dep'n c/f (310 − 190)	120,000			
		136,300			136,300

Question 3

Source of funds:
Net Profit £28,000 + depreciation £41,800 − profit on sale of assets (£12,600) =
Total generated from operations = £57,200
Other sources: issue of share capital £37,500, receipts from sale of assets £13,800
Total sources = £108,500
Applications: Purchase of fixed assets £54,000; Dividends paid £7,000; Taxation paid £9,000
Total application = £70,000; Net source of funds £38,500
Increase in working capital:

Increase in stocks	16,000
Increase in debtors	8,500
Increase in creditors	(1,500)
Movement in net liquid funds	15,500
	£38,500

Now attempt the review questions on page 308. Answers are given on page 324.

GETTING STARTED

Although the final accounts of an unincorporated business might consist of only two pages, containing trading and profit and loss accounts on one and a balance sheet on the other, a limited company must produce more detailed information to satisfy the requirements of the Companies Act, accounting standards and possibly the Stock Exchange if the company has a stock market listing. The factor which is common to all business organisations is that these accounting statements are not produced solely for the purpose of providing information for the owner or owners of the business, but are also likely to be used by other interested parties for various purposes. These include the following:

Banks, who need to know whether a business is capable of repaying loans, or is in a sound financial position if loans are being requested.

Potential investors, who may use the accounting information to decide whether or not to invest money in the business.

The Government, which must ensure that tax is paid on profits, where applicable, and that there is compliance with relevant Acts of Parliament.

Customers and suppliers, both actual and potential, who may wish to ensure that a business is solvent prior to entering a trading relationship.

Employees who have a direct interest in the financial affairs of the business for which they work.

The local community, which may be concerned about the effects of redundancies, factory closures, etc.

Business competitors, who can measure their own performance against that of their rivals.

Economic analysts, who can attempt to establish trends by an analysis of the results of particular businesses.

Members of the general public, who may require information relating to environmental, ecological or other attitudes revealed in company annual reports.

INTERPRETATION OF ACCOUNTS

WHAT INFORMATION IS AVAILABLE?

INTERPRETATION OF THE ACCOUNTS

THE FIRST STAGE: PRELIMINARY ANALYSIS

THE SECOND STAGE: RATIO ANALYSIS

THE THIRD STAGE: INTERPRETATION

THE VALIDITY OF ACCOUNTING STATEMENTS

CURRENT PURCHASING POWER ACCOUNTING

CURRENT COST ACCOUNTING

ESSENTIAL PRINCIPLES

The amount of information which is made available depends primarily upon the type of business entity.

SOLE TRADERS AND PARTNERSHIPS

One of the features of sole trading or partnership is the absence of any statutory requirement to *publish* accounts.

In practice, only a handful of 'sets' of final accounts are produced (usually by a qualified accountant), their likely destination being to the owner or partners, a bank manager, and the taxation authorities. Any wider distribution is entirely at the discretion of the owner(s).

LIMITED COMPANIES

For a limited company however, not only does each shareholder and debenture holder have a right to receive a copy of the final accounts, but also a copy must be placed on public record (in the United Kingdom by being sent to a Registrar of Companies). Members of the public may obtain copies of a particular company's accounting information on payment of a fee.

Private limited companies

A private limited company will include in its published accounts the following statements, in addition to the profit and loss account and balance sheet in the prescribed Companies Act format:

A *directors' report*, which contains a brief review of the company's results and trading activities, and certain statutory information not necessarily found in the accounting statements.

Notes to the accounts, which give additional information required by statute or accounting standards to aid the fuller understanding of the company's financial position.

An *auditor's report*, which is a statement from an independent qualified accountant as to whether the accounts show a true and fair view of the state of the company's affairs and comply with the various requirements of the Companies Act.

Note that the Companies Act gives certain exemptions from full disclosure to 'small' and 'medium-sized' companies.

Public limited companies

A public limited company subject to Stock Exchange regulations will provide additionally:

A *chairman's report*, which is a comprehensive survey of the state of the company's business, its past performance and future prospects.

A *summary of statistics*, which gives certain key financial figures for a five-year period (or longer).

A *cash flow statement*, drafted in accordance with FRS 1 (see Chapter 10).

As previously explained, the amount of information contained within the accounting statements will vary considerably according, primarily, to the type of business entity and secondly, the attitude of the business owners regarding the provision of additional, 'non-statutory' information.

Regardless of the quantity of information provided, the users of accounting statements must adopt a methodical and analytical approach if they are to gain the maximum understanding of the business's performance. This can best be demonstrated by using data from a fictitious company, Ace plc, for the two years ended 31 December 1993. For this purpose, it has been assumed that the analyst has access to the detailed, unpublished accounting statements, as well as to the published version. (See Figures 11.1(a), 11.1(b) and (11.1(c).)

The accounting statements given in Figure 11.1 contain a mass of statistical information, and in practice this would be supplemented by other information including the directors' report and the various 'notes to the accounts'. A logical approach must be adopted to ensure that the correct conclusions are drawn from the analysis, and this is best achieved by dividing the process into three distinct parts: preliminary, calculations and interpretation.

Ace plc
Trading and Profit and Loss Accounts
for the years ended 31 December 1992 and 1993

(All figures in £000)

	1993		1992	
Sales		4,500		3,600
Less: Cost of sales				
Opening stock	200		160	
Purchases	1,850		1,670	
	2,050		1,830	
Less: Closing stock	250		200	
		1,800		1,630
Gross profit		2,700		1,970
Less: Expenses				
Directors' salaries	148		127	
Wages and staff salaries	915		836	
Printing, stationery and advertising	275		223	
Postages, wrappings and sundries	61		57	
Discount (net)	36		2	
Rent and rates	31		26	
Light and heat	42		60	
Motor expenses	95		90	
Telephone and insurance	25		26	
Repairs and renewals	49		45	
Depreciation	180		170	
Audit and accountancy	19	1,876	18	1,680
Net profit on ordinary activities, before interest		824		290
Interest paid		74		50
Net profit before taxation		750		240
Less taxation		200		60
Net profit after taxation		550		180
Proposed dividends		150		60
		400		120
P&L b/f		300		180
P&L c/f		700		300

Fig. 11.1(a) Specimen accounts for analysis — trading and profit and loss accounts

Ace plc
Balance Sheets as at 31 December 1992 and 1993

(All figures in £000)

	1993	1992
Fixed assets	1,114	322
Current assets		
Stock	250	200
Debtors	434	476
Cash in hand	22	20
	706	696
Creditors: amounts due for payment within one year		
Creditors	128	101
Taxation	200	60
Dividend	150	60
Bank overdraft	350	285
	828	506
Net current assets (liabilities)	(122)	190
Net assets	992	512
Share capital		
Ordinary shares of 25p each	200	200
Reserves (P&L)	700	300
	900	500
Creditors: amounts due for payment after more than one year		
Long-term loans	92	12
Capital employed	992	512

Fig. 11.1(b) Specimen accounts for analysis: balance sheet

Ace plc
Cash flow statement
for year ended 31 December 1993

	£000	£000
Operating activities: net cash inflow (note 1)		1,023
Returns on investment and servicing of finance:		
Interest paid	(74)	
Dividends paid	(60)	
Net cash outflow from servicing of capital		(134)
Taxation		
Corporation tax paid		(60)
Investing activities		
Payments to acquire tangible fixed assets	(984)	
Receipts from sales of tangible fixed assets		12
Net cash outflow from investing activities		(972)
Net cash outflow before financing		(143)
Financing		
Issue of long term loans		80
Net cash inflow from financing		80
Decrease in cash and cash equivalents		(63)

Notes to the cash flow statement

1. Reconciliation of operating profit to net inflow from operating activities

	£000
Operating profit	824
Depreciation	180
Increase in stocks	(50)
Decrease in debtors	42
Increase in creditors	27
Net cash inflow from operating activities	1,023

2. Analysis of changes in cash and cash equivalents in the year	£000
Balance at 1 January 1993	265
Net cash flow	63
Balance at 31 December 1993	328

3. Analysis of the balances of cash and cash equivalents as shown in the balance sheet

	1993	1992	Change in year
	£000	£000	£000
Cash at bank	22	20	2
Bank overdraft	(350)	(285)	(65)
	(328)	(265)	(63)

Note:

1. The company is a retailer, with eight shops selling a wide range of household goods
2. The company bought a supermarket from a competitor during 1993.

Fig. 11.1(c) specimen accounts for analysis — cash flow statement

THE FIRST STAGE: PRELIMINARY ANALYSIS

❝❝ Find out as much as possible about the company ❞❞

This consists of obtaining sufficient background knowledge to make the user aware of the environment in which the business operates. It includes such matters as the following, with the likely source of the information in brackets:

1. Type of trade (directors' report, chairman's report, advertising).
2. Geographical trading areas (directors' report, chairman's report).
3. Financial history (five-year summary, previous years' accounts, company information services, e.g. Extel).
4. Management (directors' report).
5. Competition (trade newspapers, stock market sector analyses).
6. Quality of products (visual inspection, advertising).

The amount of information which can be gleaned will obviously depend upon many factors, but *any* preliminary research is useful if it helps to place the company and its business in an appropriate context prior to the detailed calculation of ratios and percentages.

Having obtained a general impression of the scope and nature of the business, the analyst should then take the current year's accounts and read through each statement, making careful notes of any unusual or interesting items, changes in accounting policies, qualification in auditors' reports, etc. By looking at the 'bottom lines' of the profit and loss account and balance sheet, i.e. the net profit and total capital employed, an immediate impression can be gained of the progress of the business in the year. For Ace plc, the net profit has increased from £240,000 to £750,000, whilst shareholders' funds have increased from £512,000 to £992,000. This seems to indicate that the company had a 'good year', which may or may not be borne out by the detailed calculations to be made in the second stage of the analytical process.

THE SECOND STAGE: RATIO ANALYSIS

The next step is to calculate ratios which reveal specific aspects of the financial picture of the business as a whole.

These ratios are usually grouped into three categories:

1. Operating ratios.
2. Financial ratios.
3. Investment ratios.

Operating ratios

These are extracted primarily from the trading and profit and loss accounts and also from within the working capital section of the balance sheet. All figures used are taken from Figure 11.2 (Ace plc).

1. Gross profit margin

$$\frac{\text{Gross profit}}{\text{Sales}} \times 100$$

1993 $\dfrac{2,700}{4,500} \times 100 = 60\%$

1992 $\dfrac{1,970}{3,600} \times 100 = 54.7\%$

This shows the proportion of the sales revenue which resulted in a gross profit to the company. It is affected by various factors including changing price levels and altered sales mix. The margin might be reduced by companies that wish to increase their share of a particular market. For Ace plc, however, the position strengthened in 1993 as compared with 1992.

2. Net profit margin

$$\frac{\text{Net profit}}{\text{Sales}} \times 100$$

1993 $\dfrac{750}{4,500} \times 100 = 16.7\%$

1992 $\dfrac{240}{3,600} \times 100 = 6.7\%$

The net profit margin shows the efficiency with which expenses are controlled, and it is clear that 1993 was a far better year than 1992 in this respect. However, the figure can become distorted by factors such as the company imposing rigid 'wage freezes' on employees' pay, or by drastic although temporary cut-backs in overheads, which may be storing up trouble for future years.

3. 'Mark-up'

$$\frac{\text{Gross profit}}{\text{Cost of goods sold}} \times 100$$

1993 $\qquad \dfrac{2,700}{1,800} \times 100 = 150\%$

1992 $\qquad \dfrac{1,970}{1,630} \times 100 = 120.9\%$

Directly linked to the gross profit margin, the 'mark-up' indicates the pricing policy of the business, as it shows the percentage addition made to cost prices to arrive at selling prices.

In 1993, every £100 of goods bought in by Ace plc was being sold at an average of £250. Similarly priced goods bought in 1992 were being sold at £220.

4. Return on capital employed (ROCE)
$$\dfrac{\text{Net profit before interest and tax}}{\text{Average capital employed}} \times 100$$

1993 $\qquad \dfrac{750 + 74}{992} \times 100 = 83.1\%$

1992 $\qquad \dfrac{240 + 50}{512} \times 100 = 56.7\%$

This is a measure of overall profitability, showing the percentage return from the capital employed within the company. In both years, the ROCE was exceptionally high, which might indicate that the time will come soon when new competitors emerge. The denominator used in the formula is the capital employed at the balance sheet date, but the average of capital between the start and end of the year could also be used. The ROCE can be distorted if significant loans and overdrafts have been 'netted off' when arriving at the balance sheet totals. In Ace plc's case, the revised formulae would be (adding back the overdraft):

1993 $\qquad \dfrac{750 + 74}{992 + 350} \times 100 = 61.4\%$

1992 $\qquad \dfrac{240 + 50}{512 + 285} \times 100 = 36.4\%$

Although the ROCE percentages are reduced, the returns are still high, and the revised formulae do little to change the original comment on the figures.

5. Fixed assets turnover
$$\dfrac{\text{Sales}}{\text{Fixed assets (net value)}}$$

1993 $\qquad \dfrac{4,500}{1,114} = 4.0{:}1$

1992 $\qquad \dfrac{3,600}{322} = 11.2{:}1$

The fixed assets turnover ratio measures the sales generated by each £1 of fixed assets: £11.20 in 1992 but only £4 in 1993. The purchase of the supermarket referred to in the notes to the accounts appears to have been completed in the latter part of 1993, which would seem to indicate that the sharp decline in the ratio is only temporary. When the 1994 accounts are available analysts would expect to see a reversal of the downward trend as the sales from the new premises would be recorded for the full year.

6. Rate of stock turnover ('stock turn')

$$\frac{\text{Average stockholding}}{\text{Cost of goods sold}} \times 365$$

1993 $\quad \dfrac{0.5(200 + 250)}{1,800} \times 365 = 45.6 \text{ days}$

How long does it take to sell stock?

1992 $\quad \dfrac{0.5(160 + 200)}{1,630} \times 365 = 40.3 \text{ days}$

If a company can increase the speed at which it sells its stocks, then it can generate more profit in the process, provided that the increase in turnover is not obtained by simply slashing the gross profit margin. In 1992, the business took an average of 40.3 days to sell its stock, but this had increased to 45.6 days in 1993. The drawback of this calculation is that accurate average stock figures need to be used, but those appearing in the balance sheets are likely to be at an unrealistically low level owing to the fact that most businesses choose the end of their financial year so that it coincides with their period of least activity.

7. Debtors' collection period

$$\frac{\text{Debtors}}{\text{Credit Sales}} \times 365$$

1993 $\quad \dfrac{434}{4,500} \times 365 = 35.2 \text{ days}$

How much time do debtors take to pay?

1992 $\quad \dfrac{476}{3,600} \times 365 = 48.3 \text{ days}$

The efficiency of the business's credit control department is measured here by calculating the average length of time that money is owed by debtors. The department was more efficient in 1993 than 1992, and a collection period of five weeks is considered to be a very good average.

8. Creditors' payment period

$$\frac{\text{Creditors}}{\text{Purchases on Credit}} \times 365$$

1993 $\quad \dfrac{128}{1,850} \times 365 = 25.3 \text{ days}$

How long before the company pays its creditors?

1992 $\quad \dfrac{101}{1,670} \times 365 = 22.1 \text{ days}$

In 1993, creditors were paid, on average, twenty-five days after the supplies were made. This appears to indicate that attractive discount terms were being offered in return for payment withon one calendar month of the invoice date. If no such discount were available then the company might delay payment (within reason), thus taking advantage of the interest-free credit provided by its suppliers. However, great care should be taken not to alienate suppliers through undue delays in the settling of debts.

9. Cash operating cycle

	1993 (days)	111992 (days)
Stock turn	45.6	40.3
Debtors' collection period	35.2	48.3
	80.8	88.6
Less: Creditors' payment period	25.3	22.1
	55.5	66.5

By using the results of the three previous ratios, it is possible to assess the period of time which elapses between the payment for stock received and the collection of cash from customers in respect of the sale of that stock. The shorter the length of time between the initial outlay and the ultimate receipt of cash, the less working capital needs to be financed by the company. Ways of 'speeding up' the cycle include selling stock faster by reducing margins or increasing advertising, tightening up the collection of debtors' balances, and delaying payments to creditors.

Financial ratios

These are extracted exclusively from the balance sheet, and concentrate on the liquidity, solvency and financial structure of the business.

1. Working capital ratio (or current ratio)

$$\frac{\text{Current assets}}{\text{Current liabilities}}$$

1993

$$\frac{706}{828} = 0.9{:}1$$

1992

$$\frac{696}{506} = 1.4{:}1$$

This measures the overall adequacy of the working capital. The 'ideal' ratio is often quoted as between 1.5:1 and 2:1 but this depends upon the type of business, and many thriving companies continue successfully, despite having a negative ratio. However, it is apparent that Ace plc's position has deteriorated markedly in the year, which is of concern if the company is having, or is likely to have, difficulty in meeting its debts as they fall due. This aspect is further explored by the acid test ratio (see below).

2. Acid test ratio (or 'quick assets' or 'liquidity' ratio)

$$\frac{\text{'Quick' assets}}{\text{Current liabilities}}$$

1993

$$\frac{456}{828} = 0.6{:}1$$

1992

$$\frac{496}{506} = 1.0{:}1$$

It is of obvious importance that a company should be able to meet its debts as they fall due. 'Quick assets' are those which can be converted quickly into cash as the need arises, and stocks and work-in-progress are excluded as being, generally, slow-moving assets. The 'ideal' ratio is 1:1, as recorded in 1992 by Ace plc. By 1993 the company has only 60p of quickly realisable assets to meet each £1 of its current liabilities which indicates that it might be unable to withstand a crisis whereby the majority of its creditors demand payment at about the same time. Analysts consider the acid test to be of fundamental importance when assessing the ability of a business to survive; a fact which must cause great anxiety to the directors of Ace plc.

3. Gearing ratio

$$\frac{\text{Fixed return funding}}{\text{Total long-term capital}} \times 100$$

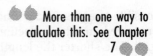

More than one way to calculate this. See Chapter 7

1993 $\dfrac{92}{992} \times 100 = 9.3\%$

1992 $\dfrac{12}{512} \times 100 = 2.3\%$

The importance of gearing was explained in Chapter 7, and it is clear that, using the formula quoted, Ace plc was 'low geared' in both of the years under review. The directors may feel that this gives them scope for further borrowing so as to alleviate their liquidity problems (see *acid test ratio*). Note, however, that there are other ways of calculating a company's gearing: for example, the level of bank borrowing is sometimes included in the numerator. For Ace plc, this would increase the gearing levels to the following percentages:

1993 $\dfrac{92 + 350}{992} \times 100 = 44.6\%$

1992 $\dfrac{12 + 285}{512} \times 100 = 58\%$

The analyst will use the formula which he or she feels gives the greatest insight into the position and trends of the company; there are no hard and fast rules as to the composition of the gearing calculation.

The first formula showed that long-term borrowing had increased in 1993 as compared to 1992, whilst the second formula shows that when the overdraft is included in the definition of 'long-term borrowing', the proportion of borrowing to total capital actually decreased in 1993.

Investment ratios

These are used primarily by potential investors when assessing the shares and dividends of publicly listed companies. For the purpose of calculating ratios 2 and 3 below it is assumed that Ace plc's current stock market price is 520p (1992 370p).

1. Earnings per share (eps)

$$\frac{\text{Net profit} - (\text{Tax} + \text{pref divs})}{\text{Number of ordinary shares in issue}}$$

1993 $\dfrac{(750 - 200)}{800} = 69\text{p}$

1992 $\dfrac{(240 - 60)}{800} = 23\text{p}$

There were no preference dividends in either of the two years, the formula thus becoming 'net profit after tax' divided by the number of ordinary shares in issue. The progress made in 1993 reflects the increased profitability obtained despite a weakening in the liquidity position. For further discussion of eps, see Chapter 7.

2. Price/earnings ratio

$$\frac{\text{Stock market price}}{\text{eps}}$$

1993
$$\frac{520\text{p}}{69\text{p}} = 8$$

1992
$$\frac{370\text{p}}{23\text{p}} = 16$$

The p/e ratio, as explained in Chapter 7, is a reflection of the way in which the stock market views the prospects of a particular company. The higher the p/e, the more optimistic are investors' views concerning future profits and dividends. The decline in Ace possibly indicates concern that the company has over-reached itself with the acquisition of the supermarket, and that the liquidity problems might force the company to cut back its operations.

3. Dividend yield

$$\frac{\text{Dividend per share}}{\text{Market price per share}} \times 100$$

1993
$$\frac{(150 \div 800)}{£5.20} \times 100 = 3.6\%$$

1992
$$\frac{(60 \div 800)}{£3.70} \times 100 = 2\%$$

This measures the actual rate of return obtained by way of dividends, assuming that the shares are purchased at the current stock market price. Although the yield from Ace has increased in 1993, this indicates the higher risk which is associated with the investment, due to factors explained previously.

4. Dividend cover

$$\frac{\text{Profit available for dividend}}{\text{Dividend}}$$

1993
$$\frac{550}{150} = 3.7 \text{ times}$$

1992
$$\frac{180}{60} = 3 \text{ times}$$

This reveals the proportion which the dividend bears to profit available for dividend, thus giving an indication as to how secure future dividend payments may be. As has been seen throughout the analysis, however, profit does not equal liquidity, and whilst Ace's profits are three times greater than the proposed dividend payments, the poor state of the company's liquid resources may well jeopardise future dividend payments.

SUMMARY OF THE RATIOS

Operating ratios		1993	1992	Trend (A = Adverse) (F = Favourable)
(a)	GP margin	60%	54.7%	F
(b)	NP margin	16.7%	6.7%	F
(c)	Mark-up	150%	120.9%	F
(d)	ROCE	83.1%	56.7%	F
(e)	Fixed assets turnover	4:1	11.2:1	A
(f)	Rate of stock turnover	45.6 days	40.3 days	A
(g)	Debtors' collection period	35.2 days	48.3 days	F
(h)	Creditors' payment period	25 days	22 days	F
(i)	Cash operating cycle	55.5 days	66.5 days	F

Financial ratios				
(j)	Working capital ratio	0.9:1	1.4:1	A
(k)	Acid test ratio	0.6:1	1:1	A
(i)	Gearing ratio	9.3%	2.3%	—

Ivestment ratios				
(m)	Earnings per share	69p	23p	F
(n)	Price/earnings ratio	8	16	A
(o)	Dividend yield	3.6%	2%	—
(p)	Dividend cover	3.7 times	3 times	F

'Pyramids of ratios'

Although the above represents the major ratios required for analysis purposes, it is possible to produce a far more detailed breakdown, whereby ratios are subdivided into their various components. This enables an analyst to make an assessment of the strengths and weaknesses of all areas within the business. One way of illustrating the inter-connection between ratios is by means of a 'pyramid', whereby the apex is progressively broken down into its supporting components (see Figure 11.2). The wider the base of the pyramid, the more detailed becomes the analysis, and specific 'problem areas' can be identified when compared with the ratios of previous years and those of other companies.

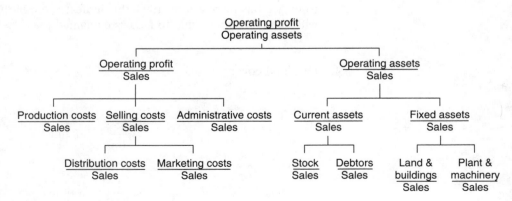

Fig. 11.2 A pyramid of ratios

THE THIRD STAGE: INTERPRETATION

The summary of the ratios reveals a stark contrast between the operating ratios and the financial ratios, clearly showing that the increased profits of the company were gained at the cost of a weakened working capital position. For example, whilst the net profit margin increased from 6.7% to 16.7%, the acid test declined from 1:1 to 0.6:1. In addition, the decline in the price/earnings ratio appears to reflect stock market anxieties that the company is over-trading, i.e. expanding its turnover and profits without sufficient working capital to meet its debts as they fall due. However, there are unanswered questions regarding the future returns from the new supermarket, and this may well prove crucial for the company in 1994. Only time will tell whether conditions will be sufficiently favourable to bring the business back on to an 'even keel'.

The cash flow statement illustrates clearly the liquidity problems facing the company as even without the extra £80,000 loans raised in the year the company's cash decreased by £63,000. Changes in debtors and creditors are in the right direction, but stock holding policy needs to be reviewed. If the cash expenditure on fixed assets can be kept under control in 1994 then the prospects for the company are good; if the company comes under pressure from creditors and lenders it may find that its quest for expansion has put it in too restricted a position to meet their demands.

THE USE OF EXTERNAL MEASURES OF COMPARISON

For a truly objective assessment of a company's results, comparisons should be made not only with the performance of previous years, but also with the performance of competitors. In many business sectors, trade organisations exist which collate data from member companies and publish key statistics which enable companies to measure their own efficiency against that of their rivals. In addition, The *Financial Times* publishes daily, in conjunction with the Institute of Actuaries and Faculty of Actuaries, a list of share indices which show average yields and p/e ratios for companies divided between various equity groups, e.g. 'building materials', 'leisure', 'stores', etc.

THE VALIDITY OF ACCOUNTING STATEMENTS

In the analysis of company statements, it is assumed that the financial information as presented is accurate and reliable and provides a suitable database for study. However, in this section it will be seen that the traditional method of accounting may well prove to be unreliable for reasons connected with the incidence of *inflation* upon the reported results.

SSAP2 'Disclosure of Accounting Policies' requires companies to disclose the specific policies adopted when preparing the accounts. These policies are listed within a 'note to the accounts' and usually commence with a statement that the accounts are drawn up 'under the historical cost convention as modified by the revaluation of certain fixed assets'.

Historical cost accounting (HCA) is the traditional method of accounting whereby all items are recorded at their purchase price at the date of acquisition. HCA has a number of advantages including:

(a) it provides a fair degree of objectivity, as measurements are based on actual costs;
(b) it lends itself to the application of double entry book-keeping;
(c) verification by auditors is relatively straightforward;
(d) it is the only system of accounting recognised for the purpose of taxation assessment;
(e) it is easy to understand by both accountants and non-accountants.

However, the disadvantages of HCA are hinted at in part by the addition of the words 'as modified by the revaluation of certain fixed assets' in the notes explaining accounting policies, previously mentioned. If HCA is such a reliable system, then why does it need to be 'modified'? The answer is that despite its advantages the use of HCA can seriously distort the results of a business owing to its inability to reflect the impact of inflation.

In times of inflation, the purchasing power of the currency is falling, which means that fixed assets and stock cost more to replace than their original (historical) cost and assets such as debtors lose value, as debtors are able to use 'devalued' currency to pay their debts. Liabilities such as creditors lose value for the same reason.

Additionally, any attempt to compare the accounts of one year with those of another will be hampered because of the different values of the monetary units used at the different dates. HCA may, therefore, result in:

(a) Overstated profits due to inadequate provisions being made for the *future replacement* prices of fixed assets.
(b) Overstated profits due to the failure to adjust for the increased replacement cost of stock.
(c) Understatement of assets due to their inclusion at their *historical* value rather than their current value at the balance sheet date; although HCA can, as we have seen, be modified to incorporate revaluations of certain fixed assets, notably land and buildings. This may further lead to:

    (i) Excessive dividend payments based on inflated profits, and over-generous pay settlements being reached with employees, which the business cannot afford.
    (ii) Inaccurate and misleading analysis of the company's performance.
    (iii) Inadequate retention of profits causing difficulty when fixed assets require replacement.

If it is acknowledged that HCA is an imperfect system, one would suppose that suitable alternative accounting systems exist to remedy the deficiencies. The accountancy profession has, for nearly two decades, been debating the pros and cons of 'current purchasing power' accounting (CPP) and 'current cost' accounting (CCA) but has not been able to persuade the majority of those who prepare and use accounts that their advantages outweigh their disadvantages, and there is at present no compulsion on companies to present accounts in any form other than HCA. However, a brief explanation of CPP and CCA follows.

CURRENT PURCHASING POWER ACCOUNTING

This is based upon the translation of 'historical cost' amounts appearing in the profit and loss account and balance sheet into inflation-adjusted values by the use of 'CPP-units', which represent stable monetary units calculated by reference to general price indices. This conversion would not apply to debtors and creditors, which represent definite amounts payable or receivable at the balance sheet date, nor to cash and bank balances.

Advantages claimed for CPP are that it provides a 'real' measure of profit and allows meaningful comparisons to be made from one year to the next. The system is based on HCA, and therefore retains the advantages of that system as previously listed. Disadvantages are that the application of 'CPP-units' based on general price indices could cause distortions when applied to specific companies, particularly those operating in highly specialised areas. Additionally, there are uncertainties over the public's perception of items expressed in terms of an artificial 'accounting currency'.

An attempt was made in 1974 in the United Kingdom to introduce CPP accounting, to be presented as supplementary statements to the HCA accounts. An SSAP was issued, but was withdrawn in the following year when a Government-appointed committee produced a report (known as 'The Sandilands Report') which favoured *current cost accounting*. A new SSAP No 16 was issued in 1980, but it was withdrawn in 1988.

CURRENT COST ACCOUNTING

The Sandilands Report proposed that companies should present CCA accounts which would include a current cost profit and loss account and current cost balance sheet. These are detailed below.

CURRENT COST PROFIT AND LOSS ACCOUNT

This is where the net profit as calculated under the historical cost convention would be subject to adjustments which show the increased costs required to maintain the *operating capability* of the business, i.e. the ability of the business to maintain the output of goods and services from its existing resources. Specifically, four adjustments are applied to the HC profit to arrive at the CC profit:

1. *The depreciation adjustment*, which reflects the extra depreciation that is required to provide for the replacement cost of fixed assets rather than the historical cost.
2. *The cost of sales adjustment*, which represents the difference between the historical cost of stock sold and the replacement value of that stock.
3. *The monetary working capital adjustment*, which is a calculation of the extra finance required to fund the increased net debtors (debtors less creditors) which are likely to result when inflation raises invoice prices.
4. *The gearing adjustment*, which is applied as a percentage reduction to the total of the previous three adjustments, recognises that for many companies, the 'burden' of inflation is carried in part by external providers of finance to the company (e.g. debenture holders) rather than by its shareholders.

CURRENT COST BALANCE SHEET

As CC accounting is concerned with the business's ability to maintain its operating capability, it follows that balance sheet values should reflect the value to the business of its assets and liabilities at the balance sheet date rather than using historical cost data which do not relate values to current conditions as affected by inflation. Consequently the CCA balance sheet shows both fixed assets and stock at replacement prices (which may be calculated by reference to price indices) and a current cost reserve is opened to record the surpluses (or deficits) caused by the revaluations from the HC figures. The reserve also carries the adjustments made in the CC profit and loss account. No amendments would be made to actual amounts owing by, or to, third parties, e.g. trade debtors and creditors, cash and bank balances, shareholders' capital and debentures.

Advantages claimed for CCA are that the accounts present a more realistic picture of the business by, on the one hand, showing the effects of inflation on HC profit, and on the other, showing the current values of assets rather than outdated ones. Proponents of CCA believe that evaluation of business performance can be made only from accounting information which is both accurate and relevant, and management are more likely to obtain relevant data from CCA statements.

Disadvantages of CCA include the difficulty of making reliable estimates of replacement values of assets, particularly when price indices are used. The inclusion of separate CC accounting statements in a company's annual report may lead to confusion for the non-expert user of the information.

EXAMINATION QUESTIONS

1 (i) The following ratios and other data have been extracted from the 1991 accounts of Plum Ltd.

Current ratio	3:1
Acid test	2:1
Days debtors	73
Gross profit %	30%
Bank balance	£30,000
Return on equity	20%
Fixed asset turnover	2:1
Sales	£600,000

(ii) The only reserve shown in the accounts is the revenue reserve.

(iii) An interim dividend of 20p per £1 ordinary share paid during 1991 has absorbed half the net profit. No final dividend is proposed.

(iv) The only current assets are stock, debtors, and the bank balance. The only liability is the amount owing to trade creditors.

You are required to:

(a) prepare a profit and loss account for the year ended 31 December 1991 and a Balance Sheet as at 31 December 1991 in as much detail as you can on the basis of the above information. *(16)*

(b) Suggest **two** external sources of information from which meaningful comparisons can be made with the ratios of Plum Ltd. *(4)*

(Northern 1992)

2 The directors of Keats & Co. Ltd. are faced with strong competition from similar companies and are seeking more information that may help them retain their trading position. It has been suggested that various ratios will give an indication of the performance of the company and help the directors to make vital decisions.

The following are the summarised financial statements of the company:

Trading and Profit and Loss Accounts for the year ended 31 December

	1990		1991	
	£000	£000	£000	£000
Turnover		9,000		12,000
less: Cost of sales		6,300		9,120
Gross profit		2,700		2,880
less Expenses		1,700		1,820
Net profit		1,000		1,060
less Corporation tax	540		580	
Dividends	420	960	460	1,040
		40		20
Retained earnings b/f		240		280
Retained earnings c/f		280		300

Balance Sheet as at 31 December

	1990		1991	
	£000	£000	£000	£000
Fixed assets (at cost less depreciation)		9,300		10,200
Current assets				
Stock	1,560		3,020	
Debtors	1,520		2,940	
Balance at bank	640		—	
	3,720		5,960	
Less Current liabilities				
Creditors	1,540		2,780	
Tax and dividends	960		1,040	
Bank overdraft	—		1,800	
	2,500		5,620	
Working capital		1,220		340
		10,520		10,540

Financed by:

Share capital (fully issued and paid up)		6,000	6,000
General reserve	1,440		1,440
Profit and loss A/C	280	1,720	300	1,740
10% Debentures		2,800	2,800
		10,520	10,540

Note: All sales are on a credit basis only.

REQUIRED

(a) Calculate **three** liquidity and **three** profitability ratios for 1990 and 1991.

(9)

(b) Comment on the company's position as revealed by these ratios. *(10)*

(c) A brief report critically evaluating the use of ratios in a business. *(6)*

(AEB 1992)

3 Donald Mince has always invested his savings in a building society or a bank, but recently he has noticed that more people are investing in companies.

The following information was presented to him and he is considering making an investment in one of the companies:

Summarised financial information as at 31 May 1991

	Meta plc £000	Retal plc £000
Authorised capital		
500,000 Ordinary shares of £1 each	500	
6,000,000 Ordinary shares of 25p each		1,500
400,000 12% Preference shares of £1 each		400
Isssued capital		
500,000 Ordinary shares of £1 fully paid	500	
5,000,000 Ordinary shares of 25p fully paid		1,250
300,000 12% Preference shares of £1 each		300
Share premium account	450	600
General reserve	200	500
Retained earnings	250	1,050
13% Debentures 1998–2000	1,000	—
Current liabilities	200	450
	2,600	4,150

Appropriation account

	£000		£000	
Retained earnings b/f		150		848
Net trading profit for 1991		150		400
Less Dividends for 1991:				
Preference	—		48	
Ordinary	50	50	150	198
Retained earnings c/f		250		1050

The prices below were extracted from a Stock Exchange list on 31 May 1991.

		£	
Meta plc	£1 ordinary shares	2	per share
	£100 13% debenture stock 1998–2000	105	per £100 unit of stock
Retal plc	£1 12% preference shares	1.30	per share
	25p ordinary shares	1.50	per share

Before making a final decision to invest. Mince wanted to ask you, as his financial advisor, a number of questions.

REQUIRED

(a) Identify the different investment opportunities that these two companies offer for Donald Mince.
   Explain the relative merits of these investments to Mince. *(8)*
(b) Explain to Mince what is meant by the term gearing. Calculate gearing ratios for both Meta plc and Retal plc.
   What significance does gearing have for an ordinary shareholder? *(7)*
(c) Calculate the ordinary share dividend yield for both Meta plc and Retal plc based on the dividends for the financial year ended 31 May 1991 and the share prices as at 31 May 1991. Use the equity capital base as at 1 June 1990. *(5)*

(AEB 1991)

4 The following financial information was available on three similar companies.

Balance sheets as at 31 December 1991

	£000	Orba Ltd £000	Pego Ltd £000	Doliva Ltd £000
Called-up capital				
£1 Ordinary shares fully paid		100	100	—
50p Ordinary shares fully paid		—	—	150
Share premium		100	50	—
General reserve		150	60	70
Retained earnings as at 1 January 1991	150		140	105
Less interim dividend paid for 1991	5	145		
Net profit for 1991		200	40	15
10% Debentures 1998		—	100	—
Current liabilities		110	260	240
		805	750	580
Fixed assets less depreciation		240	505	350
Current assets				
Stock		200	100	50
Trade debtors		110	50	95
Balance at bank		200	75	50
Cash		55	20	35
		805	750	580

Additional information.

(1) The directors of Orba Ltd had made the following recommendations for the financial year ended 31 December 1991.

    (i) An interim ordinary dividend of 5% was paid on 1 July 1991.
    (ii) A final ordinary dividend of 11% is to be paid on 15 February 1992.
    (iii) A transfer to general reserve of £60,000.
    (iv) An issue of ordinary bonus shares on a one for two basis. The issue will be made on 31 January 1992 and will be wholly financed from retained earnings.

(2) Pego Ltd revalued its land and buildings on 1 January 1992. The net book value on 31 December 1991 was £100,000, and they were revalued at £250,000.
(3) In order to raise further finance Doliva Ltd gave effect to the following.

    (i) Surplus fixed assets were sold for £65,000 cash on 10 January 1992. The net book value of the assets on 31 December 1991 was £100,000.

(ii)   A rights issue of ordinary shares on a one for three basis was made on 20 January 1992 at 60p per share, fully paid.
Only 60% of the ordinary shareholders subscribed to the rights issue, the remainder being taken up by underwriters.

(4)   There were no other transactions in the month of January 1992 for any of the companies.

REQUIRED

(a)   A profit and loss appropriation account for the year ended 31 December 1991 for Orba Ltd.   *(4)*

(b)   A revised balance sheet for Orba Ltd as at 31 January 1992.   *(5)*

(c)   A brief report on each of the three companies commenting on:
  (i)   the profitability of each company during 1991. (Use shareholders' total funds as at 1 January 1991);
  (ii)   the liquidity of each company as at 31 January 1992.   *(12)*

(d)   On 1 February 1992 the directors of Orba Ltd decided to acquire a controlling interest in both Pego Ltd and Doliva Ltd.
Explain what this means and provide suitable calculations to support your answer.   *(4)*

(AEB 1992)

5   In times of inflation historic cost accounts are often said to be unsatisfactory for a number of reasons, including:

  (i)   they overstate profit;
  (ii)   they understate the capital employed;
  (iii)   comparisons over a number of years are distorted.

Current Purchasing Power (CPP) and Current Cost Accounting (CCA) have both been seriously considered as possible solutions to these problems.
You are required to describe how each of the problems with historic cost accounts outlined above arises, and explain to what extent each of CPP and CCA solves each problem.   *(20)*

(Northern 1992)

TUTOR'S ANSWER TO QUESTION 4

(a)

Orba Limited
Profit and Loss Appropriation Account
for the year ended 31 December 1991

	£000	£000
Net profit for the year		200
Less Dividends		
Interim	5	
Proposed final	11	(16)
		184
Transfer to general reserve		(60)
Retained profit for the year		124
Retained profit brought forward		150
Retained profit carried forward		274

(b)

Orba Limited
(revised) Balance Sheet
as at 31 January 1992

	£000	£000
Fixed assets less depreciation		240
Current assets		
Stock	200	
Trade debtors	110	
Bank balance	200	
Cash	55	
	565	
Creditors: amounts due for payment within one year		
Trade creditors	110	
Proposed dividend	11	
	121	
Net current assets		444
		684
Paid up share capital		
150,000 ordinary shares of £1 each, fully paid		150
Reserves		
Share Premium	100	
General Reserve	210	
Retained earnings	224	534
		684

(c) (i) Return on Capital Employed (ROCE) in 1992 for each company is as follows:

$$\text{Orba Ltd} \quad \frac{£200}{£500} \times 100 = 40\%$$

$$\text{Pego Ltd} \quad \frac{£40}{£350} \times 100 = 11.4\%$$

$$\text{Doliva Ltd} \quad \frac{£15}{£325} \times 100 = 4.6\%$$

As can be seen, Orba's ROCE is very high, Pego's moderate whilst Doliva's is poor by comparison. Figures of one year should be treated with caution, and ideally the figures of several years are needed to establish trends. If the asset values of Orba and Doliva are not as up-to-date as Pego's, then those two companies' figures will be artificially high, as the asset base is relatively low due to unrealistic valuations.

(ii) Liquidity of the three companies can be measured by calculating the working capital ratio and acid test ratio for each company:

	Working Capital Ratio	*Acit Test Ratio*
Orba Ltd	565:121 = 4.7:1	365:121 = 3.0:1
Pego Ltd	245:260 = 0.9:1	145:260 = 0.6:1
Doliva Ltd	355*:240 = 1.5:1	305:240 = 1.3:1

*Includes £65,000 from sale of assets and £60,000 (100,000 shares @ 60p) from rights issue.

In general terms Orba Ltd has the strongest liquidity position of the three companies. It has sufficient cash reserves to pay off all of its current liabilities.

Pego's Ltd liquidity is relatively poor and it would have great difficulty in paying off its current liabilities immediately. Perhaps it should sell some fixed assets to raise cash.

Doliva's liquidity position was significantly improved by the sale of fixed assets and the rights issue. The improved liquid situation may enable Doliva to finance further business in 1992; hopefully more profitably.

(d)   A controlling interest is where one company owns at least one share more than 50% of another company's voting share capital. Once the controlling interest is obtained, the holding company can effectively control the policies of its subsidiaries, and will produce consolidated accounts to reflect the financial position of the group as a whole.

A controlling interest in Pego Ltd would need the acquisition of 50,001 shares whilst 200,001 shares in Doliva Ltd would be required.

Tutor's comment

The majority of marks in this question was for parts (c) and (d), and in an exam, time should be allocated carefully to reflect this. Notice that in parts (a) and (b) care has been taken with the presentation of the statements, and Companies Act format headings have been used where possible.

TUTOR'S ANSWER TO QUESTION 5

In times of inflation the combined effect of two traditional accounting conventions distorts historical cost accounts:

a)   The money measurement convention measures all items in the accounts by the same monetary unit. In times of inflation the significance of this unit depends on the time when it was spent, as money loses value over time. 'Current Purchasing Power' (CPP) accounting uses a different unit of measurement, the *purchasing power* of the monetary unit at the balance sheet date.

b)   The historic cost convention provides that each item in the accounts should be measured on the basis of the transaction whereby the item originally entered the accounts. Current Cost Accounting (CCA) involves revaluations of items in the accounts, normally at replacement cost, at each balance sheet date or at the time of usage.

Historic cost accounts are said to overstate profit because they match sales with earlier, and therefore lower, costs of goods consumed to earn those sales. This gives an unrealistically low expense figure, particularly for depreciation and cost of sales. CPP restates these expense items to current, higher, general price levels. CCA revalues the items consumed and is claimed to be more relevant because items consumed are charged against profit at specific price levels relevant to the changes in the price of the items in which the business deals.

Historic cost accounts are said to understate capital employed because non-monetary assets (e.g. stocks) held by the business are recorded at the price levels that applied when they were acquired rather than the higher price levels that apply when the accounts are presented. CPP adjusts these items by references to the general price level, CCA adjusts these items by reference to changes in the specific price levels relevant to the type of assets concerned.

c)   In times of high inflation a comparison of an enterprise's accounts over a number of years can be highly misleading because in successive years the significance of the monetary amounts changes. As an example, inflation may cause reported turnover to increase despite a fall in the physical quantity of (identical) goods sold. CPP updates all corresponding amounts to the value of money at the current reporting date. CCA does not offer a solution to this problem.

OUTLINE ANSWERS

Question 1

a) *Plum Ltd — Profit and loss account for the year ended 31st December 1992*

	£
Sales	600,000
Cost of Sales	420,000
Gross profit	180,000
Expenses	90,000
Net Profit	90,000
Dividend	45,000
Retained profit	45,000

Plum Ltd — Balance Sheet as at 31st December 1991

	£	£
Fixed Assets		300,000
Current Assets		
Stock	75,000	
Debtors	120,000	
Bank	30,000	
	225,000	
Current Liabilities		
Trade Creditors	75,000	
Net current assets		150,000
		450,000
Ordinary shares of £1		225,000
Revenue Reserve		225,000
		450,000

b) Useful sources for comparative ratios include:
  i) Previous years' ratios for the same company.
 ii) Recent ratios for another company in the same industry.
iii) Industrial average ratios for the industry, drawn from published figures or from an interfirm comparison exercise.

Question 2

(a) Liquidity ratios (e.g.)

(i) Current ratio

		(1990)		(1991)
$\dfrac{\text{Current assets}}{\text{Current liabilities}}$	$\dfrac{3720}{2500}$	1.48:1	$\dfrac{5960}{5620}$	1.06:1

(ii) Acid test ratio

$\dfrac{\text{Current assets less stock}}{\text{Current liabilities}}$	$\dfrac{2160}{2500}$	0.86:1	$\dfrac{2940}{5620}$	0.52:1

(iii) Debtor collection period

$\dfrac{\text{Debtor}}{\text{Average daily sales}}$	$\dfrac{1520}{9000/365}$	61.6 days	$\dfrac{2940}{12000/365}$	89.4 days*

* or $\dfrac{2230}{12,000/365}$ = 67.8 days if average debtors used.

Profitability ratios (e.g.)

(i) Return on capital employed

$$\frac{\text{Profit before tax}}{\text{Capital employed}} \qquad \frac{1000}{10520} \times 100 \quad 9.5\% \qquad \frac{1060}{10540} \times 100 \quad 10.05\%$$

(ii) Gross profit to sales

$$\frac{\text{Gross profit} \times 100}{\text{Sales}} \qquad \frac{2700}{9000} \times 100 \quad 30\% \qquad \frac{2880}{12000} \times 100 \quad 24\%$$

(iii) Net profit to sales

$$\frac{\text{Net profit} \times 100}{\text{Sales}} \qquad \frac{1000}{9000} \times 100 \quad 11.1\% \qquad \frac{1060}{12000} \times 100 \quad 8.8\%$$

(b) Liquidity

(i) & (ii) A poor liquidity ratio has worsened. The company has only about half of the resources available that are needed to meet its responsibilities. Overdraft facilities have helped to buy new assets.

(iii) Credit control has become poorer and this has led to an increase of 28 days in the time it takes debtors to pay. There is a danger of bad debts.

Profitability

(i) The return on capital employed has only increased very slightly indicating that any expansion has been financed mainly by the bank overdraft. The return on total assets would have indicated a less satisfactory position.

(ii) & (iii) A fall in these ratios suggests that despite higher sales this could have been achieved by lower prices, and profitability is weakened thus restricting a build up of resources through better profits.

(c) Advantages —

(i) They help comparison
(ii) They reveal trends
(iii) They help analysis
(iv) Relationships are made clearer
(v) Most areas of activity of a business can be covered
(vi) Assists decision making

Disadvantages —

(i) The causes of changes in ratios are not revealed
(ii) To be helpful they must be capable of comparing 'like with like' in all respects
(iii) Time factors due to seasonal trading can cause distortion and fluctuation in the current assets
(iv) Complete accuracy of relevant figures cannot be always guaranteed
(v) There is a need for consistent accounting policies to be applied
(vi) The value of money can change over time
(vii) Accounting data is limited to information having a monetary value.

Question 3

(a) Ordinary Shares — Both companies have ordinary shares available as an investment. Ordinary shares yield a dividend which may be high in times of good profits. These investments are risky and all the capital may be lost.

Also the potential for a capital gain in the longer term.

Rights issues and bonus issues may also bring a benefit.

Preference shares — Provide a more secure investment than ordinary shares. Usually have a fixed return eg 12%.

Capital may be returned — redeemable.

Dividends may be cumulative.

May be preference on return of capital.

Debentures — least risk of these three investments — really a loan. Relative security since interest must be paid. Capital may be secured on the company's assets.

(b) Gearing refers to the relative proportions of loan capital and total capital/equity capital. A suitable gearing ratio would be:

$$\frac{\text{Loan capital} + \text{preference shares}}{\text{Equity capital} + \text{reserves}} \times 100$$

Gearing Ratios   Meta plc   Retal plc

$$= \frac{1000 \times 100}{500 + 450 + 450} \qquad \frac{300 \times 100}{1250 + 2150}$$

$$= 71.4 \qquad\qquad\qquad = 8.8$$

Significance of gearing for an ordinary shareholder:
If gearing is high, i.e. high loan capital, there is a high commitment to loan charges. Risk. Return.
High profits — ordinary shareholders do well.
Low profits — ordinary shareholders do not do well.
The converse tends to apply for low gearing.

(c) Ordinary share dividend yield is:

Meta plc $$\frac{£50,000}{500,000 \times £2.00} \times 100 = 5\%$$

Retal plc $$\frac{£150,000}{5,000,000 \times £1.50} \times 100 = 2\%$$

Now attempt the review questions on page 309. The answers are given on page 324.

CHAPTER

AN INTRODUCTION TO MANAGEMENT ACCOUNTING

FUNCTIONS OF MANAGEMENT

MANAGEMENT DECISION-MAKING

COSTING SYSTEMS

ELEMENTS OF COST

PRODUCT AND PERIOD COSTS

GETTING STARTED

Financial accounting is that part of accounting which covers the classification and recording of monetary transactions in accordance with established concepts, principles, accounting standards, and legal requirements. It is concerned to present a view of the effects of these transactions during and at the end of the accounting period.

Financial accounts are required by managers within the business; and by people outside of the business – such as shareholders, banks, taxation authorities, investment analysts.

Those people whose job it is to manage the business on behalf of the owners require more and different accounting information from that derived from the financial accounts. These people require information which is produced from the business's cost and management accounts.

Cost accounting has to do with the establishment of budgets; with standard costs and actual costs of operations, activities and products; and the analysis of variances, profitability or the social use of funds.

Management accounting is an integral part of management, and is concerned with identifying, presenting and interpreting information to assist management in decisionmaking. Management accounting includes cost accounting.

The following chapters examine ways of satisfying the needs of those within the business whose task is to manage the enterprise.

ESSENTIAL PRINCIPLES

FUNCTIONS OF MANAGEMENT

The management function is based upon the five key activities of planning, organisation, co-ordination, command and control. No matter what the business, these five basic managerial activities must be present.

Business planning comprises two stages: long-term or strategic planning and short-term operational planning. Strategic planning is concerned with setting the firm's long-term objectives: where is the business to go over, say, the next five years? Long-term objectives will be in general terms, and as such will provide a policy framework within which administrative and operating decisions can be taken. These policy statements will be concerned with employment, market share, product development, and profitability. Firms will, therefore, develop policies for finance, marketing, personnel, production, procurement, and research and development.

MANAGEMENT DECISION-MAKING

Management is not a homogeneous entity. Within a business there will be senior, middle and junior managers, each contributing to the overall objectives of the firm. The main distinction between the levels of management relates to their influence upon the various decision-making processes (see Figure 12.1). It is possible to identify three levels of decision-making within an organisation: strategic, tactical and operational.

STRATEGIC DECISIONS

Tend to be taken by the Board of Directors

These are concerned with controlling the relationship between the business and its environment in order to devise overall objectives for the whole firm. These overall objectives, framed in general terms, provide a structure within which other decisions can be taken. Although the need to take or to amend a strategic decision can be perceived at any level within the organisation, such decisions tend to be taken by the board of directors acting upon the advice of senior managers.

These decisions, having resource implications, are often referred to as 'policies' and costs associated with these decisions are termed 'policy costs'. Thus, a policy decision to lease premises rather than to buy gives rise to a policy cost in terms of the rent paid: where a decision is taken to purchase the premises, the depreciation of the buildings would be a policy cost.

TACTICAL DECISIONS

These are concerned with how the overall objectives are to be met, and they are a function of management control; they ensure that the necessary inputs are acquired, and that they are used in a way most likely to achieve the firm's objectives. Broadly, this area of decision-making is that of middle management.

The area of middle management

Insofar as managerial policies need filling out and controlling this activity tends to be referred to as *administration*: the term *management* is reserved for the establishment

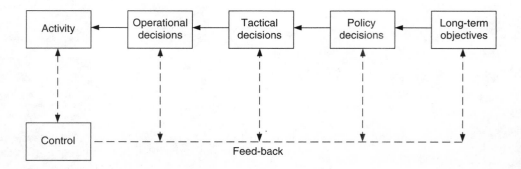

Fig. 12.1 The management process.

of policies and the framing of strategies. In reality, executives carrying out their normal duties will alternate between administering and managing.

OPERATIONAL DECISIONS

To do with specific tasks

These have to do with specific tasks. Management's job here is to ensure that the tasks are carried out effectively and efficiently in accordance with the tactical decisions already taken.

Each of these levels of decision-making requires information, but each will require different information. Because strategic decision-making operates with a long-term time horizon, it is accompanied by a high degree of uncertainty. These decisions tend therefore to be based upon informed judgement and experience. The information required for strategic management accounting comprises information on relative levels and trends in real costs and prices, volumes, market share, cash flow, and demands made generally upon the firm's total resources.

On the other hand, operational decisions take place within a very short time horizon, and such decisions can often be made on the basis of simple calculations. Falling somewhere between the two is the level of tactical decision-making, endeavouring to ensure that the day-to-day operational decisions do in fact promote the firm's stated objectives. The type of data collected, the way they are recorded and reported will therefore depend upon the purpose for which the data are required, and the level of management which requires them.

COSTING SYSTEMS

It is through the costing system that the management accountant obtains the information necessary to support management. Just what sort of costing system is adopted will depend upon the organisational structure of the business, the firm's technology, and upon the data it has decided to collect.

Because one of the main purposes of cost accounting is to help management to control expenditure, it is necessary to trace costs to those employees who are responsible for their control. The business must therefore be divided into a number of main areas which must in turn be split into departments, each department comprising a number of *cost centres*. A cost centre is the smallest unit of managerial control which can be identified.

A cost centre is the smallest unit of managerial control

It is usually not advisable to modify radically an otherwise satisfactory business structure merely in the interests of the costing system. Other benefits may be lost, and the goodwill of other managers may be sacrificed.

The technological profile will influence the costing system

The firm's technological profile will undoubtedly influence its organisational structure, and will certainly influence the costing system. A light engineering firm with a large number of small machines in its factories may gather cost data for groups of machines, rather than for each single one. Conversely, if the business is that of heavy engineering, or chemical engineering, with relatively few but large and expensive pieces of plant – such as a coking plant, chemical works, or iron works – then data may be collected for each major process, machine, or furnace.

Generally a cost centre is a location, a person or an item of equipment – or a group of these – in relation to which costs may be ascertained, and used for control purposes. Hence, there are personal cost centres, where costs are identified for a person or for a group of people; operation cost centres, which consist of machines and/or people who carry out the same operation; and process cost centres, which consist of a continuous sequence of operations. Whatever type it is, a cost centre is the point around which costs are gathered.

Service centres are cost centres which provide a service

Some costs, such as rates or rent, cannot be traced to any one cost centre directly. These costs are gathered to an overall cost centre, and are then arbitrarily apportioned to the other cost centres. Expenses incurred by service departments – canteen, safety, welfare – have to be traced to cost centres which provide a service rather than to productive cost centres. For this reason, they are sometimes known as *service centres*.

Whatever cost centres are adopted, the main purpose is to trace costs through the business to that person who has direct influence over them. In this way, the firm's management can exercise the fullest control over costs.

Much of the raw costing data will be supplied by production, research or technical staff in the course of their normal duties. It is important therefore that standard forms be used and that they be kept as simple as possible. The forms themselves could be regularly and frequently despatched to the costing department so that the data can be processed as soon as possible after the events to which they refer.

Although it is possible to distinguish financial accounting from cost and management accounting, it is less easy to draw a boundary between cost accounting and management accounting; for this reason, the terms are often used together.

Generally, cost accounting operates at a more basic level, and has to do with the determination of product or process costs. Management accounting is concerned with providing and interpreting accounting information so that management may more easily carry out its fivefold function.

ELEMENTS OF COST

The cost of a product is the amount of money incurred on or attributable to it. Thus, the cost of a desk comprises the wood, metal, glue and screws used in its manufacture; the cost of the worker's time in assembling the materials; and the overheads of the factory such as heating and lighting. These various parts of the product's cost are termed the *elements of cost*.

Direct costs are those expenses which can be identified precisely as attaching to the product or process: with the desk the direct materials comprise the wood and metal used in manufacture; the direct labour is the cost of the worker's time in putting the desk together. If a royalty of so much per item is payable to the designer of the desk, then this would constitute a direct expense. The royalties payable to the authors of this book represent a direct expense for the publisher.

> ❛❛ The cost of a product is the amount of money incurred on it ❜❜

The total of direct materials, direct labour and direct expenses constitutes *prime cost*. Generally, the term prime cost is restricted to direct production costs only, and does not normally include the direct costs of marketing or of research and development:

$$\frac{\text{Direct}}{\text{materials}} + \frac{\text{Direct}}{\text{labour}} + \frac{\text{Direct}}{\text{expenses}} = \text{Prime cost}$$

All expenses over and above prime cost are termed as overheads or indirect costs. In the USA and with some subsidiaries of American companies in other parts of the world, the term *burden* is used. Overhead, indirect cost and burden all mean the same thing; they are those costs which cannot be attributed directly to the product.

Indirect materials include cleaning materials, coolants and lubrication. On a lathe, it is not possible to measure how much cooling oil is used in producing one single component. The cooling oil used for the whole week must be costed, and that cost spread over all items produced during the period. Similarly, with indirect labour: the salaries of foremen, maintenance staff and others cannot be identified as attaching to particular products. Indirect expenses such as buildings insurance, heating, lighting and power suffer from the same problem.

> ❛❛ Overheads cannot be attributed directly to the product ❜❜

$$\frac{\text{Indirect}}{\text{material}} + \frac{\text{Indirect}}{\text{labour}} + \frac{\text{Indirect}}{\text{expenses}} = \text{Total overhead cost}$$

> ❛❛ Overheads can be identified with specific functions ❜❜

Although by their very nature overheads cannot be identified with products directly, they can be identified with specific functions. Thus, the total overhead cost is normally divided into production overhead, selling and distribution overhead, administration overhead, and research and development overhead. In each case, there may be included an element of indirect materials, indirect labour and indirect expenses:

$$\frac{\text{Factory}}{\text{indirect}} + \frac{\text{Factory}}{\text{indirect}} + \frac{\text{Factory}}{\text{indirect}} = \text{Total production overhead}$$
$$\text{material} \quad \text{labour} \quad \text{expenses}$$

Prime cost plus production overhead provides a figure for total production cost:

$$\frac{\text{Prime}}{\text{cost}} + \frac{\text{Production}}{\text{overhead}} = \text{Total production cost}$$

When overhead costs for selling and distribution, administration, and research and development are added to total production cost, the figure for total cost is calculated:

$$\text{Total production cost} + \text{Selling overhead} + \text{Administration overhead} + \text{R \& D overhead} = \text{Total cost}$$

PRODUCT AND PERIOD COSTS

Product costs are related to level of production

Period costs are unaffected by the level of production

The costs which comprise factory cost are related to the number of items which are produced: the greater the volume of production, the greater one would expect the factory cost to be. If a firm doubled its output, one would expect direct and indirect costs to increase also, although the costs may increase at differing rates, and they may not all double. If a firm can enjoy economies of scale, then costs may increase by less than production; if a firm suffers from diseconomies of scale, costs may increase by more than production.

Costs which are related to production in this way are sometimes called *product costs*. They include both direct and indirect expenses which are responsive to the volume of production.

Some costs, however, are more related to time, and are, in the short term, unaffected by changes in the level of output. Costs such as rent, rates, insurance and management salaries come into this group, and because they are time-related, they are sometimes called *period costs*. Most of the expenses appearing in the profit and loss account fall into this category.

A great amount of ground has been covered in this chapter, and it may be helpful to bring together some of the main ideas in a practical example.

Example 1

Gibbon Ltd manufactures three products, K, L and M, for which the financial accountant has produced the following statement. From the figures, the profit at £9,000 appears healthy at 12 per cent of turnover. But this statement refers to the total business: it may mask the detailed picture. In order to be useful for management decision-making, it is necessary to disaggregate the figures, to discover the situation with each of the firm's three products.

Gibbon Ltd

Trading and Profit and Loss Account for the year ended 31 December 1993

	£	£
Sales (turnover)		75,000
Less:		
Materials used	37,500	
Wages	17,500	
Factory overheads	5,000	
		60,000
Gross profit		15,000
Less:		
Selling and distribution overheads	2,000	
Administration overheads	4,000	
		6,000
Net profit		9,000

Tutor's comments

When the cost accountant has produced figures for each product as a separate cost centre, a different view emerges. Products (K) and (L) are earning healthy profits of 26 and 28 per cent of sales; but the loss on (M) is reducing total profits down to the 12 per cent level.

Armed with this information, it is now for Gibbon's management to decide what action to take. Does Gibbon stop producing (M)? What are the likely effects upon costs and revenues if it does? If customers cannot purchase (M) from Gibbon, may they go elsewhere for (K) and (L)? Does the firm, therefore, continue to produce (M) as a lossmaker to retain customer goodwill? Can the price of (M) be increased? What effect will such an increase have upon sales of (M) and other products in the range? Can the cost of (M) be reduced by more efficient working, or by restyling the product?

Gibbon Ltd
Cost statement

	Product K £	Product L £	Product M £	Total £
Materials used	12,000	9,250	16,250	37,500
Wages	3,750	6,250	7,500	17,500
Factory overheads	1,250	1,500	2,250	5,000
	17,000	17,000	26,000	60,000
Selling & distribution	500	750	500	1,750
Administration	1,500	1,750	1,000	4,250
Total cost	19,000	19,500	27,500	66,000
Sales revenue	25,600	27,000	22,400	75,000
Profit (loss)	6,600	7,500	(5,100)	9,000

These are all essentially management questions. In order to answer them, and to make the necessary decisions, management will need more than just accounting information. But at least the cost accountant has enabled management to pin-point the problem, and so frame the relevant questions.

EXAMINATION QUESTIONS

1 Management accounting operates to ensure that there is effective:

a) formulation of plans to meet objectives
b) formulation of short term operating plans
c) recording of actual transactions
d) corrective action to bring future actual transactions into line
e) obtaining and controlling finance
f) reviewing and reporting on systems and operations.

Choose any FIVE of the above, and show how management accounting seeks to meet these requirements. Use topics from your studies to illustrate your answer in each case. *(20)*
(London 1992)

2 'Financial accounting is non-dynamic, backward looking, conservative, as objective as possible, and subject to statutory and other regulation. Management accounting is future oriented, is dynamic, produces forward looking figures, and is meant to be decision and control relevant, should not be too concerned with objectivity, and is not generally subject to external regulation.'
Prof. Michael Bromwich, June, 1988.

Justify this statement, giving examples to illustrate your answer. *(20)*
(London 1990)

3 a) What is meant by the term 'elements of cost'? Illustrate your answer with examples.

b) The cost of a product or service depends upon the accounting conventions used, and the assumptions which underpin those conventions: there is thus no such thing as a true cost.

Use examples from your studies to support this statement as far as costing for materials and overheads is concerned. Fully explain all terms used. *(20)*

(London 1993)

4 'A cost is a fact, but a price depends upon a company's policy.'
   a) Define the terms 'cost' and 'policy'. *(4)*
   b) How far do you agree with the above statement? Illustrate your answer with examples. *(16)*

(London 1990)

TUTOR'S ANSWER TO QUESTION 4

a) 'Cost' is the amount of expenditure incurred on, or attributable to, a specified thing or activity.

   'Policy' is a course of action adopted by an organisation. It is usually laid down in the form of general guidelines to inform and guide corporate decision making.

b) The approach to costing depends upon the accounting conventions used, and the assumptions which underpin those assumptions. In this sense, therefore, there is no such thing as 'true' cost, and therefore a cost cannot be a 'fact'.

   Thus, the apportionment of overhead is based upon assumptions about how much is to be charged to particular departments, and the bases used for apportionment: methods include floor area, volume, number of workers. Each will give a different answer.

   The absorption of overheads depends upon whether direct labour hours or machine hours is used as a basis; and then upon an estimate of how many hours will be worked. Different bases will give different figures for costs.

   Similarly, the pricing of materials to production depends upon which method is adopted: FIFO, LIFO or AVCO. FIFO assumes that the first items to be received are issued first; LIFO assumes that the latest items to be received are issued first; whilst AVCO calculates a cost based upon an average price of receipts. All three methods are acceptable for costing purposes, but each will give a different figure for the cost of materials.

   Pricing depends upon how a business decides to approach its market, and is thus a feature of policy. A company may decide to adopt full cost or marginal cost pricing. Full cost includes all the costs attributable to a product or service, with a percentage added for profit; marginal cost uses only the additional costs incurred in producing the product or service, and writes off the fixed costs to the 'contribution'.

   The contribution is the difference between sales value and the variable costs of those sales.

   The pricing policy adopted will be based upon decisions by the company's senior management. Do they wish to maximise profits by charging what the market will bear? Or are they keen to penetrate a new market by reducing prices to the marginal cost? These are policy decisions based upon the company's aims and objectives.

   In conclusion, therefore, it is not correct to state that a cost is a fact, since it depends upon decisions taken by management; different approaches will result in different costs. In this, costs are like prices, they are creatures of management thinking.

STUDENT'S ANSWER TO QUESTION 2

According to the 'Official Terminology' financial accounting is defined as 'the classification and recording of monetary transactions of an entity in accordance with established concepts, principles, accounting standards and legal requirements and presentation of a view of the effect of those transactions during and at the end of an accounting period.'

Examples of accounting concepts and principles include among others that of materiality which states that financial statements should include items significant enough to affect business decisions; and the going concern concept which assumes that the business will continue in existence for the foreseeable future.

Accounting standards give guidelines on how particular issues should be approached. Thus SSAP 9 deals with accounting for stocks and long term contracts.

Legal requirements are found in statutes such as the Companies Acts and the 1890 Partnership Act, which govern the form of accounts for these two business types.

Management accounting is defined as an integral part of management concerned with identifying, presenting, and interpreting information used for formulating strategy, planning and controlling activities, and decision taking.

Management accounting uses information generated from within an organisation on a daily, weekly or monthly basis in order to inform decision making and to assist in the formulation of plans. In this, management accounting is forward looking: it uses data to prepare plans for the future.

But it also uses current information as a feedback to ensure that actual activity conforms to planned activity, and to investigate divergences. Thus the techniques of budgetary control and standard costing use current information to set standards against which actual performance can be measured.

Generally, it is true that management accounting is not subject to the same degree of regulation as is financial accounting. But the Chartered Institute of Management Accountants does issue recommendations which companies are urged to regard as best practice.

Each branch of accounting has a legitimate role to play; the one complementing the other. Indeed, the management accountant may well use many figures which the financial accountant has prepared.

Tutor's comments

This is a well balanced answer, and shows evidence of having been carefully planned, with each topic flowing sensibly from one to another. The candidate has clearly teased out the various strands of the question, and has answered them in turn. The candidate has also learned the relevant definitions from the 'Official Terminology' (published by CIMA) and has set out to offer examples of the concepts, principles, and legal requirements of financial accounting drawn from the syllabus. The clear definitions and the good examples will score high marks.

Similarly with management accounting: the answer is clear, concise and well focused. By knowing the formal definitions, the candidate is able to score maximum marks without unnecessary explanation.

The final paragraph shows that the candidate appreciates the complementary nature of the two branches of accounting, and these final comments conclude an excellent answer.

OUTLINE ANSWERS

1 a) long term planning: investment appraisal
  b) budgeting/profit planning
  c) financial accounting/cost accounting
  d) financial control/standard costing
  e) treasuryship: cash budgets
  f) internal audit/management audit: standard costing
3 a) Elements of cost: the constituent parts of costs according to the factors upon which expenditure is incurred – materials, labour, expenses. Examples of each.
  b) Comparison of FIFO, LIFO, AVCO – perpetual and periodic – during times of changing prices.
    Apportionment of overheads – reasons for and examples; estimates used; basis upon which absorbed by production. Give examples.
    If other examples are used, give: definition, methods, and examples.

Now attempt the review questions on page 310. The answers are given on page 324.

GETTING STARTED

In many industries a large proportion of the total production cost comprises the costs of materials used in manufacture. Not only this, but large sums of money are invested in stocks of materials and components, some of which require specialist and costly storage facilities, either to ensure the qualities of the materials or for the sake of security. For many industries, therefore, accounting for materials is an important activity.

Purchasing procedures involve;

▶ purchase requisitions — which are internal instructions to the buying department to purchase goods or services. Purchase requisitions elicit;
▶ purchase orders — which are written instructions sent to a supplier requesting the supply of particular goods or services.

Once items are received, they require the provision of stores handling procedures, and proper *stores routines* to ensure that items are properly recorded, and their security guaranteed. Some items may require specialist storage facilities.

Changes in the price levels of materials raise difficulties over *charging items to production*. Where the items retain their individuality, they can be charged out at their purchase price. Problems arise however with materials which lose their identity; here accountants have devised a number of acceptable approaches to resolve the difficulties. The accounting method adopted by a company does not necessarily have to reflect the actual physical issuing of materials.

MATERIAL COSTS

PURCHASING PROCEDURE

RECEIVING MATERIALS

STORES ROUTINE

STORES CONTROL

RE-ORDER LEVELS

RE-ORDER QUANTITY

VALUING MATERIALS ISSUES

FIRST IN, FIRST OUT (FIFO)

LAST IN, FIRST OUT (LIFO)

AVERAGE COST (AVCO)

PERPETUAL AND PERIODIC METHODS

THE ACCOUNTING SYSTEM AND STOCK ISSUES

ESSENTIAL PRINCIPLES

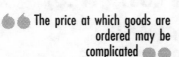 The themes in purchasing procedure are common to all businesses

Although detailed procedures adopted by particular firms may differ, there are general themes in purchasing procedure which are common to all. Thus, usually it is better for one person — or one department — to be responsible for placing all orders (see Figure 13.1). This helps to prevent duplication of ordering, enables purchasing expertise to be developed, and makes for closer control of the purchasing function.

By centralising the activity, specialist information can be maintained and regularly updated concerning catalogues, prices and suppliers, delivery dates and terms of contract for those materials commonly used by the business. Specialist legislation can be monitored, and information collected from trade associations and purchasing consortia. By routing the firm's purchasing power through one department, it may be possible to obtain better terms from suppliers through quantity discounts. Common purchasing policies can be applied, and some standardisation achieved in the items ordered.

No purchases should be allowed unless ordered on official order forms through the buyer or purchasing department, and the number of people authorised to sign official orders should be kept to a minimum to guard against misappropriation.

The ordering of materials begins when the stores department issues a requisition to the purchasing department asking them to order a given amount of a particular item. The requisition should state clearly the quantity required, the nature of the items, the suppliers, catalogue reference, and should give some indication of how urgently items are needed.

The purchasing department will then raise an order with the supplier. The order will carry all relevant details taken from the requisition, plus the current prices and contract or tender number. Delivery will be requested to a specific reception point by a certain date. Copies of the order will be sent to the stores and to the accounts department with a copy retained in purchasing. The stores can then check their copy order against their requisition to ensure that what has been ordered is what is required; any discrepancy will then be notified to the purchasing department immediately so that the order can be amended.

In some cases the purchasing department will obtain quotations from suppliers in an effort to ascertain the current price within the delivery period. When orders are placed against quotations, the relevant quotation reference should be shown clearly.

For materials that are used regularly and in quantity, forward contracts may be made with a supplier to supply a given quantity as required over a specified time period and at a fixed price. The advantages of such a contract are that the purchaser has a guaranteed price, and the supplier has a guaranteed market for his product. Orders placed against such contracts should stipulate that they are to be set against the contract and should show clearly the contract reference.

The price at which goods are ordered may be complicated

The price at which items are ordered may be complicated by value added tax (or sales taxes), by quantity, trade and cash discounts, transport and storage charges, and charges for returnable containers or packaging.

VALUE ADDED (SALES) TAXES

A number of countries, including the United Kingdom, operate value added (VAT) or sales taxes. These taxes are usually added to the cost price after other discounts have

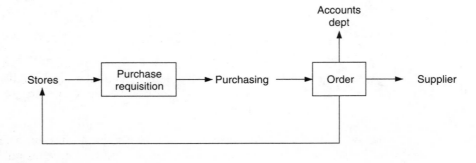

Fig. 13.1 Purchasing procedure.

been allowed. Hence, where goods valued at £200 are ordered and are subject to $2\frac{1}{2}$ per cent cash discount, and where VAT is $17\frac{1}{2}$ per cent, the pricing calculation is as follows:

	£
Goods ordered	200.00
Less: Cash discount ($2\frac{1}{2}$%)	5.00
	195.00
VAT at $17\frac{1}{2}$%	34.12
Cost price of goods	200.00
VAT	34.12
Invoice price	234.12

Note that cash discount is a financial item, and will not be shown in the cost accounts. The cost records will show the cost of the goods as £234.12. If payment is made promptly and the discount taken, £5 can be deducted from the invoice, and £229.12 will be paid. (See Cash discounts below.)

QUANTITY DISCOUNTS

Some suppliers allow discounts on large orders in an effort to encourage customers to order in quantity. Large orders enable the supplier to operate larger production runs – and these often result in lower unit costs – and reduce packing and delivery expenses. In passing on a proportion of these savings to the customer, firms hope to encourage bulk buying. A company's buyer must always take quantity discounts into reckoning when placing orders.

TRADE DISCOUNTS

Some suppliers will offer extra discounts to businesses who are in the same trade, and where the goods are to be sold on to another customer. The discount is to compensate for breaking bulk and repacking, storing and delivering small quantities to customers.

CASH DISCOUNTS

These are allowed to customers to encourage prompt payment of bills; for example, some firms will allow a discount of 5 per cent, if the account is settled within, say, seven days. It is an effort on the part of the supplier to improve his own cash liquidity. However, whether a firm takes advantage of this discount is a matter of policy for the buying firm; as such, cash discount is a financial matter, and should not be shown in the cost accounts.

TRANSPORT AND STORAGE CHARGES

The price quoted by the supplier will often include delivery to the customer's address: where price is quoted c.i.f. (cost, insurance and freight) delivery is included. But sometimes delivery and storage will be charged extra, or delivery will be restricted. Prices quoted may be:

f.a.s:	free alongside	f.o.b:	free on board
f.o.q:	free on quay	f.o.r:	free on rail

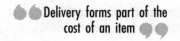
Delivery forms part of the
cost of an item

Where delivery charges do apply – charged either by the supplier, or borne directly by the purchaser – they should be added to the purchase price by the buyer, if possible, or charged by him to factory overhead. The expense of delivery does form part of the cost of an item.

CHARGEABLE PACKAGING

Sometimes special packaging or containers are charged by the supplier and a credit for all or part of the charge is granted when the packing is returned. Where this is so, the cost of packaging will not be taken into account, since it is assumed that the crates, etc. will be returned promptly – although records should be kept to ensure that this happens. That part of the value *not credited* on return should be added to the purchase price of the goods. Where the full cost of packaging is to be borne by the purchasing company, the buyer should include this sum as part of the purchase cost.

Example 1

To see just how complicated pricing calculations can be — and to see why expert knowledge is required — consider an example where a company agrees to supply material (X) on the following terms:

Quantity (units)	Unit price (£)
100	3.00
200–800	2.70
800–1,000	2.55

The material is supplied only in lots of 100 units. Trade discount is 20 per cent, and cash discount of $2\frac{1}{2}$ per cent applies if the account is settled within 14 days. Packing crates are charged at £5.00 each, and are credited at £4.00 each if returned in good condition. One container is required for every 100 units.

Required
The customer decides to purchase 700 units which attract transport charges of £28 and storage charges of £21. Prepare a price calculation.

Solution:

Price Calculation

	£	Unit cost £	Total cost £
Material (X): 700 units at £2.70 unit		2.70	1,890
Less: 20 per cent trade discount		0.54	378
		2.16	1,512
Returnable packing crates:			
7 at £5.00	35		
Less: Credited on return £4	28	0.01	7
	7	2.17	1,519
Transport charges	28		
Storage	21	0.07	49
	49	2.24	1,568

Tutor's comments

Since cash discounts are a financial item subject to managerial policy, they do not appear in the cost accounts. If the customer were to pay within 14 days, a discount of £39.20 would be allowed, and the customer could pay only £1,568 – £39.20 = £1,528.80.

RECEIVING MATERIALS

When the goods are received they should be checked against the delivery note to ensure that the note agrees with the type and quantities actually received (see Figure 13.2). Where there is a discrepancy, or where the goods are damaged, the note should be marked accordingly. One copy of the note will be left with the goods, and the delivery company will retain another copy. The delivery note may then either be kept by the stores or sent to the packing department to be married up with the copy order. Shortages or damaged items must be notified to the purchasing department immediately so that a claim may be entered with the deliverers and the suppliers made aware.

The goods may be invoiced upon receipt, or the invoice may follow in the course of a few days. In either case, the invoice should be sent to the purchasing department so that it can be checked against the copy order. Once this is done, the invoice may be sent to the stores for them to certify that the goods have been received, or where the delivery note has been despatched to the purchasing department, the check can be made by the purchasing staff. Either way the invoice itself becomes the prime document from which the purchaser's account is debited and the suppliers account credited.

Some suppliers may send monthly statements listing the invoices despatched during the month, and the total amount due for payment. Increasingly, however, customers pay upon the invoice.

Bulky raw materials will be delivered to stock yards, storing grounds or tanks, and these may be so arranged that necessary specialist equipment is permanently installed: cranes, conveyor belts, wagon hoists, pumps, steam lines, etc.

With smaller items, specific receiving points should be identified so that items can be kept safely until they can be transferred either to the stores or to the requisitioning department.

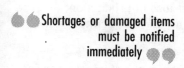 Shortages or damaged items must be notified immediately

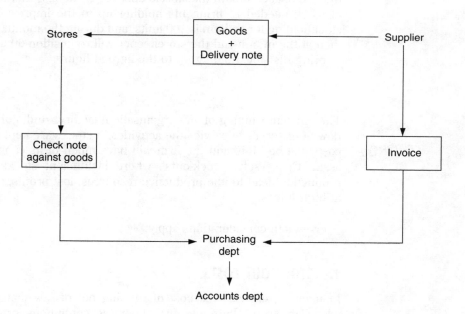

Fig. 13.2 Goods received procedure.

STORES ROUTINE

The pattern adopted for stores organisation depends largely upon the nature of the firm's activities, and the geography of the factory itself. Three general patterns can be identified:

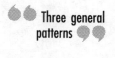 Three general patterns

1. Centralised buying and holding of stores.
2. Centralised purchasing of materials, but decentralised handling of items through stores situated around the works.
3. Decentralised buying, and handling of stores, where each storekeeper is responsible for the purchasing and handling of his own orders.

The advantages of centralised buying were discussed on p. 174, and many firms adopt such a strategy. However, the case is less clear-cut when considering the centralisation of *materials handling*.

The advantages normally cited in support of a central store are that it:

(a)   leads to economies in terms of staffing, clerical costs and storage space;
(b)   enables expertise to be developed concerning those items commonly handled by the firm;
(c)   improves supervision, security and administration;
(d)   enables better laying out of stores, with the provision of specialist facilities: bins, racks, etc.;
(e)   enables stocks to be kept to a minimum, thus reducing the amount of capital invested in stores;
(f)   improves efficiency of stock-taking and stock control.

Against these advantages may be set a number of drawbacks, depending upon the nature of the stores and the geography of the plant. Centralised storage may:

(a)   increase transport costs if the stores are some way from the user;
(b)   cause delays in obtaining materials, with consequent loss of production;
(c)   increase risk to production, in that any problems in the central store – breakdowns, fire etc – will affect all departments.

Where a firm operates a central store it may also set up sub-stores to service particular departments; with such an arrangement, an *imprest system of storekeeping* may be introduced, and in this way some of the advantages of centralisation may be enjoyed whilst some of the disadvantages may be minimised.

The imprest storekeeping system for each store operates much as the imprest system with petty cash. A level of stockholding is identified for each item of stock. At the end of each month the storekeeper requisitions from the central store that amount of stock needed to bring his holding up to the imprest level. Thus, if the agreed stockholding for an item is 100 units, and during the month the stores issued 60 items, then at the month-end the storekeeper will requisition 60 units from the central store to bring his stockholding up to the agreed figure.

STORES CONTROL

The efficient running of any organisation, factory, studio or office demands a planned flow of materials to service the activities. If stocks are kept at too high a level, storage costs will be high, and the firm will have much of its capital locked up in an illiquid asset. Conversely, 'stock-outs', where insufficient stocks are available to support production, lead to idle productive resources, lost profits, and possibly 'panic' buying at high prices.

Five main considerations apply:

1.   STOCK OUT COSTS.

In many businesses the cost of running out of raw materials can be high. This is especially true where the firm operates continuous processes rather than batch production. Indeed, many continuous processes can be closed down only by following a given sequence of operations; similarly, starting up such processes may be both lengthy and costly. Such is the situation with many chemical operations, the smelting of ores, or the production of gases. To avoid stock-outs, it is necessary to balance the rate of use and the time taken to obtain supplies. Firms will often insure against stock-outs by keeping a minimum stock, sometimes called a 'buffer stock'.

> The efficient running of any organisation demands a planned flow of materials

2.   STOCKHOLDING COSTS.

Storage space has to be found for all materials, and for some materials, expensive specialist facilities are required. Flammable liquids, corrosive and poisonous materials demand special safety precautions, often imposed by law; materials for human consumption must be kept free from contamination. With all materials insurance and deterioration impose their own expenses, whilst some materials are more vulnerable to evaporation or to theft than are others. Keeping materials in store, therefore, incurs expense.

3. PRODUCTION RATES.

Since raw materials are destined for use in manufacture, the levels of stock will rise and fall as production fluctuates. Stocks will need to be built up before any planned increase in output, although unplanned fluctuations in production will clearly have knock-on, unplanned effects upon stockholding. When planning future production, it is essential to recognise fully the consequences for stock levels.

4. PROCUREMENT COSTS.

The simple act of actually placing an order costs the firm money: clerical and accounting staff must be paid, so too must the other overhead expenses of the purchasing and accounting departments. There are also costs involved in the checking of deliveries, settling of accounts, etc. The fewer the number of orders placed, the lower such procurement costs will be. Also, as we have seen, many suppliers offer extra discounts for bulk orders. However, reductions in procurement costs, through bulk buying and reducing the number of orders placed, must be set against the stockholding costs in (2).

5. COST OF FINANCE.

Money tied up in stocks cannot be used to finance other activities, so that there is an opportunity cost involved in investing in raw materials, since other investment opportunities must be foregone: *opportunity cost* is the term used for such lost opportunities. It is difficult to measure this opportunity cost in practice, but many firms equate it with the level of external interest rates.

The whole issue of stock control, therefore, has to do with the balancing of various costs, some of which move in opposite directions. Thus, if stocks are kept low, holding costs will be small, and so will the cost of financing stocks; but the risk of stocking out will be high. Also, if orders are placed infrequently, procurement costs will be kept down, but stockholding costs may increase.

The task of monitoring the financial investment which a firm has in stocks will fall to the *stores ledger*. This will usually be kept in the cost office, and will record not just the physical receipts and issues of all items, but their monetary value also.

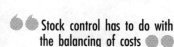 **Stock control has to do with the balancing of costs**

With large organisations, where there may be many hundreds of different items in stock, it is clearly difficult to control every type of component or material. In such situations the number and value of each stock item is analysed, and control applied to those items which account for the largest total value. For example, it may be found that 20 per cent of the quantity of stocks held account for 80 per cent of the value. Therefore, any improvement in the physical control of these items is likely to have major knock-on financial benefits. By conducting such stock analyses, control can be concentrated on those areas where savings can best be made.

RE-ORDER LEVELS

The great importance of stock control to many firms has led to the development of sophisticated operational research techniques to govern stock levels and re-order patterns. It is not the purpose of this book to examine these in detail, but a simple set of equations will be discussed by way of example: an equation to indicate *when* orders should be placed, and an equation to indicate *how much* of the material should be ordered.

The stock level at which further supplies should be ordered is determined by:

(a)   the lead time: that period of time between placing an order with the supplier and receiving the goods in the firm;

(b)   the rate of consumption of the material within the firm;

(c) the minimum stock level: this minimum level represents a buffer stock for use in emergencies. In normal circumstances, it is a level below which stock should not be allowed to fall. A minimum stock level will be set by the firm for each item of stock and for each type of raw material, using formulae based upon probability theory, i.e. the chances of particular situations occurring. For our purposes, we assume that the firm has already been able to do this to its satisfaction.

Once each of these measures is known for a particular item, the re-order level can be calculated by the formula:

66 An equation to indicate when orders should be placed 99

$$\text{Re-order level} = U \times L + M$$

Where U is the usage per period, t; L is the lead time expressed as a fraction of t; and M is the minimum stock level.

Thus, where the average usage U is 500 tonnes per month, the lead time L is $\frac{3}{4}$ month, and the minimum stock level M has been fixed at 60 tonnes, the re-order level is:

$$(500) \times (0.75) + 60 = 435 \text{ tonnes}$$

Thus, when stocks of this item fall to 435 tonnes, a further order is placed. However, for this model to operate satisfactorily it is necessary to monitor the lead time and consumption levels continuously, so that any changes can be reflected in the calculation. Minimum stock levels should also be examined regularly to discover if the figures need revising.

RE-ORDER QUANTITY

The equation given above will indicate when orders need to be placed, but the equation will not indicate how much of an item should be ordered bearing in mind procurement and holding costs, and usage rates. It costs money to place an order, but it also costs money to hold excess stocks: the two expenses need to be balanced with the rate of usage.

Assume that a firm uses a material at a constant rate and that regular orders arrive at the moment that the previously delivery has been used up. If this sequence is plotted on a graph, the 'saw-tooth graph' of Figure 13.3 is devised. Since stock moves from Q down to zero over a fixed time span, the average quantity held in stock must be $Q/2$. If the cost of holding stocks is H per unit, then the *total holding costs* are:

$$\frac{(Q)}{(2)} \times H \text{ or } \frac{(Q)}{(2)} H$$

Procurement costs similarly: if U is the rate of usage in time t, and Q is the quantity ordered, then the number of orders placed in time t will be U/Q.

If C is the cost of placing an order, the cost of ordering during time t will be:

$$\left(\frac{U}{Q}\right) \times C \text{ or } \left(\frac{U}{Q}\right) C$$

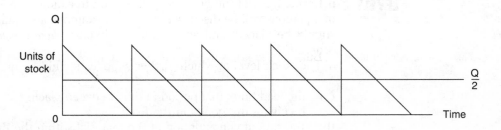

Fig. 13.3 'Saw-tooth' graph

The total costs of an order are thus the holding cost plus the procurement cost:

$$\text{Total cost of order} = \left(\frac{U}{2}\right)H \;+\; \left(\frac{U}{2}\right)C$$

holding   procurement
cost   cost

Elementary calculus enables us to differentiate in respect of Q to find the minimum total cost, which is reached at:

An equation to indicate how much should be ordered

$$Q = \sqrt{\frac{2UC}{H}}$$

By using this equation, the firm can calculate that order quantity at which procurement and holding costs will be at a minimum. Hence, if usage U is at the rate of 7,500 litres per period, the cost of ordering C is £20 per order, and holding costs H are £120 per litre, then the economic order quantity for the material is:

$$\sqrt{\frac{2\,(7,500)\times(20)}{120}}$$

$$= \sqrt{\frac{2\,(150,000)}{120}}$$

$$= \sqrt{\frac{300,000}{120}}$$

$$= \sqrt{2,500}$$

$$= 50 \text{ litres}$$

VALUING MATERIALS ISSUES

Once received by the stores, materials wait until the departments have need of them. Items required for manufacture are ordered from the stores by the production departments as necessary, usually by way of a materials requisition. These requisitions give details of the nature and amount of the items required, and the department's cost centre number, so that the department can be charged with the relevant material costs.

Where items used in production can be readily identified then the price at which they are issued to production can be the price which was paid for them. In such cases the items are marked when they are taken into stock. When they are used in production, the relevant price is attributed to them, and they are charged accordingly. This may happen when a garage orders a new engine for a customer's car: the price of the engine can be identified, and the customer charged, along with the labour and other costs for his job.

Many items brought into stock lose their individual identity

But many items brought into stock do lose their individual identity, and whilst this does not create problems when prices are stable, in times of rapid price changes difficulties do arise. In the following example Partons Ltd took delivery of two consignments of 'splash cans' during the first half of 19–7. Opening stock on 1 January 19–7 comprised seven cans at £13.80 each. During January, a delivery was made when cans cost £14.00 each, whilst in April the price had increased to £15.10.

Example 2

Partons Ltd

Splash cans

	Receipts	Issues	
10 January:	20 @ £14.00 each	14 February:	22
20 April:	10 @ £15.10 each	12 May:	6

What price should the production department be charged? Opening stock valued the cans at £13.80 each, but January's receipts cost £14.00 each. Are the 22 cans issued in February to be deemed as taken from the old stock, with 15 from the new; or all 20 from the January delivery, and only two from the opening stock?

To resolve these problems, a number of standard approaches have been developed. Three of the common ones will be examined here, but there are others.

FIRST IN, FIRST OUT (FIFO)

This approach assumes that the first items to be received will be the first to be issued, hence the name. Under this method the old stock is deemed to be issued first, so that closing stocks are valued at the more recent prices paid – (see Table 13.1).

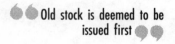 Old stock is deemed to be issued first

In February, therefore, as seen from the table, under FIFO the 22 items issued are assumed to comprise the seven of the opening stock at £13.80 each, and 15 of the January delivery at £14.00 each. In May, the six cans issued are assumed to include the remaining five from the January delivery, at £14.00, and one from the April consignment at £15.10.

The value of the cans issued during the period is assumed to be £306.60 + £85.10 = £391.70, and closing stock is assumed to comprise nine cans at £15.10, total value £135.90.

Table 13.1 (FIFO)

Date	Receipts Quantity	Price (£)	Total (£)	Issues Quantity	Price (£)	Total (£)	Stock Quantity	Price (£)	Total (£)
1 Jan		Opening stock					7	13.80	96.60
10 Jan.	20	14.0	280				7	13.80	96.60
							20	14.00	280.00
							27		376.60
14 Feb.				7	13.80	96.60	5	14.00	70.00
				15	14.00	210.00			
				22		306.60			
20 April	10	15.10	151				5	14.00	70.00
							10	15.10	151.00
							15		221.00
12 May				5	14.00	70.00	9	15.10	135.90
				1	15.10	15.10			
				6		85.10			

<table>
<tr><td>**LAST IN,
FIRST OUT
(LIFO)**</td><td>An alternative approach is to assume that the latest goods to arrive are the first to be issued: last in, first out. Here, since the more recent items are deemed to be issued first the closing stock is assumed to comprise the older items (see Table 13.2). Thus, in February, the issue of 22 cans is assumed to include all 20 of January's delivery at £14.00, and two of the opening stock at £13.80 each. In May, the six cans issued are deemed to be from the latest consignment, which in this instance is the April delivery at £15.10.</td></tr>
</table>

> ❝ More recent items are deemed to be issued first ❞

Under LIFO, the value of cans issued is assumed to be £307.60 + £90.60 = £398.20, and closing stock comprises five at £13.80 and four at £15.10, making £129.40.

AVERAGE COST (AVCO)

The third method of accounting for materials calculates the average cost of goods held in stock each time a new delivery is received (Table 13.3). Thus, when 20 cans are received on 10 January at £14.00 each, the total value of stock becomes £96.60 + £280 = £376.60. This is the value of 27 cans now in stock – the opening stock of seven, and the 20 recently received. The average value of each can is £376.60 ÷ 27 = £13.95. Now, when issues are made in February the 22 cans are issued at £13.95, so the value of February's issues is 22 × £13.95 = £306.90. Again, when April's consignment is received 10 cans at £15.10 increases the value of total stock by

Table 13.2 (LIFO)

Date	Receipts			Issues			Stock		
	Quantity	Price (£)	Total (£)	Quantity	Price (£)	Total (£)	Quantity	Price (£)	Total (£)
1 Jan		Opening stock					7	13.80	96.60
10 Jan.	20	14.0	280				7	13.80	96.60
							20	14.00	280.00
							27		376.60
14 Feb.				2	13.80	27.60	5	13.80	69.00
				20	14.00	280.00			
				22		307.60			
20 April	10	15.10	151				5	13.80	69.00
							10	15.10	151.00
							15		220.00
12 May				6	15.10	90.60	5	13.80	69.00
							4	15.10	60.40
							9		129.40

Table 13.3 (AVCO)

Date	Receipts			Issues			Stock		
	Quantity	Price (£)	Total (£)	Quantity	Price (£)	Total (£)	Quantity	Price (£)	Total (£)
1 Jan		Opening stock					7	13.80	96.60
10 Jan.	20	14	280				27	13.95	376.60
14 Feb.				22	13.95	306.90	5	13.95	69.70
20 April.	10	15.10	151				15	14.71	220.70
12 May				6	14.71	88.26	9	14.71	132.44

£151, to £220.70. Since this represents 15 cans, the average value is £220.70 ÷ 15 = £14.71. And it is at this price of £14.71 that issues are made in May.

With AVCO, therefore, the value of cans issued is assumed to be £306.90 + £88.26 = £395.16. The closing stock of nine cans is valued at £132.44.

EFFECTS ON PROFITS

By tabulating the value of issues and the value of closing stock under each method, we can analyse the effects upon profits:

	Issues (£)	Closing stock (£)
FIFO	391.70	135.90
LIFO	398.20	129.40
AVCO	395.16	132.44

Assume that the materials issued were used in products which were sold for a total of £800. The profits would appear as below:

	FIFO (£)	LIFO (£)	AVCO (£)
Opening stock	96.60	96.60	96.60
Purchases (£280 + £151)	431.00	431.00	431.00
	527.60	527.60	527.60
Closing stock	135.90	129.40	132.44
	391.70	398.20	395.16
Profit	408.30	401.80	404.84
Sales revenue	800.00	800.00	800.00

FIFO gives the highest figure for closing stock at £135.90, followed by AVCO at £132.44, and then LIFO at £129.40. Because of this, FIFO's profit is the greatest at £408.30, followed by AVCO at £404.84, and LIFO at £401.80.

In periods when prices are rising — as in the example — FIFO will show the greatest profit because it assumes that the earliest, and therefore cheapest, items are issued to production first. This reduces the cost of production, and because the latest, and more expensive items are assumed still to be in stock the closing stock figure is high, and so too are the profits.

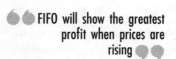 FIFO will show the greatest profit when prices are rising

Conversely, LIFO will show the smallest profit when prices are rising, since it assumes that the latest, and therefore more expensive, items are issued to production first. This increases the cost of production, and because the earlier, and cheaper, items are assumed to be in stock it depresses stock values, which in turn leads to a lower profit. LIFO in fact delays the recognition of profit in this way. AVCO falls between the two extremes, because goods are issued to production on the basis of weighted averages.

When prices are falling the opposite is the case: FIFO will show the smallest profit, and LIFO the highest profit. Once again, AVCO will be somewhere between the two.

FIFO, LIFO AND AVCO COMPARED

The FIFO method gives a more realistic figure for closing stock than does LIFO, since FIFO values stock at current prices. In the description above LIFO was still including as part of the closing stock calculation items deemed to have cost £13.80 each, when prices had risen to £15.10. However, FIFO gives the lowest figure of the three for the value of issues. In times of rapid price changes, therefore, FIFO will give a realistic figure for stock but an unrealistic figure for materials issued.

In contrast, whilst LIFO gives a low value for closing stock — because it values stock at out-of-date prices — it does give an up-to-date valuation for materials issued.

AVCO seeks to avoid the extremes of both of the other two methods by steering a mid course. In the description above, AVCO gives the second highest figure for both closing stock and materials issued: the situation would be the same even if prices were falling. However, AVCO does suffer from the disadvantage that the prices charged to production may bear no relation to any price actually paid: nowhere in Example 2 did Parton Ltd. pay £13.95 or £14.71. Also, the number and complexity of the calculations with AVCO can increase the risk of errors, and rounding-off problems occur. FIFO and LIFO are both easier to understand and to apply than AVCO.

But there is no 'right' and 'wrong' method, just as there is no one 'correct' profit among the three given. The value of stocks and of profit will depend upon the method used. All three are acceptable in management accounting, but LIFO is unacceptable in financial accounting (see SSAP9).

AVCO steers a mid course

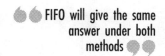

There is no right and wrong method

PERPETUAL AND PERIODIC METHODS

In the discussions of FIFO, LIFO and AVCO, the valuation of stocks changed each time new receipts were added or issues made. Because stocks were continuously changing, this method is termed the *perpetual* method. However, there are occasions when the calculation of goods issued or of closing stock may not be made until the end of the period. Such an approach is called the *periodic* method, and with it the precise dates of receipts and issues are ignored.

A summary of the receipts of Parton Ltd shows:

			£	£
Opening stock	7	@	13.80	96.60
Receipts	20	@	14.00	280.00
Receipts	10	@	15.10	151.00
	37			527.60

Throughout the period 37 items are available for issue, of which 28 were in fact issued, leaving a closing stock of nine cans.

Under FIFO periodic, the first items in stock are assumed to be the first to be issued; therefore, the closing stock of nine cans is assumed to be from the last consignment received. Under FIFO periodic, therefore, the value of closing stock is nine at £15.10 = £135.90. A comparison with the figure for FIFO perpetual will show that there is no difference: FIFO will give the same closing stock figure irrespective of whether perpetual or periodic approaches are used. Similarly with the assumed cost of goods issued: FIFO will give the same answer under both methods: £527.60 − £135.90 = £391.70.

With LIFO, the earliest items are assumed to remain in stock; therefore, under LIFO periodic, the closing stock figure is: seven at £13.80 plus two at £14.00, equals £124.60. The assumed cost of issues is £527.60 − £124.60 = £403.00. In both cases there is a difference between LIFO perpetual and LIFO periodic. This difference arises because under the periodic approach the timings of receipts and issues have been ignored, although sometimes, depending upon the pattern of goods received and goods sent out, LIFO *may* give the same answer for both perpetual and periodic approaches.

AVCO periodic uses the weighted average calculated over the whole period. Thus, with 37 cans costing a total of £527.60 the average cost is £527.60 ÷ 37 = £14.26. The value of nine cans as closing stock, therefore, is 9 × £14.26 = £128.34. With goods issued, £527.60 was available for issue, of which £128.34 remained in stock at the end of the period, the assumed value of the issues is £527.60 − £128.34 = £399.26. Again, the differences between perpetual and periodic measures arise because under periodic we have calculated an average based upon the whole period, and assumed all issues have been made at this price. With the perpetual approach, a new average is calculated with each set of receipts, and issues are costed at this new price until further receipts alter it.

FIFO will give the same answer under both methods

Perpetual and periodic methods: comparison of issues and stocks

	Issues (£)		Stocks (£)	
	Perpetual	*Periodic*	*Perpetual*	*Periodic*
FIFO	391.70	391.70	135.90	135.90
LIFO	398.20	403.00	129.40	124.60
AVCO	395.16	399.26	132.44	128.34

THE ACCOUNTING SYSTEM AND STOCK ISSUES

❝❝ There need be no direct relationship between the method used and the actual physical issue of stock ❞❞

Throughout the discussion on accounting for material issues it was carefully emphasised that stock was *assumed* to be issued on a first in, first out basis, or that the newer stock was *deemed* to be issued first.

The purpose of FIFO and LIFO is to resolve an accounting problem. *Whether in fact the materials themselves are physically used on a last in, first out basis – or on a first in, first out basis – is irrelevant for the accounts.* In some businesses – such as a fishmonger or a fruiterer, where the produce is perishable – the older stock may be used first, but in other businesses it may make no difference. There may, therefore be *no direct relationship between the accounting system used and the way in which the stock is actually issued.* Any such relationship that does exist arises from production considerations, and not from accounting ones.

Thus, a fishmonger may decide to *issue* fish on a FIFO basis, because it is perishable but to *account* for it on a LIFO basis, because of the way prices are moving.

EXAMINATION QUESTIONS

1   James Day commenced business on 1 April 1991 as a retailer of the Excel Road Master Caravan Mark II.

During the year ended 31 March 1992, James Day's dealings in caravans were as follows:

1991
April	Bought 6 caravans at £10,000 each
May	Bought 3 caravans at £11,000 each.
June	Sold 1 caravan at £16,000.
July	Sold 3 caravans at £15,500 each.
August	Bought 2 caravans at £11,200 each.
November	Sold 4 caravans at £16,200 each.

1992
January	Bought 5 caravans at £12,500 each.
March	Sold 4 caravans at £15,900 each.

During his first year's trading, James Day has not taken any money out of the business for living expenses.

The overhead expenses incurred during the year ended 31 March 1992 have amounted to £9,000.

REQUIRED

(a)   Accounting statements showing James Day's net profit or loss for the year ended 31 March 1992 using each of the following methods of stock valuation:

(i)   first in first out;
(ii)   last in first out. *(13)*

(b)   Explain the advantages and disadvantages of using each of the stock valuation methods used in *(a)* above. *(12)*

(Cambridge 1992)

2 a) In calculating a re-order quantity for materials, what is meant by the 'saw-tooth' graph? What are the assumptions upon which it is based? *(6)*

  b) Hasling Ltd keeps six weeks' supply of 'Bumol' as a minimum stock: supplies of 'Bumol' take three weeks to be delivered from the date of ordering. Each order costs £25 to place.

  Consumption of 'Bumol' for the last six months, and the costs of storage were:

Month No	Usage (tonnes)	Storage Costs £	Month No	Usage (tonnes)	Storage Costs £
8	840	12,350	11	850	12,880
9	490	7,460	12	810	12,010
10	760	11,220	13	750	11,580

Calculate:
  i) the re-order level, and
  ii) the economic order quantity. *(9)*

(London 1993)

3 a) What is meant by the imprest system of storekeeping? *(4)*

  b) Discuss the advantages and disadvantages of the three patterns of organising material stores:

  i centralised buying and holding of stores
  ii centralised purchasing of stores, but decentralised handling of materials
  iii decentralised buying and handling of stores. *(11)*

(London 1993)

TUTOR'S ANSWER TO QUESTION 1

			£
a) Purchases	6	@ £10,000	60,000
	3	@ £11,000	33,000
	2	@ £11,200	22,400
	5	@ £12,500	62,500
	16		177,900
Sales	1	@ £16,000	16,000
	3	@ £15,500	46,500
	4	@ £16,200	64,800
	4	@ £15,900	63,600
	12		190,900

16 Caravans purchased, 12 caravans sold: closing stock is thus four caravans.

	FIFO		LIFO	
	£	£	£	£
Sales		190,900		190,900
Less purchases	177,900		177,900	
Closing stock	50,000		42,500	
		127,900		135,400
		63,000		55,500
Overheads		9,000		9,000
Profit		54,000		46,500

Closing stock under FIFO represents four caravans @ £12,500 = £50,000: under LIFO the stock is one caravan at £12,500 and three at £10,000 = £42,500.

b) FIFO provides a more realistic valuation for closing stock than does LIFO – £50,000 compared to £42,500. But FIFO values the cost of goods sold at oudated prices – £127,900 compared to £135,400. The net effect of this is that FIFO shows a greater profit figure of £54,000 compared to LIFO's profit of £46,500. LIFO is not acceptable under SSAP9.

OUTLINE ANSWERS

2 a) Saw-tooth graph: relates levels of stocks held against production over time. Assumes: business uses material at a constant rate; and that regular orders arrive at the moment that the previous delivery is used up.

b i) $U \times L + M$ = $(4,500/6) \times (0.75) + (4,500/24) \times 6$
$= 750 \times 0.75 + 1,125 = \underline{1,687.5}$

ii) Firstly, calculate holding cost:

$$H = \frac{67\,500}{4\,500} = 15$$

Secondly, calculate the EOQ:

$$\sqrt{\frac{2UC}{H}} = \sqrt{\frac{2(750 \times £25)}{15}}$$

$$= \sqrt{\frac{2(18\,750)}{15}}$$

$$= \sqrt{2\,500}$$

$$= 50$$

3 a) Imprest system: a level of stockholding is identified for each store and for each item of stock in that store. At the end of an agreed period, the storekeeper requisitions that amount necessary to bring the holding up to the agreed level.

b) Centralised purchasing: enables necessary expertise to be acquired; eases control over ordering.

Centralised materials handling: can lead to economies in cost of staffing, and of storage space: enables expertise to be developed in materials handling; improves supervision, security, and administration; enables a better laying out of stores; and makes maximum use of specialist equipment such as cranes, conveyors, tanks etc.; enables stocks to be kept at a minimum; and generally improves efficiency of stocktaking and control.

Drawbacks: increased transport costs if stores are a distance from the user; possible delays in obtaining materials from central stores; increased risk that anything that disrupts central stores will disrupt all production.

Decentralised handling goes some way to reducing these risks, whilst preserving advantages of centralised purchasing; but problem with specialist equipment.

Decentralised buying and handling: reduces drawbacks of centralisation even further, but may reduce control and efficiency.

Now attempt the review questions on page 310. The answers are given on page 325.

LABOUR COSTS

WAGES SYSTEMS

TIME-WORK

PAYMENT BY RESULTS

GETTING STARTED

Just as the cost of materials is an important part of production costs, so too is labour cost. Salaries paid to administrative, supervisory and managerial staffs constitute indirect labour costs, and as such are overheads: overheads are considered in Chapter 16.

On the other hand, wages paid to direct labour — sometimes called factory wages, or production wages — represents a direct cost in that it can be readily identified with a saleable cost unit.

When direct labour is paid on hourly rates, the time actually worked by an employee forms the basis of his or her wages – and of the business's cost of labour. This form of payment is known as 'time rates'.

Where employees are paid on the basis of the amount of output they produce, they are paid on 'piece rates'.

Time rates and piece rates represent the two main types of wages systems. Each has its advantages and its drawbacks.

ESSENTIAL PRINCIPLES

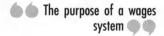

WAGES SYSTEMS

The purpose of a wages system is not merely to recompense employees for the work they have done, although, clearly, this is important. There are other factors which may be considered: wages systems can be used to increase output and to reduce overheads, to encourage efficiency or to reduce labour turnover.

In many cases minimum wage rates will be established by national agreements as a result of negotiation between employers' associations and trade unions. There may, however, be variations upon any national settlement as a result of local agreements to accommodate special circumstances. Whether an individual company can do much by itself to influence such agreements may be doubtful.

The purpose of a wages system

However, a company can ensure, through local representatives of trade unions and through its own efforts, that its employees thoroughly understand the system that it adopts. Unless the full co-operation of the work force is obtained, the potential advantages of any wages system will not be realised.

Neither is it necessarily the case that the firm which pays the lowest wages has the lowest labour cost. One firm may pay its workers £4.00 per hour, and its work force of 200 people may produce 500 units per week, giving a labour cost per unit of:

$$\frac{£4.00 \times 200}{500} = £1.60 \text{ per unit}$$

However, with a better-trained, better-motivated work force, another comparable firm paying £4.40 per hour may achieve a lower labour cost per unit because the workers are more productive, and produce 600 units:

$$\frac{£4.40 \times 200}{600} = £1.47 \text{ per unit}$$

Of itself, therefore, the cost of labour is not very meaningful; the cost must be related to the output achieved in order to give a measure of productivity.

Labour productivity, however, may be measured, not just in terms of quantities, but also in terms of quality. Where the sheer quantity of output is important wages schemes can be devised to encourage increased volumes. But there are situations where care, accuracy and a generally high standard of workmanship is required, and here wage systems based upon the volume of output may be inappropriate.

Many overheads incurred by a company are fixed in the short term: they are time related or period costs, rather than product related or product costs. And yet it is through the income generated by output that such overheads can be met. Thus the greater the output that can be achieved in a given period, the smaller the amount of fixed costs which each product has to carry (see Table 14.1).

As Table 14.1 shows, fixed costs of £500 when spread over 250 units amount to £2.00 per item, but when spread over 1,500 units the same level of fixed cost can be covered at £0.33 per item. Many wage systems, therefore, seek to encourage an increased volume of output over a given time period.

TIME-WORK

Time-work wages systems relate the number of hours worked by an employee to an agreed hourly rate.

Table 14.1 Output and costs

Output	Fixed cost (£)	Fixed cost per unit (£)
250	500	2.00
500	500	1.00
1,000	500	0.50
1,500	500	0.33

FLAT TIME-WORK OR DAY RATES

These methods calculate gross pay by multiplying the clock hours worked by the wage rate per hour:

Gross earnings = Clock hours worked × Rate per hour

Thus, if an employee works for 35 hours, and the hourly rate is £4.00, then the gross earnings are:

35 × £4.00 = £140

Usually the hourly rate for overtime includes an additional premium, often of 25 or 50 per cent of the basic rate. Sometimes, overtime rates pay 'time and a quarter' for the first few hours, and 'time and a half' thereafter. Sunday working may attract double time, i.e. twice the basic hourly rate, and work done on special holidays, such as Christmas day, may attract 'treble time'.

Assume that a woman works for 45 hours in a week. The hourly rate for a basic 35-hour week is £3.60; thereafter, overtime is paid at time-and-a-quarter for the first five hours, and time-and-a-half for the remainder. The woman's hourly rates are:

		£
Basic hourly rate:		3.60
Initial overtime rate	£3.60 × 1.25 =	4.50
Full overtime rate:	£3.60 × 1.5 =	5.40

The woman's gross earnings are therefore:

Basic working week:	35 × £3.60 =	126.00
Initial overtime:	5 × £4.50 =	22.50
Full overtime:	5 × £5.40 =	27.00
	45	175.50

Many companies find that a wages system based upon flat-time rates is very successful. Wages are easy to calculate, and the employees have little difficulty in understanding the system; they can also rely upon earning regular sums each week. For activities where increases in output are secondary to quality of production, then the method is quite satisfactory. Indeed, many indirect workers, such as cleaners, labourers, canteen assistants, night watchmen, etc., are paid on time rates. However, flat rates do little to encourage employees to improve output: people may do no more than is necessary, waiting between jobs until instructed what to do, and 'spinning out' tasks from one workbreak to another.

HIGH DAY RATES

In an effort to overcome some of these disadvantages, many firms have introduced methods based upon high day rates. The justification for these methods is that low wage rates do not necessarily mean low labour costs; conversely, high wage rates may not mean high labour costs. If a firm can increase wage rates to attract efficient employees, then the increases in output may *more than* compensate for the increased rates.

Under such systems standards of quality and of production are established by the firm's management, so that particular tasks must be satisfactorily completed within a given period of time. The standards so set should be realistic, such that a competent and conscientious worker can reasonably be able to attain them day after day. Where the work moves through the factory on a conveyor belt, particular activities must be completed before the work reaches specified points. Inspections of work quality will be regular and strict, and absences from the work place for 'natural breaks' will be

Relate hours worked to an agreed rate

Flat time rates are very successful

Low wage rates do not necessarily mean low labour costs

carefully monitored. In return for such close supervision, and for the additional effort, the hourly rates of pay are higher than they otherwise might be. It is unusual for employees to work overtime if such a system is in operation.

MEASURED DAY-WORK

A further refinement of high day rates is where the firm pays an agreed hourly rate for a specified level of performance. It is claimed that although this method offers no incentive to increase output, it does lead to better relations between management and employees.

PAYMENT BY RESULTS

All forms of time-work are based upon the relationship between the hours worked and the hourly rate: wages are related to the time spent in the factory. There is no attempt made to encourage workers to greater efficiency. Any improvement in productivity accrues to the employers, but equally any deterioration in productivity is for them to bear.

> **Payment by results relates wages to output**

With schemes based upon 'payment by results', wages are related to output. Any gain or loss arising from the employee's efficiency affects that employee's wages directly. The employee therefore has an incentive towards greater efficiency in a way that is not obtainable under time-work systems. However, it is important that quality of output is maintained in the drive for greater volume, and where piece-work systems do apply, close inspection of work is essential. Piece-work systems thus lend themselves to tasks which are simple and repetitive, and where the quality of output is determined more by the raw material and the machines than by operator skill.

Secondly, no matter what monetary incentive is offered, many employees will decide for themselves what constitutes a reasonable week's work in terms of effort expended and wages received. Disincentives towards greater effort, such as the incidence of taxation, may also operate against maximum effort. The result may be that employees will not be prepared to work a full week: they may take time off or leave early, knowing that they have earned sufficient for their own needs. Where the firm seeks to recover overheads on the basis of labour hours worked, such an approach can have serious consequences. Because of this, employees being paid on piece rates should also be required to clock-in, so that information upon hours actually worked may be collected for use in overhead calculations.

> **Employees on piece rates should be required to clock in**

STRAIGHT PIECE WORK

Under straight piece work, the employee is paid a rate for each item, or batch of items produced. The wage rates set are usually higher than would be the case under flat time rates, in order to constitute an incentive to greater output. In setting the necessary rates, work study techniques are used so that the levels set may be reasonable in terms of achievement for the employee and in terms of output for the firm.

Example 1

Assume that the firm has traditionally paid £3.20 per hour on day rates, but that now, after consultation with the trade unions and the employees, it has been decided to convert to piece rates. The previous hourly output per employee was 20 units, and it is felt that an improvement of 20 per cent might be achieved under the new system, i.e. 24 units. Under the day-rate system, the rate per unit was £3.20 ÷ 20 = £0.16. As an incentive under the new piece-rate system, the unit rate is to be increased to £0.165, but the hourly rate is to be reduced to £2.97, representing 18 units at the new rate. At the expected new level of output, the employee will receive wages of 24 × £0.165 = £3.96 per hour.

With piece-rate systems newly appointed employees usually begin on straight time rates during their training period, and convert to piece rates when they have reached a standard where their earnings under day rates would equal their pay under piece rates. In Example 1 outputs per hour in excess of 18 units would give rise to piece rates, since it is at this level that day and piece rates diverge. Also, where workers are idle through no fault of their own, hourly rates are paid. The level of such rates will be the subject of negotiation with the trade union before the system is introduced.

PREMIUM BONUS SCHEMES

The straight piece-work system holds constant the payment per item produced, so that an employee earns more by producing more items at this set rate. In Example 1 the rate per item was £0.165: to increase earnings, the employee endeavours to produce as many as possible at this price.

Premium bonus schemes work on a different principle: the bonus is given based upon the time saved in doing a job when compared to the set time for that job. The standard times are fixed by reference to work study surveys, past records, etc.

Bonus paid on time saved

Both the employees and the management have incentives under such schemes. The employees have an incentive to save time and to earn bonus; and the management has an incentive to reduce overhead costs by ensuring efficient systems of work and well laid out and maintained plant. Indeed, it is the saving on overhead which provides the 'fund' out of which the bonus is paid.

There exist a number of premium bonus schemes, differing largely in the proportion of the savings made available to the employee. The *Halsey* scheme pays 50 per cent of the time saved to the employee, whereas the *Halsey–Weir* scheme pays 30 per cent of the time saved.

COLLECTIVE BONUS SCHEMES

Schemes operated on a group basis

Thus far we have considered bonus schemes based upon an individual employee's performance. In many factories, however, bonus schemes are operated on a group basis, either for separate groups within the factory or for all workers in separate factories. Such collective schemes are often easier to administer than a range of separate bonuses; workers who are only indirectly concerned with production can be included as part of the 'team', and working arrangements within the group can be made more flexible. However, people who wish to work at a pace different from that of the group may not be welcome, inefficient members may be 'carried' by their more efficient colleagues so that the incentive element may not be so pronounced, and it may prove difficult to negotiate the level of bonus which members of the group shall receive.

As with many of these schemes, various forms exist: the *Rucker* scheme is based upon the notion of added value, defined as the increase in realisable value resulting from an alteration in form, location or availability of a product or a service. Added value excludes the cost of purchased materials and services. Thus, if materials and services are bought in at £1,000 and the goods so produced are sold for £1,500, then the added value amounts to £500.

The Rucker scheme uses records of past earnings and added value to establish a relationship between the two. Whenever there is a reduction in the ratio of earnings to added value, then bonus payments accrue.

PROFIT-SHARING SCHEMES

Cultivates feeling of commitment

In an effort to cultivate within employees a feeling of commitment to the firm, some companies have introduced profit-sharing schemes. Here, employees who have completed a minimum length of service – say two years – receive an agreed proportion of the profits remaining after the preference shareholders have been paid, and after a fixed dividend has been paid on ordinary shares. If there are insufficient profits to cover these sums, then no bonus is paid.

One drawback to such schemes is that the bonus cannot be paid until after the firm's accounts have been audited and agreed and this may take some considerable time after the end of the financial year. However, since the bonus is aimed at reducing labour turnover and engendering a long-term commitment to the firm, this criticism is possibly misplaced. Certainly, the prospect of receiving a large annual bonus based upon performance has been found to be attractive for staff.

Some companies incorporate into their schemes an arrangement whereby the bonus can be converted into non-voting shares attracting a fixed level of dividend. Although such shares usually carry the restriction that they shall be sold only to the trustees of the fund, they do nevertheless contribute to the overall aim of allowing employees to have a stake in the enterprise for which they work.

EXAMINATION QUESTIONS

1   a)   Distinguish between (i) collective and (ii) premium bonus schemes of remuneration.   *(5)*
    b)   Under Sturton Manufacturing Co's premium bonus scheme, employees receive a bonus equivalent to half of the time saved on the job. Three workers are given a similar job to do, the set time for which is six hours. Daniels completes the task in three hours, Ericson in four hours, and Frith in six hours. The hourly rate of pay is £5.00.
         i)   Calculate the earnings for each of the workers for that job.
         ii)   Assuming that Daniels and Frith work at the above speed throughout a 35 hour week, calculate who would earn the most. State why.   *(10)*

(London 1990)

2   A company decides to introduce a bonus system whereby the workers receive as a bonus a constant proportion of the 'added value' for the year. It is agreed that the average figure for added value as established over the three years 1987, 1988, 1989 is to be used as the basis for the calculation.

Year	1987	1988	1989	1990
Direct labour	220,300	233,500	239,200	251,400
Production overheads	54,100	63,300	67,400	61,300
Gross profit	13,600	15,200	17,400	21,700

It is agreed that the bonus is to be shared out on the basis of 2 per cent of added value, and is to be payable whenever the base ratio is reduced, no matter how small the reduction might be.

a)   Define the term 'added value'   *(4)*
b)   Calculate:
     i)   the amount of added value in each of the three 'base' years,
     ii)   the ratio of earnings to added value in the base years,
     iii) the ratio of earnings to added value during 1990,
     iv)   the amount of bonus payable in 1990 (if any). If no bonus is payable, state reasons clearly.   *(11)*

(London 1991)

3   a)   Show how the following documents are used as part of a time rate method of remuneration:
         i)   clock cards
         ii)   time sheets
         iii) job cards   *(10)*
    b)   Examine five purposes of wages systems, showing how (i) time rates and (ii) piece rate systems achieve these purposes.   *(10)*

(London 1991)

4 a) Distinguish between wages systems based upon (i) time rates and (ii) piece rates, and give examples of where each method may be appropriately adopted. *(7)*

b) It is sometimes thought that wage systems based upon time rates offer no incentives to employees to improve output. Use (i) high day rates and (ii) measured day work methods to show how this may be a misconception. *(6)*

c) Show how for a company, the payment of high wages may not always be a bad thing. *(7)*

(London 1993)

TUTOR'S ANSWER

1 a) Collective bonus schemes apply to groups of workers as opposed to individual employees: workers under collective schemes receive a bonus depending upon how the whole group have performed.

Premium bonus schemes apply to wages systems which recognise that gains and losses in labour efficiency are shared by the employer and the employee jointly. Such schemes therefore reward workers with a bonus based upon the percentage of time that is saved.

b i)

	Time (hours)				Wages (£)			
	Allowed	*Taken*	*Saved*	*Bonus*	*Basic*	*Bonus*	*Total*	*£/hr*
D	6	3	3	1.5	15	7.5	22.5	7.5
E	6	4	2	1.0	20	5.0	25.0	6.25
F	6	6	—	—	30	—	30.0	5.0

ii) Over a 35 hour week at the same hourly rate:

D = £7.5 × 35 = £262.5
F = £5.0 × 35 = £175.0

Difference   £87.5

Daniels would earn £87.50 more than Frith because his/her hourly rate is £2.50 more than Frith's.

STUDENT'S ANSWER

2 a) Added value is the increase in realisable value resulting from an alteration in form, location, or availability of a product or service, excluding the cost of purchased materials and services.

b) i)

Year	Earnings (£000)	Added Value (£000)
1987	220.3	288.0
1988	233.5	312.0
1989	239.2	324.0
Total	693.0	924.0

ii) Ratio earnings to added value $= \dfrac{693}{924} \times 100 = 75\%$

iii) Ratio of earnings to added value in 1990: $\dfrac{251.4}{334.4} \times 100 = 75.18\%$

iv) There is no bonus payable, since the ratio on 1990 at 75.18% is greater than the base ratio 75%.

Tutor's comments

A well presented answer which will score highly. The definition in (a) should include not only products but also services, since the notion of added value applies to services as well. Otherwise, an excellent answer.

OUTLINE ANSWERS

3a) i) Clock cards: each employee has own card to record time arrives for work, and time they leave. Cards are punched by a time clock which prints start and finish times. Overtime often printed in red, as too is lateness. Cards are used to calculate number of hours worked at basic and overtime rates.

ii) Time sheets: used to show what employee was doing whilst at work. Each employee has own time sheet upon which is recorded the work done and the particular job numbers. These sheets are used to charge labour costs to the relevant jobs.

Time sheets may also refer to booking-in sheets where workers' signatures are verified by a supervisor.

iii) Job card: used to record all costs of a particular job — labour, materials, and overheads (usually as a rate per labour or machine hour).

b) — recompense employees for work done; time worked or output achieved
— increase output: time rates not good here
— reduce overheads: time rates not good because no incentive to increase output
— encourage efficiency: piece rates better because of incentive effects
— reduce labour turnover: level of earnings important here; either method acceptable subject to work being done.

4 a) Time rates: reward employees for the time worked, irrespective of output achieved. Can be used where accuracy or quality is more important than output e.g. research laboratories.

Piece rates: reward employees based upon the level of output. Act as motivators to increased production but must be aware of quality issues. Useful where repetitive activities concerned.

b) High day rates: employees are still paid on a time basis, but their output is expected to be higher than normal in return for higher wages. Close supervision and checks on quality.

Measured day work: firm pays a higher hourly rate in return for a specified — and higher — level of performance.

c) High wages may be acceptable when accompanied by high output. It is the wage cost per unit of output that is important rather than the overall level of wages. Concept of productivity; definition and explanation.

High wages can attract — and keep — skilled workers, and enable the company to compete in the market.

Now attempt the review questions on page 311. The answers are given on page 325.

GETTING STARTED

Overhead cost is the cost of indirect materials, indirect labour and indirect expenses. These are termed *indirect costs* because they cannot easily be allocated to particular items or batches of production.

Overheads can be divided into production overhead, administration overhead, and selling and distribution overhead. Production overheads include the salaries of foremen and supervisors; the costs of heating, lighting and cleaning the factory areas; rent, rates, and insurances paid on factory premises; and depreciation on factory plant and machinery.

Administration overheads comprise all the costs of running the company's offices — other than any factory office. Administrative overheads thus include the salaries paid to office staff; the lighting, heating, and cleaning of office areas; rent, rates and insurances paid on offices; and the depreciation on office equipment.

Selling and distribution overheads include all the costs of selling the company's product: sales staff salaries; the cost of the company's fleet of cars for sales representatives; warehousing and transport costs.

Each of these groups of overheads can also be divided into fixed, semi-fixed and variable overheads. See Fig. 15.1 and page 229.

OVERHEAD APPORTIONMENT

CLASSIFICATION OF OVERHEAD

COST ALLOCATION AND COST APPORTIONMENT

APPORTIONING OVERHEADS

SERVICE DEPARTMENTS: INTER-SERVICE TRANSFERS

OVERHEAD ABSORPTION

OVERHEAD ADJUSTMENT ACCOUNT

ESSENTIAL PRINCIPLES

CLASSIFICATION OF OVERHEAD

Overhead	Fixed	Semi-fixed	Variable
Production	✓	✓	✓
Administration	✓	✓	✓
Selling and distribution	✓	✓	✓

Fig. 15.1 Classification of overheads.

INDIRECT MATERIALS

Indirect materials are those which cannot be traced through into the finished product. In the making of spanners, the steel of the spanner itself is a direct cost, but the dies used by the drop-forging machines are an indirect cost, and they will be included as a production overhead.

In some industries various raw materials may be used in such small amounts that although technically qualifying for inclusion as a direct cost, they are in fact treated as an overhead. Many garden implements have their handles glued on and affixed with a small nail: such glue and nails, although traceable directly to the implement, are of such an insignificant value compared to the total that they may be treated as an overhead in production.

With industries such as brick making, potteries or steelmaking, where heat is used in the production process, although the fuels themselves do not enter the finished product, at least the heat produced by the fuel does act upon the other materials; indeed without the heat, the items would not be produced at all. Thus, although at first sight such fuel may be considered as an indirect expense, it is often treated as a direct cost.

Examples of indirect materials include cleaning rags and cotton waste, cleaning equipment such as brushes and dusters, and cleaning materials such as polish and soap. Cooling and lubricating oils, too, are indirect materials, as are light tools such as drills, files, saws, taps and dies, and reamers; office stationery and packing materials also qualify for inclusion.

INDIRECT LABOUR

Under this heading comes all remuneration paid to administrative, maintenance, managerial, research, sales and security staff. Usually, such staff will be 'salaried' in that they will be paid a fixed sum monthly rather than weekly, the amount remaining fixed, irrespective of the level of output. Even with sales staff, who may be paid an element of commission, their pay usually includes a basic level of salary. The term 'salary' itself derives from the days when Roman soldiers were paid part of their reward in salt; this was later converted to 'salt money', from whence 'salary'.

INDIRECT EXPENSES

Many indirect expenses, such as rent, rates and insurance, may apply to the business as a whole rather than to particular products or departments. In such cases the expenses have to be apportioned to departments on some agreed basis. There are, however, some indirect expenses which can be identified with particular areas of the firm: depreciation of factory machinery, plant maintenance and office stationery can usually be so identified. Here the overheads can be allocated directly to the department concerned.

UNUSUAL ITEMS

There are also some expenses which cannot be reasonably included as cost items. Abnormal losses arising from wastage or faulty production or from obsolescence are usually excluded: so too are income taxes, bonuses paid to employees as an apportionment of profit, and dividends. Sometimes cash discounts – allowed and received – are excluded, although some businesses include them. These extraordinary items are transferred to special accounts – obsolescence, taxation, etc. – and from these to the profit and loss account at the end of the period.

COST ALLOCATION AND COST APPORTIONMENT

❝❝ Where a cost has to be divided amongst cost centres ❞❞

Cost allocation refers to the charging of discrete, identifiable items of cost to cost centres or cost units. Thus, direct costs can be allocated to cost centres because whole items of cost such as direct labour or direct materials can be readily identified. Some indirect costs can also be allocated, as where fuel is metred to a production department. However, where a cost has to be divided among two or more cost centres in proportion to the benefit received this is known as *cost apportionment*. Many overhead costs benefit more than one department, and so these costs must be apportioned on some agreed basis.

APPORTIONING OVERHEADS TO DEPARTMENTS

If you took a car to a garage to have a new alternator fitted, the garage owner can quite easily calculate the cost of the materials used on the job, and the number of hours which the mechanic spent working on the car. The direct costs, therefore, should present few problems in calculation. However, it is a different matter when the indirect or overhead expenses are being considered.

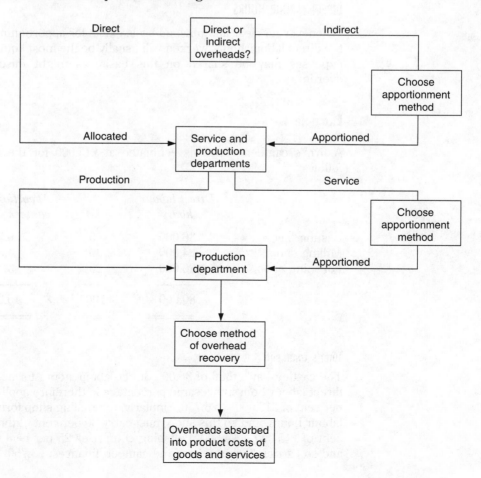

Fig. 15.2 Allocation, apportionment and absorption of overheads.

Many overhead costs will not be known for certain until the end of the accounting period, perhaps 12 months away. The garage could, of course, send a bill for the parts and labour, and follow this with a supplementary account later, when the indirect expenses are known. Generally, the customer would not be happy with this, and it would involve the office staff at the garage in additional paperwork.

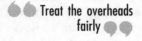

Overheads are estimated

In order to recover overheads, therefore, it is first necessary for the garage to estimate in advance what the overheads are likely to be for the coming period. In forming such an estimate the owner will look back at the figures for previous periods and adjust for levels of inflation and output. Second, this estimated amount of total overhead has to be apportioned to the production departments in some agreed manner. For example, the costs of the garage's office will have to be carried by the body shop, the paint shop and the service bay. Third, the overheads apportioned to each production department must be allocated to each item of production which passes through that department. It is, therefore a three-stage process:

1. Appointing overheads to all departments: production and service departments.
2. Apportioning the overheads of the service departments to the production departments.
3. Allocating the total production overhead to items of production.

Treat the overheads fairly

There are various ways of apportioning overheads to departments. Whichever method is used will depend upon circumstances and the policy of the firm. In all cases the aim should be to treat the overheads fairly between departments without creating unnecessary complications for the accounting system:

DIRECT CHARGES

It may be that certain items such as electricity, fuel and water are metered separately to individual departments. The time spent on repairing plant or the salaries of foremen working wholly in a section can be traced easily to particular departments. In such cases the departments can be allocated the whole of the overhead cost without any need to apportion between departments.

DIRECT LABOUR HOURS

Whenever no clear and obvious basis exists for apportionment, a division based upon the direct labour hours worked will usually be the most equitable. Welfare and canteen expenses may be shared on this basis, as might miscellaneous overheads and overtime.

Example 1

A firm's canteen expenses estimated at £15,000 for the year may be allocated as follows:

	Direct labour hours	%	Apportionment of canteen costs (£)
Casting bay	36,000	45	6,750
Milling shop	24,000	30	4,500
Polishing shop	20,000	25	3,750
	80,000	100	15,000

Tutor's comments

The casting bay's total of 36,000 direct labour hours forms 45 per cent of the total of direct labour hours; this same percentage is therefore applied to the canteen costs: 45 per cent of £15,000 = £6,750. Similarly, the milling shop forms 30 per cent of the direct labour hours, and so this shop must carry 30 per cent of the canteen expenses: 30 per cent of £15,000 = £4,500. Polishing comprises 25 per cent of the direct labour hours and so carries 25 per cent of the canteen finances: £3,750.

MACHINE HOURS

Where the production processes are more capital intensive, then an apportionment based upon machine hours may be better. If jobs are split between bench work, which is labour intensive, and machining, which is capital intensive, then some attempt should be made to devise separate totals.

WAGES PAID

Overheads are often apportioned on the basis of the total of wages paid to workers in the respective departments. In general, this approach should be avoided, and its use reserved only for those expenses which vary directly with the wages actually paid. In practice, very few expenses are influenced in this manner.

NUMBER OF WORKERS

This is a better basis than the wages bill, and may be used for dividing lighting expenses, time-keeping and wages departments, welfare and canteen costs – if not apportioned under any other method.

CAPITAL VALUES

The capital values of buildings and plant may be used for apportioning overheads such as depreciation, fire insurance, rates.

FLOOR AREA

Some overheads can be more fairly apportioned using the floor area – or the volume – of the departments' buildings. When lighting and heating are not separately metered, this method may be adopted. Rent, wages to security staff and fire prevention costs are also expenses which may be apportioned in this way, as too might depreciation of buildings.

APPORTIONING SERVICE DEPARTMENT OVERHEADS TO PRODUCTION DEPARTMENTS

💬 Service departments' costs to the production departments 💬

Having completed the first stage of apportioning overheads to particular departments, the second stage must now be embarked upon: that of apportioning service departments' costs to the production departments.

In the previous section, the various bases used were examined to divide total overheads among all departments: overheads were apportioned to production and to service departments alike. But *all* overhead has to be covered by the revenue generated by production, therefore, all of the overhead allocated to the service departments must find its way to the production departments.

Often, service departments will keep their own records of work done for the production departments, and these records can be used as the basis for apportionment. Where such records are not kept, then some estimate must be made based either upon the views of the managers concerned, or better still, upon some short investigation. Usually, the apportionment of service departments' costs to production departments is done using percentages.

Example 2

Chesterton plc has three production departments and two service departments; it estimated monthly overheads for the coming year at £36,300, divided as follows:

Chesterton plc

	Production depts			Service depts	
	U	V	W	Y	Z
Indirect labour (£)	10,000	8,000	4,000	2,000	1,500
Other indirect expenses (£)	5,000	3,000	1,500	800	500
	15,000	11,000	5,500	2,800	2,000

The task is to apportion the service departments' overheads to the production departments.

Tutor's comments

The firm's records show that department (Z) serves (Y) as well as serving the production departments. The agreed percentages are:

	U	V	W	Y	Z
(Z)'s expenses (%)	40	30	25	5	—
(Y)'s expenses (%)	45	35	20	—	—

Armed with this information, the service departments' indirect expenses can be apportioned to the production departments. First, department (Z), whose £2,000 of indirect expenses is apportioned in the percentages shown: 40 per cent of the £2,000 goes to (U) to increase that department's expenses by £800 to £15,800; 30 per cent goes to (V) to bring (V)'s total to £11,600; 25 per cent to (W) making £6,000; and £100 to (Y) bringing its figure to £2,900.

The total of these increases should equal the total of (Z)'s overheads:

£800 + £600 + £500 + £100 = £2,000
40% + 30% + 25% + 5% = 100%

Chesterton plc

	Production depts			Service depts	
	U	V	W	Y	Z
Indirect labour (£)	10,000	8,000	4,000	2,000	1,500
Other indirect expenses (£)	5,000	3,000	1,500	800	500
	15,000	11,000	5,500	2,800	2,000
DEPT (Z)'s expenses (£)	800	600	500	100	—
	15,800	11,600	6,000	2,900	—
DEPT (Y)'s expenses (£)	1,305	1,015	580	—	—
	17,105	12,615	6,580	—	—

Next, (Y)'s expenses are apportioned. Note, however, that (Y)'s expenses are now £2,900, *and not* £2,800 because (Y) has had to carry some of (Z)'s overheads. Thus, when applying the percentages to (Y) the £2,900 total is used. Hence, (U) carries £1,305, (V) £1,015 and (W) £580. The total of these figures should equal (Y)'s total overheads:

£1,305 + £1,015 + £580 = £2,900
45% + 35% + 20% = 100%

The total overhead to be carried by each of the production departments is:

£17,105 + £12,615 + £6,580 = £36,300
 (U)   (V)   (W)

The total of £36,300 equals the total monthly overhead for the whole firm, since *all* overhead is now carried by the production departments. The production departments carry not only their own overhead, but also an agreed proportion of the overheads from the service departments.

SERVICE DEPARTMENTS: INTER-SERVICE TRANSFERS

In Example 2, service department (Z)'s expenses were apportioned in part to service department (Y), but none of (Y)'s expenses were apportioned to (Z). This made the calculations relatively simple. But there are many occasions when service departments will service each other: the safety officers, working from the safety department, which is a service department, may inspect and advise the canteen, another service department, whilst the canteen itself offers meals and refreshments to members of the

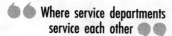
Where service departments service each other

safety department. Some way must therefore be found to handle inter-departmental transfers of this kind.

There are two methods in common use:

1. Elimination method.
2. Continuous apportionment.

To show how the methods operate, the following example will be used: Caldigate Engineering has estimated monthly overheads for 1993 of £35,000, allocated as shown:

Caldigate Engineering

	Production depts			Service depts	
	K	L	M	P	Q
Overheads (£)	12,000	10,000	7,000	3,500	2,500
Apportionment (%) (P)	40	30	20	—	10
(Q)	30	40	25	5	—

ELIMINATION METHOD

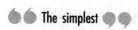
The simplest

This is the simplest of the two. The overhead figures of the service departments are compared, and that department with the largest total is apportioned first. In the example this is department (P), whose overheads are apportioned in the usual way according to the agreed percentages.

Caldigate Engineering

	Production depts			Service depts	
	K	L	M	P	Q
Overheads (£)	12,000	10,000	7,000	3,500	2,500
(P)'s expenses (£)	1,400	1,050	700	—	350
	13,400	11,050	7,700	—	2,850
(Q)'s expenses (£)	855	1,140	713	(142)	—
	14,255	12,190	8,413	—	—

When department (Q) is reached, these overheads, which now total £2,850, are apportioned to production as agreed, 30:40:25; but the 5 per cent to be apportioned to (P) is ignored.

It was stated earlier in the chapter that the apportionment of overheads to departments is based upon estimates and accounting conventions. To say, therefore, that the elimination method gives an 'inaccurate' result is to misunderstand – or to ignore – the accuracy of the figures handled. In the example, total overheads are *estimated* at £35,000: of this, the elimination method is ignoring £142 – five per cent of £2,850. The amount ignored represents 0.41 per cent of the total. If the estimates made for overheads turn out to be within plus or minus 0.205 per cent, most accountants would be delighted!

Note, also, that it is because the apportionment of the second service department's overheads to the first service department tends to be ignored that the method begins with that service department which shows the largest overhead.

CONTINUOUS APPORTIONMENT

This method apportions overheads continuously between service departments until the amounts outstanding become small enough to ignore:

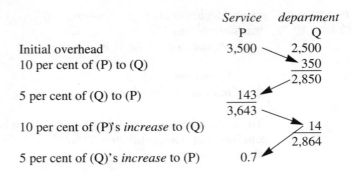

	Service	department
	P	Q
Initial overhead	3,500	2,500
10 per cent of (P) to (Q)		350
		2,850
5 per cent of (Q) to (P)	143	
	3,643	
10 per cent of (P)'s *increase* to (Q)		14
		2,864
5 per cent of (Q)'s *increase* to (P)	0.7	

The 10 per cent of (P)'s overhead is added to (Q)'s figure: £2,500 + £350 = £2,850. Then, 5 per cent of this is added to (P): £3,500 + £143 = £3,643. Note that the 5 and 10 per cent were the proportions originally agreed for apportioning overheads between the service departments.

66 **Amounts small enough to ignore** 99

After the first two calculations the percentages are based upon the *increase* in the figures. Hence, the next round sees 10 per cent of (P)'s increase added to (Q): £143 × 10 per cent = £14. Five per cent of this to be added to (P) to complete the second round is £0.7 – a figure significantly small to be ignored:

Caldigate Engineering

	Production depts			Service depts	
	K	L	M	P	Q
Overheads (£)	12,000	10,000	7,000	3,643	2,864
(P)'s expenses (£)	1,457	1,093	729	—	(364)
	13,457	11,093	7,729	—	2,864
(Q)'s expenses (£)	859	1,146	716	(143)	—
	14,316	12,239	8,445	—	—

The total overheads to be apportioned to the production departments thus becomes £3,643 for (P) and £2,864 for (Q). These figures can now be allocated to the production departments in the agreed proportions. Department (P)'s overheads of £3,643 are apportioned in the ratios 40:30:20:10. Once apportioned, the £364 going to (Q) is ignored, since the interdepartmental allocation between the service departments has been allowed for already.

Next (Q)'s overheads are apportioned in the agreed ratios of 30:40:25:5. Again, since the interdepartmental allocation between (Q) and (P) has been incorporated in the figures, the £143 for (P) can be ignored. As a check, once the service departments have had their overheads apportioned, the total overheads being carried by the production departments can be totalled:

£14,316 + £12,239 + £8,445 = £35,000

Thus the whole of the £35,000 of overhead has been allocated to the production departments.

OVERHEAD ABSORPTION

After overheads have been *apportioned* to the production departments they must be *absorbed* into the production costs of the firm's goods or services. Overheads are absorbed by means of absorption rates based either upon direct labour hours or upon machine hours, depending upon whether overheads are thought to be related to labour input or plant input. The decision to use absorption rates – also known as overhead recovery rates – based upon labour hours or machine hours is one for the firm's management to make.

66 **Overheads must be absorbed into production costs** 99

In the previous section, the elimination method apportioned Caldigate Engineering's overheads to production departments. In (K) and (M) overheads are thought to accrue to direct labour hours, whilst in (L) they are deemed a function of machine hours:

Caldigate Engineering

	K	L	M
Total overheads (£)	14,255	12,190	8,413
Direct labour hours worked (estimated)	570	—	467
Machine hours worked (estimated)	—	381	—
Overhead recovery rate per:			
Direct labour hour	$\dfrac{£14,255}{570}$		$\dfrac{£8,413}{467}$
	= £25		= £18
Machine hour		$\dfrac{£12,190}{381}$	
		= £32	

To calculate the overhead recovery rate for each direct labour hour, the total overheads in (K) and (M) are divided by the estimated number of direct labour hours to be worked in each department during the period. In (L) total overheads are divided by the estimated number of machine hours to be worked. These calculations give overhead recovery rates for the departments of £25, £32 and £18 respectively.

Thus, every job that passes through (K) has added to its direct costs of labour and materials an amount of £25 for every direct labour hour it attracts, and this amount goes towards covering that department's overheads. Similarly in (M) £18 is added for every hour of direct labour. In (L), for every hour that a job is on a machine, £32 is added to cover overheads.

Assume that a job comes into (K) where it receives £260 of direct materials, and 10 hours of direct labour at £3.60 per hour. It then passes to (L) where it receives eight hours of direct labour at £3.80 per hour, and four machine hours. The cost of the job would be calculated as follows:

			£
Dept K:	Direct materials		260
	Direct labour: 10 hours at £3.60		36
	Overheads: 10 hours at £25		250
			546
Dept L:	Direct labour:	8 hours at £3.80	30.4
	Overheads:	4 hours at £32	128
			704.4

In (K) overheads are recovered on the basis of direct labour hours, of which the job attracted 10; hence 10 × £25 = £250. In (L) overheads are recovered using machine hours, of which the job attracted four: 4 × £32 = £128.

OVERHEAD ADJUSTMENT ACCOUNT

The absorption of overheads into production costs is based upon estimates and assumptions. Before the financial period, estimates are made of the total of indirect expenses to be incurred by the production and service departments. Once these estimates have been made, the service departments' overheads are apportioned to production departments on some agreed basis. These overheads, which now lie wholly with the production departments, are then absorbed into production via overhead recovery rates.

Clearly, at the end of the accounting period there are likely to be differences between overheads actually incurred, and those absorbed by production. These differences may arise because production was more or less than was assumed would be the case; or because indirect costs actually incurred were different from those estimated.

Based upon estimates and assumptions

Such differences, either over-recovered or under-recovered overheads, are transferred to the overhead adjustment account. Over-recovered overheads represent a profit, and are credited to the account: under-recovered overheads represent a loss and are debited to the account. At the end of the period the balance on the overhead adjustment account is transferred to the profit and loss account.

EXAMINATION QUESTIONS

1   As the accountant of a manufacturing company you have prepared the annual budgets for the forthcoming year and presented them to the board of directors for approval.

The managing director is alarmed at the increase in the production overhead recovery rate, which has risen from 150% to 300% of direct labour.

You are required to:
(a)   explain what is meant by the term 'overhead recovery rates', and indicate how they are calculated and applied;   *(6)*
(b)   give two possible causes for the above increase;   *(2)*
(c)   define the following terms:
    (i)   absorption
    (ii)   allocation
    (iii)   apportionment;   *(6)*
(d)   suggest how the following three overhead costs might be apportioned:
    (i)   rent and rates
    (ii)   maintenance of machines
    (iii)   canteen costs;   *(3)*
(e)   using an overhead recovery rate based on labour hours, calculate the overhead over or under absorption for department X, details of which are as follows:

Budgeted overhead costs	£20,000
Actual overhead costs	£21,250
Budgeted labour hours	5,000
Actual labour hours	4,950

                                                                                    (3)

(Northern 1992)

2   Hi-Life Limited manufactures suspended ceilings and the figures shown below have been estimated for the year ended 31 December 1993.

	£000
General heating and lighting	24
Raw materials	900
Salesmen's salaries and commissions	140
Salesmen's expenses	16
Indirect wages and related costs	296
Depreciation of production machinery	230
Rent and rates	64
Carriage inwards on raw materials	46
Carriage outwards	12
Direct wages	720
Advertising	49
Security	16
General management and administration	349
Inspection and testing (production)	70
Maintenance of: machinery	36
buildings	32
Power (for machines)	40

Additional information is as follows:
1. Budgeted sales for the year ended 31 December 1993 are £3,900,000.
2. The company's premises extend to 200,000 square metres. 75% of floor space is used for production and the remaining 25% is occupied equally between the sales department and the general administrative function.
3. The following hours are expected to be worked in the year ended 31 December 1993.

Direct labour hours	120,000
Machine hours	75,000

REQUIRED

(a) Prepare a schedule analysing the budgeted overhead costs for the year ended 31 December 1993 according to the following classification:

   (i) Production overhead to be absorbed by direct labour hours
   (ii) Production overhead to be absorbed by machine hours
   (iii) Selling and distribution costs
   (iv) General and administrative costs   *(12)*

(b) Calculate the rates of absorption for each of the categories (i) to (iv) above. (8)
(c) Compute the total cost of the following job expected to be undertaken during the year ended 31 December 1993.

	£	
Direct material costs	4,000	
Direct labour costs	3,000	(for 500 direct labour hours)

It is expected that the job will require 450 machine hours and when completed will sell for £15 000.   *(5)*

(Cambridge 1992)

3 R. E. Lee Ltd. is a company that manufactures building equipment. It has three production departments and a service department and has produced the following budgeted cost of production for the year ended 31 March 1992:

		£	£
Production cost	Direct materials	240,000	
	Carriage inwards	10,000	
	Direct wages	200,000	450,000
Indirect wages	Dept. X	8,000	
	Dept. Y	12,000	
	Dept. Z	18,300	
	General Service Dept.	6,700	45,000
Other costs	Consumable stores	32,000	
	Rent	21,000	
	Light and heat	14,000	
	Power	36,000	
	Depreciation	80,000	
	Insurance—machinery	2,000	185,000
			680,000

The following is a set of data relating to the physical and performance aspects of the company:

Department	Area m²	Book Value of Plant £	Stores Requisitions	Effective Horse Power	Direct Labour Hours	Direct Labour Cost £	Machine Hours
X	15,000	140,000	180	80	100,000	50,000	70,000
Y	22,500	180,000	120	100	80,000	60,000	90,000
Z	20,000	10,000	100	5	220,000	90,000	10,000
Service	12,500	70,000	—	15	—	—	—

The general service department is apportioned to the production departments on the basis of direct labour cost.

REQUIRED

(a) An overhead analysis sheet for the departments, showing clearly the basis of apportionment.   *(13)*

(b) A computation (correct to three decimal places) of hourly cost rates of overhead absorption for each production department using the performance data given.   *(6)*

(c) A critical assessment of the methods used in (b) above.   *(6)*

TUTOR'S ANSWER

2 (This is a somewhat involved question. It demands that candidates are quite clear about the conventions surrounding the calculation of overhead recovery rates, since a number of the steps in calculation are left for the candidate to decide. The first part of the answer shows the value of using an analysis statement to allocate figures to particular departments.)

a) *Hi-Life Ltd: Schedule of Overhead Costs (£000)*

	Labour	Machine	Selling	Admin	Total
Heat and light	18		3	3	24
Salesmens' salaries			140		140
Salesmens' expenses			16		16
Indirect wages	296				296
Depreciation		230			230
Rent and rates	48		8	8	64
Carriage outwards			12		12
Advertising			49		49
Security	12		2	2	16
Managt. and admin.				349	349
Inspection	70				70
Machinery maintenance		36			36
Buildings maintenance	24		4	4	32
Power		40			40
Totals	468	306	234	366	1,374

b) *Absorption Rates*

Direct labour hours: $\dfrac{468}{120} = £3.90$

Direct machine hours: $\dfrac{306}{75} = £4.08$

(The denominator in each of the above is taken from information in Note 3 of the question.)

$$\text{Selling \& distrib.:} \quad \frac{234}{3\,900} = 6\%$$

(The denominator is taken from Note 1 of the question.)

$$\text{General and admin.:} \quad \frac{366}{2\,440} = 15\%$$

The denominator is derived by adding:

	£	
Raw materials	900	
Carriage on materials	46	
Direct wages	720	
Indirect labour	468	— from the schedule above
Machine indirect	306	— from the schedule above
	2440	

c) *Job Cost*

	£
Direct materials	4,000
Direct labour	3,000
Overhead absorbed by labour hours: 500 hours × £3.90	1,950
Overhead absorbed by machine hours: 450 × £4.08	1,836
	10,786
Selling overheads: 6% × £15,000	900
General and admin overheads: 15% × £10,786	1,618
Total cost	13,304

STUDENT'S ANSWER

1 a) Overhead recovery rates are the means of applying indirect costs to products. They are calculated by dividing the predetermined costs by the total predetermined levels of activity, measured by means such as units of production, labour hours or machine hours. This rate is then applied to each product based on the content of the product's base element e.g. direct labour hours, machine hours etc. If more or less activity takes place than was forecast, or expenditure is higher or lower than anticipated then over or under recovery will result.

 b) Increased costs, or decreased direct labour.

 c) i)   The means of applying a proportion of the overheads to the product.

   ii) The identification of specific overhead costs with a particular department or cost centre.

   iii) The sharing of general/non-specific overhead costs amongst departments.

 d) i)   Area

   ii) Machine running hours

   iii) Number of employees.

 e) $\dfrac{£20,000}{5,000} = £4.00$ per labour hour

Tutor's comment

This is a clearly presented answer: it is accurate in content, and it flows well. The candidate knows the subject, and has taken some thought to prepare the answer. Note how each stage of the question builds on itself.

OUTLINE ANSWER

3 a)

R E L ee L td Overhead Analysis Sheet

		Department			
Overhead	Basis of Apportionment	X	Y	Z	Service
Ind. Wages	Direct	8,000	12,000	18,300	6,700
Cons stores	Requisitions	14,400	9,600	8,000	—
Rent	Area	4,500	6,750	6,000	3,750
Light & heat	Area	3,000	4,500	4,000	2,500
Power	Horse power	14,400	18,000	900	2,700
Depreciation	Book value 20%	28,000	36,000	2,000	14,000
Insurance	Book value	700	900	50	350
		73,000	87,750	39,250	30,000
Service	Direct labour cost	7,500	9,000	13,500	(30,000)
		80,500	96,750	52,750	–

b) *Computation of Hourly Cost Rates of Overhead Absorption*

Absorption rates based on:

Direct labour hours:		80,500	96,750	52,750
		100,000	80,000	220,000
	=	£0.805	£1.209	£0.24
Machine hours:		80,500	96,750	52,750
		70,000	90,000	10,000
	=	£1.15	£1.075	£5.275

c) Labour hour rates: applicable if work is labour intensive. Relates to time, and overcomes fluctuating wage rates and different grade of worker. Disadvantage may be the time and cost of maintaining labour records.
Machine hour rates: applicable where work is capital intensive. Relates to time and can be analysed to individual machine or group of machines. Disadvantages may be the calculations themselves, and the time and cost of collecting data.

Now attempt the review questions on page 313. The answers are given on page 326.

PRODUCT COSTING

GETTING STARTED

Product cost is the cost of a finished item built up from its cost elements. Product cost, therefore, will comprise the direct labour, direct materials, direct expenses, and those overheads applicable to the product. The method of determining product costs and of collating and presenting the information is influenced greatly by the demands of the production processes and by custom and practice within an industry.

Where work consists of separate contracts, jobs, or batches, each of which is authorised by a special order or contract, then *specific order costing* may be used. Where, however, a product or service results from a sequence of continuous or repetitive operations or processes, *continuous, operation, or process costing* may be necessary. Product costing, therefore, breaks down into:

Specific order costing: job costing
                                               batch costing
                                               contract costing
Operation costing: process costing
                                                 service costing

Whichever approach is adopted to ascertain costs, the basic principles of determining costs will still apply: it is the *manner* of collecting and presenting cost data which differs.

ESSENTIAL PRINCIPLES

JOB COSTING AND BATCH COSTING

💬💬 Special requirements .... short duration 💬💬

Job costing is used where work is undertaken to a customer's special requirements, and where each order is of a comparatively short duration. Thus, where a garage is repairing a customer's car, job costing may be used: no two jobs will be precisely similar, and the tasks carried out can be completed relatively quickly. Job costing may also be used by printers, decorators, tailors, etc.

Each order will be given a distinguishing job number, and all costs relating to that order will be charged to that job number. Where a garage services a customer's car, all costs relating to the service will be gathered together on a cost sheet as follows:

Job 8T / 104

materials:	$3\frac{1}{2}$ litres engine oil	4.55	
	1 oil filter	2.46	
	1 air filter element	2.86	
	4 spark plugs	5.04	
		———	
			14.91
labour:	4 hours at £3.20 hour		12.80
overheads:	£3.50 per direct labour hour		14.00
			———
			41.71
			=====

Materials ordered from the stores on materials requisition forms will show not only the items issued and their cost, but also the job number to which the materials are to be charged. Similarly, wages – either day rate, piece rate or bonuses – will be charged to the job number from time sheets or piece-work tickets. Because employees are likely to be spending different times on different jobs, it is essential that time-sheets or piece-work tickets should show the relevant job numbers clearly. Overheads will be charged on the basis of direct labour hours or machine hours. In this way, the cost of the job will be built up from its elements.

💬💬 Similar articles manufactured together 💬💬

Where similar articles are manufactured together in batches, a method similar to job costing is employed. In essence, each batch is regarded as a 'job' and costs are collected for each batch. This approach tends to be used by bakeries, potteries, etc.

CONTRACT COSTING

💬💬 Special requirements .... long duration 💬💬

As with the previous two methods, contract costing is used where work is undertaken to a customer's specific requirements. The essential difference, however, is that in contract costing the orders tend to be of a much longer duration, as in building construction and shipbuilding.

The method of collecting costing data is similar to that of job costing, but the nature and duration of the work does raise particular problems. For example, where some of the work is sub-contracted to other firms, the total cost of the sub-contract must be debited to the main contract. Where amounts of materials issued to the contract are greater than those actually used, the surplus should be returned to the stores, and the value of this surplus credited to the contract.

Wages will be calculated from time-sheets, and overheads recovered on the basis of direct labour hours or machine hours, as agreed.

Machinery and tools sent to a building site or used on the job are debited to the contract account at their estimated value. When the items are returned to store, the valuation on return is credited to the contract: the difference between the two figures is the depreciation to be charged to the contract. Alternatively, the firm may calculate a daily 'hire' rate for all plant, based upon depreciation, maintenance, running costs, etc. The contract will then be debited with this hire rate for each day that the equipment is on the job. This approach has the advantage that the contract account is not overburdened with figures for capital items which are afterwards credited on return: the approach also encourages site managers to return unwanted items to the stores as quickly as possible.

Where any of the plant issued to a contract is used to do jobbing work not connected to the contract, then any payment received for such work should be credited to the contract account.

Where the contract extends over a long period, money by way of stage-payments may be received by the contractor. How and when these monies are to be paid will be stipulated in the contract before work commences. As the work progresses, the architect, surveyor, or clerk of works employed by the customer will issue certificates authorising payments to be made to the contractor. These payments are credited to the contract account.

Often, large civil engineering contracts will specify that a proportion – 10 or 15 per cent – of the total contract sum be held back for an agreed period to allow any inherent defects in the work to show. This proportion is known as *retention money*. After this period – say, a year – the customer's representative will inspect the work, and agree with the contractor such remedial work as is necessary. Only when this work has been satisfactorily completed, will the balance of the monies be released.

Following the general accounting concept of prudence, profits on contracts are not taken until the contract has been completed. However, with very long contracts, i.e. those taking more than a year to complete, this can cause problems. If profit is not credited until the end of the contract, then the profit and loss account will show, not profits on that period's activities, but profits on contracts which have ended during the period. SSAP 9 therefore requires that credit should be taken for profit on long-term contracts whilst they are still in progress.

In such cases a conservative estimation of profit may be credited to the profit and loss account. The basis of calculating such profit may vary from one firm to another, but usually the difference between the *value* of work certified and the *cost* of work certified is used as a basis, as follows:

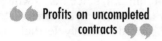
Profits on uncompleted contracts

$$\text{Profit on uncompleted contract} = \text{Value of Work Certified} \times \text{Cost of Work Certified}$$

Where a retention is kept in lieu of remedial work the profit figure is reduced accordingly. Thus, where the value of the work certified is £480,000, the cost of the work certified is £362,700, and the retention is 15 per cent, the profit taken on the contract is:

$$(£480,000 - £362,700) = 117,300$$

Reduction for 15 per cent retention:

$$85\% \times £117,300 = £99,705$$

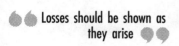
Losses should be shown as they arise

The profit taken on the contract, therefore, is £99,705. SSAP 9 also requires that work-in-progress on long-term contracts should be valued at cost plus attributable profit less foreseeable losses. Any progress payments received or receivable should be shown as a deduction from this figure. Where foreseeable losses on a contract are greater than the costs to date less payments received, then the difference should be shown as a provision. In general, losses should not be apportioned, as are profits, but should be shown in total as they arise. See question 2, later in this chapter, for a worked example.

PROCESS COSTING

In specific order costing, each job, batch or contract is costed separately. Where, however, products are produced in a single process, or where the product of one process becomes the material of a second process, a different costing system is needed, since products can no longer be identified individually.

Under process costing the firm is divided into departments which tend to be limited to one process or operation. Thus, in ironmaking, one department will prepare the iron ore for the furnaces, another will prepare the fuel, and a third may raise the hot air blast.

Accounts are kept for each process, the materials, labour, expenses and overheads being debited to the process, and scrap and by-products being credited to the process. Note that whereas in job costing costs were kept for each order, under process costing costs are gathered around identifiable processes. These differences in approach are imposed by the technology of production, and not merely by accounting considerations. Process costing methods tend to be used by firms in the chemical industry, distillation and the food industry.

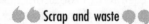

In most processes there is a degree of wastage which is inherent in the production process itself. Depending upon the process, such *normal loss* may take the form of ash, evaporation, swarf or unavoidable spoilage. By experience and/or calculation, firms are able to allow for normal losses arising in production, and such losses are seen as a legitimate production expense to be borne by the 'good' items produced.

Losses in excess of normal wastage – *abnormal losses* – are recorded separately, to enable the firm's management to identify the cost of inefficiency and poor working so that necessary investigations can be mounted into likely causes. Abnormal losses are written off to the profit and loss account.

Sometimes, a happy combination of circumstances – good process conditions, quality raw materials and an experienced operating team – will be able to produce more good items than would normally be expected from a given quantity of raw material. Such *abnormal gains* are also recorded separately, since it is as important to investigate their cause as to enquire after abnormal losses. Abnormal gains are credited to the profit and loss account.

In process costing, the terms *scrap* and *waste* have particular meanings. Scrap refers to material which has some recovery value, and which is usually either disposed of without further treatment, or is reintroduced into the production process in place of raw materials. In contrast, waste refers to discarded substances which have no value at all.

It is vitally important that scrap and waste are kept to a minimum, since items which are processed and subsequently discarded do incur labour and overhead charges up to the point when they are rejected. Clearly, the later in the production cycle that the rejection occurs, the more of the labour and overhead charges attach to the items, and the greater is the loss. Example 2 explains the relevant issues.

Example 1

Borough Products processes its product through four separate stages. In the primary processing plant, 5,000 kg of raw material is introduced at a cost of £0.40 kg. Labour costs are £450 and production overheads are £250. Normal process losses are estimated at 10 per cent. Actual production was 4,000 kg.

Required

Prepare the primary process account.

Solution:

Primary process account

	kg	kg	£	£
Direct materials		5,000	2,000	
Direct labour			450	
Production overhead			250	
		5,000	2,700	
Less: Normal loss	500		–	
Abnormal loss	500		300	
	1,000		300	
Transferred to secondary process		4,000	2,400	

Tutor's comments

In process accounts it is usual to show physical quantities as well as monetary amounts, hence the columns for kilos.

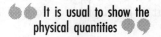
It is usual to show the physical quantities

The direct materials, direct labour, and production overheads are added to give a total production cost of £2,700. From actual production is deducted the normal loss of 10 per cent of 5,000 kg, i.e. 500 kg. Note that there are no entries in the monetary column, since the cost of the normal loss is to be carried by the good production. Had all gone well, the primary process should have produced 4,500 kg of product, i.e. the original material input less normal loss: 5,000 − 500 = 4,500 kg. In fact, only 4,000 kg was produced. The difference 4,500 − 4,000 = 500 kg, represents the quantity of the abnormal loss:

Abnormal loss = total loss − normal loss.

To calculate the *value* of the abnormal loss, the cost of the good production has to be calculated: £2,700 was spent, and this should have produced 4,500 kg of product. The cost per kilo, therefore, should have been:

$$\frac{£2,700}{4,500} = £0.6 \text{ kg}$$

The abnormal loss is thus valued at 500 kg times £0.6 kg = £300. Note that the cost of the abnormal loss comprises not just the material cost of £0.40 kg but also an element of the labour and overhead charges. The sum of £300 is credited to the process account, and debited to the abnormal loss account, (page 217). When these adjustments have been made, 4,000 kg costing £2,400 passes to the next process.

Example 2

In the secondary process, Borough Products uses a further £1,600 of material, £518 of direct labour, £262 of direct expenses, and £350 of production overheads. Output is 3,900 kg, and normal losses are expected to be 5 per cent.

Required
Prepare the secondary process account.

Solution:

Secondary process account

	kg	kg	£	£
Transferred from primary process	4,000			2,400
Direct materials			1,600	
Direct labour			518	
Direct expenses			262	
Production overhead			350	2,730
				5,130
Abnormal gain	100			135
	4,100			5,265
Less: Normal loss	200			—
Transferred to tertiary process		3,900		5,265

Tutor's comments

The account begins with the quantity and value transferred from the previous process: 4,000 kg and £2,400. To these are added the direct and indirect costs incurred by the secondary process: £1,600 + £518 + £262 + £350 = £2,730.

It was estimated that the normal process losses should have been 5 per cent, or 200 kg, giving an output of $4,000 - 200 = 3,800$. In fact, 3,900 kg was produced: actual output was greater than expected output by 100 kg: $3,900 - 3,800 = 100$ kg. There was thus an abnormal gain of 100 kg. To find the value of this, the cost of the secondary process (£5,130) has to be divided by the *expected* output of good product, to give a value per kilo:

$$\frac{£5,130}{3,800} = £1.35 \text{ kg}$$

Since the *quantity* of the abnormal gain was 100 kg, the *value* of the gain is $100 \times £1.35 = £135$. Note that in performing the calculation, the figure for expected output 3,800 was used and *not* the figure for actual output, 3,900. The whole of the balance on the account was also used, £5,130, not merely those costs which refer solely to the secondary process. This is because the gains are calculated on the full cost of production up to the completion of the secondary process, and these include the cost of products introduced from the primary process.

The value of the abnormal gain is debited to the process account, and credited to the separate abnormal gain account (page 218).

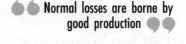
Normal losses are borne by good production

The anticipated normal loss of 200 kg is deducted from the quantity produced, but as before, no figure appears in the monetary columns because normal losses are borne by the good production. Thus, 3900 kg of output is transferred to the tertiary process at a cost of £5,265. Note that the cost per kilo of the abnormal gain £1.35 is the same as the cost per kilo of the output transferred to the tertiary process:

$$\frac{£5,265}{3,900} = £1.35 \text{ kg}$$

Example 3

During the tertiary process direct labour costs of £824 are incurred, together with £441 of direct expenses, and £373 of production overheads. Estimated normal losses are 10 per cent, and all scrap from this process can be sold at £1.50 kg. Actual output is 3,400 kg.

Required
Prepare the tertiary process account.

Solution:

Tertiary process account

	kg	kg	£	£
Transferred from secondary process		3,900		5,265
Direct labour			824	
Direct expenses			441	
Production overheads			373	
				1,638
		3,900		6,903
Less: Normal loss	390		585	
Abnormal loss	110		198	
		500		783
Transferred to finishing process		3,400		6,120

Tutor's comments

The 3,900 kg costing £2,265 is transferred from the secondary process, and to this are added the labour, direct expenses and overheads to give a total of £6,903.

Normal loss at 10 per cent of 3,900 kg is 390 kg: the actual loss was 500 kg (3,900 − 3,400 = 500 kg). The difference between the actual loss and the normal loss, therefore, gives the amount of the abnormal loss: 500 − 390 = 110 kg.

Income from normal losses is credited Usually, there is no value placed against normal loss, since it is regarded as a legitimate production expense to be carried by the good output. However, where some or all of the normal loss is sold, the income generated from such sales is credited to the process account to lessen the cost of production. In the example all scrap arising can be sold at £1.50 kg. The value of the normal loss to be credited, therefore, is 390 × £1.50 = £585. The cost of the good output, is thus £6,903 − £585 = £6,318.

In contrast, the value of abnormal losses is shown in the process account at *cost* price. To compute abnormal losses the cost per kilo of expected good output must first be calculated: estimated output was 3,510 kg which cost £6,318 to produce. The cost per kilo, therefore, is:

$$\frac{£6,318}{3,510} = £1.8$$

The value of the abnormal loss of 110 kg is:

110 × £1.8 = £198

The abnormal loss of £198 is also credited to the process account. Thus, losses of 500 kg are deducted from the physical quantities, and £783 is deducted from the monetary column. When these adjustments have been made 3,400 kg of good product is transferred to the finishing process at a cost of £6,120, or £1.8 kg.

Income from abnormal loss The figure of £198 for abnormal loss also appears on the debit of the abnormal loss account (see below). The income derived from selling the abnormal loss appears on this account as a credit entry: 110 kg at £1.50 = £165.

Abnormal loss account

	£	£
Primary process	300	
Tertiary process	198	
		498
Less: Income from sale of tertiary scrap		165
Transferred to debit of profit and loss account		333

Thus, income from the sale of normal loss appears on the process account itself, but income from the sale of abnormal loss appears on the abnormal loss account.

Example 4

In the finishing process losses are expected to be 10 per cent. Actual output, however, is 3,200 kg. Direct materials used cost £762, direct labour £908, and production overheads are £506. All rejects from the finishing process can be sold at £1.9 kg.

Required

Prepare the finishing process account.

Solution:

Finishing process

	kg	kg	£	£
Transferred from tertiary process	3,400			6,120
Direct materials			762	
Direct labour			908	
Production overheads			506	
				2,176
				8,296
Abnormal gain	140			350
	3,540			8,646
Less: Normal loss	340			646
Transferred to finished stock account		3,200		8,000

Tutor's comments

The production costs incurred in finishing (£2,176) are added to the cost of the items transferred from the tertiary process (£6,120) to give the total of £8,296.

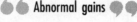 **Abnormal gains**

With normal losses at 10 per cent, estimated production from an input of 3,400 kg was 3,060 kg. But actual production was 3,200 kg. There were thus abnormal gains of 140 kg; since actual output was 140 kg more than expected.

To calculate the value of this abnormal gain, the cost of expected output must first be calculated. All rejects from the process can be sold at £1.9 kg. Hence, the normal loss of 340 kg can be sold for 340 × £1.9 = £646. The cost of normal production, therefore, is reduced by the sale of normal loss, so that the cost of normal production is £8,296 − £646 = £7,650. Normal output was expected to be 3,060 kg, thus the cost per kilo of normal output was expected to be:

$$\frac{£7,650}{3,060} = £2.5 \text{ kg}$$

The quantity of the abnormal gain was 140 kg; its value at £2.5 kg is therefore 140 × £2.5 = £350. This figure is then added to the cost of production £8,296 to give £8,646. From this figure the value of normal losses is deducted, to give an output of 3,200 kg costing £8,000. Note that the unit cost of final output at £2.5 kg is the same as the unit value of the abnormal gain:

$$\frac{£8,000}{3,200} = £2.5 \text{ kg}$$

The figure for the abnormal gain is credited to the abnormal gain account:

Abnormal gain account

	£	£
Secondary process	135	
Finishing process	350	
Transferred to credit of profit and loss account		485

The balance on the finishing process account is transferred to the debit of the finished product account, to be added to any outstanding balance there. As items are sold, so the finished product account is credited and the debit balance on the account diminishes, until further output is transferred to the account. The balances on the abnormal loss and abnormal gain accounts are transferred to profit and loss account:

Finished product account

	kg	£
Transferred from finishing process	3,200	8,000

Profit and loss account

	£	£
Abnormal gains account	485	
Less: Abnormal losses account	333	
Balance to credit of profit and loss account		152

WORK-IN-PROGRESS

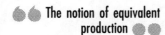 **The notion of equivalent production**

At the end of any financial period it is likely that there will be partly finished items passing through the production sequence. Clearly, some of the period's costs relate to the partly finished items as well as to the completely finished products. To help to spread the costs equitably over fully finished and partly finished products, the notion of *equivalent production* can be used.

Suppose that at the end of the financial period production of finished goods stood at 4,000 items, with a further 500 units only half completed. The total equivalent production for the period would be:

$$4,000 + \tfrac{1}{2}(500)$$
$$= 4,000 + 250$$
$$= 4,250 \text{ units}$$

The period's total costs can therefore be spread over finished and partly finished items alike. If the total costs for the period were £14,875, then the cost per unit would be:

$$\text{Cost per unit} = \frac{\text{Total cost}}{\text{Total equivalent production (units)}}$$

$$= \frac{£14,875}{4,250}$$

$$= £3.5 \text{ per unit}$$

Where units are only half completed, therefore, their cost is £1.75. If work-in-progress (WIP) had comprised 1,000 items one quarter completed, then the cost of WIP per unit would have been £0.875 (£3.5 ÷ 4 = £0.875). Sometimes, however, an overall estimate of completion is either not possible or not desirable. In such cases it may be necessary to consider the percentage completion of each of the cost elements separately – materials, labour and overheads. The principle is the same as that used above, except that the data are disaggregated.

Example 5

Assume that in a given period total output was 5,000 fully finished items plus 600 partly finished items.

	Cost element			
	Materials	*Labour*	*Overheads*	*Total*
Total cost (£)	10,412	7,504	6,360	24,276
WIP degree of completion (%)	80	60	50	—

Required:

Calculate the total equivalent production, the cost per complete unit and the value of the WIP.

Solution:

	Cost element			
	Materials	*Labour*	*Overheads*	*Total*
WIP (equivalent units)	600 × 80% = 480	600 × 60% = 360	600 × 50% = 300	
Fully finished units	5,000	5,000	5,000	
Total production	5,480	5,360	5,300	
Total cost (£)	10,412	7,504	6,360	24,276
Cost per unit (£)	1.9	1.4	1.2	4.5

Tutor's comments

From the table, one completed unit costs £4.5, thus, 5,000 completed items cost:

5,000 × £4.5 = £22,500

The value of the WIP must therefore equal total costs less the value of the completed production:

£24,276 − £22,500 = £1,776

The answer could have been approached in a different way, by multiplying the number of equivalent units in the WIP of each element of cost by the cost per unit. The same answer would result:

	Cost element			
	Materials	*Labour*	*Overheads*	*Total*
WIP (Equivalent units)	480	360	300	
Cost per unit (£)	1.9	1.4	1.2	4.5
Value WIP (£)	912	504	360	1,776

In the above, the material included in the WIP was the material introduced into each process *as production progressed*. There was no opening WIP. However, the value of the closing WIP for one period forms the value of the opening WIP in the following period, and it must be accounted for.

BY-PRODUCTS

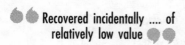 Recovered incidentally .... of relatively low value

A by-product is one which is recovered incidentally from materials used in the manufacture of the recognised main product. By-products have either a net realisable value or a usable value which is relatively low when compared to the sales value of the main product. Examples of by-products are furnace slag from iron and steel manufacture: the slag is sold for cement and brickmaking and for hard core for road construction.

Where by-products are of very little value it is pointless calculating a cost for each unit produced. In such circumstances, any monies earned from the sales of the by-product may be treated as a profit and credited to the profit and loss account. Alternatively, the income may be credited to the process account for the main product to reduce the cost of production.

In cases where the sales of by-products are significant the value of the by-products may be calculated using one of three approaches:

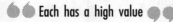 **Three approaches**

1. Market value.
2. Comparative price.
3. Standard price.

With the first method the value of the by-product is based upon current market values, and the necessary amount is credited to the process account. Any further refining or processing needed to make the by-product saleable is deducted from the income earned from the by-product.

Example 6

In producing its main product, a firm produces 500 tones of by-product, which after £200 worth of further processing has a market value of £1.50 per tonne.

Required

Calculate the sum to be credited to the main product's process account.

Solution:

	£
Sales revenue (500 × £1.50)	750
Less: Processing costs	200
Sum to be credited to main product's process account	550

Tutor's comments

The problem with using market values is that these fluctuate, causing the amount credited to the process account to vary. Such variable figures may hide any poor working in the processing plant itself, and thus delay any remedial action.

The comparative price approach is similar to the first one, but instead of using market values, the prices of comparable products are used instead. Where, for example, an integrated iron and steel works uses furnace gas to heat its offices, it may charge the gas out to the various departments at the price it would have to pay were it to buy in the gas.

In the first method, with market values, the firm uses the price it would receive: in the second method it uses the price it would pay. Since prices fluctuate, however, the second method suffers from the disadvantages of the first.

Standard costs

To avoid fluctuation caused by price changes, some firms set standard costs for the by-product, perhaps using past records to help fix the value. Once fixed, the value may be applied to all units of that by-product produced that year. At the end of the year the standard may be revised in the light of more recent experience.

JOINT PRODUCTS

Each has a high value

Joint products arise where two or more products which are separated in the course of the same processing each have a sufficiently high sales value to warrant recognition as a main product. The difference between joint products and by-products is that by-products tend to have comparatively little value compared to the main product, whereas with joint products each has a comparatively high value.

Joint products arise in oil refining, where crude oil is cracked to produce different fuels and lubricants. In coal mining, various grades of coal may be produced at the same time from the same seams.

By definition, joint products emerge from a common processing. The point at which the products take on their separate identity is known as the *separation point* or *split-off point*. After the point of separation, conventional methods of process costing apply: difficulties arise, however, whilst the products are still joint, before the point of separation. Three approaches can be adopted for apportioning the joint costs:

1. Market value.
2. Sales value.
3. Physical measurement.

The market value method ascertains the value of the products just after the split-off point, and apportions all costs up to that point on this basis. Where further processing is likely to incur disproportionate costs, the approach can be useful.

Thus, where two joint products (A) and (B) are known to have market values at split-off of £12 and £8 per litre respectively, the joint costs are apportioned 12/20 and 8/20 or 3/5 and 2/5.

Sales value uses the relative values of the *finished products* as a weighting. This method is acceptable where processing costs after the split off point are comparable: where they are not, the method may be inequitable.

Where pre-separation costs are £9,000 and the sales revenues of (C) and (D) are £16,000 and £14,000 respectively, the apportionment of joint costs will be:

$$Product\ (C) \qquad £9,000 \times \frac{£16,000}{£30,000} \qquad Product\ (D) \qquad £9,000 \times \frac{£14,000}{£30,000}$$

$$= £4,800 \qquad\qquad\qquad\qquad = £4,200$$

In (C) the £16,000 sales revenue is divided by the total joint revenue of (C) and (D): £16,000 + £14,000 = £30,000. The joint costs attributable to (C) are thus £4,800. Similarly, £4,200 is attributable to (D). In this way, the total of the pre-separation costs are allocated: £4,800 + £4,200 = £9,000.

The third approach is to compare the physical amounts of each product after the point of separation, and to use this comparison as a basis for apportionment. However, the method is not applicable when comparing liquids and gases; neither may it be equitable where one product is much more valuable than another.

SERVICE COSTING

The costing of specific services is different from that used when costing production departments. The differences lie mainly in the way the cost data is collected and the way costs are then allocated to cost units.

With services, it is often the definition of cost units that causes difficulties. Often, such units are composites, so that in hospitals a 'patient-day' may be used; in hotels, the number of beds occupied; with transport the number of 'passenger-miles', or 'tonne-kilometres'; colleges and universities may use 'full-time equivalent students'.

There really is no general rule for determining cost units: each organisation must decide for itself depending upon its circumstances, and the use it wishes to make of the cost data. Clearly, if similar organisations adopt similar units, then comparisons can be made across organisations.

Whatever decision is made, the calculation of unit cost is similar to the calculation used in production:

$$\text{Cost per service unit} = \frac{\text{Total costs for the period}}{\text{Number of service units supplied in the period}}$$

Thus, if a college has a full-time student equivalent population of 1,500, and an annual budget of £3.15m, the cost of each full-time student equivalent is:

$$\frac{£3,150,000}{1,500} = £2,100$$

EXAMINATION QUESTIONS

1 a) What is meant by the term 'specific order costing'?   *(3)*

  b) In what ways does specific order costing differ from process costing?   *(6)*

  c) The Acme Shelving Co manufactures shelving brackets in batches of 300. During May, Batch No 23 was machined at a rate of 15 per hour. Sixty of the brackets failed to pass inspection, but of these, 40 were thought to be rectifiable: the remaining 20 were scrapped, and the scrap value was credited to the Batch cost account. Rectification work took nine hours.

Batch No 23

	£
Raw materials per bracket	1.60
Scrap value per bracket	0.86
Machinists' hourly rate	4.20
Machine hour overhead rate (running time only)	3.60
Setting up of machine: normal machining	21.00
rectification	18.00

  Calculate:
  i) the cost of a full batch, in total and per unit, if all units pass inspection,
  ii) the actual cost of batch no 23, in total and per unit, after crediting the recovery value of the scrapped components, and including the rectification costs,
  iii) the loss incurred because of defective work.   *(16)*

(London 1991)

2 a) What is meant by the term 'product cost'?   *(2)*

  b) In product costing what are the main differences between specific order costing and continuous operation/process costing? How are these differences reflected in the cost accounts?   *(10)*

  c) The following information refers to contract number 10/92 in the books of Hauxton Contracting:

Contract No 10/92

Contract price	850,000
Direct materials issued to site	125,850
Materials returned to stores	1,340
Materials on site 31 December, 1992	15,560
Direct wages	145,000
Wages owing at 31 December, 1992	4,320
Plant issued to contract (at valuation)	87,450
Plant value at 31 December, 1992	80,890
Sub-contractors' charges	24,380
Head office expenses	71,210
Direct site expenses	39,470
Direct expenses owing at 31 December, 1992	5,670
Work certified by architect	485,000
Cost of work not yet certified	35,440

  Payment received from the client by 31 December, 1992 was equal to the value of the work certified less an agreed retention of 15 per cent. In calculating profits on uncompleted contracts, Hauxton Contracting uses the figure of 75 per cent.

  Prepare the contract account for contract number 10/92 as it would appear in the books of Hauxton Contracting as at 31 December, 1992. Show clearly the value of retentions, and the profit still to be taken on the work to date. *(13)*

(London 1993)

3 The Universal Glue Co makes two products Stickytak and Takolene. The products pass through the same primary and secondary processes, after which they are separated for different tertiary processes. Joint costs are divided between the products in proportion to their respective weights at the point of separation. Because of the nature of the processes, no product is left partly finished at the end of a week's activity.

Week ending 12 January, 1992

	Primary Process £	Secondary Process £
Materials introduced (10,000 kg)	20,000	—
Direct labour	5,000	7,525
Overheads	8,250	10,530

Normal losses as a percentage of each process's input are expected to be 5 per cent for Primary, and $2\frac{1}{2}$ per cent for Secondary. Lost output from the Secondary process can be sold at £4 per kg; this revenue is to be credited to the Secondary process account.

Output actually achieved during the week was 9,200 kg from Primary, and 9,100 kg from Secondary: the Secondary process's output comprised 5,460 kg of Stickytak and 3,640 kg of Takolene.

Costs incurred during the Tertiary processes were;

	Stickytak £	Takolene £
Direct labour	6,400	5,200
Overheads	7,300	6,900

a) Prepare process accounts for the Primary and Secondary processes, and for the two Tertiary processes. *(18)*

b) What are the difficulties inherent in apportioning joint costs on the basis of the products' physical measurement? How can these difficulties be overcome? *(7)*

(London 1992)

4 a) Define the term 'equivalent production' and state when the principle is used. *(4)*

b) During May 1991, M Wurzel & Co's output was 4,000 finished items plus 600 partly finished items. The details were:

	Materials	Labour	O/heads	Total
Total cost (£)	8,172	7,120	5,196	20,488
WIP degree of completion %	90	75	55	–

Calculate:
  i) the total equivalent production for each cost element,
  ii) the cost per complete unit, and
  iii) the value of the Work in Progress *(11)*

(London 1991)

TUTOR'S ANSWER

1 a) Specific order costing is the basic costing method applicable where the work consists of separate contracts, jobs, or batches, each of which is authorised by a special order or contract.

b)   Process costing is the basic costing method where goods or services result from a sequence of continuous or repetitive operations or processes to which costs are charged before being averaged over the units produced during the period.

Since individual units of output are not easily identified the process itself therefore becomes the cost centre rather than the unit of output. The costs are collected for each process and averaged over the output of that process for the period.

c)   i)

	COST (£)	
	Unit	Total
Raw materials (1.60 × 300)	1.60	480
Wages (£4.20 × 20 hrs)	0.28	84
Overheads (20 × £3.60)	0.24	72
Setting up costs	0.07	21
Cost of full batch	2.19	657

ii)

Cost of full batch		657.00
Add: Rectification costs		
Wages (9 hrs × £4.20)	37.8	
Overheads (9 hrs × £3.60)	32.4	
Set-up costs	18.0	
		88.20
		745.20
Less income from scrapped components 20 × £0.86		17.20
Total cost of 280 brackets		728.00
Cost of batch per unit: 728/280	=	£2.60

iii)

280 units should have cost 280 × £2.19	=	613.20
Actual cost	=	728.00
Loss:		114.80

STUDENT'S ANSWER

2   a)   Product cost is the cost of a finished product built up from its cost elements.

b)   (The student then gave the definitions of specific order and process costing as given in question 1 above.)

In specific order costing, costs attributable to a particular job, batch or contract are collected against a particular order number, and recorded on a job, batch or contract account.

With continuous operation or process costing on the other hand, the costs are collected for a process or operation in a process account, and the costs are averaged out over the whole output for the period.

c)

Hauxton Contracting

Contract No 10/92

Direct materials		125,850	
Less: returns	1,340		
on site 31.12.92	15,560	16,900	108,950
Direct wages		145,000	
Add owing		4,320	149,320
Direct site expenses		39,470	
Add owing		5,670	45,140
Sub-contractors' charges			24,380
HO expenses			71,210
Plant issued to site		87,450	
Less value at 31.12.92		80,890	6,560
			405,560
Less work not certified			35,440
Cost of work certified			370,120
Profit taken*		73,236	
Profit in suspense	28,720		
Retention	12,924	41,644	114,880
Value of work certified			485,000

*Note:

Profit	taken:	= £86,160
$\frac{3}{4}$ (£485,000 − £370,120)		
Retention: 15% × £86,160		= £12,924
Profit taken		= £73,236

Tutor's comments

This answer is well presented in the form of a vertical contract account. The figures are clearly shown, with the adjustments properly displayed. The candidate uses a footnote to show how the figure for profit has been calculated. An answer presented in this orderly format immediately indicates to an examiner that the candidate knows the subject, and even where minor arithmetical errors might arise, a candidate will score highly on 'principle' marks.

OUTLINE ANSWERS

3a)

Primary Process a/c

	kg	kg	£	£
Direct materials		10,000	20,000	
Direct labour			5,000	
Overheads			8,250	
				33,250

Less:

Normal losses	500*		
Abnormal losses	300	800	1,050
To Secondary		9,200	32,200

Secondary Process a/c

From Primary	9,200	32,200
Direct labour		7,525
Overheads		10,530
		50,255
Abnormal gain	130	(718)	715*
	9,330	(50,973)	50,970
Normal losses	230		920#
To Tertiaries	9,100	(50,053)	50,050

Tertiary Process a/cs

		Stickytak		Takolene
From Secondary (60%)	(30,032)	30,030		
(40%)			(20,021)	20,020
Direct labour		6,400		5,200
Overheads		7,300		6,900
		43,730		32,120

*Note:

Normal Loss: $9,200 \times 2\frac{1}{2}\%$ = 230
Output expected: 9,200 − 230 = 8,970
Output achieved: 9,100
Abnormal gain: 130

50,255/9,100 = £5.5
Value of abnormal gain: 130 kg × £5.5 = £715 (or £718)
Note:

230 kg sold at £4 kg = £920

   b) Difficulties: joint products may be different physical measurement e.g. gases and liquids. Also, assumes joint products are equally valuable — they may not be.

      Use either: i) *market value at point of separation* but may be inequitable if further processing costs are not comparable and some semi-finished items have no easily determinable market values.

      or ii) *Sales value of finished products:* acceptable unless further processing costs are disproportionate.

4 a) A notional quantity of finished units substituted for an actual quantity of incomplete units in progress.

      Use when operation costs are being apportioned between WIP and completed output.

   b) i)

		Matls	Labour	O/head
WIP (Equiv units)	600 × 90%	540		
	600 × 75%		450	
	600 × 55%			330
Finished units		4,000	4,000	4,000
Total		4,540	4,450	4,300

ii)

Total cost (£)	8,172	7,120	5,196
Cost/unit (£)	= 1.8 +	1.6 +	1.2 = 4.6

iii) Total value WIP:

Cost of finished output = 4,000 × £4.6 = £18,400
Total cost   = 20,488
Cost of WIP   = 20,488 − 18,400 = £2,088

OR:

540 × £1.8 + 450 × £1.6 + 330 × £1.2
= 972 + 720 + 396
= £2,088

Now attempt the review questions on page 314. The answers are given on page 327.

GETTING STARTED

Absorption and marginal costing are techniques concerned primarily with the effect of overheads upon a business's profits: they are not costing systems in their own right as are job costing and process costing. A firm using job costing (or process costing) may still use absorption costing (or marginal costing) in valuing closing stocks.

Overhead costs comprise the cost of indirect labour, indirect materials and indirect expenses: they are those types of cost which cannot be charged directly to a product. In the USA and in some American firms operating in Britain, the term *burden* is used instead of overhead: it is the same thing.

In Chapter 15, it was seen how overheads can be divided either into production, administration, and selling overhead; or into fixed, semi-fixed and variable overhead. In each case the total of indirect expenses was the same: merely reclassified to suit different purposes.

Fixed overheads are those which accrue with the passing of time, and which, within certain limits of output and turnover, tend to be unaffected by fluctuations in the levels of activity. Sometimes the terms *period cost* or *policy cost* are used. Examples are rent, rates, insurances and management salaries.

Semi-fixed overheads – or semi-variable overheads – are those which contain both fixed and variable elements, and which in consequence are partly affected by fluctuations in the levels of activity. Examples include electricity, and metered water supplies, where charges levied comprise a fixed element to be paid irrespective of usage, plus a variable levied element for each unit consumed.

Variable overheads are those which do fluctuate with the level of activity. Examples include packing charges, carriage and sales commission.

ABSORPTION AND MARGINAL COSTING

FIXED, SEMI-FIXED AND VARIABLE OVERHEADS

ABSORPTION COSTING

MARGINAL COSTING

THE CONTRIBUTION

COST-VOLUME-PROFIT ANALYSIS

BREAK-EVEN CHARTS

PROFIT GRAPH

PRICING DECISIONS

ACCEPT-REJECT DECISIONS

MAKE OR BUY DECISIONS

ABSORPTION AND MARGINAL COSTING COMPARED

ESSENTIAL PRINCIPLES

FIXED, SEMI-FIXED AND VARIABLE OVERHEADS

When considering overheads it is important to distinguish between their behaviour over total output and their behaviour per unit of output. Assume that a firm's fixed costs are £1,000 per month in the output range 0–100 units (Table 17.1). Because these costs remain fixed throughout the range, a graph relating total cost to total output will show fixed costs as a horizontal line in Figure 17.1(a). However if fixed costs are plotted *per unit of output*, it can be seen that the graph slopes downwards to the right (see Figure 17.1(b)).

At an output of one unit, the whole of the fixed costs accrue, so the fixed costs per unit are £1,000. At 40 units, costs are spread at £25 per unit, whilst at 100 units fixed costs are £10 per unit.

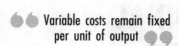

Variable costs remain fixed per unit of output

Conversely, variable costs, whilst remaining fixed per unit of output over limited ranges, do increase in total as output rises. Thus, where variable costs per unit are £5.00, the total variable costs will rise as output increases: at an output of 10 units, total variable costs are £50 (10 × £5); at 80 units total variable costs are £400 (80 × £5), Figure 17.2(a). However, if a graph of variable costs per unit is plotted it can be seen that the graph gives a horizontal line (Figure 17.2(b)).

Semi-variable costs can adopt many patterns of behaviour: *total* semi-variable costs may be linear (Figure 17.3(a)); curvilinear and concave (Figure 17.3(b)); or curvilinear and convex (Figure 17.3(c)). In each case the range (O–F) represents the fixed element of the overhead.

When plotted as semi-variable costs *per unit*, the curves usually slope downwards to the right, the slope of the curve depending upon the behaviour of the cost.

Some costs show a stepped feature

Some costs show a stepped feature, remaining fixed for particular levels of activity and then changing for different activity levels (Figure 17.4). This may arise with fixed costs, when, in order to expand output, an additional workshop has to be rented. The cost of this workshop remains fixed whether it is used for just one day per week or seven days per week.

Table 17.1

Output (units)	Fixed cost per unit (£)	Variable cost per unit (£)
1	1000	5
10	100	50
20	50	100
40	25	200

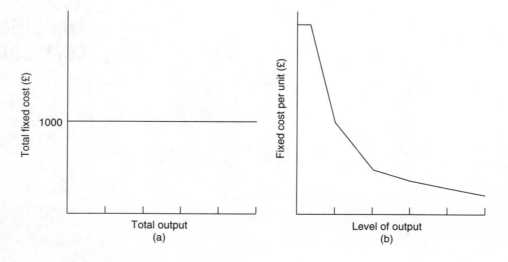

Fig. 17.1 The behaviour of fixed costs.

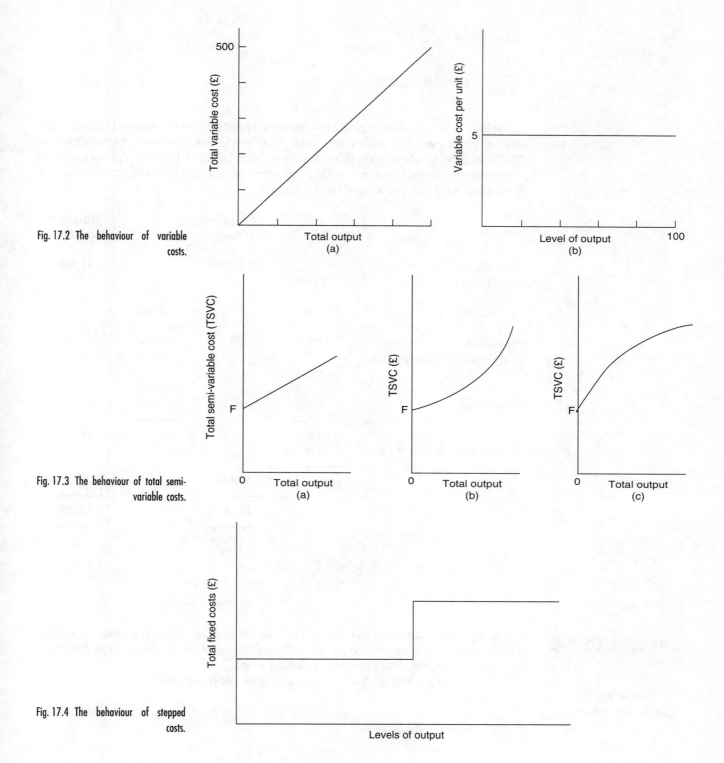

Fig. 17.2 The behaviour of variable costs.

Fig. 17.3 The behaviour of total semi-variable costs.

Fig. 17.4 The behaviour of stepped costs.

ABSORPTION COSTING

❛❛ Assumes fixed costs attach to products ❜❜

Absorption costing assumes that fixed costs attach to products, so that they can transfer to subsequent periods by way of closing and opening stocks. The following data relates to a company in 1992. There are no opening stocks:

Sales: 800 units at £40 unit.
Production: 1,000 units.
Direct materials £7,000; direct labour £5,000; variable overheads £3,000.
Fixed factory overheads: £4,800.

The accounts appear on page 232. Using absorption costing, the fixed costs are added to the prime cost (£15,000 + £4,800 = £19,800) and the value of the closing stock is calculated on the result. With 1,000 items produced and 800 sold, closing stock must be 200 units (1,000 − 800). This, as a proportion of total output is applied to the total cost as follows:

$$\frac{200}{1,000} \times £19,800 = £3,960$$

The value of closing stock is deducted from total production cost to give £15,840 as the cost of producing the 800 units sold. The profit for the period, therefore, is £32,000 − £15,840 = £16,160. Note, however, that SSAP 9 permits the inclusion of production overheads but not selling or administration overheads. In valuing the closing stocks, fixed costs have been included.

	£	Absorption costing £	£	Marginal costing £
Sales: 800 @ £40		32,000		32,000
Less: Direct materials	7,000		7,000	
Direct labour	5,000		5,000	
Variable overheads	3,000		3,000	
Prime cost	15,000		15,000	
Closing stock (Marginal)			3,000	
			12,000	
Fixed costs	4,800		4,800	
	19,800			16,800
Closing stock (absorption)	3,960			
		15,840		
Profit		16,160		15,200

MARGINAL COSTING

❝❞ Assumes that fixed costs attach to time periods ❞❞

Marginal costing assumes that fixed costs attach to time periods, so that in valuing closing stocks, only *variable costs* are included. None of 1992's fixed costs find their way into subsequent years as part of closing stock.

In the example, closing stocks are valued solely at prime cost:

$$\frac{200}{1,000} \times £15,000 = £3,000$$

Only after allowance has been made for stocks (see above) is the figure for fixed costs added in, to give the cost of producing 800 items at £16,800. The profit for the period becomes £32,000 − £16,800 = £15,200.

The difference in the profit figures is £960:

Profit (£)

Absorption costing	16,160
Marginal costing	15,200
Difference	960

This can readily be explained. In absorption costing, the closing stock figure included an element for the fixed costs: the element was proportional to the ratio of closing stock units to total production:

$$\frac{200}{1,000} \times £4,800 = £960$$

The difference in profit arises solely because absorption costing includes fixed costs in the closing stock valuation.

EXAMPLE 1

The following information relates to the same company, but for 1993:

Sales: 1,200 units at £42 per unit
Production: 1,100 units
Direct materials £8,050; direct labour £5,750; variable overheads £3,450
Fixed factory overheads: £5,520
The firm values closing stock on the basis of FIFO.

Required
Show the profit using (a) absorption and (b) marginal costing.

Solution:

	Absorption costing		Marginal costing	
	£	£	£	£
Sales: 1,200 @ £42		50,400		50,400
Less: Direct materials	8,050		8,050	
Direct labour	5,750		5,750	
Variable overheads	3,450		3,450	
Prime cost	17,250		17,250	
Add: Opening stock (marginal)			3,000	
			20,250	
Less: Closing stock (marginal)			1,568	
			18,682	
Add: Fixed costs	5,520		5,520	
	22,770			24,202
Add: Opening stock (absorption)	3,960			
	26,730			
Less: Closing stock (absorption)	2,070			
		24,660		
Profit		25,740		26,198

TUTOR'S COMMENTS

With absorption costing, the prime costs are calculated and fixed costs are added to give £22,770. Opening stock is then added to give £26,730. Since the firm had an opening stock of 200 items from the previous year, physical stocks held at the end of

1993 are:

	Units
Opening stock	200
Add: Production	1,100
	1,300
Less: Sales	1,200
Closing stock	100

The value of closing stock using FIFO is therefore:

$$\frac{100}{1,100} \times £22,770 = £2,070$$

Note that closing stock is calculated on the total production costs of the period before adjustments are made for opening stock. The cost of goods sold is £24,660, giving a profit of £25,740 (£50,400 − £24,660 = £25,740).

By contrast, the marginal costing approach values stocks at variable costs only, thus closing stocks are calculated:

$$\frac{100}{1,100} \times £17,250 = £1,568$$

Opening stocks are added to the prime cost, closing stocks deducted, and only then are the period's fixed costs added: £5,520. The cost of goods sold in this approach is £24,202, giving a profit of £26,198 (£50,400 − £24,202 = £26,198).

Note that in 1993 the profits under marginal costing were greater than under absorption, whereas in the previous year profits using absorption costing were the greater. Do not, therefore assume that either approach always gives a greater or less profit figure: much depends upon the figures used.

◖◗ Neither approach always gives a greater profit ◖◗

	Profits (£)	
	1992	1993
Absorption costing	16,160	25,740
Marginal costing	15,200	26,198
Difference	960	(458)

The profit figures for 1993 can be reconciled to show the relative effects of fixed costs:

Physical closing stock as fraction of total output	= 1/11
Fixed costs	= £5,520.
Proportion allocated to closing stocks	= £5,520 × 1/11
	= £502.
Less: From 1992	£960
	− £458

The negative sign indicates that marginal costs' profits have grown greater than those of absorption costs.

In the example it was assumed that the firm used FIFO when valuing closing stocks: the firm could, of course, have used AVCO or LIFO.

THE CONTRIBUTION

The marginal cost of an item is that cost which would be avoided if the unit was not produced or the service not provided. Since fixed costs remain fixed irrespective of the level of output, the marginal cost of an item is the variable cost of a product or service. In the example below, the extra cost of producing the second unit is £140 − £120 = £20; and this equals the amount of the added variable cost:

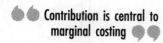
Contribution is central to marginal costing

Output (units)	Fixed cost (£)	Variable cost (£)	Total cost (£)	Marginal cost (£)
1	100	20	120	
2	100	40	140	20

The notion of the contribution is central to marginal costing. The contribution is defined as:

Contribution = Sales value − variable cost of sales.

It represents the surplus available to defray fixed costs, once variable costs have been met. Remember, fixed costs have to be paid even at zero output: anything that reduces fixed costs will reduce losses or increase profits.

By redrafting the information in Example 1, the marginal cost of £18,682 can be highlighted and the *contribution* of £31,718 calculated. This latter sum is available to contribute towards fixed costs and profit:

1993	£	£
Sales: 1,200 @ £42		50,400
Less: Prime cost	17,250	
Add: Opening stock	3,000	
	20,250	
Less: Closing stock	1,568	
Marginal cost		18,612
Contribution towards fixed costs and profit		31,718
Less: Fixed costs		5,520
Profit		26,198

In the example the contribution is:

£50,400 − £18,612 = £31,788
sales value − variable cost of sales = contribution

The contribution per unit is:

$$\text{Contribution per unit} = \frac{\text{Contribution}}{\text{Total sales (units)}}$$

In the example:

$$\frac{£31,788}{1,200} = £26.49$$

The contribution per unit plus the marginal cost per unit, should equal the selling price per unit. The marginal cost per unit equals £18,612 ÷ 1,200 = £15.51.

£26.49 + £15.51 = £42

By using the idea of the contribution, marginal costing enables the firm's management to calculate the level of profit if sales vary: absorption costing cannot do this.

EXAMPLE 2

Assume that the firm wishes to increase sales from 1,200 to 1,500 units. Recall, that in the short run, variable costs per unit do not change.

Required
Using the figures from the 1993 accounts above, calculate the anticipated profit figure.

Solution:

	£
Total sales: 1,500 × £42	63,000
Less: Anticipated marginal cost:	
$\dfrac{1,500 \times £18,612}{1,200}$	23,265
Contribution:	39,735
Less: Fixed costs	5,520
Anticipated profit	34,215

TUTOR'S COMMENTS

The anticipated marginal cost figure for 1,500 units assumes that the marginal cost per unit does not change. Thus, 1,500 units at £15.51 equals £23,265. When the new marginal cost is deducted from the income, the new contribution is calculated; this is the amount available for fixed costs and profit. When fixed costs are deducted – remember they are assumed to be unchanging over the range of output – then the anticipated profit figure emerges.

COST–VOLUME– PROFIT ANALYSIS

Cost–volume–profit (CVP) analysis uses many of the principles of marginal costing in explaining the relationship between costs, revenues, levels of output and profit. CVP is based upon some restrictive assumptions, which effectively limits the usefulness of CVP analysis to short-term and small-scale changes. Even then, CVP can offer only approximate guides for decision-making. These assumptions are:

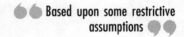
Based upon some restrictive assumptions

1. All costs are either fixed or variable: semi-variable costs are not considered to exist.
2. Fixed costs remain fixed over time, and variable costs per unit remain constant.
3. All costs and revenues are linear.
4. Volume is the only factor affecting either costs or revenues.
5. The technology of production, and productive efficiency remain unchanged.
6. The firm produces one product or a constant product mix.
7. There are no changes in stock levels.

The break-even point

A firm's break-even point is that point where total sales revenue just equals total costs: it is a point of zero profit and zero losses. Using CVP analysis, the break-even point in terms of either units produced, or the value of sales, can readily be found:

(a) $\text{Break-even point (units)} = \dfrac{\text{Fixed costs}}{\text{Contribution per unit}}$

(b) $\text{Break-even point (£ sales)} = \dfrac{\text{Fixed costs}}{\text{Contribution per unit}} \times \text{Unit sales price}$

The contribution to sales (C/S) ratio is widely called the profit/volume (P/V) ratio, although the term (C/S) ratio is now preferred. This ratio shows the relationship between the contribution and sales:

(c) $\text{C/S ratio} = \dfrac{\text{Contribution per unit}}{\text{Unit sales price}} \times 100$

CVP can also indicate the level of sales – in physical units or in monetary values – which is necessary to earn a given profit figure:

(d)   Sales (units) for required profit $= \dfrac{\text{Fixed cost} + \text{required profit}}{\text{Contribution per unit}}$

(e)   Sales (£) for required profit $= \dfrac{(\text{Fixed cost} + \text{required profit})\ \text{unit sales price}}{\text{Contribution per unit}}$

Assume a firm manufactures a single product which sells at £50. Its marginal cost is £30, and fixed costs are £200,000.

Using these figures, the contribution is:

$$\text{Contribution} = \text{Sales value} - \text{marginal costs}$$
$$= £50 - £30$$
$$= £20$$

(a)   Break-even point (units) $= \dfrac{£200,000}{£20} = 10,000 \text{ units}$

(b)   Break-even point (£ sales) $= \dfrac{£200,000}{£20} \times £50 = £500,000$

(c)   C/S ratio $= \dfrac{£20}{£50} \times 100 = 40\%$

(d)   Sales (units) to earn £100,000 profit $= \dfrac{£200,000 + £100,000}{£20} = 15,000 \text{ units}$

(e)   Sales (£) to earn £100,000 profit $= \dfrac{£200,000 + £100,000}{£20} \times £50 = £750,000$

Note that after the break-even point has been reached the contribution per unit becomes net profit per unit. Thus, since 10,000 units are needed to break-even, the extra 5,000 units in (d) would earn a profit equal to their contribution:

$$5,000 \times £20 = £100,000 \text{ profit}$$

BREAK-EVEN CHARTS

A compilation of three graphs

It is sometimes useful to show a firm's break-even point using graphical methods, rather than by using equations. Although there are a number of forms which a break-even chart can take, they all indicate approximate profit or loss at different levels of sales volume within a limited range. Usually, sales and costs are represented on the vertical (y) axis, and output on the horizontal (x) axis. Table 17.2 shows data for a firm's output at five different levels, and this information is used in the charts which follow.

The break-even chart is really a compilation of three graphs. Figure 17.5 shows costs and revenues at various levels of output and sales. Variable costs are £0.4 per unit, and selling price £1.2 per unit.

Figure 17.5(a) is the graph for fixed costs: as fixed costs are constant at £2,000, so the line is horizontal. In 17.5(b) the total costs are shown; fixed costs plus variable costs. The angle of the line is a measure of the variable costs. Note that at zero output only fixed costs are incurred: the total cost line thus begins at £2,000. In (c) the sales revenue line begins at the origin when sales are zero, and slopes upwards to £6,000 when sales are 5,000 units.

When these three graphs are superimposed on to one graph (Figure 17.6) the break-even point, where neither profits nor losses accrue, is shown at (E) where the total revenue line cuts the total cost line. The area to the left of break-even point shows the area of loss; to the right, the area of profit. The break-even point occurs at an output

Output (000)	1	2	3	4	5
Fixed costs (000)	2.0	2.0	2.0	2.0	2.0
Variable costs	0.4	0.8	1.2	1.6	2.0
Total costs	2.4	2.8	3.2	3.6	4.0
Sales	1.2	2.4	3.6	4.8	6.0

Table 17.2

of £2,500 units and at an income of £3,000. This can be verified by using the equations (a) and (b) on page 236.

The *margin of safety* is the distance between current output (5,000 units) and the break-even output, 2,500 units: (MS) on the graph. If the distance (MS) is large it indicates that the firm can reduce output substantially without making losses. If the distance is short, it indicates that a large reduction in output may cause the firm to make losses.

In financial terms the margin of safety can be calculated using the formula:

Margin of safety = Profit ÷ (C/S) ratio

The (C/S) ratio is contribution per unit divided by unit sales price. In the example therefore the margin of safety at an output of 5,000 units is:

$$£2,000 \div \frac{£0.8}{£1.2}$$

$$= £2,000 \times 3/2$$
$$= £3,000$$

This can be verified from the graph. Income at break-even point is £3,000; income at 5,000 units is £6,000. The margin of safety, therefore is £6,000 − £3,000 = £3,000.

The *angle of incidence* is the angle at which the total revenue line cuts the total cost line: θ in Figure 17.6. If the angle is large, it suggests that profits are being earned at a high rate; if the angle is small, profits are more difficult to achieve.

❝❝ A large angle of incidence and a high margin of safety indicates a strong position ❞❞

When combined with the margin of safety, a large angle of incidence and a high margin of safety indicates a strong position: profits earned at a high rate, and the ability to reduce output greatly without incurring losses. Conversely, a low angle of incidence and a small margin of safety spells a weak position: profits difficult to earn, and output not much above break-even levels.

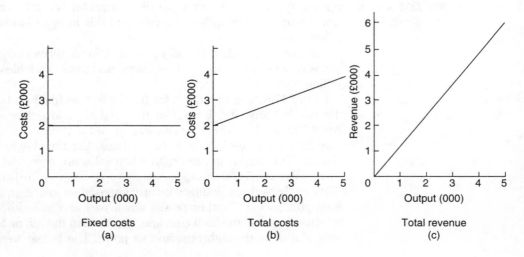

Fig. 17.5 Constituents of break-even charts.

| Fixed costs (a) | Total costs (b) | Total revenue (c) |

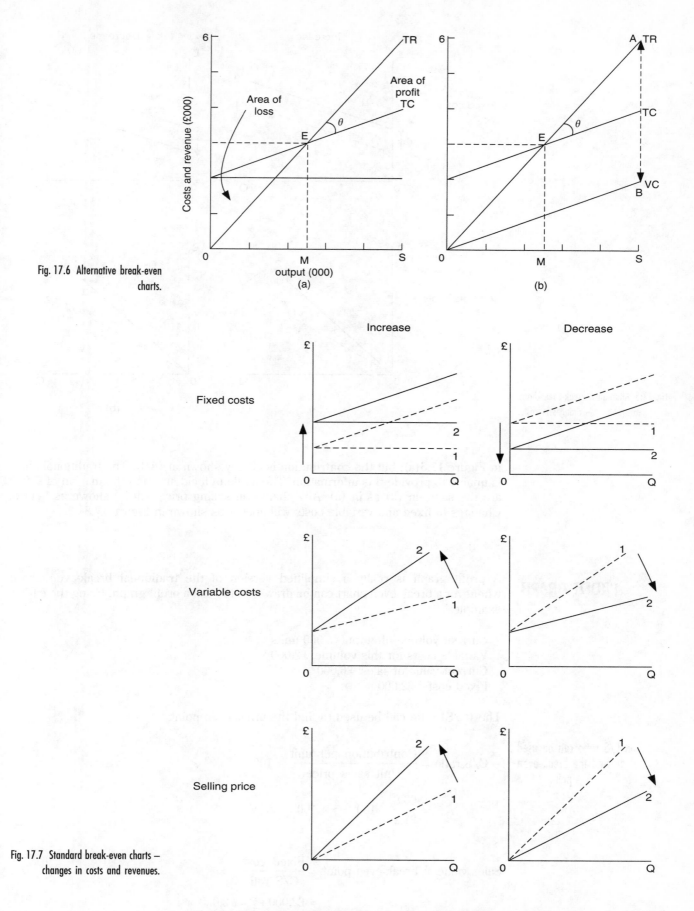

Fig. 17.6 Alternative break-even charts.

Fig. 17.7 Standard break-even charts – changes in costs and revenues.

Clearly, if there is a change in fixed costs, variable costs or selling price, the position and/or shape of the lines will change; and so too may the break-even point. Figure 17.7 indicates the effects of increases and decreases upon the break-even chart.

An alternative method of drawing break-even charts, and one which emphasises the role of the contribution, appears in Figure 17.6(b). The break-even point is the same as

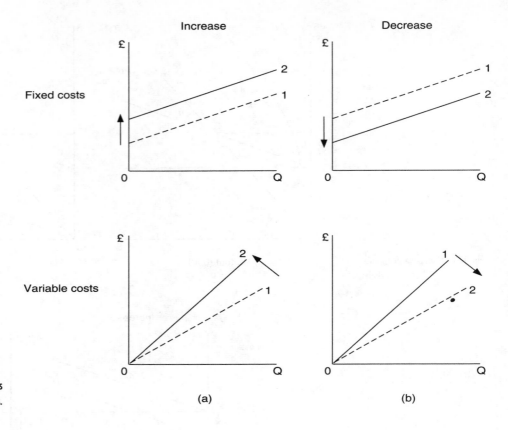

Fig. 17.8 Alternative break-even charts – changes in costs.

in Figure 17.6(a), but the contribution is clearly shown at (AB). The traditional chart is unable to provide this information. The angle of incidence and the margin of safety are the same in (b) as in (a). Any change in selling price will be shown as before. Changes in fixed and variable costs will appear as shown in Figure 17.8.

PROFIT GRAPH

A profit graph is really a simplified version of the traditional break-even chart: whenever a break-even chart can be drawn, so too can a profit graph. Using the earlier example:

Current volume of output: 5,000 units
Variable costs for this volume: £2,000
Current value of sales: £6,000
Fixed costs: £2,000

The (C/S) ratio can be used to find the break-even point:

> The C/S ratio can be used to find the break-even point

$$\text{C/S ratio} = \frac{\text{Contribution per unit}}{\text{Unit sales price}} \times 100$$

$$= \frac{£0.8}{£1.2} \times 100 = \tfrac{2}{3} \times 100 = 66.7\%$$

$$\text{Sales value at break-even point} = \frac{\text{Fixed costs}}{\text{C/S ratio}}$$

$$= £2,000 \div \tfrac{2}{3} = £2,000 \times \tfrac{3}{2}$$

$$= £3,000$$

The profit graph (Figure 17.9) shows sales on the horizontal axis: below this, on the vertical axis represents losses; above represents profits. Thus, fixed costs at zero sales is shown as a full £2,000 loss. As sales are made, and contributions are received

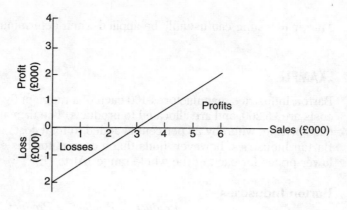

Fig. 17.9 Profit graph.

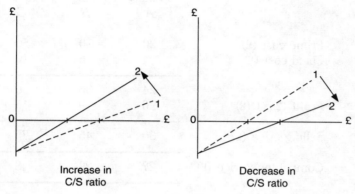

Fig. 17.10 Profit graph – changes in c/s ratio.

Increase in
C/S ratio

Decrease in
C/S ratio

towards fixed costs, so the loss diminishes. At the break-even point, the loss disappears altogether, and to the right of the break-even point, profits are earned. If the (C/S) ratio is increased, it shows that the contribution towards fixed costs has also increased. In Figure 17.10, the line pivots upwards. If the (C/S) ratio decreases, the line points downwards.

The (C/S) ratio will increase (decrease) if:

(a)   selling prices increase (decrease);
(b)   if direct and indirect costs reduce (increase);
(c)   if the product mix is changed towards products with a greater (lesser) c/s ratio.

Any reduction (increase) in fixed overheads will not affect the (C/S) ratio, and thus will not alter the *slope* of the line, but it will increase (decrease) the profit available, thus moving the whole line to the right or left, and changing the break-even point (Figure 17.11).

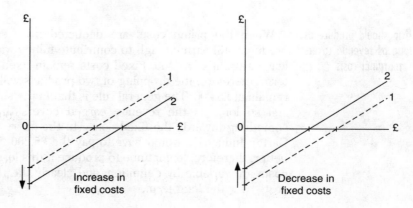

Fig. 17.11 Profit graph – changes in fixed costs.

Increase in
fixed costs

Decrease in
fixed costs

PRICING DECISIONS

Marginal costing can usefully be applied when determining prices.

EXAMPLE 3

Barton Industries manufactures 100 each of a range of five products per month. Fixed costs are £5,200, and are allocated to products. The firm also operates cost-plus, or full cost, pricing, whereby 25 per cent is added to total costs to calculate the selling price. Barton Industries, however, finds that a competitor has entered the market charging lower prices for each of the whole range (A) to (E).

Barton Industries

	Product A	Product B	Product C	Product D	Product E
Prime cost (£)	20	30	50	70	90
Fixed cost (£)	4	6	10	14	18
	24	36	60	84	108
Profit (25%) (£)	6	9	15	21	27
Selling price (£)	30	45	75	105	135
Competitor's price (£)	27	29	48	91	128

Required

Prepare a costing in order to work out which of the five products, if any, Barton Industries should continue to produce.

TUTOR'S COMMENTS

A careful study of the above table shows that although the competitor charges less than Barton for all products, he charges less than prime costs only for (B) and (C). In all other cases, Barton can sell at the same price as the competitor, make a contribution towards the fixed costs, and earn a profit, albeit a lower profit than previously. The following shows the profit calculation if 100 each of (A), (D) and (E) are produced and sold at the competitor's prices:

Barton Industries

	£	£
Sales: 100 (£27 + £91 + £128)	24,600	
Less: Prime cost 100 (£20 + £70 + £90)	18,000	
Contribution towards fixed costs and profit		6,600
Less: Fixed costs		5,200
Profit		1,400

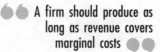

A firm should produce as long as revenue covers marginal costs

When the prime costs are deducted from sales revenue the three remaining products still earn enough to contribute fully towards the fixed costs of £5,200 and to leave a profit of £1,400. Fixed costs remain fixed irrespective of output: in the short term, therefore, the dropping of two products will not reduce total fixed costs, which remain at £5,200. The general rule is that in the short term, a firm should produce and sell so long as the revenue earned covers the marginal costs, and contributes something towards the fixed costs. In the short run fixed costs cannot be changed: Barton Industries would have to pay the £5,200 fixed costs even at zero output. It is better, therefore, to continue to produce if this loss can be reduced. In the long run all costs are variable by definition, and clearly the firm must endeavour to cover all its costs over the long term.

ACCEPT–REJECT DECISIONS

Marginal costing can also help where a firm is offered an additional order over and above its normal output.

EXAMPLE 4

Grantchester Engineering currently manufactures 200 items per month of a product, which sells at £50 per item. Prime costs per unit are £27.50, and total monthly fixed costs are £2,500.

The firm's sales department is approached by a foreign buyer who wishes to order 100 similar items per month, but at a price of £40 per item. Grantchester could accommodate the order without any threat to existing markets, by working overtime at the normal prime costs plus £750 per month. Additional machinery and storage space would need to be rented at £100 and £40 per month respectively.

Required:
Prepare a costing in order to advise Grantchester to accept the order.

Solution:

Grantchester Engineering

	Without export order		With export order	
Sales: 200 @ £50	10,000		10,000	
100 @ £40			4,000	
			14,000	
Less: Prime costs: 200 @ £27.50	5,500	5,500		
100 @ £27.50		2,750		
overtime premium		750		
			9,000	
Contribution	4,500		5,000	
Less: Fixed costs	2,500	2,500		
Machinery and storage		140		
			2,640	
Profit	2,000		2,360	

TUTOR'S COMMENTS

The general rule is that provided the new order covers its additional costs, then the order should be accepted. In the example, the acceptance of the order increases profits from £2,000 to £2,360 per month. The 'normal' fixed costs of £2,500 are already covered by existing output: provided the new order covers the additional prime costs, the overtime premium, and the extra rental charges, then the order can begin to add to profit. In fact, the lowest possible price that Grantchester could accept would be:

$$\frac{£2,750 + £750 + £140}{100} = £36.40 \text{ unit}$$

The difference between this price and the price actually charged amounts to the increased profit earned:

£40 − £36.40 = £3.60 unit
Profit on 100 units = £360

MAKE OR BUY DECISIONS

When a firm is deciding whether to make a component itself, or to buy it in, the comparison of costs should use marginal costs and not full costs. Suppose a firm has the option of buying in 1,000 units at £8.20 unit, whereas to manufacture in-house costs £11

	£
Prime cost	7.60
Fixed overhead	3.40
	11.00

Assume also that if the components are not manufactured the spare capacity made available cannot be used for any other activity.

In these circumstances, since the prime cost is less than the buying-in price: £.760 compared to £8.20 – the firm should manufacture. The fixed costs of £3.40 × 1,000 = £3,400 cannot be absorbed by any replacement output, and so they must fall upon any other products currently being made. By producing the components in-house, at least £8.20 – £7.60 = £0.60 per item is being earned towards the fixed costs.

The position is slightly different when a firm must displace existing output to produce the components: in such cases the loss of contribution from the displaced output must be considered. Suppose that 1,000 items can be bought in for £5.30 per unit, whilst the marginal costs of producing in-house are £4.80 per unit. At first sight, it might appear wise to manufacture in-plant; however, this would displace items with a contribution of £1,700:

	£
Marginal cost of in-house production (£4.8 × 1000)	4,800
Add: Loss of contribution from displaced output	1,700
	6,500
Buying-in price £5.30 × 1,000	5,300

On these figures there is a saving of £1,200 from buying in rather than from producing in-plant (£6,500 – £5,300 = £1,200).

ABSORPTION AND MARGINAL COSTING COMPARED

A number of advantages are claimed for marginal costing as a routine method of ascertaining costs:

(a) It may be simple to operate, although with some job costing situations this is questionable.
(b) It makes unnecessary the arbitrary apportionment of fixed costs to products or departments.
(c) It shows a constant net profit where sales are constant, even if output is fluctuating: absorption techniques in such cases would show a varying profit.
(d) It largely avoids the problem of under or over absorption of overheads.
(e) Since fixed overheads tend to be time-related, it seems more equitable to write them off during the period in which they are incurred.
(f) Accounts produced on marginal cost bases reflect more closely the firm's true cash flow position.

However, there are drawbacks:

(a)   Marginal costing may give the impression that fixed costs are in some way divorced from production, or are of less importance than variable costs. This is a false impression, more especially with increasingly capital intensive industries.

(b)   Many firms endeavour to maintain even production flows, allowing sales to fluctuate, since these are less easy to control. In such circumstances, profits will vary less with absorption than with marginal costing.

(c)   Where the build up of stocks is an integral part of the production cycle – such as in maturing wines and spirits, seasoning timber etc. – it is more acceptable to include fixed costs in stock valuations.

(d)   In price setting, the emphasis on contribution may lead to prices being fixed lower than is necessary to cover total costs. Absorption costing makes this less likely because it includes fixed costs.

(e)   SSAP 9 (stocks and long term contracts) recommends the use of absorption costing for financial accounts, because costs and revenues must be matched in the period when the revenue arises and not when the costs are incurred. The statement also recommends that stock valuations should include the production overhead incurred in the normal course of business, regardless of the fact that the overhead might be time-related. The production overhead must be based upon normal output.

The position, therefore, is that either absorption or marginal costing can be used for internal purposes, but SSAP 9 makes it clear that absorption costing should be used for financial accounts. In fact, research suggests that full marginal costing systems used in routine costing procedures are very rare in practice. This does not mean, however, that the principles of marginal costing are unimportant. Marginal costing is a useful management tool in decision-making, and depending upon the circumstances, the insights it provides can be most valuable.

EXAMINATION QUESTIONS

1   Barmik plc manufactures a single product which has a selling price of £60 per unit. The unit product cost is as follows:

	£	£
Direct materials		10
Direct labour		15
Manufacturing overheads		
Variable	5	
Fixed	10	15
		40

The unit fixed manufacturing overhead cost has been calculated based on a quarterly budgeted expenditure of £200 000 at the normal level of production.

Selling and distribution costs are:

Variable	10% of sales
Fixed	£80,000 per annum.

There was an opening stock of 5,000 units of finished goods at the beginning of the first quater. By the end of the first quarter the stock had risen to 12,000 units. The closing stock at the end of the second quarter was 6,000 units.

Actual sales for the first and second quarters were 16,000 and 24,000 units respectively.

Currently the company is using an absorption costing system.

There was no work in progress at the beginning or the end of either of the quarters and actual fixed overheads were as budgeted.

You are required to:

(a)   determine the normal level of production;   *(2)*
(b)   identify the actual production, in units, in each of the two quarters;   *(6)*
(c)   prepare a statement showing the profit or loss for each quarter using the current system of absorption costing;   *(16)*
(d)   recalculate the profit or loss for each quarter using a marginal costing system;   *(8)*
(e)   reconcile the profits or losses calculated in (c) and (d) for each quarter giving an explanation of the reasons for the differences.   *(8)*

(Northern 1992)

2   Quacker Limited makes mascots for football supporters and its trading results for the year just ending (31 December 1992) are expected to look as follows:

	£ 000	£ 000
Sales (200,000 mascots)		1,800
Cost –		
Materials – Direct, Variable	400	
Labour – Direct, Variable	240	
– Indirect, Fixed	70	
Other Production overheads – Variable	100	
– Fixed	160	
Selling overheads – Variable	120	
– Fixed	90	
Distribution overheads – Variable	70	
– Fixed	30	
Administration overheads – Fixed	150	1,430
Expected Net Profit 1992		370

Quackers is currently planning next year's activity and its forecasts for 1993 are as follows:

1.   A reduction in selling price to £8 per mascot is expected to increase sales volume by 50%.
2.   Material prices per unit will remain unchanged except that because of the increased quantities being purchased, a 5% quantity discount will be obtained.
3.   Hourly direct wage rates will increase by 10% but labour efficiency will remain the same.
4.   Variable selling overheads will increase in total in line with the increase in sales revenue.
5.   Variable production and distribution overhead expenses will increase in line with the 50% increase in sales volume.
6.   All fixed costs will increase by 20% but will then remain fixed until production volume reaches 350,000 units.

(a)   Prepare a Budget Profit statement for 1993 using a marginal cost approach. Show clearly total sales and total costs for the year and also full cost and net profit per unit.   *(12)*
(b)   Calculate the break-even points for the two years and explain why the break-even point has changed. Comment on the margin of safety in both years.   *(6)*
(c)   Calculate the sales volume required (using the new selling price) in order to achieve the same net profit in 1993 as in 1992.   *(2)*
(d)   One director says 'This net profit per unit is very useful. All we now have to do to work out our budgeted profit is to multiply the net profit per unit by the number of units we want to sell'.
    Why is the director wrong and what would the profits be if sales and production volumes were increased by 60% instead of 50%?   *(5)*

(Cambridge 1992)

3 a) What are the differences between (i) marginal cost pricing and (ii) full cost pricing? *(4)*

b) How far is it true to state that marginal cost pricing is a short term strategy? *(4)*

c) A. S. Teroid Ltd make five different products – Ceres, Eros, Hermes, Icarus, and Vesta. The various costs per unit of the products are respectively: direct labour, £14, £8, £22, £18, and £26; direct materials, £8, £10, £13, £12, and £17; variable overheads, £11, £9, £16, £15, and £19.

The fixed expenses for the month are estimated at £82,000, and this has been allocated to the units produced as Ceres £17, Eros £13, Hermes £19, Icarus £15, and Vesta £18. The company adds 20 per cent onto the total cost of each product by way of profit.

i) calculate the prices based upon full cost pricing,

ii) advise the company on which products to produce, if competition forces the prices to Ceres £59, Eros £25, Hermes £80, Icarus £44, and Vesta £92.

iii) assuming that output for the month amounts to 100 units of each model – and that unused capacity cannot be used for other products – calculate the profit or loss if the company continued to produce the whole range at the new prices, AND if the company followed your advice in (ii) above.

(17)

(London 1991)

4 a) What are (i) the uses and (ii) the limitations of the traditional break-even chart? *(8)*

b) The following graphs refer to Mutt Ltd and Jeff Ltd each of which is a one-product company. The graphs are drawn to the same scale. Use the graphs to compare and contrast the two companies. *(7)*

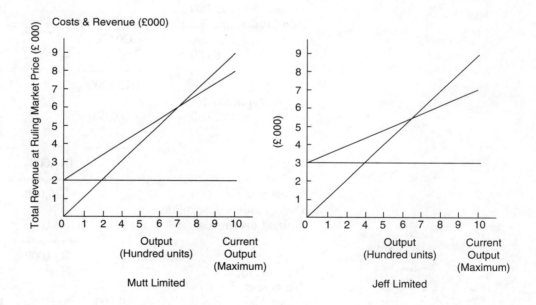

(London 1992)

TUTOR'S ANSWER

1 This is a very complicated question, covering much of the syllabus devoted to absorption and marginal costing. It is for this reason that it has been included here for a Tutor's Answer. The time spent working through the question will serve to reinforce many important aspects of this part of the syllabus.

a) *Barmik Ltd*
    The normal level of production:

$$\frac{\text{Total budgeted fixed manufacturing overhead}}{\text{Fixed manufacturing overhead per unit}} = \frac{£200,000}{£10} = \underline{20,000 \text{ units}}$$

b) Actual production (units):

	QUARTER I	II
Sales	16,000	24,000
Add closing stock	12,000	6,000
	28,000	30,000
Less opening stock	5,000	12,000
Production	23,000	18,000

c) Profit statement (absorption costing):

	£	£	£	£
Sales @ £60: 16 000		960,000		
: 24 000				1,440,000
Opening stock @ £40:				
: 5 000	200,000			
: 12 000			480,000	
Add production @ £40:				
: 23 000	920,000			
: 18 000			720,000	
	1,120,000		1,200,000	
Less closing stock				
@ £40 : 12,000	480,000			
: 6,000			240,000	
		640,000		960,000
Gross profit		320,000		480,000
Over/(under) absorption of fixed overheads*:		30,000		(20,000)
		350,000		460,000
Less selling & dist costs#:				
variable	96,000		144,000	
fixed	20,000		20,000	
		116,000		164,000
Net profit		234,000		296,000

* Note:

	QUARTER	
	I	II
Actual production	23,000	18,000
Normal production from (a)	20,000	20,000
	3,000	(2,000)
Fixed overhead over/under recovered @ £10/unit	30,000	(20,000)

\# Note:

	QUARTER	
	I	II
Selling and distribution costs:		
Variable costs = 10% of sales:		
£960,000 × 10%	96,000	
£1,440,000 × 10%		144,000
Fixed costs = £80,000 p.a.		
Three months thus:	20,000	20,000

d)   Profit statement (marginal costing):

	£	£
Selling price/unit		60
Less variable costs:		
Production	30	
Selling &c	6	
		36
Contribution/unit		24

	QUARTER	
	I	II
Contribution/unit @ £24/unit:		
16 000	384,000	
24 000		576,000
Less fixed costs*:		
Production	200,000	200,000
Selling &c	20,000	20,000
	220,000	220,000
Net profit	164,000	356,000

* Note:

Fixed production overhead is given as £200 000 *per quarter*.
Fixed selling and distribution costs are £80 000 *per annum*:
Three months costs are thus £20 000.

e)   Profit reconciliation statement:

	QUARTER	
	I	II
Marginal cost profit	164,000	356,000
Fixed overhead content of:		
Stock increase: 7 000 × £10	70,000	
Stock decrease: 6 000 × £10		(60,000)
Absorption cost profit	234,000	296,000

Under absorption costing, fixed overheads are included in the product cost. When stocks increase, a proportion of the fixed costs are carried forward into the next period, relieving the current period of the burden. The current period's profits therefore increase. When stocks decrease, profits will also decrease.

Under marginal costing, all fixed costs are written off in the period in which they are incurred; they are not included in the stock valuations.

STUDENT'S ANSWER

2   a)   *Quacker Ltd: Budgeted profit statement:*

	COSTS		
		TOTAL	UNIT
	£000	£000	£
Sales (300 000 × £8)		2,400	8.00
Materials	570		
Labour	396		
Variable selling o/h			
(£120 + 1/3)	160		
Production o/h	150		
Distribution	105		
		1,381	4.60
Contribution		1,019	3.40
Fixed costs (£500 + 20%)		600	2.00
Budgeted profit		419	1.40

b)   Break-even points:

1992 contribution:

	Cost £000	Cost/unit £
Sales revenue: £1,800,000/200,000		9.00
Less variable costs:		
Materials	400	
Labour	240	
Production o/h	100	
Selling o/h	120	
Distribution o/h	70	
	930	4.65
Contribution		4.35

	1992	1993
Break-even output (units):	£500,000	£600,000
	£4.35	£3.4
=	114,943	176,471

The break-even point has changed because of;
a) reduced selling price, which has reduced the contribution per unit by £1 and
b) a 20 per cent increase in fixed costs.

Margin of Safety:

Percentage:	114,943	176,471
	200,000	300,000
=	57.5%	=59%
Units:	200,000 − 114,943	300,000 − 176,471
=	85,057 units	123,529 units

Whilst the margin of safety has been slightly increased, there is doubt over whether the new level of sales – 300 000 units – will be achieved.

c) *Desired sales volume:*

$$\frac{\text{Break-even point} + \text{desired profit}}{\text{Contribution}}$$

$$= \frac{£600,000 + £370,000}{£3.40}$$

= 285,294 units

OR   £2,282,352 at £8 unit

d) *Director's error:*
The director is wrong because net profit per unit is a combination of fixed costs and variable costs. Since fixed costs are constant, the cost per unit is valid only at a given level of output, and will change as more or less units are produced.

At 60% volume increase:

Contribution: 320,000 × £3.40	1,088,000
Less fixed costs	600,000
Profits	488,000

TUTOR'S COMMENTS

This is an excellent answer. The candidate has set the calculations out logically, and shown all the ancilliary workings. Thus, even if an arithmetical mistake were to have been made, the examiner is able easily to see where a mistake has arisen, and can award full principle marks.

OUTLINE ANSWERS

3 a) i) Marginal cost: price based upon variable cost of a product, i.e. cost which would be avoided if product not made or service not provided. Excludes fixed costs, because these already 'sunk' costs, to be incurred irrespective of level of output.

    ii) Full cost: price based upon variable costs and fixed costs.

b) In the long run, all costs must be covered: thus, marginal cost pricing can be seen as a short term approach. But, in long run all costs are variable, depends upon what is included in definition of variable costs.

c)

PRODUCT	C	E	H	I	V
Direct labour	14	8	22	18	26
Direct matls	8	10	13	12	17
Variable o/h	11	9	16	15	19
Marginal cost	33	27	51	45	62
Fixed costs	17	13	19	15	18
Total costs	50	40	70	60	80
Profit 20%	10	8	14	12	16
Full cost prices	60	48	84	72	96
Market prices	59	25	80	44	92
Make (*)	*		*		*

	(All)		(Recommended)	
	£	£	£	£
Sales (@ new mkt prices)		30,000		23,100
Less var costs	21 800		14 600	
fixed costs	8,200		8,200	
		30,000		22,800
Profit		NIL		300

4 a) i) Shows approximate profit or loss at different levels of sales volume within a limited range, by illustrating the relationship between costs, and revenues at different levels of output.

    ii) Limitations derive from the restrictive assumptions upon which B/E chart is based:
      – costs can be divided easily into fixed and variable costs
      – firm makes one product or product mix stays constant
      – there are no opening or closing stocks
      – there exists a linear relationship between costs and revenues.

b) M lower fixed costs than J; M higher variable costs than J; M breakeven at 7, J breakeven at 6; M margin of safety 3, J margin of safety 4; M profit of 1, J profit of 2.

Now attempt the review questions on page 315. The answers are given on page 327.

GETTING STARTED

A *budget* is a plan couched in monetary terms. It relates to a defined period of time and is drawn up and approved well before the period to which it refers. Usually, the plan will show the income which it is hoped to generate, and the expenditure likely to be incurred. It may also show the capital to be employed in achieving a stated objective.

Budgetary control refers to the establishment of financial plans which relate the responsibilities of individual managers to the requirements of a policy or course of action. An essential element of budgetary control is the continuous comparison of the actual results achieved with those budgeted (or planned) for. This comparison serves either to ensure that policy objectives are achieved, or to provide a basis for those objectives to be revised.

Chapter 12 described two of the essential activities of management as those of planning and control. Once the strategic plan has identified long-term objectives more detailed operational plans are needed to ensure that the agreed objectives are met: to ensure that decisions taken within individual departments do in fact help progress towards the firm's stated objectives.

A firm may therefore have many plans in force at the same time, some concerned with improving the quality of the product or service, some with employee relations or market share, others relating to research and development. The nature of each plan will largely determine how it is expressed: plans concerning product design may be couched in technical terms; plans about employee welfare may be in human relations terms. The budget, concerned with financial matters, appears in monetary terms, and since accounting is being studied here, it is financial plans that are discussed. Remember, however, that the budget may be just one of a number of plans which the firm may have devised.

BUDGETS AND BUDGETARY CONTROL

THE BUDGET PROCESS

CLASSIFICATION OF BUDGETS

THE LIMITING FACTOR

OPERATING BUDGETS

SALES BUDGETS

PRODUCTION BUDGETS

CASH BUDGETS

THE MASTER BUDGET

ADDITIONAL BUDGETS

FLEXIBLE BUDGETS

PURPOSE OF BUDGETS

ESSENTIAL PRINCIPLES

THE BUDGET PROCESS

In smaller businesses the drafting of a budget may be a relatively informal affair. Indeed, the budget may be no more than a few notes on a piece of paper – the sort of quick expenditure plan which many people make before going on holiday.

In medium and large firms the budgeting process is more formalised. Perhaps a budget committee chaired by the chief executive will be established, charged with the oversight of the budget preparation. The detailed budgeting operations may be made the responsibility of a senior member of the accounting staff who will act as the budget manager. The committee itself may comprise senior people from various departments: sales, purchasing, production, technical services, personnel. The committee will draft a general approach to be used when preparing the budget, and the budget manager will then adopt this approach when producing the budget proper.

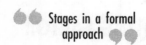 Tends to become the task of senior management

In smaller firms the chief accountant or the cost accountant may undertake the preparation of the budget. In any event, the budget tends to become the task of a firm's senior management.

The period for which a budget is prepared and used – the *budget period* – may be any length of time. In practice, budgets are usually prepared for periods of three, six or twelve months, usually to coincide with the firm's financial periods.

Irrespective of the method used, or of the budget period, any formal approach will normally incorporate the following stages:

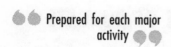 Stages in a formal approach

1. Issuing of instructions to departments to ensure a uniform presentation of information, and to ensure that deadlines are met.
2. Offering of historical and other information to help managers in their forecasting.
3. Receipt and checking of budget estimates from the departments.
4. Helping managers to resolve any difficulties they encounter, and assisting them to revise estimates where necessary.
5. Submitting departmental budgets to the budget committee and producing any necessary explanations.
6. Preparation of a master budget from the departmental submissions. A master budget summarises the departmental budgets, and as such it forms an expression of the firm's overall objectives for the period.

Thus, budgets are prepared for each of the major activity areas, and are revised in the light of general policy decisions. Budgets may be prepared for:

Prepared for each major activity

(a) Sales.
(b) Production.
(c) Purchasing.
(d) Cash.
(e) Research and development.
(f) Personnel.
(g) Administration.

Each of these departmental budgets will contribute towards the firm's master budget.

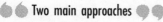 Two main approaches

There are two main approaches to the drawing up of budgets. Budget managers can either devise the budget themselves, and seek to get senior colleagues to impose it upon the organisation, or they can involve as many managerial colleagues as possible in an effort to engage them in setting their own budgets. The first approach is likely to be resented by those upon whom the budget is imposed, and the whole system of budgetary control will be brought into disrepute; it is far better to harness the knowledge and expertise of the managerial team as a whole in an effort to obtain some consensus over budgetary levels.

CLASSIFICATION OF BUDGETS

Budgets can be classified into two types:

1. *Operating budgets* which have to do with sales, production, and day-to-day cash budgets.
2. *Capital budgets* which have to do with the long-term provision of resources. They include such matters as fixed assets, working capital, equity and loan capital, and long-term cash budgets.

Whilst operating budgets may be prepared for a six- or twelve-month period, depending upon the nature of the business and market conditions, capital budgets can be prepared for up to 20 years ahead. This is especially true in capital-intensive industries such as iron and steel-making, mining and shipbuilding. The preparation of capital budgets will be considered in Chapter 20.

THE LIMITING FACTOR

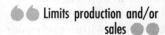 Limits production and/or sales

When compiling budgets it is important to consider the *limiting factor*, sometimes called the *principal budget factor* or *key factor*. This is the factor which limits production, and/or sales. It may be that the firm can sell as much of a product as it wishes, in which case its productive capacity will probably be the limiting factor. Alternatively, the firm may be able to make all that it can sell, in which case sales will be the limiting factor. Most firms are constrained by at least one limiting factor. Where there is more than one constraint, the key factor is the most important limiting factor at any one time. Examples of such factors are:

(a) *Materials*: availability of supply; legal or trade restrictions arising from quotas, licences, etc.
(b) *Labour*: general shortage; shortage of specific types of labour.
(c) *Productive capacity*: shortage of plant; lack of capital to finance plant; lack of physical space to accommodate new plant.
(d) *Management*: policy decisions, such as maintaining price by limiting output; shortage of trained management personnel.
(e) *Finance*: general lack of finance; lack of right sort of finance; debt or equity; long or short term.
(f) *Sales*: consumer demand; ineffective or insufficient advertising; shortage of good sales people.

It is important to assess the nature and influence of the limiting factor so as to ensure that operational budgets can be fulfilled. There is little point in a firm planning to sell half a million units if it has the capacity to make only a quarter of a million. Similarly, if the firm can obtain the materials, plant and labour to produce one million units, there is little point in planning to increase production to this level if only half a million units can be sold.

OPERATING BUDGETS

If sales are the limiting factor, then the operating budgets will be prepared by working from the sales budget. If the firm can estimate how many units of each product it can sell month by month during the period, then it can work back from this figure to estimate production and stock levels. If more is produced than can be sold, stocks will increase: if sales exceed production, then stocks will decrease (Figure 18.1).

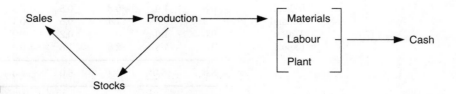

Fig. 18.1 Sequence of operating budgets.

Once an estimate is made of monthly production levels, then the firm's requirements for materials, labour and plant can be estimated. With this information, and information concerning sales, a cash budget can be drawn up, showing the firm's flow of cash over the period.

If, however, it is productive capacity which is the limiting factor, then the sales budget will be determined by output, as will the materials and labour budgets.

SALES BUDGETS

The sales budget is one of the most difficult to prepare, since it is not easy to forecast customers' future demands, nor the effect of a competitor's action upon a firm's share of the market. Two approaches can be adopted:

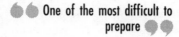 **One of the most difficult to prepare**

1. The firm can draw up a statistical forecast based upon the effects of the general economic climate upon its own markets and upon how it is thought competitors will react.
2. The firm can take an introspective stance and obtain the views of its sales force about likely future trends.

In practice, a firm is likely to combine both approaches in producing its sales budget. The budget may be produced either in terms of physical units, or in terms of monetary values.

Estimates will be needed for each of the firm's products, for sales within each sales area, and for sales made by each sales person. Information concerning past periods will be used as a basis from which to make projections, and month by month figures will be produced, since the actual timing of sales has a distinct bearing upon a firm's cash flow.

A firm's sales budget for the first six months of 1994 may therefore have been prepared as Table 18.1 where forecasted monthly sales are shown by type of product.

Similar budgets may be produced for each product, and a secondary summary prepared showing sales, for each area and each product (Table 18.2).

Note that sales in Scotland show an increase in March, because the firm hopes to supply a major customer. During February, March and April a large export order is

Table 18.1

Edgar Industries plc
Sales budget: Jan–June 1994 — product (00 tonnes)

	J	F	M	A	M	J
Brass	8	10	12	6	4	4
Copper	14	12	10	8	4	2
Nickel	12	14	16	14	8	6
Lead	10	8	10	6	6	4
Tin	16	18	20	12	8	6
	60	62	68	46	30	22

Table 18.2

Edgar Industries plc
Sales budget: Jan–June 1994 sales of brass by area (00 tonnes)

	J	F	M	A	M	J
N. England	2.2	2.6	3.6	1.6	1.2	1.2
S. England	2.6	2.8	2.8	1.2	1.0	0.8
Ireland	0.8	1.0	0.8	0.8	0.4	0.4
Scotland	1.0	0.8	1.4	0.6	0.4	0.6
Wales	0.6	1.0	0.6	0.2	0.2	0.4
Export	0.8	1.8	2.8	1.6	0.8	0.6
	8.0	10.0	12.0	6.0	4.0	4.0

anticipated. Generally, however, sales are seen to fall as the year progresses, since it is felt that demand will weaken.

PRODUCTION BUDGETS

Where sales is the limiting factor, then the production budget will follow on from it. Again, the production budget, like the sales budget, may be expressed either in terms of physical units or in financial terms. Whichever approach is adopted – and in practice summaries in both forms may be produced – the firm will need to make a decision about stock levels, since items produced but not sold will go into stock, whilst items will be drawn from stock where sales exceed output. Stocks thus tend to be the buffer by which sales and output are matched.

In industries where sales fluctuate from one season to another, a firm may decide to produce for stock in slack periods, and to draw from stock during busy times. In this way production levels can be evened out over a period. Generally, management and production staff favour even production flows since it makes planning much easier, regular times can be set aside for maintenance, and the work force knows what hours will be required: it makes for a settled life.

EXAMPLE 1

Edgar Industries wishes to maintain an even production flow of copper items, with a maximum output per month of 800 tonnes.

Required:
Calculate what the stock levels need to be at the beginning of 1994 if the sales budget figures shown in Table 18.1 are to be met.

Solution:

Edgar Industries plc

Copper: production budget: Jan–June 1994 (00 tonnes)

	J	F	M	A	M	J
Opening stock	12	6	2	Nil	Nil	4
Add: Production	8	8	8	8	8	8
	20	14	10	8	8	12
Less: Sales	14	12	10	8	4	2
Closing stock	6	2	Nil	Nil	4	10

TUTOR'S COMMENTS

Begin by assuming a nil stock at the beginning of 1994. The production budget would be as Table 18.3.

Table 18.3

Edgar Industries plc
Copper: production budget: Jan–June 1994 (00 tonnes)

	J	F	M	A	M	J
Opening stock	—	(6)	(10)	(12)	(12)	(8)
Add: Production	8	8	8	8	8	8
	8	2	(2)	(4)	(4)	—
Less: Sales	14	12	10	8	4	2
Closing stock	(6)	(10)	(12)	(12)	(8)	(2)

During January 800 tonnes are to be produced – the maximum output – but 1,400 tonnes are to be sold according to the sales budget. This gives a deficit at the end of January of 600 tonnes. This deficit is carried forward to February, when a further 800 tonnes are produced, and 1,200 tonnes sold: giving a deficit of 1,000 tonnes. In March, the deficit rises to 1,200 tonnes, which is maintained during April, before falling to 800 tonnes in May and 200 tonnes in June.

If it is required to maintain normal working during 1994 without resorting to overtime, the firm must have a stock of copper products on hand at the beginning of January 1994 of at least 1,200 tonnes – the maximum shortfall predicted. With such an opening stock, the production budget becomes as in the solution above.

Should the firm not wish to run stocks down to zero in March and April, then opening stocks in January would need to be increased by the minimum stock level required.

It may not, of course, be possible to build up such stocks by the beginning of January. Accordingly, arrangements may be made to work overtime to build up stocks during January and February. If the maximum stock figure which could be built up by the beginning of January 1994 was 800 tonnes, then at least an additional 400 tonnes would need to be produced in January and February to maintain sales. If also we assume that Edgar Industries do not wish stocks to fall below 200 tonnes, and that overtime working is to be equalised over January and February:

	Tonnes
Minimum stock requirements at 1 Jan 1994	1,200
Less: maximum possible at 1 Jan 1994	800
	400
Add: Minimum stock required	200
Extra production necessary	600

Therefore, an extra 300 tonnes per month would need to be produced, during January and February to give a revised budget as Table 18.4.

Table 18.4

Edgar Industries plc
Copper: production budget: Jan–June 1994 (00 tonnes)

	J	F	M	A	M	J
Opening stock	8	5	4	2	2	6
Add: Production	11	11	8	8	8	8
	19	16	12	10	10	14
Less: Sales	14	12	10	8	4	2
Closing stock	5	4	2	2	6	12

In some industries it is not possible to produce large stocks for periods of peak demand. Certain food products must be consumed within specific periods after manufacture. In such cases, production must be varied to keep stocks at a minimum.

EXAMPLE 2

A yogurt factory has the following estimated sales pattern; the figures are given in thousands of hectolitres.

March	10	June	18
April	12	July	20
May	16	August	22

Required:
Assume that stocks are to be kept at 2,000 hl until the end of May, and at 4,000 hl thereafter. Calculate what the production should be if the opening stock in March is 2,000 hl.

Solution:

Yoghurt: production budget, March–Aug 1994 (000 hl)

	M	A	M	J	J	A
Opening stock	2	2	2	2	4	4
Add: Production	10	12	16	20	20	22
	12	14	18	22	24	26
Less: Sales	10	12	16	18	20	22
Closing stock	2	2	2	4	4	4

TUTOR'S COMMENTS

As the budget shows, production must equal sales until June, when an additional 2,000 hl must be produced to raise the desired stock level from 2,000 hl to 4,000 hl.

By planning in this way, firms can estimate when their peak production times are likely to be. They can then ensure that the necessary labour and materials are available to meet requirements. This is especially important where production has to vary from month to month, and where there is a time lag in the receipt of raw materials. Hence it may be that the yogurt firm has to order its flavouring materials two months in advance. By drafting its production budget in the manner shown, the firm can see just how much flavouring to order in June to support August's production.

CASH BUDGETS

Since both sales and production budgets have an influence upon the firm's cash flow, it is important to produce an estimate of likely cash balances at the end of each month for the period covered by the budget.

Cash budgets include a firm's cash and bank balances. These balances perform three functions:

1. They help to ensure that sufficient cash is available when needed.
2. They reveal any expected cash shortage, so that a loan or an overdraft can be negotiated in good time.
3. They reveal cash surpluses which can then be loaned or invested.

Producing a cash budget is a three-stage process, comprising:

(a) receipts schedule;
(b) payments schedule;
(c) cash budget summary.

The receipts schedule shows how each month's cash inflows are to be built up: receipts from customers, tax rebates, additional capital received, sale of assets, etc. In contrast, the payments schedule shows likely cash outflows each month: payment for labour, materials, overheads etc. The budget summary brings both of these schedules together to reveal the net effect each month of estimated inflows and outflows. Note that the cash budget records estimates of *actual* receipts and outgoings: non-cash expenses such as depreciation are not included.

EXAMPLE 3

Comberton Products has produced the following estimates for the first half of 1994.

Comberton Products

Estimated receipts & payments: Jan–June 1994 (£000)

Month	Sales	Materials	Wages	Overheads
Jan	172.4	39.6	7.4	119.0
Feb	179.3	41.8	7.7	116.4
Mar	196.6	46.3	8.5	127.5
Apr	133.5	29.6	5.8	86.2
May	87.3	19.2	3.7	57.6
Jun	68.2	14.5	2.5	41.7
	837.3	191.0	35.6	548.4

The cash balance on 1 January was expected to be £11,000. During April major plant repairs are planned; these will cost £21,000 and will be paid for in May. Generally, materials are paid for after three months and customers pay after two months. Materials payments outstanding at 1 January 1994 were expected to be: October £38,200, November £33,400, December £26,500. Debts from customers outstanding were estimated to be: November £127,600, and December £105,300. Wages are paid in the month they fall due, and overheads are paid one month after they have been incurred: December's were £98,200.

TUTOR'S COMMENTS

The first stage in constructing the cash budget is to prepare the receipts schedule. Since all of Comberton's income derives from sales, this is quite straight forward. Customers are expected to take two months to pay, thus November's sales should be received in January; December's in February, etc. Had the firm expected any other income, it would be recorded on the schedule for the month of its expected receipt:

Receipts schedule (£000)

	J	F	M	A	M	J
Sales	127.6	105.3	172.4	179.3	196.6	133.5

The payments schedule is a little more involved, since payments will be made for materials (three months in arrears), for labour, and for overheads (one month in arrears). October's materials are to be paid in January; November's in February, etc. Similarly, December's overheads are payable in January; January's in February, etc. We must also allow for the payment of the plant repairs in May:

Payments schedule (£000)

	J	F	M	A	M	J
Materials	38.2	33.4	26.5	39.6	41.8	46.3
Labour	7.4	7.7	8.5	5.8	3.7	2.5
Overheads	98.2	119.0	116.4	127.5	86.2	57.6
Repairs					21.0	
	143.8	160.1	151.4	172.9	152.7	106.4

Once separate schedules have been produced for monthly receipts and payments, the two schedules can be brought together to provide a cash budget summary. The summary begins with the opening balance of £11,000 to which receipts are added, and from which payments are deducted, to give a closing balance at the end of January of £5,200 overdrawn. The closing balance of January becomes the opening balance of February, to which February's receipts are added, and from which February's payments are deducted.

By making monthly adjustments in this way the summary shows the anticipated state of the firm's finances at each month end. Remember, however, that we are dealing with *estimates*, not actual figures: we are projecting into the future. Actual figures may turn out to be different.

Solution:

Comberton Products
Cash budget summary: Jan–June 1994 (£000)

	J	F	M	A	M	J
Opening balance (overdrawn)	11.0	(5.2)	(60.0)	(39.0)	(32.6)	11.3
Add: receipts	127.6	105.3	172.4	179.3	196.6	133.5
	138.6	100.1	112.4	140.3	164.0	144.8
Less: payments	143.8	160.1	151.4	172.9	152.7	106.4
Closing balance (overdrawn)	(5.2)	(60.0)	(39.0)	(32.6)	11.3	38.4

From the solution it can be seen that Comberton Products is in need of additional funds to finance overspending from January until April, unless, of course, customers can be persuaded to pay more quickly, and creditors can be made to wait longer. Only in May, when sales made in February begin to work their way through the cycle, does the firm begin to balance its cash flows.

Equipped with the budget, Comberton's management can see the effects of the timing of receipts and payments upon the firm's cash balance. For example, how farsighted not to pay for the plant repairs until May: had the money been paid in April, the deficit then would have been even greater, although May's balance would have been larger, too. Comberton can now attempt to build up its cash reserves during 1993 in an effort to generate a larger opening balance on 1 January 1994, and thus to reduce, or remove, the deficits; or it can approach a bank for a loan or an overdraft to finance the overspending until May.

THE MASTER BUDGET

When all of the operational budgets have been completed – and only three have been studied here: there will be many more in a firm – then the budget manager, or whoever is carrying out these functions, will drawn them all together into a *master budget*. This is really a budgeted set of final accounts prepared for the full budget period (see question 3, p. 265).

Once the budget has been agreed, it acts as a guide to management: if individual results are not as planned, then enquiries must be mounted to discover the reasons. Each operational manager has his or her own budget: via the master budget, operational budgets are aggregated to see the total effect upon the firm. With such a framework, decisions taken within departments can be kept in accord with the firm's overall aims.

ADDITIONAL BUDGETS

Reference was made above to budgets other than sales, production and cash budgets: a few of these additional budgets are now briefly examined. Whether a firm uses all, some or none of them will depend upon its perception of their usefulness.

The *selling and distribution* budget will show the cost of selling and distributing the quantities of product identified in the sales budget. Any increase in sales is likely to bring increases in distribution costs.

The *purchases budget* relates the consumption of raw materials to stock levels and to purchases; in doing so it is intimately related to the production budget.

When the production budget is couched in financial terms, it may be known as a *production cost budget*. Such budgets may be devised for products or for departments. Deriving from the production cost budget may be budgets for raw materials, labour and overheads.

The *plant usage budget* shows the machinery requirements necessary to meet the production budget. The plant usage budget identifies the machine loading in each department, and in doing so it highlights over- and under-loading well in advance, enabling the rescheduling of work to be planned.

An overloading in the plant usage budget may need to be met by the purchase of new equipment: the *capital expenditure budget* lists planned expenditure here. It also identifies modifications to existing plant, improvements, replacements and extensions. Clearly, such investment will require funding, and there will be a direct impact upon the firm's cash budget.

FLEXIBLE BUDGETS

The value of a budgetary control system lies in the comparison which it allows between actual results and planned results. However, actual and budgeted figures may be different for two reasons.

First, although the balance of output and sales may be as planned, cost differences may arise. To the extent that these are within the control of individual managers, it seems reasonable that they should be accountable for such differences.

But differences may arise because although costs have remained as planned, the *volume* of output has changed. Such changes may arise largely as a result of senior management's decisions, and it would be wrong to hold individual managers responsible for differences arising from policy changes.

Consider the information in Table 18.5. The ore crushing manager would feel aggrieved if he were expected to incur the same variable overhead costs at an output of 6,000 tonnes as he was budgeted to incur at 4,000 tonnes. In an effort towards realistic cost control, therefore, many firms produce a series of budgets, each applicable to a particular activity level. Table 18.5 shows the ore crushing department's manufacturing overheads using a flexible approach. In practice, the budget would be far more detailed than is shown here.

The crushing department's overheads increase as output increases, but they do not vary in direct proportion to output: if they did, the variable overhead attributable to an output of 6,000 tonnes would be half as much again as at 4,000 tonnes i.e. £7,500 rather than £6,200. If the crushers' overheads are recovered on the basis of crusher hours worked, the rate at 4,000 tonnes is £7,500 ÷ 300 = £25; at 7,000 tonnes, the recovery rate reduces to £21.33 per crusher hour.

By using a flexible budget of this kind, the ore crushers' manager knows that if production is 4,000 tonnes, he must not incur variable overheads greater than £5,000; if production increases to 7,000 tonnes, the limit on variable overheads is £7,100.

PURPOSE OF BUDGETS

Budgets are concerned with planning and control. Planning involves drawing up a comprehensive and properly co-ordinated plan for the whole business: it is not just an array of unconnected aspirations. But plans are useless unless responsibility for various elements is allocated to individual managers, with performance standards clearly laid down. Thus, each departmental manager will be presented with a budget as a guide. By checking actual performance against planned performance, any differences are emphasised, and it is possible to mount any necessary investigations. It is this very feature – identifying the questions to be asked, and fixing responsibility for answering them – which is the very essence of budgetary control.

Table 18.5   **Ore Crushing Dept**

Manufacturing overhead budget: Jan–June 1993

	Weekly production (000 tonnes)			
	4	5	6	7
Variable overhead (£000)	5.0	5.5	6.2	7.1
Fixed overhead (£000)	2.5	2.5	2.5	2.5
	7.5	8.0	8.7	9.6
Crusher hours	300	350	400	450
Overhead rates per hour (£)	25	22.86	21.75	21.33

EXAMINATION QUESTIONS

1 a)   For each of the following, state three reasons why a firm may wish to keep:
   i)   a minimum stock level of finished goods; and
   ii)   an even level of production in the face of fluctuating demand.   *(6)*

   b)   The sales forecast for Douglas & Co for July–December 1993 is:

	J	A	S	O	N	D
Units	280	200	260	360	400	420

   Produce a production budget showing monthly opening and closing stock figures if the firm wishes to maintain an even level of producing 300 units each month, AND a minimum stock level of 150 units.
   What must the opening stock be at 1 July to achieve this?   *(5)*

   c)   Under what circumstances, in budgetary control, may a firm's productive capacity prove to be its limiting factor?   *(4)*

   (London 1990)

2   Springtime Ltd own a retail store that sells clothes.
   The company's summarised balance sheet as at 31 March 1992 was as follows.

	£000
Called-up capital	
200 000 £1 Ordinary	
shares fully paid	200
General reserve	150
Retained earnings	250
Current liabilities	90
	690
Fixed assets less	
depreciation	458
Current assets	
Stock and debtors	120
Balance at bank	112
	690

The company decided to open a branch store in a neighbouring town. The branch is to be opened on 1 May 1992 in newly acquired freehold premises which cost £100,000. Half of this cost will be paid on 1 May 1992, and the remainder on 1 July 1992. The refurbishment of these premises will cost £20,000, and this amount is due to be paid on 1 July 1992. All these amounts are paid by the company's main store.

Additional information.

(1)

		1992				
	ACTUAL SALES			FORECAST SALES		
	FEB	MAR	APR	MAY	JUN	JUL
	£	£	£	£	£	£
Main store	160 000	150 500	153 000	149 500	158 000	161 000
Branch	–	–	–	8 000	19 000	24 000

Main store: cash from sales is received two months after the month of sale.
Branch: cash from sales is received one month after the month of sale.
The branch will operate its own bank current account and receipts from debtors will be banked each day. The account was opened on 1 April 1992 with an initial balance of £20,000.

(2) The following fixed costs are paid:

Main store £15,000 every month.
Branch   £1,000 every month, except April.

As a cost transfer the company allocates £2,500 of the main store fixed costs every month (except April) to the branch.

(3) The company pays variable costs as follows:

	MAR	APR	MAY	JUN	JUL
	£	£	£	£	£
Main store	25,000	30,000	33,000	31,000	29,000
Branch	—	—	2,500	2,700	1,900

All variable costs are paid one month in arrears except that in May the branch is required to pay them in that month.

(4) The main store will be required to pay £5000 legal costs on 1 July 1992 in respect of the new freehold premises.

(5) Staff salaries paid:
Main store   £12,000 every month.
Branch   £1,000 every month, except April.

(6) Springtime Ltd are due to pay an interim ordinary share dividend of 5% on 1 July 1992.

(7) All goods for re-sale are bought by the main store and are charged to the branch store at cost price.

	FEB	MAR	APR	MAY	JUN	JUL
	£	£	£	£	£	£
Goods purchased by Main store	61,000	58,000	153,000	48,000	49,500	152,000
Goods received at Branch Store	—	—	8,000	12,000	23,000	24,000

Springtime Ltd receives two months credit on all of its clothing purchases. The branch remits payment for its goods to the main store by credit transfer at the end of the month of receipt.

(8) In order to fund further business development Springtime Ltd plans to issue £100,000 of 11% debentures at par on 1 July 1992. The issue is expected to be fully subscribed and the cash will be received on the same date.

(9) The branch store is scheduled to earn a 50% mark-up on cost.

REQUIRED

(a) Separate monthly cash budgets for each store for the four months ending 31 July 1992. *(15)*

(b) For the forecast period ending 31 July 1992:
   (i) A profit and loss statement for the branch;
   (ii) A report giving an assessment of the branch's expected profitability during this period. *(10)*

(AEB 1992)

3. The following information has been extracted from the books of Issa Ltd for the financial year ended 31 December 1990.

Trading and Profit and Loss Account
for the year ended 31 December 1990

	£000s		£000s
Opening stock	90		
Purchases	490	Sales	750
	580		
Less closing stock	80		
Cost of goods sold	500		
Gross profit	250		
	750		750

Administration		Gross profit	250
expenses	60		
Selling and distribution			
expenses	50		
Financial charges	20		
Depreciation of fixed			
assets	20		
Net profit	100		
	250		250

Balance sheet as at 31 December 1990

	£000s	£000s		£000s	£000s
Fixed assets			£1 Ordinary shares.		
at cost		750	Fully paid		200
less aggregate			9% £1 Preference		
depreciation		144	shares. Fully paid.		100
		606			
Current					
Stock		80	Share premium		150
Trade debtors	75		Retained earnings		350
Less provision					
for doubtful			Current liabilities		
debts	5	70	Trade creditors	50	
Balance at			Accrued expenses	6	56
bank	100	250			
		856			856

The company had commenced the preparation of its budget for the year ending 31 December 1991 and the following information is the basis of its forecast.

(1) An intensive advertising campaign will be carried out in the first six months of 1991 at a cost of £15,000. It is anticipated that as a result of this, sales will increase to £900,000 in 1991.

(2) The gross profit/sales ratio will be increased to 35%.

(3) A new stock control system is to be installed in 1991 and it is expected that the stock level will be reduced by £15,000 as compared to the 1990 closing stock.

(4) Land and buildings which cost £50,000 (nil depreciation to date) will be sold in 1991 for £200,000 cash. Half of the proceeds will be used to buy ordinary shares in another company, Yates Ltd, at an agreed price of £4 per share. (Ignore share commissions etc.)

(5) The company planned to capitalise some of its reserves on 1 April 1991. New ordinary shares are to be issued on a 1 for 2 basis. Half the funds required will be drawn from the share premium account and the remainder will be taken from retained earnings.

(6) Preference share dividends will be paid on 1 May 1991 and 1 November 1991.
The company planned to pay an interim ordinary share dividend on the increased share capital of 2.5p per share on 1 July 1991.
No final dividend is proposed.

(7) Owing to inflation revenue expenses are expected to rise as follows:
Administration expenses will increase by 6%.
Selling and distribution expenses will increase by 8%.
The advertising campaign expenses are in addition to the increase above.
Financial charges will increase by 4%.
These percentage increases are based on the figures for the year ended 31 December 1990.

(8) With the projected sales increases trade debtors are expected to rise to £100 000 by 31 December 1991. The provision for doubtful debts is to be adjusted to $7\frac{1}{2}\%$ of forecast trade debtors.

(9) Other forecast figures as at 31 December 1991.

	£000s
Balance at bank	350.1
Trade creditors	56.0
Expense creditors	15.0

(10) Depreciation of 10% per annum on cost is to be provided on £600,000 of the company's fixed assets.

REQUIRED

(a) A budget trading, profit and loss and appropriation account for the year ending 31 December 1991.
Show the full details of the trading account.   *(10)*

(b) A budgeted balance sheet as at 31 December 1991.   *(8)*

(c) What advantages accrue to a business by preparing a budget with respect to
  (i) forecast profitability;
  (ii) forecast liquidity?   *(7)*
(AEB 1991)

4 a) Define the terms;
    – budget
    – budgetary control   *(3)*

   b) What is meant by the term 'flexing' a budget?   *(3)*

   c) From the following information, calculate the overhead recovery rates per blending hour for each level of activity, showing clearly how the differences arise in the rates calculated;

Blending Department
Manufacturing Overhead Budget: September–December, 1993

	Monthly Production (000 kg)		
	3	5	6
Variable overheads (£000)	6.5	7.2	8.1
Fixed overheads (£000)	3.5	3.5	3.5
Hours worked	320	360	400

(6)

   d) Explain the significance of the differences calculated in (c) above.   *(3)*
(London 1993)

TUTOR'S ANSWER

2 a)

SPRINGTIME LTD: MAIN STORE

	A	M	J	J
Receipts:				
Balance b/f	112,000	167,000	164,500	127,500
Sales	160,000	150,500	153,000	149,500
Goods to branch	8,000	12,000	23,000	24,000
Debentures	—	—	—	100,000
	280,000	329,500	340,500	401,000
Payments:				
Premises	—	50,000	—	50,000
Refurbishment	—	—	—	20,000
Fixed costs	15,000	15,000	15,000	15,000
Variable costs	25,000	30,000	33,000	31,000
Legal costs	—	—	—	5,000
Salaries	12,000	12,000	12,000	12,000
Purchases	61,000	58,000	153,000	48,000
Interim dividend	—	—	—	10 000
	113,000	165,000	213,000	191,000
Balance c/f	167,000	164,500	127,500	210,000

SPRINGTIME LTD: BRANCH STORE

	A	M	J	J
Receipts:				
Balance b/f	20 000	12 000	(4 500)	(21 500)
Sales	—	—	8 000	19 000
	20 000	12 000	3 500	2 500
Payments:				
Fixed costs	—	1 000	1 000	1 000
Variable costs	—	2 500	—	2 700
Salaries	—	1 000	1 000	1 000
Main store: goods	8 000	12 000	23 000	24 000
	8 000	16 500	25 000	28 700
Balance c/f	12 000	(4 500)	(21 500)	(31 200)

b) i)

Springtime Ltd
Branch Store Profit & Loss Statement
for the Three Months Ending 31 July 1992

Sales		51,000
Less: Cost of sales		34,000
Gross profit:		17,000
Staff salaries	3,000	
Variable costs	7,100	
Fixed costs	3,000	
Allocated costs	7,500	
		20,600
Net loss		3,600

ii) Whilst sales are expected to rise significantly over the period, earning a $33\frac{1}{3}$ per cent gross profit, overall the branch is expected to record a net loss for the period. This may be acceptable during the initial stages of a newly-established business, but will require careful monitoring.

In particular, the variable expenses should be kept under review. Deducting the allocation costs of £7,500 results in a net profit of £3,900; and generally, the branch would appear to be sufficiently promising for it to continue.

STUDENT'S ANSWER TO QUESTION 3

a)

Issa Ltd
Budgeted Trading and Profit and Loss Appropriation
Account for the year ending 31 December 1991

	£	£
Sales		900,000
Less		
Opening stock	80,000	
Purchases	570,000	
	650,000	
Less closing stock	65,000	
		585,000
Gross profit		315,000
Administrative Exp	63,600	
Selling & distribution		
exps 54,000		
+Advertising 15,000	69,000	
Increase in provision		
for doubtful debts	2,500	
Financial charges	20,800	
Depreciation of fixed		
assets	60,000	215,900
		99,100
Add profit on sales of		
land & buildings		150,000
Net profit		249,100
Add retained earnings 1.1.90		350,000
		599,100
Less bonus issue		50,000
		549,100
Dividends		
Interim: Preference	4,500	
Ordinary	7,500	
Final: Preference	4,500	16,500
Retained earnings		532,600

(b)

Issa Ltd
Forecast Balance Sheet
as at 31 December 1990

	AT COST £000	AGGREG. DEP £000	NET £000
FIXED ASSETS	700	204	496
Investment: 25 000			
Shares in Yates Ltd			100
			596
CURRENT ASSETS			
Stock		65	
Trade debtors	100		
less provision for			
doubtful debts	7.5	92.5	
Balance at bank		350.1	
		507.6	
Less			
CURRENT LIABILITIES			
Trade creditors	56		
Expense creditors	15	71.0	
			436.6
			1,032.6
Financed by			
£1 ordinary shares. Fully paid			300
9% £1 Preference shares. Fully paid			100
			400
Share premium			100
Retained earnings			532.6
			1,032.6

c) i) Advantages accruing:
Business can aim to make a profit and take managerial action to achieve it.
With profit planning the control and development of a business may be exercised rather than leaving it to chance.
Enables a whole range of planning decisions to be made:
e.g. capital expenditure decisions
tax planning
dividend forecasts
financing of strategy planning
product development

ii) Manage working capital to accommodate peaks/troughs of funds flow.
Manage cash balances to best effect
Finance deficits
Invest surpluss
Finance fixed asset purchases
Can ensure that business resources are available for –
Revenue payments
Stock purchases
Make decisions on the control of debtors/creditors.

TUTOR'S COMMENTS

Note how clearly the candidate has presented the answer. The headings are unambiguous, and the adjustments appear on the face of the accounts/statements. It would have been better to have identified the Cost of Goods Sold figure of £585,000 in the trading account; and the Working Capital figure of £71,000 in the balance sheet; don't forget these simple matters. Part (c) seemed rushed and written in note form, but all major parts were covered nevertheless. Otherwise, a very good answer.

OUTLINE ANSWERS

1 a) Minimum stock: stockholding costs; meet surges in demand; insurance against breakdowns in production, strikes; interruptions to obtaining supplies of parts, materials; control price of finished items.

Even production: employees may prefer it; enables planned maintenace; eases purchasing of materials, stockholding; eases employment of labour and acquisition of equipment; eases planning generally.

b) Production: $6 \times 300 = 1,800$; less sales of 1,920 gives a shortfall of 120. Thus open production budget with 120 as opening stock;

	J	A	S	O	N	D
Opening stock	120	140	240	280	220	120
Production	300	300	300	300	300	300
	420	440	540	580	520	420
Sales	280	200	260	360	400	420
Closing stock	140	240	280	220	120	—

December gives stock-out, thus increase opening stock to meet minimum stock level requested: $120 + 150 = 270$;

Revised	290	390	430	370	270	150

c) Limiting factor: a factor which at any time or over a period may limit the activity of a business. Production may be the limiting factor when the firm's plant is unable to produce sufficient quantities to meet demand.

4 a) *Budget:* a plan qualified in money terms, prepared and approved prior to a defined period of time. *Budgetary control:* the establishment of budgets relating the responsibilities of executives to the requirements of a policy, and the continuous comparison of actual with budgeted results.

b) Flexible budget: a budget which recognises the difference in behaviour between fixed and variable costs in relation to fluctuations in output, turnover, or other variable factors such as number of employees, and which changes appropriately with such fluctuations.

c)

Blending Department
Manufacturing Overhead Budget: September–December, 1993

	Monthly Production (000 kg)		
	3	5	6
Variable o/h per hour	20.3125	20.00	20.25
Fixed o/h per hour	10.9375	9.72	8.75
	31.25	29.72	29.00

d) Output produced during a month when 3,000 kg was produced would attract overheads of £31.25 per hour whereas output produced when 4,000 was produced would attract overheads of £29.00 per hour. The budget recognises the difference in behaviour between total variable overheads – which increase as production increases and total fixed overheads – which remain constant as production increases.

Now attempt the review questions on page 316. The answers are given on page 328.

CHAPTER 19

GETTING STARTED

Previous chapters have been concerned with the *actual* costs incurred in production: materials, labour, and overheads. Standard costing is concerned with what costs *ought* to have been. Standards are set in advance for levels of performance and prices of resources. Actual levels of performance and the actual prices paid are then compared with the standards: any differences between the standard and the actual values are known as *variances*.

The benefit of standard costing arises in that it prompts questions to be asked as to why the variances have arisen: if there is a variance, something has not gone according to plan. And in this respect, actual costs that are less than standard costs merit just as much investigation as where actual costs are greater than standard.

Standard costing also enables organisations to adopt the practice of *management by exception*, so that management's attention can be concentrated upon those areas which differ from the plan, on the assumption that for most of the time, most of the areas remain as planned.

STANDARD COSTING

VARIANCES

MANAGEMENT BY EXCEPTION

SETTING STANDARDS

THE STANDARD HOUR

MATERIAL VARIANCES

LABOUR VARIANCES

OVERHEAD VARIANCES

VARIABLE OVERHEADS

FIXED OVERHEADS

THE VARIANCE ACCOUNT

ESSENTIAL PRINCIPLES

In previous chapters the discussion has been mainly concerned with the actual costs incurred during production: materials, labour and overheads. However, using actual costs can lead to difficulties.

EXAMPLE 1

Hauxton Industries has undertaken two identical jobs – (X) and (Y) – for the same customer. Hauxton fixes its prices by adding 20 per cent to the total costs incurred. The details of the two jobs are as follows:

Hauxton Industries

		(X)		(Y)	Differences
Primary process		£		£	£
Direct materials		150		150	
Direct labour	10 @ £5	50	12 @ £5	60	10
Overheads	10 @ £6	60	12 @ £6	72	12
		260		282	22
Secondary process					
Direct materials		46		48	2
Direct labour	8 @ £4.50	36		36	
Overheads	6 @ £8	48	8 @ £8	64	16
		390		430	40
Profit 20%		78		86	8
		468		516	48

Required:
Show how the differences in selling price have arisen.

TUTOR'S COMMENTS

Overheads in the primary process are recovered on the basis of £6 for each direct labour hour; since job (X) takes 10 hours, the overhead incurred is 10 × £6 = £60. Job (Y) takes 12 labour hours, so that overheads here are 12 × £6 = £72. Therefore, with the £10 difference in labour costs and the £12 difference in overheads, job (Y) costs £22 more than job (X) when leaving the primary process.

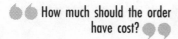
How much should the order have cost?

In the secondary process machine hours provide the basis for overhead recovery: job (X) incurs six machine hours, which at £8 per hour attracts overheads of 6 × £8 = £48. Job (Y) incurs eight machine hours, to attract 8 × £8 = £64. By the time the jobs have left the secondary process, the cost difference has grown to £40.

When the 20 per cent is added for profit, it is seen that identical jobs performed by the same firm in the same factory give two different prices: £468 for (X) and £516 for (Y). How can Hauxton justify the £48 difference to the customer?

To explain that labour was less efficient in working on (Y) than on (X) in the primary process would not be acceptable to the client. To argue that there was a greater waste of material on (Y) than on (X) in the secondary process, resulting in an additional two hours of machine time, would equally find disfavour with the customer.

In order to avoid these situations, and to increase managerial control over activities, many firms operate a system of *standard costing*. What Hauxton Industries need to know is, how much *should* the orders (X) and (Y) have cost, and why were actual costs different?

By determining in advance what costs should be under particular working conditions, and by comparing actual costs with these standards, *variances* are produced. The firm must decide in advance what costs ought to be for each item of production and for each stage of production. Thus, the firm calculates for each item and for each production activity a standard cost made up of a standard material cost, a standard labour cost, and a standard overhead cost, as follows:

Variance	=	Standard cost − actual cost
Favourable or positive variance	=	Actual cost is less than standard cost
Adverse or negative variance	=	Actual cost is more than standard cost

Variances act as indicators

By examining the variances, a firm's management can identify those factors which have caused the differences between actual costs and standard costs, and can decide what action to take to remedy matters. Variances, therefore, act as indicators of those areas requiring management attention. Note that favourable (positive) variances demand the same diligent investigation as adverse (negative) (sometimes called 'unfavourable') variances, since they also represent a departure from the standards set.

MANAGEMENT BY EXCEPTION

A system of standard costing enables a firm to operate the principle of '*management by exception.*' This assumes that for most of the time most of the activities are proceeding as planned, so that management's attention can concentrate upon those activities which are diverging from the plan. Since these should be the minority, they should also be the exceptions.

Many managers in industry and commerce find themselves inundated with information, much of it of a routine nature merely confirming that matters are going according to plan. The adoption of the management-by-exception approach helps to screen out the bulk of the information, leaving managers free to concentrate upon those areas where problems are developing.

Concentrates on divergencies from the plan

With standard costing, the production of any kind of variance – favourable or adverse – acts as a trigger for management action. When a variance is produced it indicates a difference between planned and actual cost. Management is therefore alerted to mount the necessary investigations to find the reasons for the differences. Where planned cost and actual cost coincides, there will be no variance emerging, and managers can assume that the agreed plans are being followed.

Note that management by exception is not the same as *management by crisis*. Management by crisis arises where managers' attention is constantly being diverted to the latest urgent problem. There is little or no planned approach and almost no real sense of direction. Management by exception, on the other hand, is a deliberate policy of concentrating on those areas where plans are not being met. With management by exception allied to standard costing, all aspects of the firm's operations are planned in some detail so that day-to-day operations further the overall objectives of the organisation.

Not the same as 'management by crisis'

SETTING STANDARDS

When establishing what costs ought to be, three levels of activity can be used as a basis:

1. *Average expected level of activity*. This standard is based upon past experience. It is seen as being easily attainable, and as a result it may lead to inefficient working and the condoning of complacency.
2. *Maximum possible level of activity*. This is based upon the maximum levels that are theoretically possible: the output of the best worker; the best ever production run of a type of machine. However, standards that are barely attainable tend to discourage people, and can bring the whole system into ridicule.
3. *Efficient working level of activity*. This standard is based upon what can reasonably be expected with efficient management. It is a far more realistic level to aim for, since with effort it marks a standard which can reasonably be achieved.

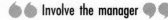

Involve the manager

Generally, in standard costing, the standards will be set by the firm's cost accountant after discussions with other colleagues. The manager of the department for which standards are being set should be involved, as will work study engineers, production engineers, buyers and personnel staff.

Standards will be agreed for each process in each department under the headings of: direct material; direct labour; variable overhead; fixed overhead. These standards may be recorded upon a *standard cost card* – one card for each product and for each process. The card will show the detailed build-up of the standard costs, and a summary. With computerised methods, such information is unlikely to be kept on actual cards, but on computer files instead.

The materials content of each product will be based upon technical specifications; these will include not just the basic raw materials, but also items bought in, sub-units, etc. Allowance will also be made for normal losses by way of evaporation, machine loss, scrap, etc.

Once the quantities have been calculated by the production engineers, the buying department will calculate the anticipated prices to be paid over the budget period. Past experience may be used as a guide, but it is not generally acceptable merely to take past costs and to adjust for price changes; this will merely compound any errors or inefficiencies in previous practice. The prices used must relate to future buying policies, discounts likely to be offered by suppliers, price movements, delivery and packing charges.

Labour standards must be based upon the agreed methods of production, and will identify the grade of labour to be used, and the times to be taken on various tasks. Once these have been established, the personnel section can estimate, for each grade of worker, the wage rates likely to be in force during the budget period.

Overhead absorption rates, as discussed in Chapter 15, will be applied to products on the basis either of the standard labour hours or of the standard machine hours. Usually, to enable effective control, overheads are sub-divided into their fixed and variable elements, and separate absorption rates calculated for each. In setting standards for overheads it is necessary to agree the level of planned activity within the firm for the budget control.

The setting of the firm's selling prices is usually a top management decision, based upon their view of the market, the likely plans of competitors, production costs and expected consumer demand. The information provided by the firm's sales force will be crucial here. Once a standard selling price has been established for each product, the *standard sales margin* can be calculated:

$$\text{Standard sales margin} = \text{Standard price} - \text{Standard cost}$$

Standards must be reviewed periodically

Once standards are fixed, they must be reviewed from time to time to keep them relevant to current conditions, but the task of revision can be a lengthy one, and much of the value of standard costing lies in the ability to identify trends. Thus, in practice, small changes in wage rates, prices or materials usage are generally ignored over the short term, and once established standards tend not to be revised more than every three or six months. Once a revision is agreed, it is likely that the firm will wish to revise all of its standards at the same time, rather than opt for piecemeal revision, which would make comparisons between periods more difficult.

THE STANDARD HOUR

Production is often measured in terms of litres, kilograms or tonnes, and while this may be acceptable in certain circumstances there are occasions when it is less suitable. Thus, when considering different types of products which may be expressed in different measures, it may be more convenient to use a measure common to them all. With standard costing, especially in relation to standards for labour and overheads, production is often expressed in terms of *standard hours*.

A standard hour is the amount of work which can be done at a standard level of performance; it is expressed as a standard unit of work in a standard period of time. Note that standard hours are measures of the amount of work done in one hour; the term is not a measure of time.

For example, if 50 units of (A) can be produced in 10 hours, and 30 units of (B) in 15 hours, then a standard hour represents five units of (A) or two units of (B). Similarly, an output of 100 units of (A) or 40 units of (B) represents 20 standard hours. Various ratios can be used based upon the concept of standard hours.

The *productivity ratio* measures the efficiency with which the firm is operating. The ratio is calculated as:

$$\text{Productivity} = \frac{\text{Actual production (standard hours)}}{\text{Actual hours worked}} \times 100$$

Assume that a firm produces and sells garden sheds. The 'Rutland' can be made in 5 hours, the 'Westmoreland' in 15 hours. During May actual production is 25 'Rutland' and 10 'Westmoreland'.

The actual hours worked were 220:

		Standard hours
Rutland	25 at 5 hours	125
Westmoreland	10 at 15 hours	150
Actual production		275

The productivity ratio is:

$$\frac{275}{220} \times 100 = 125\%$$

The *production volume ratio* measures the level at which the firm is operating:

$$\text{Production volume} = \frac{\text{Actual production (standard hours)}}{\text{Budgeted production (standard hours)}} \times 100$$

If in the above example budgeted production in standard hours was:

		Standard hours
Rutland	20 at 5 hours	100
Westmoreland	12 at 15 hours	180
		280

the production volume ratio is:

$$\frac{275}{280} \times 100 = 98.2\%$$

A *capacity ratio* can be calculated, relating the actual number esf working hours to the budgeted number. In the example:

$$\frac{220}{280} \times 100 = 78.57\%$$

The answers to each of the three ratios can be checked using the relationship:

$$\frac{\text{Production}}{\text{volume}} = \frac{\text{Capacity}}{\text{ratio}} \times \frac{\text{Productivity}}{\text{ratio}}$$

$$\frac{275}{280} = \frac{220}{280} \times \frac{275}{220}$$

Cancelling out, the following is obtained:

$$\frac{275}{280} = \frac{275}{280}$$

$$= 98.2\%$$

MATERIAL VARIANCES

Material variances can be divided into price variances and usage variances. A *price variance* arises because the actual price paid for the material is different from the standard price. A *usage variance* arises where more or less of the material is used than has been allowed:

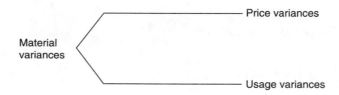

Consider the following:

	A	B	C
Standard price (litres)	£1.30	£1.20	£1.60
Standard usage (litres)	200	250	270
Actual price (litres)	£1.50	£1.20	£1.40
Actual usage (litres)	200	230	280

In producing a paint (A) a firm estimates that it should have incurred material costs of:

$$\underset{\text{standard price}}{£1.30} \times \underset{\text{standard usage}}{200 \text{ litres}} = £260$$

The actual material costs incurred were:

$$\underset{\text{actual price}}{£1.50} \times \underset{\text{actual usage}}{200 \text{ litres}} = £300$$

The difference between the standard cost £260 and the actual cost £300 is £40, and this arises solely because the price paid at £1.50 litre was greater than the standard price of £1.30. The amount used remained constant at 200 litres. Thus, we have an *adverse price variance* of £40. We know it is adverse because the actual price of £300 is greater than the planned price of £260.

If (B) applies to a second paint order, the standard cost here is:

$$\underset{\text{standard price}}{£1.20} \times \underset{\text{standard usage}}{250 \text{ litres}} = £300$$

The actual cost is:

£1.20 × 230 litres = £276
actual price   standard usage

Because the actual price is the same as the standard price, the difference arises only through a difference in usage. Since the actual cost incurred (£276) is less than the standard cost (£300) we have a *favourable usage variance* of £24, meaning that the firm has produced the paint using £24 worth less of the raw material than was planned.

In most practical cases, both actual price and actual usage will differ from standard. In such circumstances, the separate variances can be obtained by using the formulae:

$$\text{Price variance} = \left\{ \begin{matrix} \text{Standard} \\ \text{price} \end{matrix} - \begin{matrix} \text{Actual} \\ \text{price} \end{matrix} \right\} \times \begin{matrix} \text{Actual} \\ \text{quantity} \end{matrix}$$

$$\text{Usage variance} = \left\{ \begin{matrix} \text{Standard} \\ \text{quantity} \end{matrix} - \begin{matrix} \text{Actual} \\ \text{quantity} \end{matrix} \right\} \times \begin{matrix} \text{Standard} \\ \text{price} \end{matrix}$$

When using these formulae a positive variance denotes a favourable variance, whilst a negative variance denotes an adverse variance. Note also that:

$$\begin{matrix} \text{Price} \\ \text{variance} \end{matrix} + \begin{matrix} \text{Usage} \\ \text{variance} \end{matrix} = \begin{matrix} \text{Total material} \\ \text{variance} \end{matrix}$$

In (C) above the total variance is: £

Standard price × standard usage = £1.60 × 270 litres = 432
Actual price × actual usage   = £1.40 × 280 litres = 392

Total variance (favourable)   40

The actual cost was less than the planned cost, so that a favourable variance emerges. This total variance arises by the price and usage variances operating together. Using the formulae, therefore:

                                                £

Price variance = (£1.60 − £1.40) × 280   =   56
Usage variance = (270 − 280) × £1.60   = − 16

Total variance (favourable)   40

The price variance is favourable at £56, meaning that the firm paid less for the material than it planned. However, the usage variance is adverse at £16, indicating that the firm used more of the material than it estimated. Together, the effect of the two variances is to give a favourable variance of £40 which was devised earlier (£56 − £16 = £40).

It was previously mentioned that one of the values of standard costing was that it raised questions for management attention: management was required to explain the reasons for the emergence of any variances. With material variances, price variances may arise because the prices actually paid were different from those planned; this may arise because of general market changes, or it may arise because of quantity discounts. Where discounts are not being taken, the price variance may become adverse; where discounts are greater than anticipated, the price variance may become favourable.

Purchasing materials of a different quality than planned may also affect price variances, as too may the purchasing of substitute material. Note also that changes in the quality of raw material may also affect usage variances.

Usage variances reflect the yield of good product obtained from the raw material. This may have something to do with the quality of raw material, with the production practices, or with the grade of labour being employed. Poor storage conditions and lax security may also cause an increase in material wastage.

Only by asking the relevant questions – once the variance has triggered the enquiry – will the firm be able to trace responsibility and to exercise control.

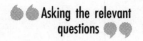 **Asking the relevant questions**

LABOUR VARIANCES

Just as the material variances can be divided into price and usage variances, so too can labour variances, although here the variances are called wage rate and efficiency variances. The *wage rate variance* measures the cost of labour whilst the *efficiency variance* measures how much labour – in terms of labour hours – has been used, as follows:

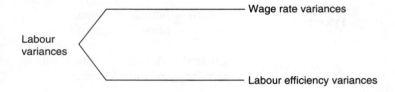

The following formulae apply:

$$\text{Wage rate variance} = \left\{ \begin{matrix} \text{Standard} \\ \text{wage rate} \end{matrix} - \begin{matrix} \text{Actual} \\ \text{wage rate} \end{matrix} \right\} \times \begin{matrix} \text{Actual} \\ \text{hours} \end{matrix}$$

$$\text{Efficiency variance} = \left\{ \begin{matrix} \text{Standard} \\ \text{hours} \end{matrix} - \begin{matrix} \text{Actual} \\ \text{hours} \end{matrix} \right\} \times \begin{matrix} \text{Standard} \\ \text{wage rate} \end{matrix}$$

Consider, therefore, the situation:

Standard hours	45
Standard wage rate per hour	£4.40
Actual hours	50
Actual wage rate per hour	£4.20

The total labour variance is:

		£
Standard hours × standard wage rate	= 45 × £4.40	198
Actual hours × actual wage rate	= 50 × £4.20	210
Total variance (adverse)		12

The total variance is adverse, because the actual cost at £210 is greater than the standard cost of £198. This total variance can be divided into:

		£
Wage rate variance	= (£4.40 − £4.20) × 50 =	10
Efficiency variance	= (45 − 50) × £4.40 =	− 22
		− 12

The wage rate variance is favourable at £10, showing that the firm paid less in wages than it planned. However, the efficiency variance is adverse at £22, showing that the work took longer to produce than was estimated.

Wage rate variances arise because higher – or lower – wages were paid than were planned. Perhaps the job was performed by different grades of worker than had been intended, or perhaps unplanned overtime or bonuses were paid. Any of these would produce a wage rate variance. Since wage rates tend to be fixed by negotiation with trade unions at national or company level, changes here tend to be outside the control of departmental managers. However, departments may be able to exercise control where more expensive labour is used on a task than was planned. If urgent orders have not been scheduled properly, highly paid workers may be required to perform lower grade duties.

The use of incorrect grades of labour might also produce an efficiency variance: so, too, might lax supervison, poor materials, or equipment difficulties. Some of these, such as improved working methods and regular maintenance, are controllable within departments, but other influences, such as the way a worker feels, family or personal problems, the approach of holidays – all have a bearing upon labour efficiency, and yet are outside the control of management.

Labour efficiency also has an influence upon overhead variances, as can be seen below.

OVERHEAD VARIANCES

Variable overhead variances can be divided into expenditure variances and efficiency variances:

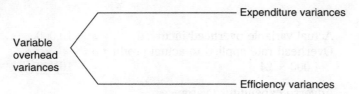

Fixed overhead variances can be divided into expenditure variances and volume variances:

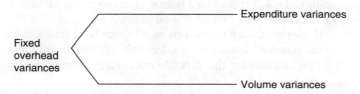

Thus we have:

1. *Spending or expenditure variances.* These occur whenever actual cost differs from planned cost. The variance can be calculated for fixed and for variable overheads.
2. *Efficiency variances.* These apply solely to variable overheads. They arise because of changes in the level of activity. Strictly, they are part of the volume variances, but because they apply to variable overheads, they are examined separately.
3. *Volume variances.* These apply solely to fixed overheads and they arise because the volume of actual output is different from that which was planned.

Overhead variances are more complicated than material or labour variances, largely because overheads are absorbed by means of predetermined overhead absorption rates applied to particular levels of production (see Chapter 15). In standard costing, production levels need to be expressed in terms of a measure which is common to all products: the most usual measure is the 'standard hour' as discussed above. Remember, that the standard hour is the quantity of output or the amount of work which can be performed in one hour. It is a measure of output, not of time.

VARIABLE OVERHEADS

EXPENDITURE VARIANCE

This variance shows the difference between the actual overhead incurred and that which would have been incurred had the budgeted overhead been adjusted to actual output.

The variable overhead variances can be calculated from the following figures:

Budgeted variable overhead (£)   20,000
Actual variable overhead (£)   19,000
Standard machine hours   5,000
Actual machine hours   4,000

First, it is necessary to calculate the standard machine hour rate; this is the rate at which variable overhead is incurred per standard hour. In our example:

$$\frac{£20,000}{5,000} = £4 \text{ per standard machine hour}$$

For every standard machine hour worked, £4 of variable overheads are incurred.

Second, this rate per standard hour must be applied to the actual number of machine hours worked, and the answer compared to the actual variable overhead incurred:

	£
Actual variable overhead incurred	19,000
Overhead rate applied to actual production	
4,000 × £4	16,000
Adverse expenditure variance	3,000

The result is an adverse expenditure variance of £3,000. At the level of output actually achieved – 4,000 standard hours – the overhead incurred should have been £16,000. In fact, £19,000 was incurred – an overspending of £3,000.

If overheads are recovered on a labour hour basis, then the calculation will be based upon standard labour hours, but the calculation remains the same.

The formula for the variable overhead expenditure variance is:

$$\text{Variable overhead expenditure variance} = \left\{ \text{Actual hours} \times \text{Variable overhead rate} \right\} - \text{Actual variable overhead}$$

In our example: $= (4,000 \times £4) - £19,000$
$= £16,000 - £19,000$
$= £\ 3,000 \text{ (adverse)}$

EFFICIENCY VARIANCE

This variance applies to variable overheads, and not to fixed overheads. The overhead absorption rate will be based either upon machine hours worked or upon direct labour hours worked. Since there will usually be a difference between the number of hours planned for production and the number of hours actually taken, this difference will affect the variable overheads.

Assume that a company has a standard of five hours to produce each unit. In fact 3,000 units are produced in 1,400 hours. If the standard variable overhead rate is £7 per hour, then the variance is:

	£
Actual hours × standard rate (14,000 × £7)	98,000
Standard hours × standard rate (15,000 × £7)s	105,000
Favourable efficiency variance	7,000

The firm was more efficient than expected in producing these items. It should have taken 5 × 3,000 = 15,000 hours to produce this quantity, whereas it took only 14,000 hours. One thousand hours saved at the standard rate of £7 per hour gives a favourable variance of £7,000.

The formula to be used is:

$$\text{Efficiency Variance} = \left\{ \begin{array}{c} \text{Standard} \\ \text{input volume} \end{array} - \begin{array}{c} \text{Actual input} \\ \text{volume} \end{array} \right\} \times \begin{array}{c} \text{standard variable} \\ \text{overhead rate.} \end{array}$$

The input volume will be measured by either direct labour hours or by machine hours. In our example:

= (15,000 − 14,000) × £7
= 1,000 × £7
= £7,000 (favourable)

FIXED OVERHEADS

EXPENDITURE VARIANCE

With fixed overheads, the expenditure variance is merely the difference between budgeted fixed overhead and actual fixed overhead. Thus:

	£
Budgeted fixed overhead	90,000
Actual fixed overhead	85,000
Favourable expenditure variance	5,000

The firm has spent £5,000 less on fixed overheads than it had planned.

VOLUME VARIANCE

Volume variances apply solely to fixed overheads. Fixed costs accrue largely on the basis of time, and are not affected by the level of output: rent, rates, insurances, staff salaries etc. have all to be paid in the short term irrespective of the level of production.

However, fixed overheads are *absorbed* by production on the basis of the relationship existing between budgeted *costs* on the one hand, and budgeted *volume* on the other. A standard amount of fixed overhead, therefore, is assumed to apply to each unit produced. Thus, if the level of activity changes, this will affect the amount of fixed overhead recovered. The more that is produced, the more fixed overhead that is recovered.

Assume:

Fixed overhead (£)	60,000
Budgeted standard hours	10,000
Actual standard hours achieved	11,000

Thus, the budgeted fixed overhead rate:

$$= \frac{£60,000}{10,000} = £6 \text{ per standard hour}$$

If the actual standard hours achieved was 11,000, the volume variance would be:

		£
Actual standard hours × standard rate	11,000 × £6	66,000
Budgeted standard hours × standard rate	10,000 × £6	60,000
Favourable volume variance		6,000

The actual amount recovered is more than was budgeted for, so the variance is:

$$= (6,000 \times £50) - £275,000$$
$$= £300,000 - £275,000$$
$$= £25,000 \text{ (favourable)}$$

Efficiency variance: $\left\{ \begin{array}{l} \text{Standard} \\ \text{input volume} \end{array} - \begin{array}{l} \text{Actual input} \\ \text{volume} \end{array} \right\} \times \begin{array}{l} \text{Standard variable} \\ \text{overhead rate} \end{array}$

$$= (210 \times 25 - 6,000) \times £50$$
$$= (5,250 - 6,000) \times £50$$
$$= \underline{£37,500} \text{ (adverse)}$$

The adverse variance for variable overheads is thus made up of a favourable expenditure variance of £25,000 and an adverse efficiency variance of £37,500, giving a net adverse variance of £12,500.

The total variance for fixed overheads is:

	£
Actual overhead	395,000
Fixed overhead allocated to production	
210 units × 25 hours × £80	420,000
Favourable variance	25,000

This total fixed overhead variance can be divided into:

Expenditure variance: Budgeted overhead − actual overhead
$$= £400,000 - £395,000$$
$$= £5,000 \text{ (favourable)}$$

Volume variance: $\left\{ \begin{array}{l} \text{Actual quantity} \\ \text{of work done} \end{array} - \begin{array}{l} \text{Standard quantity} \\ \text{of work done} \end{array} \right\} \times \begin{array}{l} \text{Standard fixed} \\ \text{overhead rate} \end{array}$

$$= (210 \times 25) - 5,000 \times £80$$
$$= (5,250 - 5,000) \times £80$$
$$= \underline{£20,000} \text{ (favourable)}$$

The favourable expenditure variance of £5,000 plus the favourable volume variance of £20,000 produced the total favourable variance of £25,000.

The very process of absorbing overheads into production costs, of itself causes overhead variances to be more complicated than are the simpler labour and materials variances. Overhead absorption rates are calculated from estimates – of both expenditure and levels of production. Any differences between these estimates and actual levels – of expenditure and production – will give rise to variances.

Differences in labour efficiency may also create overhead variances, since overheads are often absorbed into production through labour hours. Overhead efficiency variances, therefore, may arise through differences in labour efficiency.

Overhead expenditure variances occur when actual expenditure differs from planned expenditure. These differences may occur because of changes in the costs of supplies – or services – with changes in the wages paid to indirect labour, or because of the misuse of services.

The volume variance arises because of the efficiency of production and because of differences between actual and planned capacity. These last differences may arise because of changes in demand; shortages of labour or materials; absenteeism, strikes, sickness; and machine breakdowns or improvements.

THE VARIANCE ACCOUNT

Where a firm operates a full standard costing system the costs which appear in the firm's records will be standard costs. Since actual costs will usually be different from standard costs, the differences must be recorded in the profit and loss account. Adverse variances are debited to the profit and loss account, whilst favourable variances are credited.

To reduce the number of such entries in the profit and loss account itself, many firms operate a separate variance account to which adverse variances are debited and favourable variances are credited. At the end of the period only the balance on the variance account needs to be transferred to the profit and loss account: debit balances being debited to the profit and loss account, and credit balances on the variance account being credited to the profit and loss account.

EXAMINATION QUESTIONS

1

	Standard	Actual
Price of materials (litre)	£1.50	£1.60
Usage of materials (litres)	220	200
Labour hours worked	45	48
Wage rate/hour	£5.30	£5.00

a) From the figures above calculate:
  i) the total labour variance,
  ii) the wage rate variance,
  iii) the labour efficiency variance,
  iv) the total materials variance,
  v) the materials price variance,
  vi) the materials usage variance.
  In each case state clearly whether the variance is adverse or favourable. *(6)*
b) Why is a favourable labour variance and a favourable materials variance not always desirable? *(9)*
(London 1992)

2 Retlaw plc manufactures foam-backed carpet in rolls of uniform size. Within the company's standard costing system raw material stocks are held at standard cost. During the month of May 1991 the following variances were transferred to the profit and loss account.

£

Material price variances	
Material A	366 Adverse
Material B	274 Favourable
Material usage variances	
Material A	498 Adverse
Material B	95 Favourable
Direct labour variances	
Rate	517 Favourable
Efficiency	1,064 Adverse

Additional information for May 1991 is as follows:

Materials purchased
  A 49,000 kg   invoiced at £37,116
  B 19,200 kg   invoiced at £23,726

Materials issued to production
A   48,164 kg
B   18,924 kg
Actual direct wages   £37,122
Actual direct hours worked   10,754
Production 1900 rolls of foam-backed carpet

There was no opening or closing work in progress.

You are required to prepare a standard cost sheet detailing the standard prime cost for one roll of foam-backed carpet.   (20)

(Northern 1992)

3 a) From the following information calculate:

i)   the standard machine hour rate,
ii)   the standard hours per unit,
iii)   the variance overhead expenditure variance,
iv)   the variable overhead efficiency variance.

Budgeted variable overhead	£30,000
Actual variable overhead	£21,000
Budgeted machine hours	500
Actual machine hours	600
Budgeted production	20 units
Actual production	21 units

(6)

b) Explain fully the meaning of your answer to all parts of (a) above.   (9)

(London 1990)

TUTOR'S ANSWER

2   Prime cost consists of materials and labour costs. For each roll of carpet, therefore, it is necessary to calculate the price of each material, and its quantity; the hourly wage rate and the number of labours.

Retlaw plc
Standard price:
Material A: Actual price − Standard price = Variance
$$£37,116 \quad - £x \qquad = £366 \text{ adverse}$$
$$£x \qquad = £37,116 - £366$$
$$= \underline{£36,750}$$

Divide by actual quantity: $\dfrac{£36,750}{49,000} = \underline{0.75 \text{ kg}}$

Material B: $£23,726 - £x \qquad = £274$ fav.
$$£x \qquad = £23,726 + £274$$
$$= \underline{£24,000}$$

Divide by actual quantity: $\dfrac{£24,000}{19,200} = \underline{£1.25 \text{ kg}}$

Standard Quantity:

Material A: Actual quantity   − Standard quantity = Variance
$$48,164 \text{ kg} \times £0.75 - £x \qquad = £495 \text{ adv.}$$
$$£36,123 \qquad - £x \qquad = £495 \text{ adv}$$
$$£36,123 \qquad - £495 \qquad = £35,625$$

Divide by standard price: $\dfrac{£35,625}{£0.75} = \underline{47,500 \text{ kg}}$

Material B: 18,924 kg × £1.25 − £x = £95 fav
   £23,665   − £x = £95 fav
   £23,655   + £95 = £23,750

Divide by standard price: $\dfrac{£23,750}{£1.25} = \underline{19,000 \text{ kg}}$

Divide by 1,900 rolls produced:

Material A: $\dfrac{£47,500}{1,900} = \underline{25 \text{ kg/roll}}$

Material B: $\dfrac{19,000}{1,900} = \underline{10 \text{ kg/roll}}$

Labour rate: £37,122 − £x   = £517 fav
    £37,122 + £517 = £37,639

Divide by direct hours actually worked:

$\dfrac{£37,639}{10,754} = \underline{£3.5 \text{ per hour}}$

Labour efficiency: 10,754 × £3.5 − £x   = £1,064 adv
        £37,639   − £1,064 = £36,575

Divide by hourly rate: $\dfrac{£36,575}{£3.50} = \underline{10,450 \text{ hours}}$

Hours per roll: $\dfrac{10,450}{1,900} = \underline{5.5 \text{ hours}}$

Standard Prime Cost per Roll of Carpet

Materials:

A: 25 kg @ £0.75		18.75
B: 10 kg @ £1.25		12.50
		31.25
Labour: 5.5 hours @ £3.50 hour		19.25
Standard prime cost		51.50

STUDENT'S ANSWER

3 a)   i) *Standard machine hour rate:*

$\dfrac{30\,000}{500} = £60$ std machine hour

   ii) *Standard hours/unit:*

$\dfrac{500}{20} = 25$

iii) *Expenditure variance:*

Actual o/h incurred	21,000
O/h rate applied to production: 600 × £60	36,000
Favourable variance	15,000

iv) *Efficiency variance:*

Actual hours × std rate: 600 × £60	36,000
Budgeted hours × std rate: (21 × 25) × £60	31,500
Adverse variance	4,500

b) i) *Standard machine hour rate:* for every standard machine hour worked, £60 of variable overheads are assumed to be incurred.

ii) *Standard machine hours per unit:* the time it should take to produce one item.

iii) *Expenditure variance:* actual production should have incurred variable overheads of £36,000; in fact actual production incurred overheads of only £21,000: a favourable variance of £15,000.

iv) *Efficiency variance:* it should have taken 21 × £25 = 525 hours to produce 21 items: in fact it took 600 hours, a difference of 75 hours: 75 × £60 – the o/h rate – gives the variance of £4,500.

TUTOR'S COMMENTS

Note how the candidate has presented the workings. In part (b) the candidate's own figures are referred to in the answer; the examiners will award credit for this. Even if the figures in part (a) have been wrongly calculated, providing that they have been correctly used in part (b) full marks may still be awarded for this section.

OUTLINE ANSWERS

1 *Total labour variance:* (45 × £5.30) − (48 × £5.00) = £238.5 − £240 = £1.5 adv. *Wage rate:* (£5.30 − £5.00) 48 = £14.4 fav. *Efficiency:* (45 − 48) £5.30 = £15.9 adv.

Total materials variance: (£1.5 × 220) − (£1.6 × 200) = £330 − £320 = £10 fav. *Materials price:* (£1.50 − £1.60) 200 = £20 adv. *Usage:* (220 − 200) £1.5 = £30 fav.

b) *Favourable labour variance:* may not be desirable because could indicate unskilled labour being used – possibility of high wastage, low quality output. Reduced labour hours – work being skimped.

Favourable materials variance: low priced, low quality materials, could lead to low quality output. Less quantity of materials being used, also affects quality.
　　Either could indicate that standards wrongly set.

Now attempt the review questions on page 317. The answers are given on page 328.

GETTING STARTED

Chapter 18 studied sales, production and cash budgets, but did not discuss budgeting for fixed assets.

The decision to invest in fixed assets is not an easy decision. Fixed assets are bought with the intention that they should last for a long time: if, therefore, a firm makes a mistake in its purchase of fixed assets the mistake may be with it for years.

When deciding whether to commit finances to a long-term investment, the firm's management must consider the following:

1. What the future is likely to hold: how items such as costs, revenues and interest rates are likely to move, and why. How technology is likely to develop; how markets are likely to change. The view taken by the managers of one firm may be different from those of another, partly because of their perceptions based upon past experience, and partly because of the nature of the information available to them.
2. How does the firm assess the likely risks involved? What risks is the firm prepared to take, and how far? Generally, managers tend to be adverse to risk, i.e. they prefer safer options with lower returns than more risky options offering high returns.
3. What are the alternative opportunities in which to invest? It is in an effort to evaluate these alternatives that the methods discussed in this chapter have been developed.

If all things were equal, then the firm might choose to invest in the cheapest alternative available to it: the cheapest building, the cheapest new machine. But things are not equal. Cheaper machinery may be of poorer quality, and may demand greater maintenance than the more expensive equipment: low maintenance costs and the reduced costs of 'down time', i.e. the time the equipment is out of action, might render a seemingly expensive machine the cheaper option.

When the time comes to invest in new plant the firm must decide whether to consolidate its position in its existing markets, or whether to diversify into new ones.

These are not decisions which the accountant can take alone. The firm's sales personnel should be consulted to give a view of market trends: production staff must be involved, since any departure from existing practices or production may mean the introduction of new or different technologies. New plant and new methods may require the recruitment of staff with different skills, and/or the training of existing staff; there are also likely to be negotiations with trade unions. Thus, the personnel department will have an input, too.

The process of evaluating capital projects and of estimating the costs and revenues associated with them is known as *investment appraisal* – sometimes called capital budgeting. It is a complex subject, and this chapter is merely an introduction.

The term 'project' in investment appraisal can have many meanings. It may mean the acquisition of a new lathe at a modest cost, or the construction of a large manufacturing complex costing millions of pounds. Remember, however, that not every investment undertaken by a commercial firm is aimed at increasing profits directly. Investments in welfare and recreational activities may influence company earnings only indirectly: the construction of a new canteen or rest area, for example. However, attention is restricted here to those projects aimed at generating profits.

INVESTMENT APPRAISAL

COMPOUND INTEREST

PRESENT VALUE

VALUATION OF FIXED ASSETS

NET PRESENT VALUE (NPV)

YIELD

NPV COMPARED TO YIELD

COST OF CAPITAL

PAYBACK

ESSENTIAL PRINCIPLES

COMPOUND INTEREST

One of the basic concepts of investment appraisal is that of the *time value of money*, and this has to do with the paying and receiving of interest.

Assume that £100 is invested for a year at 10 per cent compound interest per annum; then, at the end of the first year, the investment will have grown to £110; at the end of the second year it will have grown to £121:

> The time value of money is connected to interest

			£
Year 1	January 1	Initial investment	100
	December 31	Interest at 10 per cent per ann	10
Year 2	January 1	Investment	110
	December 31	Interest at 10 per cent per ann	11
			121

Thus, after the first year, the investment has grown to £110, and the whole of this becomes the investment for year 2; so that in the second year the interest is calculated on the full £110. This process of calculating interest on the initial investment *plus* the interest is known as *compound interest*.

Where small amounts of money are concerned, over relatively short time spans, it may be easy to calculate the interest as in our example. However, for more complicated calculations, tables such as that in Figure 20.1 are used. The compound table shows just how much £1 will grow if compounded for various periods at various rates of interest. Interest rates appear along the top of the table, and the time periods down the side. Thus, it is seen from the table that £1 invested for five periods at 8 per cent compound interest grows to £1.469. Hence, £100 invested for five periods at 8 per cent interest compounded, would give:

£100 × 1.469 = £146.9

Similarly, £423 invested for 15 periods at 13 per cent interest per period will grow to:

£423 × 6.258 = £2,647.134

Period	1%	2%	3%	4%	5%	6%	7%	8%	9%	10%	11%	12%	13%	14%	15%
1	1.010	1.020	1.030	1.040	1.050	1.060	1.070	1.080	1.090	1.100	1.110	1.120	1.130	1.140	1.150
2	1.020	1.040	1.061	1.082	1.102	1.124	1.145	1.166	1.188	1.210	1.232	1.254	1.277	1.300	1.322
3	1.030	1.061	1.093	1.125	1.158	1.191	1.225	1.260	1.295	1.331	1.368	1.405	1.443	1.482	1.521
4	1.041	1.082	1.126	1.170	1.216	1.262	1.311	1.360	1.412	1.464	1.518	1.575	1.631	1.689	1.749
5	1.051	1.104	1.159	1.217	1.276	1.338	1.403	1.469	1.539	1.611	1.685	1.762	1.843	1.925	2.011
6	1.062	1.126	1.194	1.265	1.340	1.419	1.501	1.587	1.677	1.772	1.870	1.974	2.083	2.195	2.313
7	1.072	1.149	1.230	1.316	1.407	1.504	1.606	1.714	1.828	1.949	2.076	2.211	2.353	2.502	2.660
8	1.083	1.172	1.267	1.369	1.477	1.594	1.718	1.851	1.993	2.144	2.304	2.476	2.659	2.853	3.059
9	1.094	1.195	1.305	1.423	1.551	1.689	1.838	1.999	2.172	2.358	2.557	2.773	3.005	3.252	3.803
10	1.105	1.219	1.344	1.480	1.629	1.791	1.9067	2.159	2.367	2.594	2.838	3.106	3.396	3.707	4.046
11	1.116	1.243	1.384	1.539	1.710	1.898	2.105	2.332	2.580	2.853	3.150	3.479	3.838	4.226	4.652
12	1.127	1.268	1.426	1.601	1.796	2.012	2.252	2.518	2.813	3.138	3.497	3.896	4.337	4.818	5.350
13	1.138	1.294	1.469	1.665	1.886	2.133	2.410	2.720	3.066	3.452	3.882	4.363	4.901	5.492	6.153
14	1.149	1.319	1.513	1.732	1.980	2.261	2.579	2.937	3.342	3.797	4.309	4.887	5.538	6.261	7.076
15	1.161	1.346	1.558	1.801	2.079	2.397	2.759	3.172	3.642	4.177	4.783	5.474	6.258	7.138	8.137

Fig. 20.1 Compound amount of 1.

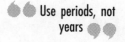

> Use periods, not years

Note that the term 'periods', and not 'years' has been used in discussion of the table. This is because time spans of other than a year may sometimes be used. Interest paid at 10 per cent per annum is different from interest paid at 10 per cent per half year:

	A 10% per annum	B 10% half year	C 20% per annum
Initial investment	200	200	200
First period's interest	20	20	40
	220	220	240
Second period's interest		22	
		242	

In the description above, the period is a year in (A) at the end of which the investment has grown to £220. In (B) the period is six months: at the end of a year, therefore, two periods' interest has accrued, taking the investment to £242. Note, too, that two lots of 10 per cent is better than one lot of 20 per cent. In (C) interest at the end of the period is £40, whereas in (B) total interest received over the same year is £42.

Check Figure 20.1 to verify the figures in Table 20.1.

			Compound Interest	
1 Amount (£)	*2* Periods	*3* Interest (%)	*4* Compound amount of £1	*5* **Total** col. 1 × col. 4 (£)
22	4	8	1.360	29.92
78	8	10	2.144	167.23
130	11	15	4.652	604.76
261	5	12	1.762	459.88

Table 20.1

PRESENT VALUE

Consider the situation where interest rates are 10 per cent per annum. There is a choice of either (a) £100 in a year's time or (b) £100 today. Irrespective of inflation, which would have been chosen?

If (a) is chosen £100 is guaranteed in 12 months' time. However, if (b) is chosen, £100 received today could be invested at 10 per cent, and at the end of the year the investment would have grown to £110. If the finances are to be maximised (b) would be chosen: *not because of inflation, but because of the existence of interest rates.*

Consider, now, a choice between (a) £95 in one year's time, or (b) £87 now. If interest rates are 15 per cent, which one would be chosen? If (a), we are sure to have £95 in a year's time. But if (b), we could invest £87 at 15 per cent interest, so that in 12 months' time it will have grown to:

	£
Original investment	87
Interest at 15 per cent	13.05
	100.05

By choosing (b) one has gained more than the £8 difference between £87 and £95.

Another way of stating the situation is to say that when interest rates are 15 per cent, the *present value* of £100 receivable in a year's time is £87. Thus, with interest rates at 15 per cent, the value of £87 *now* equals £100.05 in a year's time.

One could calculate the present value stage by stage for each set of figures, using relevant formulae, but it is far easier to use present value tables instead (Figure 20.2). Again, the interest rates appear along the top, and the time periods down the left-hand side. By using the table, we can see that at 18 per cent interest the present value of £1 receivable in six periods' time is £0.370. Thus, the present value of £240 receivable in six periods' time is

£240 × 0.370 = £88.8

Period	1%	2%	3%	4%	5%	6%	7%	8%	9%	10%
1	0.990	0.980	0.971	0.961	0.952	0.943	0.935	0.926	0.917	0.909
2	0.980	0.961	0.943	0.925	0.907	0.890	0.873	0.857	0.842	0.826
3	0.971	0.942	0.915	0.889	0.864	0.840	0.816	0.794	0.772	0.751
4	0.961	0.924	0.889	0.855	0.823	0.792	0.763	0.735	0.708	0.683
5	0.9051	0.906	0.863	0.822	0.784	0.747	0.713	0.681	0.650	0.621
6	0.942	0.888	0.838	0.790	0.746	0.705	0.666	0.630	0.596	0.564
7	0.933	0.871	0.813	0.760	0.711	0.665	0.623	0.583	0.547	0.513
8	0.923	0.853	0.789	0.731	0.677	0.627	0.582	0.540	0.502	0.467
9	0.914	0.837	0.766	0.703	0.645	0.592	0.544	0.500	0.460	0.424
10	0.905	0.820	0.744	0.676	0.614	0.588	0.508	0.463	0.422	0.386
11	0.896	0.804	0.722	0.650	0.585	0.527	0.475	0.429	0.388	0.350
12	0.887	0.788	0.701	0.625	0.557	0.497	0.444	0.397	0.356	0.319
13	0.879	0.773	0.681	0.601	0.530	0.469	0.415	0.368	0.326	0.290
14	0.870	0.758	0.661	0.577	0.505	0.442	0.388	0.340	0.299	0.263
15	0.861	0.743	0.642	0.555	0.481	0.417	0.362	0.315	0.275	0.239

Period	11%	12%	13%	14%	15%	16%	17%	18%	19%	20%
1	0.901	0.893	0.885	0.877	0.870	0.862	0.855	0.847	0.840	0.833
2	0.8123	0.797	0.783	0.769	0.756	0.743	0.731	0.718	0.706	0.694
3	0.731	0.712	0.693	0.675	0.658	0.641	0.624	0.609	0.593	0.571
4	0.659	0.636	0.613	0.592	0.572	0.552	0.534	0.516	0.499	0.482
5	0.594	0.567	0.543	0.519	0.497	0.476	0.456	0.437	0.419	0.402
6	0.535	0.507	0.480	0.456	0.432	0.410	0.390	0.370	0.352	0.335
7	0.482	0.452	0.425	0.400	0.376	0.354	0.333	0.314	0.296	0.279
8	0.4345	0.404	0.376	0.351	0.327	0.305	0.285	0.266	0.249	0.233
9	0.391	0.361	0.333	0.308	0.284	0.263	0.243	0.226	0.20-9	0.194
10	0.352	0.322	0.295	0.270	0.247	0.227	0.208	0.191	0.176	0.162
11	0.317	0.287	0.261	0.237	0.215	0.195	0.178	0.162	0.148	0.135
12	0.289	0.257	0.231	0.208	0.187	0.169	0.152	0.137	0.124	0.112
13	0.258	0.229	0.204	0.182	0.163	0.145	0.130	0.116	0.104	0.094
14	0.232	0.205	0.181	0.160	0.141	0.125	0.111	0.099	0.088	0.078
15	0.209	0.183	0.1060	0.140	0.123	0.108	0.095	0.084	0.074	0.065

Fig. 20.2 Present value of 1.

Another way of saying this is that £88.8 invested for six periods at 18 per cent will grow to £240. This can be verified by compounding:

£88.8 × 2.7 = £239.76 (rounding errors account for the difference).

The process of working backwards to find the present value of a future sum is known as *discounting*.

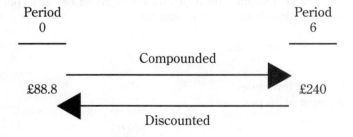

Period
0

Compounded

£88.8   £240

Discounted

Use Figure 20.2 to check the figures in Table 20.2.

		Present Value (PV)Z		
Amount (£)	Periods	Interest (%)	PV of £1	PV of amount col. 1 × col. 4 (£)
162	4	5	0.823	133.33
227	9	9	0.460	104.42
723	11	14	0.237	171.35
561	6	16	0.410	230.01

Table 20.2

Note that whereas the compounded amount of a sum of money is always greater than the initial sum, the present value is always less than the original sum. Also, the longer the period before the money accrues, the lower the present value. Thus the present value of £500 at 5 per cent in five periods is £392, whereas in ten periods the present value is £307. The promise of money in the future is worth less than the promise of money now, and the further into the future, the less the value.

Present value is always less than the original sum

VALUATION OF FIXED ASSETS

The valuation of fixed assets largely depends upon the purpose for which the valuation is required: different values arise using cost, cost less depreciation, scrap value, replacement value. With investment appraisal, an asset is valued not in terms of its cost, but in terms of its earning power, since fixed assets are purchased specifically to be used within the business to generate income.

A firm purchases a new machine for £1,000. It is estimated that the machine will last for three years, after which time its scrap value will be zero. During its life it is estimated that its net yearly earnings will be £300, £500 and £600. If the machine is to be valued, not in terms of its cost, but in terms of its earning power, then what valuation is to be put on the machine? Clearly it is not sufficient to add the income streams together (£300 + £500 + £600 = £1,400) since it is known that money received in the future is worth less than money received now. It is also known that this difference arises because of interest rates irrespective of inflation.

Discounting the cash flow

In order to find the machine's value, the income flow must be converted into present value terms, a process known as *discounting the cash flow*. Using the present value table, and assuming an interest rate of 15 per cent, the necessary discount factors can be applied (Table 20.3).

	1 *Year*	*2* *Cash flow (£)*	*3* *PV of £1*	*4* *PV of cash flow* *col. 2 × col. 3 (£)*
Table 20.3	1	300	0.870	261
	2	500	0.756	378
	3	600	0.658	394.8
				1,033.8

The present value of the income which the machine will generate amounts to £1,033.8. In other words, if the firm were to invest £1,033.8 for three years at 15 per cent compound interest, and the firm were to withdraw, by way of earnings, amounts equal to the yearly cash flow, then the investment would redeem itself at the end of the third year (Table 20.4).

The initial investment, valued in present value terms, is £1,033.8. It attracts interest at 15 per cent, to give £1,188.87, from which is deducted the first year's earnings of £300. The residue of £888.87 becomes the opening investment for year 2; it also attracts interest at 15 per cent, to give £1,022.2. When the earnings of £500 are deducted, £522.2 goes forward to year 3. It earns interest of £78.33, to give £600.53, from which the third year's earnings are taken. At the end of this third year, the investment has redeemed itself: the £0.53 arises from rounding-off errors.

	Year 1 £	Year 2 £	Year 3 £
Opening investment	1,033.80	888.87	522.20
Add: Interest (15%)	155.07	133.33	78.33
	1,188.87	1,022.20	600.53
Less: Earnings withdrawn	300.00	500.00	600.00
	888.87	522.20	0.53

Table 20.4

NET PRESENT VALUE (NPV)

The present value of the income flows generated by the machine was £1,033.8. If the initial cost is deducted from this, we derive the net present value (NPV). NPV is the present value less the original investment. In the example, NPV is £1,033.8 – £1,000 = £33.8. Thus, by spending £1,000 now, the firm obtains an income stream with a present value of £33.8 more.

When assessing an invesment project, the general rule is that projects with a positive NPV are acceptable, those with negative NPV's are not. Projects with higher NPV's are preferable to those with lower NPV's.

Table 20.5

Year	Discount factor	Machine A Cash flow (£)	PV (£)	Machine B Cash flow (£)	PV (£)	Machine C Cash flow (PV)	PV (£)
0	1.0	(10,000)	(10,000)	(13,000)	(13,000)	(15,000)	(15,000)
1	0.893	3,000	2,679	4,000	3,572	5,500	4,911.5
2	0.797	4,000	3,188	6,000	4,782	6,500	5,180.5
3	0.712	5,500	3,916	7,000	4,984	8,200	5,838.4
NPV			−217		+338		+930.4

Consider the situation in Table 20.5. The firm has a choice of three machines, but it can afford only one. The interest rate is 12 per cent. Machine (A) costs £10,000; machine (B) costs £13,000; and machine (C) £15,000. None of the machines is likely to have any scrap value at the end of the third year.

With machine (A), the present value amounts to £9,783 (£2,679 + £3,188 + £3,916 = £9,783). When the initial investment is deducted, the NPV becomes negative at −£217 (£9,783 – £10,000 = −£217). Using the earlier rule, (A) is rejected, since any project with a negative NPV is not acceptable. Note the convention that the initial investment is made at the end of the year 0 i.e. the beginning of year 1. Machine (B) does have a positive NPV: the sum of the present values is £13,338, which after deducting the initial investment leaves £338. Provisionally, therefore (B) is acceptable.

Machine (C) also has a positive NPV: the sum of the present values is £15,930.4, giving an NPV of £930.4. Since the firm can afford only one machine, and since (C)'s NPV is greater than (B)'s, the choice for the firm should be machine (C).

Where a firm has to choose, say, four projects from a list of seven, each of which has a positive NPV, then the firm should rank the projects in order of their NPVs, and take the first four. Remember, therefore, that generally projects with positive NPVs are acceptable, whilst those with negative NPVs are not. Higher positive NPVs are preferred to lower positive NPVs.

> ❝ Any project with a negative NPV is not acceptable ❞

> ❝ Higher positive NPV's are preferred ❞

YIELD

If a firm invests £2,000 in fixed interest securities which pay £200 per annum then the return on the investment is easy to calculate: it is 10 per cent per annum. Problems arise, however, when a firm is investing money in a project where the annual cash flow varies.

Consider the situation in Table 20.6. The project costs £10,000 and the net annual cash flows are as shown. When discounted at 5 per cent, the project gives a positive NPV of £199.2. When discounted at 6 per cent, NPV approaches zero: discounted at 7 per cent, the NPV becomes negative at £194.2.

Table 20.6

	Net cash flows (£)	Interest Rate 5% Discount factors	PV (£)	6% Discount factor	PV (£)	7% Discount factor	PV (£)
Year 0	(10,000)	1.0	(10,000)	1.0	(10,000)	1.0	(10,000)
1	3,000	0.952	2,856	0.943	2,829	0.935	2,805
2	4,000	0.907	3,628	0.890	3,560	0.873	3,492
3	4,300	0.864	3,715.2	0.840	3,612	0.816	3,508.8
NPV			199.2		1		−194.2

If the firm must borrow money to finance the project, the project is only worth considering if the interest payable on the loan is less than 6 per cent. At a cost of finance greater than 6 per cent, the project yields a negative NPV. Thus, a positive NPV means that the rate of return of the project is greater than the cost of finance, whilst a negative NPV means that the return is less than the cost of finance. Where the NPV is zero, the rate of return just equals the cost of finance. Another way of stating this is that a project's NPV is zero when it is discounted by its yield.

NPV is zero when project is discounted by its IRR

Calculating a rate which gives a zero NPV demands the use of a complicated formula: usually, the calculation is performed by trial and error. If in a first calculation the rate produces a positive NPV, then increase the rate to reduce the NPV. If a first calculation gives a negative NPV, then reduce the rate to increase the NPV.

As far as investment appraisal is concerned, the rule is that where a project earns a return which is greater than the cost of capital, the project is acceptable: where the yield is less than the cost of capital, the project should be rejected. Where a number of projects have yields greater than the cost of capital, and the firm can afford to invest in only a few of them, it should choose those projects with the highest yields. (Another term for yield is 'internal rate of return' or IRR.)

NPV COMPARED TO YIELD

NPV and yield methods each adjust the income flows to allow for the time value of money. Such adjustment is known as discounting, and methods which adjust for time values are known as *discounting methods*.

There are problems whether to choose NPV or yield to evaluate projects. Generally, NPV provides the better approach, and is the one to favour. Normally, the rate of interest to use in the NPV calculation should be the best rate which the company could earn if it invested its money outside of the business. By adopting such a rate, only projects earning a return in excess of this would be accepted. Projects earning less than this rate would be rejected, since the firm would do better to invest its money in external organisations.

Generally NPV provides a better approach

COST OF CAPITAL

When discussing investment appraisal a figure for the cost of capital was assumed, and this was applied to NPV and yield calculations. It is now possible to go a stage further, to see how a firm with a complex capital structure can calculate its cost of capital.

From the discussion so far it is seen that the cost of finance may differ depending upon the type of finance employed. Usually, equity capital, because it carries the most risk, will be more expensive than preference capital, which in turn will cost more than debentures. Study Table 20.7: three firms, each with capitals of £600,000, but each with different capital structures. Because the cost of each *type* of capital is different, the overall cost of capital of the three firms will also be different. Company (A) is financed only by ordinary shares, the holders of which expect a return of 15 per cent; thus, company (A)'s cost of capital is 15 per cent. Firm (B) obtains finance from ordinary shares at 15 per cent, and from preference shares at 12 per cent. The company, however, is financed two thirds by ordinary shares and one-third by preference shares: any calculation of the cost of capital needs to reflect this weighting. A simple average, therefore, of $(15 + 12) \div 2 = 13.5$ per cent is not acceptable.

If the proportions of each type of finance are used, 4:2 can be used as weights, and can be applied to the cost of each type of finance: $4 \times 15 = 60$; $2 \times 12 = 24$. By adding

	Cost of Capital: Capital Structures		
Table 20.7	Company A £000	Company B £000	Company C £000
Ordinary shares 15%	600	400	350
Preference shares 12%	—	200	150
Debentures 10%	—	—	100
	600	600	600

Table 20.8

	Cost of Capital: Weighted Averages			
	Company B		Company C	
	Proportion Rate		Proportion Rate	
Ordinary shares	4 × 15 = 60		3.5 × 15 = 52.5	
Preference shares	2 × 12 = 24		1.5 × 12 = 18	
Debentures	— —		1 × 6 = 6	
	6	84	6	76.5
Cost of capital	$\dfrac{84}{6} = 14\%$		$\dfrac{76.5}{6} = \underline{12.75\%}$	

these results, and dividing the answer by the total of the weights ($84 \div 6 = 14$ per cent), the weighted average cost of capital for company (B) is obtained. In any calculation for company (B) concerned with investment appraisal, therefore, the cost of capital figure to use would be 14 per cent. This would remain so until either the firm's capital structure changed or the costs of the various sources of finance changed; the figures would then need to be reworked (Table 20.8).

Company (C) is financed by ordinary shares, preference shares and debentures in proportions 3.1:1.5:1. Before these proportions can be applied to the rates, it must be remembered that debenture interest is an allowable expense against corporation tax. In order to reflect this, the cost of debentures must be amended, by employing the formula:

Allowable expense against corporation tax

$$r = R(1 - t)$$

where r is the after-tax interest rate, R is the rate before tax, and t the tax rate as a decimal. With company (C) and corporation tax at 40 per cent, the after-tax cost of debentures would be:

$$r = 10(1 - 0.40)$$
$$= 10 \times 0.6$$
$$= \;6 \text{ per cent}$$

Therefore, in the example, the cost of debentures is 6 per cent, and it is this figure that is used in the calculations. The proportions of the different types of finance – 3.5:1.5:1 – are applied to their respective rates – 15, 12 and 6 per cent – and the results added to give 76.5. This figure is then divided by the sum of the proportions to give the company's cost of capital of 12.75 per cent.

Note that company (C)'s cost of capital is less than company (B)'s, with company (A) the most expensive. By using a weighted average, note has been taken of the different costs of funds; and by allowing for the taxation benefits attaching to debentures, a more precise cost of capital figure can be calculated. The figures thus calculated for the respective companies would be the ones to use in any investment appraisal calculation.

PAYBACK

Time values rely heavily on estimates

Methods of investment appraisal which consider time values of money rely heavily upon estimates: the life of the project, the rate of interest which will obtain throughout that life, and the level of net earnings all need to be estimated. Each of these estimates demands an ability to forecast; and the further into the future one goes the greater is the risk that the forecasts will be wrong. Because of this, and the complexities of discounting methods, many firms still use methods which ignore time values. Such methods are called *non-discounting methods*, and the most common of these is *payback*. The payback approach ignores interest rates and time values altogether, and looks solely at how long the investment takes to pay for itself.

Table 20.9

	Payback (£)		
Year	Project X	Project Y	Project Z
0	(15,000)	(15,000)	(15,000)
1	3,000	4,000	2,000
2	4,000	5,000	4,000
3	5,000	6,000	9,000
4	6,000	6,000	7,000
5	10,000	6,000	7,000
6	16,000	6,000	7,000

Study Table 20.9. A firm has a choice of three projects; each has a life of six years, and each costs £15,000. Project (X) pays for itself in three and a half years, whereas (Y) and (Z) pay for themselves in three years. Using payback, therefore, (X) would be rejected and (Y) and (Z) would be equally preferred. If one looks closely at (Z), however, it is seen that over half of the payback earnings arise in the third year, and one knows that the value of money declines as one goes into the future before receipt. Also, looking beyond the payback period it is seen that (Z) goes on to earn a further £21,000 in the final three years, whereas (Y) earns only £18,000. Payback completely ignores earnings accruing outside of the payback period. Project (X), which was originally rejected, goes on to earn £31,000 after the payback period of $3\frac{1}{2}$ years: perhaps (X) should have been accepted after all?

 **Many firms use payback**

Notwithstanding these criticisms, many firms do use payback as a method of selecting investment projects. They argue that forecasting more than two or three years ahead is so risky that the risks completely outweigh any other advantages of using NPV.

EXAMINATION QUESTIONS

1 a) Why do ordinary shareholders usually expect a greater return than the holders of preference shares, and the holders of preferences share a greater return than the holders of debentures? *(3)*

  b) By carrying a lower rate of return, debentures may be regarded as a cheaper source of finance than are ordinary shares. What limits the amount of debentures a company can carry in its capital structure? *(3)*

CAPITAL STRUCTURE (£000)		
	AJAX	BORG
Ordinary shares (16%)	700	300
Preference shares (14%)	200	200
Debentures (12%)	100	500

  c) i) Calculate the weighted average cost of capital for each of the companies above, on the assumption that debenture interest is an allowable expense against corporation tax, which stands at 40 per cent.

     ii) Explain fully the reasons for any differences in the weighted average cost of capital for the two companies. *(9)*

  d) Ajax and Borg both have an opportunity to invest in project Cymberline which requires an initial investment of £300,000, and which is thought will generate the following net cash flows:

CYMBERLINE (£)	
Year 1	55,000
Year 2	60,000
Year 3	145,000
Year 4	170,000

i) What is the maximum cost of finance that can be considered when investing in this project?

ii) From the information given, state with reasons whether you would advise either of the two companies to invest in Cymberline.

Note: Assume that the cash inflows arise at the end of each year. (10)

(London 1990)

2 a) The two companies A Brown Ltd and C Dawes Ltd have the following capital structures:

	AB £000	CD £000
Ordinary £1 shares fully paid	2,000	800
Preference shares (14%)	1,100	500
Debentures (12%)	900	2,700

Debenture interest is an allowable expense against corporation tax, which for 19–9 and 1990 stands at 45 per cent. For both companies, the return on capital employed during 1989 was 25 per cent and during 1990 it was 10 per cent. All profits remaining after the payment of debenture interest, corporation tax, and preference dividend are paid to the holders of the ordinary shares.

Calculate the percentage return on the ordinary shares for each company for 1989 and 1990. (18)

b) Use your answer to (a) above to illustrate:
i) the value of incorporating some gearing into a company's capital structure, and
ii) the factors which may limit the proportion of debt capital to equity within a company's capital structure.

Be careful to define your terms. (7)

(London 1991)

3 Vernon Chemicals plc were considering the installation of a new processing plant.

The two plants under consideration were:

Plant A The capital cost of this plant was £5M. The plant had a proven track record for operating efficiency, but its method of processing tended to be costly.

Plant B This newly designed plant cost £10M.

One of Vernon's directors was very enthusiastic about this plant since in operations elsewhere it had proved relatively profitable. However, it was known that the plant did tend to have some pollutive effect on the environment and the atmosphere.

Forecast information for each of the plants was produced as follows:

	PLANT A		PLANT B	
	Revenue Receipts £M	Operating Payments £M	Revenue Receipts £M	Operating Payments £M
YEAR 1	3.8	2.0	6.5	2.9
YEAR 2	5.1	2.6	7.2	3.1
YEAR 3	6.4	3.9	9.3	4.8
YEAR 4	6.9	4.7	9.9	5.2
YEAR 5	8.1	5.2	11.4	5.8

Additional Information:
(1) A modification to Plant B to treat the pollution would need an extra capital cost of £1.5M. In addition, operating payments would increase in each year by £200,000.

The director was convinced that this modification would eliminate the pollution.

(2)   The Chief Environmental Health Officer of the region consulted a team of government scientists about the pollutive effect. The scientists agreed that the plant modifications would reduce the level of pollution but they could give no precise figures to support the company's claim that it would be eliminated.

(3)   The company's cost of capital is 10% per annum.

(4)   The following extract is from the present value table for £1 at 10% per annum.

YEAR 1	£0.909
YEAR 2	£0.826
YEAR 3	£0.751
YEAR 4	£0.683
YEAR 5	£0.621

(5)   It should be assumed that all operating payments and revenue receipts occur at the end of each year.

REQUIRED

(a)   Net present value calculations for each of Plants A and B for the five year period.

For Plant B provide computations for the plant in its basic form and also with the modification to treat pollution.   *(11)*

(b)   Write a report advising Vernon Chemicals plc which plant should be purchased.

Give careful consideration to:

(i)   any factors about which you may have reservations.

(ii)   the social accounting aspects of the project.   *(14)*

(AEB 1991)

4   Rimham plc is considering investing in a new capital project and has a choice of three alternatives, only one of which can be implemented.

The following data is availale:

Capital project	1	2	3
	£	£	£
Initial outlay	400,000	460,000	360,000
Residual value	20,000	30,000	16,000
Net cash inflow			
Year 1	160,000	200,000	110,000
Year 2	140,000	140,000	120,000
Year 3	130,000	100,000	190,000
Year 4	120,000	100,000	200,000
Year 5	110,000	100,000	—

The company's cost of capital is 14%.

Extract from Discount tables:

Year	Present value factor for 14%
1	0.877
2	0.769
3	0.675
4	0.592
5	0.519

Project 2 has a higher labour content than the other two projects. Project 1 is powered by solid fuel whereas projects 2 and 3 utilise electricity.

Assume that capital outlays occur immediately and net cash flows occur at each year end.

You are required to:

(a) calculate the net present value of each project;   (10)
(b) calculate the pay back period of each project;   (3)
(c) state which project should be accepted based on financial considerations, giving your reasons;   (2)
(d) identify five other factors which might influence management's decision.(5)

                                                                                          (20)

                                                                          (Northern 1992)

TUTOR'S ANSWER

3 a)

Vernon Chemicals plc
New Chemical Processing Plants
Net Present Value Calculations

Year	Disc Fact.	Plant A		Plant B			
		Net Cash Flow	Disc Flow	Net Cash Flow Unadj	Disc Flow	Net Cash Flow Adj	Disc Flow
		£m	£m	£m	£m	£m	£m
1	0.909	1.8	1.636	3.6	3.272	3.4	3.091
2	0.826	2.5	2.065	4.1	3.387	3.9	3.221
3	0.751	2.5	1.878	4.5	3.380	4.3	3.229
4	0.683	2.2	1.503	4.7	3.210	4.5	3.074
5	0.621	2.9	1.801	5.6	3.478	5.4	3.353
Totals			8.883		16.727		15.968
Capital cost			5.000		10.000		11.500
NPV			3.883		6.727		4.468

b) i) On the basis of the raw data, the NPV calculations show the highest return for plant (B) whether modified or not. Thus, an initial recommendation may be to choose (B), since the decision rules require that the plant with the highest NPV be selected.

It may also happen that the plants may not operate as efficiently as predicted; the company's cost of capital may change; the plants may become obsolete before the income streams are realised. Neither is any information given about the plants' relative length of productive life. Indeed, nothing is known beyond the predictions for the first five years.

Are the plants equally reliable? What scope is there for expansion with each model?

ii) Profitability may not be the sole criterion: social aspects may need to be considered. Amongst the most important of these are the environmental effects of pollution. These are especially important if government scientists cannot give unqualified support to the company' plans for plant (B). The risks associated with the plant may just be too great.

Even if the plant can be supported, the location must also be considered: is it to be sited on a well established industrial estate, in a green belt, on the coast, or near to a residential area? Different environmental criteria may apply to each.

Generally, the evidence points towards the need for more technical investigations to be conducted into (B) order to inform the investment decision. Especially, since the more proven plant (A) is only marginally less profitable than the modified plant (B).

STUDENT'S ANSWER

4 a)

| | | PROJECT | | | | | |
| | | 1 | | 2 | | 3 | |
Yr	PV Factor	Cash Flow	PV Cash Flow	Cash Flow	PV Cash Flow	Cash Flow	PV Cash Flow
1	0.877	160 000	140 320	200 000	175 400	110 000	96 470
2	0.769	140 000	107 660	140 000	107 660	120 000	92 280
3	0.675	130 000	87 750	100 000	67 500	190 000	128 250
4	0.592	120 000	71 040	100 000	59 200	216 000	127 872
5	0.519	130 000	67 470	130 000	67 470	—	—
			474 240		477 230		444 872
Less investment			400 000		460 000		360 000
NPV			74 240		17 230		84 872

b)

| | PROJECT | | | | | |
| | 1 | | 2 | | 3 | |
	Years	Days	Years	Days	Years	Days
Payback:	2	281	3	73	2	307
Or	2.77		3.2		2.84	

c) Project (3) has a higher NPV than either of the others, and should therefore be selected using the NPV criteria. Using payback, Project (1) is the more attractive, since it pays for itself in a shorter time than either of the others.

d) Payback period, as a measure of liquidity; availability of finance; perceived accuracy of forecasts; environmental effects; availability of labour for project (2); provision of employment.

TUTOR'S COMMENT

The candidate has tackled the question well. Note especially how the residual values of the projects have been used to adjust the cash flows in the final year. In section (c) good use has been made of the answers to (a) and (b); the candidate has pointed out that NPV and payback give different results for the most favoured project. The comments in (d) are a little sketchy, and could profitably be expanded; nevertheless, the main points have been made, and the answer should score well.

OUTLINE ANSWERS

1 a) Ordinary shares receive dividend only after preference and debenture holders have been paid: thus a greater element of risk that they may receive nothing. Preference shares riskier than debentures, since debentures are loans to the company, and must receive their interest first. Often, too, debentures are secured upon specific fixed assets. Debentures are loans; interest must be paid irrespective of profit.

b) Limit to number of debentures fixed by level of confidence in the market that a company can generate sufficient profits year on year to service the debt. Since the interest must be paid whatever the level of profit, interest represents a fixed cost.

c) i)

COMPANY		A		B
Ord	7 × 16	112	3 × 16	48
Pref	2 × 14	28	2 × 14	28
Deb	1 × 7.2	7	5 × 7.2	36
		147		112
Weighted average		15		11

Note: $r = r(1 - t)$
            $= 12(1 - 0.4)$
            $= 12 \times 0.6$
            $= 7.2$

ii) Difference arises because of different capital structures, and effect of tax shield upon debenture interest paid.

d) i)   CYMBERLINE
                        13%

Year 1	55,000	0.885	48,675
Year 2	60,000	0.783	46,980
Year 3	145,000	0.693	100,485
Year 4	170,000	0.613	104,210
	Present value		300,350
	Cost		300,000
	NPV		350

Maximum cost of finance is 13% since at this level the NPV approaches zero.

ii) Ajax cost of capital is 15% - is greater than Cymberline's IRR, thus do not recommend for (A).
But Borg's cost is 11%; project may be recommended.

2 a)

	AB	CD
1989		
Profit 25%	1,000	1,000
Less	108	324
	892	676
Corp tax 45%	401.4	304.2
	490.6	371.8
Pref div 14%	154.0	70.0
	336.6	301.8
Return on ordinary shares	16.83	37.725
1990		
Profit 10%	400	400
Less deb int 12%	108	324
	292	76
Corp tax 45%	131.4	34.2
	160.6	41.8
Pref div 14%	154.0	70.0
	6.6	(28.2)
Return on ordinary shares	0.33	—

b) i) Because debenture interest can be set off against corporation tax, the company's burden of servicing the debt is reduced. Thus, when profits are high as in 1989, that company with some gearing accrues better returns to the ordinary shares than the company without.

ii) However, debenture interest is a fixed charge which must be paid irrespective of the level of earnings. Thus, when profits fall, the fixed charge bears heavily and may swallow all the profits, leaving none for the shareholders. The higher the proportion of debt to equity, the greater the risk that this may occur: debenture holders therefore demand increasing returns to compensate them for the added risk, to the extent that either the debentures become too expensive for the company to service, or the investing public refuses to purchase them.

Now attempt the review questions on page 319. The answers are given on page 329.

On the following pages you will find 'Review Sheets' for Chapters 3 to 20. You may like to cut these sheets out of the book, and place them in a revision folder. Write your answers on separate sheets of paper, and keep these in your folder, too. This will help you with revision nearer the exams. Answers are provided at the end of the book.

REVIEW SHEET FOR CHAPTER 3

1) Books of prime entry are the first stage in the book-keeping process. Which of the following are books of prime entry? _____

    Journal   Sales Day Book   General Ledger   Petty Cash Book

2) Name and explain the six types of error which may still be present even though a trial balance's totals agree.

3) Stocks are usually valued at the 'lower of cost and net realisable value'. If a business has opening stock of £10,000 and closing stock of £15,000, show the stock account for the year, including transfers to the final accounts.

4) An accrual is a liability for an expense owing at the year-end, show an Electricity account in a general ledger which starts the year with an accrual of £200, has cheque payments of £2,300, and a closing accrual of £300.

5) A prepayment is an asset, representing an amount paid in advance at the end of the financial year.
    Show a Rent account, where there was a prepayment of £600 at the start of the year, cheques paid totalling £4,400 during the year, and a prepayment of £700 at the end of the year.

6) Capital expenditure = fixed assets purchased. State which of the following are items of capital expenditure and which are items of revenue expenditure.
    i) A telephone bill _____
    ii) A new telephone _____
    iii) Motor car insurance _____
    iv) Repairs to a motor car _____
    iv) A new radio for a motor car _____

7) Depreciation is the loss in value of a fixed asset due to such factors as usage, time or obsolescence. Calculate the depreciation for 1993 in each of these two situations:

    i) A car is bought on 1 January 1992 for £8,000, and is expected to last for five years when it will have a disposal value estimated at £500. Depreciation is calculated on the straight line basis.
    ii) A computer is bought on 1 January 1992 for £2,000 and is depreciated at 60% per annum on a reducing balance basis.

8) A provision is an amount set aside out of profits to either reduce the recorded value of an asset or to cover an expected liability. Show the provision accounts in a general ledger for the following:

    i) Opening provision for doubtful debts £2,000; closing provision £3,500
    ii) Opening provision for doubtful debts £4,000; closing provision £3,700

9) When a fixed asset is sold, a calculation is made of any under- or over-provision for depreciation. Show the disposal of fixed assets account for the following:

    i) A car bought for £6,000, and sold for £1,500 when it had been depreciated by £4,000
    ii) A machine bought for £9,000 and sold for £500 when it had been depreciated by £7,000.

10) A journal shows a summary of the book-keeping entries for some specialised transactions. Show a journal entry for transferring a misposted expense of £500, which should have been posted into a Rent account instead of a Rates account.

REVIEW SHEET FOR CHAPTER 4

1. Under the revaluation method, depreciation is calculated by simply comparing a closing valuation with an opening valuation. Can you state a situation where this method might be the most appropriate?

2. The machine-hour method of depreciation links depreciation to actual usage.
    A machine costs £8,000 and has an expected residual value of £1,000. It is expected to be in use

8 hours per day, 300 days per year for five years. In Year 1 its actual usage is 2,200 hours, in year 2 it is 1,700 hours. What depreciation would be charged in each of those two years?

3. The establishment of a sinking fund helps a company to find the cash to replace assets at the end of their lives. Why do very few firms use sinking funds?

4. An appropriation account starts with the net profit, and shows what has happened to it. Name a type of business organisation where you would *not* expect to see an appropriation account as part of the final accounts.

5. In a manufacturing business, it is usual for 'stocks' to comprise three separate categories. What are they?

6. Explain the meaning of 'splitting the profit' in a manufacturing business.

7. A provision for unrealised profit account is needed where finished stocks in the manufacturing account are valued at cost plus a notional profit.
A company shows £145,000 as a provision for unrealised profit at the start of a year. During the year, its closing stock of finished goods is valued at £392,000, which includes a notional mark-up on manufacturing cost of 40%. Show the provision for unrealised profit account for the year.

8. A receipts and payments account is a summary of the cash and bank transactions. Why is this unsatisfactory for presentation to a club's members at an Annual General Meeting?

9. To follow usual double-entry principles, a club should prepare an Income and Expenditure account and a balance sheet. Why doesn't a club balance sheet show 'Capital', and what takes its place?

10. To arrive at a figure for subscriptions, adjustments often have to be made for amounts owing and owed at the start and end of a year.
A club with a membership of 400 people charged an annual subscription of £30 per annum. 12 members owed subscriptions at the start of the year (all paid during the current year) and 14 at the end. 2 members had prepaid at the start of the year, and 3 at the end. Calculate the amount to be shown as 'subscriptions' in the Income and Expenditure account for the current year.

REVIEW SHEET FOR CHAPTER 5

A control account is often used where it is necessary to find a missing figure and where records are incomplete. From the following lists of balances, draw up separate control accounts. Insert any missing figures as appropriate.

Purchase Ledger Control Accounts	£
1. Opening creditors	87,600
Opening debit balances	520
Cash and cheques paid	74,200
Goods returned to suppliers	160
Discount received	1,700
Contras to sales ledger	550
Interest charged by suppliers	80
Purchases	60,410
Closing creditors	71,300
Closing debit balances	340
2. Opening creditors	12,417
Opening debit balances	100
Cash and cheques paid	24,300
Discount received	600
Purchases	?
Closing creditors	15,400
Closing debit balances	200
3. Opening creditors	22,000
Cash and cheques paid	?
Goods returned to suppliers	140
Contras to sales ledger	200
Purchases	38,600
Closing creditors	23,300

4.
Opening creditors	58,062
Opening debit balances	304
Cash and cheques paid	79,900
Goods returned to suppliers	600
Discount received	1,472
Contras to sales ledger	480
Interest charged by suppliers	100
Purchases	74,593
Closing creditors	?
Closing debit balances	84

Sales Ledger Control Accounts

5.
Opening debtors	31,750
Opening credit balances	240
Cash and cheques received	59,920
Goods returned by customerts	1,060
Discount allowed	2,500
Bad debts written off	320
Sales	64,650
Closing debtors	32,660
Closing credit balances	300

6.
Opening debtors	81,725
Cash and cheques received	101,474
Goods returned by customers	2,590
Bad debts written off	600
Sales	94,330
Closing debtors	?

7.
Opening debtors	8,020
Opening credit balances	100
Cash and cheques received	?
Goods returned by customers	240
Discount allowed	750
Bad debts written off	180
Interest charged to customers	60
Sales	14,040
Closing debtors	10,700
Closing credit balances	56

8.
Opening debtors	29,314
Opening credit balances	282
Cash and cheques received	78,200
Discount allowed	370
Interest charged to customers	100
Sales	?
Closing debtors	31,760
Closing credit balances	200

9. Suspense accounts are temporary accounts which are closed when they are no longer needed. Give two situations which might require a suspense account to be opened.

10. Incomplete records are book-keeping records which are less than full double-entry. State the disadvantages of incomplete records.

REVIEW SHEET FOR CHAPTER 6

1. Although sole trading has a number of advantages including few legal formalities, there are also disadvantages. List four of these.

2. Occasionally, partners fail to agree over their financial arrangements. In the absence of any express or implied agreement, is any interest allowed to partners who have contributed loans in excess of their agreed capital?

3. A partnership appropriation account shows how profits (or losses) are allocated to partners according to their partnership agreement.

   Prepare a (vertical) appropriation account from the following information for the partnership of Adam and Barker:

   Net Profit: £45,000, Interest on Drawings: Adam £1,300, Barker £2,500, Salary to Barker: £10,000, Drawings: Adam £25,000, Barker £22,000, Profit shares divided Adam (3/5ths), Barker (2/5ths).

4. Many partnerships maintain both capital accounts and current accounts, with the former recording only original capital contributed, and additions and withdrawals of capital, and the latter showing all other financial matters affecting partners.

    Prepare current accounts for the partnership of Adam and Barker (see 3 above), assuming that the opening current account balances were: Adam £900, Barker £800 (debit).

5. Goodwill has been defined as the difference between the value of a business as a whole and the value of its separate assets less liabilities. Why might a partnership *not* want to record its goodwill value?

6. If new partners are admitted to the partnership, it is usual to revalue goodwill. Any increase in the recorded value is transferred to the existing partners, and 'charged' to the incoming partners, as the price which they have to pay for the privilege of sharing profits in the future.

    Whose accounts are debited, and whose are credited with the change in value?

7. The end of a partnership may come about for a number of reasons. Name two of these reasons.

8. When a partnership is dissolved, the closing entries in the partnership's books are entered in a Realisation Account, with the final profit or loss transferred to the individual partners. To which side of the account are the book values of assets transferred?

9. A partnership might decide to convert itself into a limited company. If the allocation of shares to the partners does not exactly match the partners' closing balances within the partnership, how will the partnership books be closed?

10. What is the rule in *Garner v. Murray*?

REVIEW SHEET FOR CHAPTER 7

1. What might happen to professional accountants who fail to follow accounting standards?

2. SSAP 2 *Disclosure of Accounting Policies* names four fundamental concepts. What are they?

3. The 1985 Companies Act requires separate items to be valued separately, rather than being aggregated.
    A business with three stock items records the following cost values and net realisable values at its year-end. What value should be shown in the balance sheet?

	Cost £	Net Realisable Value £
Widgets	32,000	12,000
Truckles	24,000	32,000
Farfles	18,000	20,000

4. There are a number of theoretical models for pricing stock, including LIFO, FIFO and AVCO. If a company sells fresh cream cakes, which of these models might be the most appropriate?

5. SSAP 9 *Stocks and Long Term Contracts* requires an expected loss on a long term contract to be recognised (i.e. taken into the profit and loss account) as soon as it is foreseen. Why?

6. SSAP 13 *Research and Development Expenditure* requires all research expenditure to be written off to Profit and Loss Account, but development expenditure can be carried forward on the balance sheet as a deferred asset under certain circumstances.
    What would be the effect on (a) profit and (b) total net assets if £100,000 was treated as a deferred asset rather than being written off?

7. Post balance sheet events can be either 'adjusting' or 'non-adjusting'. The former changes the figures for the financial statement ending on the balance sheet date, whilst the latter only requires a note to be appended to the statements.
    Which of the following are 'adjusting' post balance events, and which are 'non-adjusting'? The balance sheet date is 30 June, and the directors are expected to approve the accounts on 22 September.
    1) A takeover bid received on 6 July.
    2) Property owned by the company falls in value by a material amount in July and August.
    3) Fire damages a warehouse on 18 July

4) Major new issue of shares on 24 September

5) Stock valued at cost in the balance sheet can only be sold at less than cost on 15 August

8. A contingency is a condition which exists at the balance sheet date, where the outcome will be confirmed only by the occurrence or non-occurrence of one or more uncertain future events.
   A company has a court case pending at the balance sheet date, and the costs have so far totalled £250,000. No judgement has been given, but the company's legal advisors think that it is probable that the jury will decide in the company's favour, and damages of at least £10m will be awarded. How, if at all, should this be shown in the balance sheet?

9. SSAP 21 *Accounting for leases and hire purchase contracts*, identifies two types of lease agreements: finance and operating.
   A finance lease is likely to be relatively long-term whereas an operating lease may be only for a few days or weeks. If an asset is used under a finance lease agreement, how is it shown in the financial statements of the lessee?

10. What is the expression used to justify the inclusion of leased assets (finance lease) on a lessee company's balance sheet, even though the company does not legally own them?

REVIEW SHEET FOR CHAPTER 8

1. The conversion of an unincorporated business into a limited company means that far more legal requirements have to be followed. What, then, is the major benefit of carrying on business as a limited company?

2. All companies which have their shares traded on a Stock Exchange are public limited companies. What is the main difference between these and *private* limited companies?

3. Dividends to holders to ordinary shareholders are normally expressed as a number of pence per ordinary share. How are dividends to *preference* shareholders usually stated?

4. It is said that a dividend is an appropriation of profits, but debenture interest is a charge against profits. What does this mean?

5. Reserves can either be distributable (revenue) or non-distributable (capital). Give two examples of each.

6. Gearing is the relationship between a company's risk capital (ordinary shares) and its fixed return funding (debentures, etc). If a company is said to be 'low geared', does this mean that in times of generally falling profits it is safer or riskier than a high geared company, and why?

7. Why do the directors of a highly geared company have less flexibility regarding the appropriation of profits than a low geared one?

8. All companies must produce 'unpublished' as well as 'published' accounts. Why?

9. There are a number of formats for published accounts which are laid down by the Companies Act. What is the main purpose of formats?

10. FRS 3 virtually abolished 'extraordinary items'. This means that it is far harder for companies to present unrealistically high eps figures. What is 'eps', and why is it so important?

REVIEW SHEET FOR CHAPTER 9

1. When recording the issue of shares for cash to the general public, it is usual to open an *application and allotment* account in the ledger. What entries are likely to appear on the credit side of this account?

2. A bonus issue is made to transfer reserves to ordinary shareholders.
   If a company issues £400,000 of bonus shares, what effect will this have on the company's bank account?

3. A rights issue gives existing shareholders the right to subscribe for more shares, on a pro rata basis.
   If a company makes a rights issue of shares with a value of £400,000, what effect will this have on the company's bank account if 90% of the shareholders take up their rights?

4. It is an advantage for company directors to have the maximum flexibility regarding the use of reserves.
   What does this mean in practice for a company which is considering a bonus issue?

5. If a company's share price becomes very high, then there is a way of reducing the value to more realistic levels without affecting the value of the company in any way. What is this device called, and how does it work?

6. It is a statutory requirement that a capital redemption reserve is created if shares are redeemed other than out of the proceeds of a new issue of shares.
   What is the situation if debentures are redeemed?

7. Debentures might be redeemed at a *premium*, at *par*, or at a *discount.*
   Explain what these three terms mean.

8. Some companies have ordinary shares which are redeemable. How does Company Law prevent a situation where a company might end up with no shareholders if all the ordinary shares are redeemed?

9. A minority interest is the proportion of shares of a subsidiary not held by the holding company.
   If at 31 December, the minority interest of Oasis plc was £120m, how would this be shown on the consolidated balance sheet?

10. When producing consolidated accounts, unrealised profit on stocks must be eliminated. Explain the meaning of *unrealised*, and why must this adjustment be made?

REVIEW SHEET FOR CHAPTER 10

1. The objective of FRS1 *Cash Flow Statements* is for companies to report on a standard basis their cash generation and cash absorption for a period.
   Even though cash flow statements are seen as an improvement on 'funds flow' statements, they are not an infallible guide to future performance. Why is this?

2. Cash flow statements must follow a standard format, which contain five headings. What are those headings?

3. Every cash flow statement starts by showing the net cash flow from operating activities, but it is optional to show certain additional information, known as the 'direct method'.
   What additional information is given by the 'direct method'?

4. Every cash flow statement has a note which reconciles the operating profit (or loss) to the net cash inflow (or outflow) from operating activities.
   Depreciation and any profit or loss on sales of assets are shown as adjustments in this note. Why?

5. In the note which reconciles the operating profit (or loss) to the net cash inflow (or outflow) from operating activities, the effects on cash flow of changes to stocks, debtors and creditors are shown as adjustments to the operating profit.
   How would the following be shown in the note: as outflows (i.e. shown in brackets) or inflows (i.e. not shown in brackets):

   Increase in debtors _____

   Decrease in stocks _____

   Decrease in creditors _____

6. 'Returns on investments and servicing of finance' includes dividends paid during the year.
   If a company started the year with a proposed dividend of £10,000, paid an interim dividend of £6,000, and ended with a proposed dividend of £11,000, what figure would be shown in the cash flow statement?

7. 'Taxation' includes tax actually paid during the year.
   If a company started its year with a provision for tax of £24,000, paid an agreed tax figure of £23,500, and ended with a provision of £30,000, what figure would appear on the cash flow statement?

8. Fixed assets bought in a year will be shown under the heading 'Investing activities'.
   If a company starts its year with fixed assets having a net book value of £20,000, ends with £24,000, charged depreciation in the year of £5,000 and sold assets for £3,500 which had a net book value of £3,000, what amount will appear on the cash flow statement as 'purchase of fixed assets'?

9. What other figures from the information in question 8 will appear in the cash flow statement?

10. What figures from the information in question 8 will appear in the note which reconciles the operating profit to the net cash flow from operating activities?

REVIEW SHEET FOR CHAPTER 11

Use this information to answer questions 1–3 below.

| | \multicolumn{4}{c}{Company:} | | | |
	A	B	C	D
Sales	48,000	126,000	59,000	68,000
Purchases	21,000	58,000	30,000	45,000
Opening Stock	6,000	12,000	20,000	30,000
Closing Stock	7,000	6,000	24,000	25,000

1. The gross profit margin should be fairly constant from year to year, unless the sales mix has changed, or changes in purchase prices are not being reflected in similar changes in sales prices. Unexplained changes in the gross profit margin might be caused by theft of stock, or sales being unrecorded.
   Calculate the gross profit margins for each of the companies A–D above.

   A _____ B _____ C _____ D _____

2. The rate of stock turnover (stock turn) shows how quickly or slowly a company is able to sell its stocks. A company makes more profit if it can sell stock more quickly without having to greatly reduce its gross profit margin.
   Calculate the rate of stock turnover (in days) for each of the companies A–D above.

   A _____ B _____ C _____ D _____

3. Many companies fix their selling prices by adding a mark-up to cost prices. Calculate the mark-up for each of the companies A–D above.

   A _____ B _____ C _____ D _____
   Use this information to answer questions 4–6 below.

| | \multicolumn{4}{c}{Company:} | | | |
	E	F	G	H
Stock	72,000	16,000	30,000	50,000
Debtors	26,000	60,000	50,000	20,000
Bank	11,000	30,000 (o/d)	30,000	20,000
Creditors (Current)	35,000	65,000	10,000	20,000
Debentures	40,000	—	60,000	50,000
Capital employed	240,000	190,000	100,000	200,000

4. The current ratio shows the overall adequacy of working capital by comparing a company's current assets with its current liabilities.
   Calculate the current ratio for each of the companies E–H above.

   E _____ F _____ G _____ H _____

5. The acid test is a key measure of a company's liquidity, as it shows how well a company is able to meet its liabilities as they fall due.
   Calculate the acid test for each of the companies E–H above.

   E _____ F _____ G _____ H _____

6. Gearing is the relationship of fixed return funding to the company's total long-term capital.
   Using the formula

   $$\frac{\text{Fixed return funding, including bank borrowing}}{\text{Total capital employed}}$$

   Calculate the gearing percentage for each of the companies E–H above.

   E _____ F _____ G _____ H _____

7. If a company has a very strong working capital ratio, this may not necessarily be a good thing. Why not?

8. A price earnings ratio indicates the strength of a company's stock market price when compared with its earnings per share.
   If a company's eps is 14p per share and its stock market price is £2.24, what is its p/e ratio?

9. A company's dividend yield shows the return which can be obtained by investing at a particular price.
   A company's dividend yield has risen from 3% to 8% in a year and yet its dividend per share has stayed constant. What can one deduce about its market price?

10. Under Current Cost Accounting (CCA), four adjustments are made to convert a historical cost profit into a Current Cost profit.
    What is the purpose of the *depreciation* adjustment?

REVIEW SHEET FOR CHAPTER 12

1. Define the terms;

   a financial accounting: _____

   b management accounting: _____

   c elements of cost: _____

   d prime cost: _____

   e direct costs: _____

   f overheads: _____

2 List the five functions of management;

   a _____

   b _____

   c _____

   d _____

   e _____

3 Distinguish between;
   a strategic planning and operational planning;

   b produce and period costs; _____

   c cost centre and service centre; _____

4 'Cost accounting is part of management accounting.' Explain this statement.

5 Complete the following equations;

   a Direct Materials + _____ + Direct Expenses = Prime Cost

   b Indirect Materials + Indirect Labour + Indirect Expenses = _____

   c _____ + _____ + _____ = Total Production Overhead

   d _____ + _____ + _____ = Total Production Cost

   e Total Production Cost + _____ + _____ + R & D Overhead = Total Cost

6 What part do business systems play in converting raw data into information?

7 Give an example of:

   a a direct material cost; _____

   b a direct labour cost; _____

   c a direct expense; _____

8 Give an example of:

   a an indirect labour cost; _____

   b an indirect material cost; _____

   c an indirect expense; _____

REVIEW SHEET FOR CHAPTER 13

1 List the three general approaches to stores organisation:

   a _____

b _____

c _____

2 What five considerations apply to stores control?

a _____

b _____

c _____

d _____

e _____

3 Calculate the re-order levels from the following;

	Usage/month	Lead time (months)	Minimum Stock	Re-order Level
a	300	0.5	70	_____
b	400	0.25	80	_____
c	600	0.75	100	_____
d	800	2.5	240	_____

4 Calculate the economic order quantities from the following;

	Usage/month	Holding Cost/unit	Procurement Cost/order	EOQ
a	5,000	£100	£4	_____
b	16,200	£20	£5	_____
c	12,250	£125	£25	_____

5 State whether the following statements are true or false;
   a FIFO assumes that the first items to be received will be the first to be issued
   b Under LIFO closing stock is valued at current prices
   c When prices are rising LIFO will show the greatest profit
   d The profits under AVCO are between those of LIFO and FIFO whether prices are rising or falling
   e It is not necessary for the actual issue of stock to conform to the accounting method used

6 What is the difference between the perpetual and the periodic methods of valuing stocks?

7 Calculate the value of closing stock using the periodic method:

Opening Stock	Receipts	Issues
8 @ £20	20 @ £21	25
	40 @ £25	30

   a FIFO _____
   b LIFO _____
   c AVCO _____

8 Why is it necessary to adopt methods such as LIFO, FIFO and AVCO in accounting for materials issues?

9 What is the purpose of the stores ledger?

10 What are the two assumptions underlying the 'saw-tooth' graph?

   a _____
   b _____

REVIEW SHEET FOR CHAPTER 14

1 State the function of;

   a clock cards _____

   b time sheets _____

   c job tickets _____

   d piece work tickets _____

2 What is the fundamental difference between time rates and piece rates?

3   What are the disadvantages of a) time rates and b) piece rates?

a _____

b _____

4   A company operates a time rate system of paying its workers. The standard working week is 37 hours payable at £4.40 per hour; thereafter, the first five hours worked are paid at 125% of the standard rate, and any remainder at 150% of the standard rate. How much did Jill earn in the week when she worked 48 hours?

5   Under a business's premium bonus scheme, employees receive 50 per cent of the time saved as a bonus. Three workers are given identical tasks to perform, the standard time for which is eight hours at £5.20 per hour. Freda completes the job in four hours, Georgia in six hours, and Helen in eight hours. Assuming that they each work at this rate for a full 40 hour week, what would their earnings be?

Time (hrs)				Pay (£)				
Al'd	Took	Saved	Bonus	Basic	Bonus	Total	Rate/hour	Week

F _____

G _____

H _____

6   A company operates a collective bonus scheme based upon passed earnings and added value. Whenever the ratio is reduced from the agreed 75 per cent, a bonus of 1.5 per cent of added value is payable. Calculate the amount of bonus due from the following figures;

Year	Added Value £000	Earnings £000	Ratio E:AV	Bonus Payable
19–3	400	290	_____	_____
19-4	700	530	_____	_____
19–5	900	670	_____	_____

7   A company's profit sharing scheme provides 8 per cent of the profits be issued to employees after allowing for the full dividend on preference shares and a 15 per cent dividend on the ordinary shares. Calculate the amount due to the profit sharing scheme.

Company	A £000	B £000	C £000
Ordinary shares of £1	800	1 400	2 200
12 per cent pref shares of £1	200	600	800
Profit	300	400	600
Pref div	_____	_____	_____
Ordy div	_____	_____	_____
Distributable profits	_____	_____	_____
To profit sharing scheme	_____	_____	_____

8   Identify one main advantage and one main disadvantage of profit sharing schemes;

Advantage _____

Disadvantage _____

9   List five purposes of a wages system;

a _____

b _____

c _____

d _____

e _____

REVIEW SHEET FOR CHAPTER 15

1 Give examples of;

   a fixed overheads _____

   b semi fixed overheads _____

   c variable overheads _____

2 Define overhead;

   a allotment _____

   b apportionment _____

   c absorption _____

3 List eight bases which may be used to apportion overheads amongst departments, and give examples of when each might be used;

        Basis   *Example*

   a _____

   b _____

   c _____

   d _____

   e _____

   f _____

   g _____

   h _____

4 a) Apportion the service departments' overheads to the production departments, on the basis that (G's) overheads are to be apportioned: (A) 40%; (B) 25%; (C) 20%; (H) 15%. And (H's) overheads are to be split; (A) 30%; (B) 40%; (C) 25%; (G) 5%.

	Production			Service	
	A	B	C	G	H
Total overheads	10 000	8 000	4 000	2 000	1 000
G's o/h					
Total					
H's o/h					
Total					

   b) Calculate the overhead absorption rate if (A) works 592 machine hours; (B) works 600 direct labour hours and (C) works 390 machine hours during the period.

5 List the three approaches for dealing with inter service department transfers;

   a _____

   b _____

   c _____

6 Use the elimination method to apportion the following overheads. (S's) overheads are to be apportioned: (L) 40%; (M) 35%; (N) 20%; (T) 5%. (T's) overheads: (L) 30%; (M) 20%; (N) 40%; (S) 10%.

	Production			Service	
	A	B	C	G	H
Total overheads	12 000	10 000	6 000	3 000	2 000
S's o/h					
Total					
T's o/h					
Total					

7   Use the figures in (6) above to apportion the service departments' overheads using the continuous apportionment method.

	SERVICE DEPARTMENT	
	S	T
Initial overhead	3,000	2,000
5% of (S) to (T)		
Total		
10% of total to (S)		
Total		
5% of (S's) *increase* to (T)		
Total		
10% of (T's) *increase* to (S)		
Total		

8   Why is it meaningless to state that one method of apportioning overheads is less accurate than another?

9   What is the function of the overhead adjustment account?

REVIEW SHEET FOR CHAPTER 16

1   What forms may (a) specific order and (b) operation costing take?

   a   specific order costing _____

   b   operation costing _____

2   What are the essential differences between job costing and contract costing? Give examples of each.

3   Identify two reasons why recorded profits on contracts in progress may be reduced.

   a _____

   b _____

4   Calculate the profit to be taken on a contract where;
   Value of work certified; £500 000
   Cost of work certified;   £420 000
   Retention rate: 15%

5   What is the essential difference between specific order costing and process costing?

6   In process costing, why is it usual to show separate accounts for abnormal losses and abnormal gains, but not for normal losses?

7   At the end of the month a business had produced 7,000 completed items, with 500 items semi-finished. The details were:

	COST ELEMENT			
Total cost (£)	13,275	8,790	10,080	32,145
WIP degree completed	75	65	40	

   Calculate (a) the total equivalent production and the cost per completed unit; and (b) the value of the WIP.

| | COST ELEMENT | | | |
	Materials	Labour	O'heads	Total
WIP equiv units				
Finished items				
Total production				
Total cost (£)				
Cost/unit (£)				

Cost of 7 000 finished items = _____

Total cost less cost of finished items = _____

WIP value = _____

8 Distinguish between;

   a waste and scrap _____

   b by-product and joint product _____

9 List three ways in which joint costs might be apportioned to *by-products*.

   a _____

   b _____

   c _____

10 List three ways in which joint costs might be apportioned to *joint products*.

   a _____

   b _____

   c _____

REVIEW SHEET FOR CHAPTER 17

1 Identify the graph which shows;

   a fixed costs per unit; _____

   b variable costs per unit; _____

   c total variable costs; _____

   d total fixed costs; _____

2 State whether the following statements are true or false;

   a absorption costing assumes that fixed costs attach to products _____

   b under marginal costing, no fixed costs find their way into subsequent periods _____

   c absorption costing values stocks at variable cost _____

   d the stock valuation under marginal costing is always less than under absorption costing

   e profits under marginal costing are always greater than under absorption costing _____

3 Complete the following accounting statements; there was no opening stock at the beginning of the period.

	ABSORPTION		MARGINAL	
	£	£	£	£
Sales: 1,200 units @ £50		60,000		60,000
Less prime cost: 1,500 units	24,000		24,000	
Less closing stock: marginal			....	
Fixed costs	15,000		15,000	
	—————		—————	
		....		34,200
Less closing stock: absorb	....			
	—————			
		....		
		—————		—————
Profit		....		....

4 Prepare a statement showing how the difference in profits in (3) has arisen;
Profit under marginal costing

	£
Profit under marginal costing	....
....	....
Profit under absorption costing	....

5 Complete the following equations;

a contribution = _____

b contribution per unit = _____

c break-even point (units) = _____

d break-even point (£ sales) = _____

e sales (£) for required profit = _____

REVIEW SHEET FOR CHAPTER 18

1 List the six main stages in preparing a budget:

a _____

b _____

c _____

d _____

e _____

f _____

2 Define the terms:

a operating budget _____

b capital budget _____

c limiting factor _____

3 a Complete the following production budget (units):

	J	F	M	A	M	J
Opening stock	210	____	____	____	____	____
Production	420	540	660	630	780	700
Sales	420	430	870	600	760	810
Closing Stock	____	____	____	____	____	____

b   What would the opening stock need to be if closing stock during the period was to be at least 150 units?

4   What three functions does a cash budget perform?

a _____

b _____

c _____

5   List the three stages in preparing a cash budget:

a _____

b _____

c _____

6   Define the terms:

a   master budget _____

b   flexible budget _____

7   Complete the following flexible budget:

MANUFACTURING OVERHEAD BUDGET: July–December, 1994

	Monthly output (000 kg)			
	7	8	9	10
Variable overhead (£000)	10.0	11.2	12.8	14.6
Fixed overhead (£000)	4.0	4.0	4.0	4.0
Total (£000)				
Machine hours	160	190	220	250
Overhead rates/hour (£)				

8   Assume that two identical jobs were completed in consecutive months; one when output was at 7000 kg, and one when output was 9000 kg. Labour costs for each were 8 hours at £5.60/hour; material costs were £210; and machine time was 16 hours. What was the cost of the job?

	JOB	
	X	Y
Materials	_____	_____
Labour	_____	_____
Overheads	_____	_____
Total	_____	_____

REVIEW SHEET FOR CHAPTER 19

1   Define the terms;

a   variance _____

b   adverse variance _____

c   favourable variance _____

d   management by exception _____

e   standard hour _____

2   What three levels of activity may be used when setting standards?

a _____

b _____

c _____

3   Complete the following equations;

a productivity ratio = _____ × 100

b production volume ratio = _____ × 100

c capacity ratio = _____ × 100

4 If actual production = 390 std hrs; actual hours worked = 420; and budgeted production = 400; calculate

   a the productivity ratio _____

   _____

   b the production volume ratio _____

   _____

   c the capacity ratio _____

5 Calculate the variances from the following;
   Standard price £2.40 kg; Actual price £2.60 kg; standard usage 80 kg; actual usage 78 kg.

   a *Total variance*

                                                          £

   Std price × std usage _____ = _____

   Act price × act usage_____ = _____

   Total variance   = _____

   b *Price variance*

   (Std price − Act price) × Act quant _____ = _____

   c *Usage variance*

   (Std quant − Act quant) × Std price _____ = _____

6 Perform the following calculations from the information given;

Total variable overhead (£)	420 000	435 000
Total fixed overhead (£)	300 000	290 000
Volume of production (std hrs)	6 000	7 000
Units produced	250	270

   Standard variable overhead rate _____

   Standard fixed overhead rate _____

   Standard hours per unit produced _____

   Total variable overhead variance

   Actual overhead _____

   Budgeted o/h for actual production _____

   Favourable overhead _____

   Expenditure variance

   $\left\{ \text{Actual volume} \times \begin{array}{l}\text{Variable} \\ \text{o/h rate}\end{array} \right\} - \begin{array}{l}\text{Actual} \\ \text{Variable o/h}\end{array}$

   Efficiency variance

   $\left\{ \begin{array}{l}\text{Standard input} \\ \text{volume}\end{array} - \begin{array}{l}\text{Actual input} \\ \text{volume}\end{array} \right\} \times \begin{array}{l}\text{Std variable o/h} \\ \text{rate}\end{array}$

   Total fixed overhead variance

   Actual overhead _____

   Fixed o/h allocated to production _____

   Favourable variance _____

   Expenditure variance

   Budgeted overhead − Actual overhead

Volume variance

$$\left\{ \begin{array}{l} \text{Actual quantity of} \\ \text{work done} \end{array} - \begin{array}{l} \text{Standard quantity} \\ \text{of work done} \end{array} \right\} \times \begin{array}{l} \text{Standard fixed} \\ \text{overhead rate} \end{array}$$

REVIEW SHEET FOR CHAPTER 20

1 How much interest will be earned over two periods by £1 000 invested at 10 per cent per period if the money is invested;

   a at simple interest _____

   b at compound interest _____

2 Show how £2 000 invested at 5 per cent interest compounded half yearly earns more than £2 000 invested at 10 per cent per year.

   _____

3 Complete the following table;

Amount (£)	Periods	Compound Interest Rate of Interest	Compound amount of £1	Total
19	3	5	_____	_____
22	7	2	_____	_____
43	10	8	_____	_____
172	12	11	_____	_____
346	15	14	_____	_____

4 Define;

   a time value of money _____

   b discounted cash flow _____

   c net present value _____

   d internal rate of return _____

5 Complete the following table;

Amount (£)	Periods	Present Value Rate of Interest	PV of £1	Total
24	5	3	_____	_____
67	8	6	_____	_____
92	10	9	_____	_____
146	13	15	_____	_____
315	14	18	_____	_____

6 Find the rate at which the following project's NPV approaches zero;

	Net cash flows (£)	Discount factor	PV (£)
Year 0	(20 000)	_____	(20 000)
1	6 800	_____	_____
2	8 600	_____	_____
3	8 100	_____	_____
NPV			_____

7 Calculate the rate of return per ordinary share for Exe Ltd and Wye Ltd. Each company expects a return on capital of 20 per cent. Debenture interest is allowable against corporation tax which stands at 30 per cent.

Capital Structure	EXE Ltd (£)	WYE Ltd (£)
Ordinary shares (£1)	800 000	500 000
12% Debentures	—	300 000
	800 000	800 000
20 per cent return on capital	_____	_____
Less debenture interest		_____
		_____
Less corporation tax at 30%	_____	_____
Available to ordinary shares	_____	_____
Rate of return per share	_____	_____

8 Calculate the after-tax cost of debentures;

	Debenture Interest (%)	Corporation Tax (%)	After-tax Rate (%)
a	8	20	_____
b	10	30	_____
c	12	40	_____
d	14	50	_____

9 Calculate the weighted average cost of capital for each of the following companies. Debenture interest is allowable against corporation tax which is at 50 per cent.

Company	L £000	M £000	N £000
Ordinary shares 16%	1 000	600	500
Preference shares 14%		400	100
Debentures 12%			400
	1 000	1 000	1 000

	Prop-ort'n	L Rate %	P × R	Prop-ort'n	M Rate %	P × R	Prop-ort'n	N Rate %	P × R
Ordy									
Pref									
Deb									
Total		_____			_____			_____	
Cost capital		_____			_____			_____	

ANSWERS TO REVIEW SHEET QUESTIONS

CHAPTER 3

1. Journal, Sales Day Book, Petty Cash Book
2. COPCOR: see text
3.

Stock Account

Opening stock b/f	10,000	Trading a/c	10,000
Trading a/c	15,000	Closing stock c/d	25,000
	25,000		25,000
Opening stock b/d	15,000		

4.

Electricity Account

Cheque payments	2,300	Accrual b/f	200
Accrual c/d	300	P&L a/c	2,400
	2,600		2,600
		Accrual b/d	300

5.

Rent Account

Prepayment b/f	600	P&L a/c	4,300
Cheques paid	4,400	Prepayment c/d	700
	5,000		5,000
Prepayment b/d	700		

6. (ii) and (v) are capital expenditure items. The others are revenue items.
7. (i) Depreciation is £1,500 [(£8,000 − £500)/5]
   (ii) Depreciation is £480 [(£2,000 − £1,200) × 60/100]
8. (i)

Provision for Doubtful Debts Account

		Provision b/f	2,000
Provision c/d	3,500	P&L a/c	1,500
	3,500		3,500
		Provision b/d	3,500

(ii)

Provision for Doubtful Debts Account

P&L a/c	300	Provision b/f	4,000
Provision c/d	3,700		
	4,000		4,000
		Provision b/d	3,700

9.

Disposals of Fixed Assets Account

Cost of assets disposed		Proceeds of sale	
– car	6,000	– car	1,500
– machine	9,000	– machine	500
		Depreciation	
		– on car sold	4,000
		– on machine sold	7,000
		P&L a/c	
		(underprovision)	2,000
	15,000		15,000

10. Journal
    DR Rent Account 500
    CR Rates Account 500
    – Transfer of misposted item from Rent Account to Rates Account.

CHAPTER 4

1. Where there are large numbers of relatively small items (e.g. cutlery and glassware in a restaurant.
2. Depreciation per machine hour $= \dfrac{(£8,000 − £1,000)}{(8 \times 300 \times 5)}$

   $= 58.3p$

   Year 1: 58.3 × 2,200 = £1,283
   Year 2: 58.3 × 1,700 = £991
3. Cash tied up in sinking funds can normally be put to better use within the company itself.
4. Sole traders
5. Stocks of raw materials, stocks of work-in-progress, and stocks of finished goods.
6. The gross profit is split between that earned from manufacturing, and that earned from selling.

7.
Provision for Unrealised Profit Account

P&L a/c	33,000	Provision b/f	145,000
Provision c/d	112,000		
	145,000		145,000
		Provision b/d	112,000

(stock of finished goods is shown on the balance sheet at cost, £280,000)

8. A Receipts and Payments accounts fails to show assets, liabilities, surplus income or expenditure, accumulated funds, depreciation of assets etc.

9. A club doesn't have owners, so the concept of owners' capital is not applicable. 'Accumulated Funds' is the term substituted.

10.
Subscriptions

Subs owed b/f	360	Subs prepaid b/f	60
Income and	12,000	Cash (balancing figure)	11,970
Expenditure Account			
Subs prepaid c/d	90	Subs owed c/d	420
	12,450		12,450
Subs owed b/d	420	Subs prepaid	90

CHAPTER 5

(Missing figures only)

2. 27,783
3. 36,960
4. 50,083
6. 71,391
7. 10,206
8. 80,998
9. Suspense accounts are used where a trial Balance fails to agree, as a temporary resting place for the difference until the causes are found. They can also be used where there is some doubt about the correct treatment of a particular item, again as a temporary home prior to transfer to the correct account.
10. See text.

CHAPTER 6

1. See text.
2. Section 24 of the Partnership Act 1890 allows interest of 5% to be paid in such circumstances.
3.

Net Profit			45,000
Add interest on Drawings			
Adam		1,300	
Barker		2,500	3,800
			48,800
Less Salary to Barker			10,000
			38,800
Profit divisible			
Adam (3/5)		23,280	
Barker (2/5)		15,520	38,800

(Drawings not shown in the appropriation account)

4.
Partners' Current Accounts

	Adam	Barker		Adam	Barker
Opening balance		800	Opening balance	900	
Drawings	25,000	22,000	Share of profit	23,280	15,520
Interest on Drawings	1,300	2,500	Salary		10,000
Closing balance c/d		220	Closing balance c/d	2,120	
	26,300	25,520		26,300	25,520
Opening balance b/d	2,120		Opening balance b/d		220

5. See text.
6. DR Incoming partners' accounts CR Existing partners' accounts (DR 'New', CR 'Old')
7. See text.
8. Assets are debited to the Realisation Account

9. Individual partners will either pay in or draw out cash to close off their accounts.
10. If an individual partner is unable to pay off a debit balance on his or her account with the partnership, the loss is shared between the solvent partners in the proportions of their *capital* balances, not their profit or loss sharing ratios.

CHAPTER 7

1. In extreme cases, they might be expelled from their profession, or have to pay fines.
2. Going concern/Accruals/Consistency/Prudence.
3.

Widgets	12,000
Truckles	24,000
Farfles	18,000
	54,000

4. The *type* of stock is irrelevant to the decision on the pricing model, so the choice would be the one most likely to produce a 'true and fair' valuation.
5. This is in line with the prudence concept.
6. (a). Profit would be £100,000 higher.
   (b). Total net assets would be £100,000 higher.
7. Adjusting post balance sheet events are (2) and (5)
   Non-adjusting post balance sheet events are (1) and (3)
   (4) is not a post balance sheet event, as it falls outside the defined post balance sheet period.
8. As the contingent gain is *probable* but not *certain*, it cannot be accrued in the financial statements, but should be referred to in a note. Provision should be made for all legal costs.
9. An asset used by a lessee under a finance lease arrangement is treated as follows:
   A proportion of the total finance charge payable is written off to Profit and Loss account, the value of the leased asset is shown on the balance sheet as a fixed asset, and the liability for future rentals is shown as a liability on the balance sheet.
10. 'Substance over form'.

CHAPTER 8

1. The liability of shareholders to meet the company's debts in the event of liquidation is *limited* to the amount unpaid (if any) on their shareholdings.
2. Private limited companies are not allowed to offer their shares for sale to the public.
3. As a fixed percentage of the nominal value.
4. Debenture holders have lent money to the company, usually in return for some security. They are not shareholders, so the interest charged is an overhead expense reducing profits available for the shareholders. The shareholders receive part (an 'appropriation') of these profits in the form of a dividend.
5. Revenue (e.g.) P&L account, General Reserve
   Capital (e.g.) Share Premium Account, Capital Redemption Reserve, Revaluation Reserve
6. It is safer to be in a low geared company, as a lower proportion of profit is committed to paying interest or fixed dividends than a high geared company. Shareholders in the low geared company are more likely to receive *some* dividend, even when profits are low.
7. A greater proportion of profits must be paid out as interest or fixed dividends before the directors have any say in the matter of profit appropriation.
8. See text.
9. To aid comparability between companies, and to stop companies misleading the user by presenting information in an unusual way.
10. Eps is 'earnings per share'. It is one of the prime indicators of a company's performance used by stock market analysts. Companies who showed extraordinary profits or losses were able to distort their eps figure, as before FRS 3, extraordinary items were excluded from the calculation.

CHAPTER 9

1. Cash received from shareholder when applying for the shares, and cash received when the allotment monies are due.
2. None, as the shares are issued free. (Though there may be a relatively small amount of expense in connection with printing the share certificates and notifying the shareholders.)

3. The bank balance will increase by £360,000, less any expenses connected with the share issue.
4. The directors will use capital reserves (e.g. Share premium account) before using revenue reserves, as the former cannot be used for paying dividends, unlike the latter.
5. A share split, whereby the nominal value is reduced, with the number of shares increasing proportionately. The share price is also reduced, but the overall value of the company stays the same due to the greater number of shares in issue.
6. There is no statutory requirement for a debenture redemption account to be opened, but some companies might create one, on the grounds of prudence.
7. Premium = above nominal value
   Par = nominal value
   Discount = below market value
8. A company must have ordinary shares which are *not* redeemable, as well as having redeemable ordinary shares.
9. It will be shown as a liability on the balance sheet.
10. *Unrealised* means not arising through a sale to a third party outside the group. The adjustment is needed because 'real' profit can only be made by selling outside the group and not within it. So if stock has been transferred internally at a price above cost, the 'profit' element must be eliminated, to bring it back to the cost price to the group.

CHAPTER 10

1. Because, like 'funds flow' statements, they are based on historical data.
2. 'ORTIF'.
3. Cash received from customers; cash payments to suppliers; cash paid to and on behalf of employees; other cash payments.
4. To get to the cash flow from operations, any amounts charged or credited in the profit and loss which do not involve the movement of cash (such as depreciation) must be adjusted.
5. Outflows: Increase in debtors, decrease in creditors
   Inflows: Decrease in stocks
6. £16,000
7. £23,500
8. Outflow of £12,000 ([24,000 + 3,000 + 5,000] − 20,000)
9. Inflow of £3,000, proceeds of sale of fixed assets
10. Depreciation £5,000 (added to operating profit). Profit on sale of fixed asset £500 (deducted from operating profit)

CHAPTER 11

1.	A: 58.3%	B: 49.2%	C: 55.9%	D: 26.5%
2.	A: 119 days	B: 51 days	C: 309 days	D: 201 days
3.	A: 140%	B: 96.9%	C: 126.9%	D: 36%
4.	E: 3.1:1	F: 0.8:1	G: 11:1	H: 4.5:1
5.	E: 1.06:1	F: 0.6:1	G: 8:1	H: 2:1
6.	E: 16.7%	F: 15.8%	G: 60%	H: 25%

7. It may mean that too much is tied up in stocks or that credit control procedures are weak (customers not paying their debts). Also, it could mean that not enough is being invested in long term assets.
8. 16
9. If the dividend yield has increased, then the market price must have fallen during the year.
10. The depreciation adjustment shows the effect of depreciating on the basis of replacement costs rather than historic costs.

CHAPTER 12

1. a) Financial accounting: that part of accounting which covers the classification and recording of business transactions according to established principles and legal requirements.
   b) Management accounting: the provision of information to management for such purposes as the formulation of policies; planning and controlling activities; decision making.

    c) Elements of cost: the constituent parts of costs according to the factors upon which expenditure is incurred: materials, labour and expenses.

    d) Prime cost: the total of direct materials, direct labour, and direct expenses.

    e) Direct costs: those expenses which can be identified precisely as attaching to the product or process.

    f) Overheads: those costs which cannot be attributed directly to the product.

2. Planning, organisation, co-ordination, command, and control.

3. a) Strategic planning: the setting of long term objectives
Operational planning: how the overall objectives are to be met.

    b) Product cost: costs which relate to production e.g. direct materials.
Period costs: costs which relate to time e.g. rent, insurance.

    c) Cost centre: smallest unit of managerial control e.g. a single machine.
Service centre: a cost centre which provides a service to production e.g. canteen, safety.

4. Cost accounting is concerned with establishing budgets, standard costs and actual costs, with the analysis of variances. It provides the data upon which management accounting can formulate decisions.

5. a) Direct labour; b) total overhead cost; c) factory indirect material + factory indirect labour + factory indirect expenses; d) prime cost + production overhead; e) selling overhead + administrative overhead.

6. Business systems help the business to make sense of its environment by screening, processing and converting data into information.

7. a) Wood used in furniture making; b) wages of staff operating furniture making machines; c) royalties payable to the designer of the furniture.

8. a) Wages payable to the factory supervisors; b) cost of cleaning materials; c) cost of lighting and heating.

CHAPTER 13

1. a) Centralised buying and holding; b) centralised buying, decentralised holding; c) decentralised buying and holding.

2. a) Stock out costs; b) stockholding costs; c) production rates; d) procurement costs; e) costs of finance.

3. a) 220; b) 180; c) 550; d) 2,240.

4. a) 20; b) 90; c) 70.

5. a) T; b) F; c) F; d) T; e) T.

6. The perpetual method recalculates the stock valuation after each stock movement. The periodic method recalculates at the end of a period.

7. a) 13 @ £25 = £325; b) 8 @ £20 + 5 @ £21 = £265; c) 68 items available at a total cost of £1,580 gives an average cost of £23.235 per unit: closing stock of 13 items = 13 × £23.235 = £302.055.

8. Many stock items lose their identity in the stores, thus causing difficulties during times of changing price levels. LIFO, FIFO and AVCO are accounting methods which seek to address these problems.

9. The store ledger records physical receipts and issues, together with their monetary values.

10. a) The business uses materials at a constant rate; b) regular orders arrive at the moment when the previous delivery has been used up.

CHAPTER 14

1. a) Clock cards record the time workers arrive for and leave work. The hours actually worked and the pay due can thus be calculated; b) time sheets show what the worker was doing whilst at work; c) job tickets apply where each job has its own ticket, and the worker signs for the work done and the time spent; d) piece work tickets are used to record each job or batch worked on by the employee to enable wages to be calculated.

2. Time rates reward workers for the time spent at work. Piece rates reward workers for output achieved.

3. a) Time rates – offer no incentive to increase output; b) piece rates may encourage output at the expense of quality.
4. Standard hours $37 \times £4.40 = £162.80$. Five hours at $£5.50 = £27.5$. Six hours at $£6.60 = 39.60$. Total earnings $= £229.90$.
5.

	Time (hrs)				Pay (£)				
	Al'd	Took	Saved	Bonus	Basic	Bonus	Total	Rate/hour	Week
F	8	4	4	2	20.8	10.4	31.2	7.8	312
G	8	6	2	1	31.2	5.2	36.4	6.07	242.8
H	8	8	–	–	41.6	–	41.6	5.2	208

6.

Year	Ratio E:AV	Bonus Payable
19-3	72.5	6,000
19-4	75.71	—
19-5	74.4	13,500

7.

Company		A		B		C
Profit			300		400	600
Pref div		24		72		96
Ordy div		120		210		330
			144		282	426
Distributable profits			156		118	174
To profit sharing scheme			12.48		9.44	13.92

8. Advantage; reduce labour turnover by encouraging commitment to the business; disadvantage; profits may not be known until well after the period to which they relate.
9. a) Compensates employees for work done; b) increase output; c) reduce overheads; d) encourage efficiency; e) reduce labour turnover.

CHAPTER 15

1. a) Fixed overhead is a cost which is incurred for a period, and which within certain output and turnover limits tends to be unaffected by fluctuations in the levels of activity; rents, rates, insurance.
   b) A cost containing both fixed and variable components and which is thus partly affected by fluctuations in the levels of activity. Thus, any expense which has an element of a standing charge, plus a rate per unit of usage; electricity charges, gas, water.
   c) A cost which cannot be identified with a specific saleable cost unit, but which varies with the level of output; hours of factory supervisors; materials handling costs.
2. a) The charging of identifiable overheads to specific cost centres.
   b) The dividing of overhead costs to departments in proportion to the assumed benefits received.
   c) Overheads charged to produces or services by means of absorption rates.
3.

	Basis	Example
a	direct charges	water, steam, electricity, oil
b	direct labour hours	welfare, canteen
c	machine hours	capital intensive processes
d	wages paid	general method, best avoided
e	number of workers	lighting, timekeeping, welfare canteen
f	capital values	depreciation, fire insurance, rates
g	floor area	rent, security wages, fire prevention
h	technical estimates	electricity, steam, water, oil

4. a)

	PRODUCTION			SERVICE	
	A	B	C	G	H
Total overheads	10,000	8,000	4,000	2,000	1,000
G's o/h	800	500	400	—	300
Total	10,800	8,500	4,400	—	1 300
H's o/h	455	520	325	—	—
Total	11,255	9,020	4,725	—	—

b) OAR (£) 19.01   15.03   12.12
5. a) elimination method; b) continuous apportionment; c) simultaneous equation or algebraic method.

6.

	PRODUCTION			SERVICE	
	L	M	N	S	T
Total overheads	12 000	10 000	6 000	3 000	2 000
S's o/h	1 200	1 050	600	—	150
Total	13 200	11 050	6 600	—	2 150
T's o/h	645	430	860	(215)	—
Total	13 845	11 480	7 460	—	—

7. (S's) overheads = £3,216.075; (T's) overheads = £2,160.75.
8. Overheads are based upon estimates of costs and output, and on accounting conventions. Since we are dealing with estimates, notions of accuracy are misplaced.
9. The overhead adjustment account is used to record the over and under recovery of overheads during the period.

CHAPTER 16

1. a) Specific order costing: job, batch and contract costing. b) Operation costing: process costing, service costing.
2. Job costing is where work is done to a customer's specific requirements, and is of a short duration e.g. motor car repairs. Contract costing is similar, but is of a long duration e.g. ship building.
3. a) Retention monies; b) conservative/prudent estimation.
4. $(\frac{3}{4}[500,000 - 420,000]) \times 15\% = £9,000$
5. Specific order costing: jobs/products can be individually identified as cost centres. Process costing: output loses its individual character within the process, and the processes thus become the cost centres.
6. Because normal losses are regarded as part of the legitimate costs of production; they therefore appear in the process account itself.
7. a)

	COST ELEMENT			
	Materials	Labour	O'heads	Total
WIP eqiv units	375	325	200	
Finished items	7,000	7,000	7,000	
Total production	7,375	7,325	7,200	
Total cost (£)	13,275	8,790	10,080	32,145
Cost/unit (£)	1.8	1.2	1.4	4.4

b) Cost of 7,000 finished items = £30,800
Total cost less cost of finished items = £32,145 − £30,800 = £1,345. WIP value thus = £1,345.

8 a) Waste: output which has no recovery value. Scrap: output which does have recovery value
   b) By-product: a product of low value produced incidentally in the process of producing a main product. Joint product: two or more valuable products produced simultaneously from the same processes.
9. Market value; comparative price; standard price.
10. Market value; sales value of finished items; physical measurement.

CHAPTER 17

1. C; A; D; B.
2. a) T; b) T; c) F; d) T; e) F.
3. Marginal: closing stock = (£24,000/1,500) 300 = £4,800; profit = £25,800. Absorption: closing stock = (£39,000/1,500) 300 = £7,800; profit = £28,800.
4.

	£
Profit under marginal costing	25,800
Add difference in closing stock valuation	
(£7,800 − £4,800)	3,000
Profit under absorption costing	28,800

5. a) Contribution = sales value − marginal costs; b) contribution per unit = contribution/total sales (units); c) break-even point (units) fixed costs/contribution per unit; d) break-even point (£ sales) (fixed costs/contribution per unit) unit sales price; e) sales (£) for required profit = [(fixed cost + required profit) unit sales price]/contribution per unit.

CHAPTER 18

1. a) Issue instructions; b) provide information; c) receive and check departments' estimates; d) resolve difficulties; e) submit budgets to budget committee; f) prepare master budget.
2. a) Operating budget: has to do with day-to-day functions; b) capital budget: has to do with long term capital and cash; c) limiting factor: that factor which limits production or sales.
3. a) Closing stock at the end of June = 150 units; b) opening stock would need to be 250 units.
4. a) Helps to ensure sufficient cash is available; b) reveals likely cash shortages; c) reveals cash surpluses for investment.
5. a) Receipts schedule; b) payments schedule; c) cash budget summary.
6. a) Master budget: a summary of all operating budgets – takes the form of a budgeted set of final accounts; b) flexible budget; reflect impact upon costs of different levels of activity.
7. Overhead rates/hour (£)   £100; £80; £76.4; £74.4
8.

	JOB	
	X	Y
Materials	210.0	210.0
Labour	44.8	44.8
Overheads: 16 × £100	1,600.0	
16 × £76.4		1,222.4
Total	1,854.8	1,477.2

CHAPTER 19

1. a) The difference between planned and actual cost; b) where actual cost is greater than planned; c) where actual cost is less than planned; d) assumes that for most of the time, most of the activities are progressing as planned; effort can thus be spent on those issues where problems are arising; e) amount of work that can be done at a standard level of performance.
2. a) average expected; b) maximum possible; c) efficient working.
3. a) productivity ratio $= \dfrac{\text{Actual production (std hrs)}}{\text{Actual hours worked}} \times 100$

   b) production volume ratio $= \dfrac{\text{Actual production (std hrs)}}{\text{Budgeted production (std hrs)}} \times 100$

   c) capacity ratio $= \dfrac{\text{Actual hours worked}}{\text{Budgeted production (std hrs)}} \times 100$

4. a) $\dfrac{390}{420} \times 100 = 92.86\%$; b) $\dfrac{390}{400} \times 100 = 97.5\%$; c) $\dfrac{420}{400} \times 100 = 105\%$

5. a) Total variance = (Std price × std usage = £192) − (Act price × act usage = £202.8) = £10.8 adverse; b) price variance = (£2.40 − £2.60) × 78 = £15.6 adverse; c) usage variance = (80 − 78) × £2.40 = £4.80 favourable.

6. Standard variable overhead rate $= \dfrac{£420,000}{6,000} = £70$

   Standard fixed overhead rate $= \dfrac{£300,000}{6,000} = £50$

   Std hours to produce one unit $= \dfrac{6,000}{250} = 24$

   Total variable overhead variance: (Actual overhead = £435,000) − (Budgeted overhead for actual production = 270 × 24 × £70 = £453,600) = £18,600 favourable. Expenditure variance: (Actual volume × Variable overhead rate) − Actual variable overhead = (7,000 × £70) − £435,000 = £55,000 favourable. Efficiency variance: (Standard input volume − Actual input volume) × Standard variable overhead rate = (270 × 24 − 7,000) × £70 = £36,400 favourable. Total fixed overhead variance: (Actual

overhead = £290,000) − (Fixed overhead allocated to production =
270 × 24 × £50 = £324,000) = £34,000 favourable. Expenditure variance: (Budgeted overhead = £300,000) − (Actual overhead = £290,000) = £10,000 favourable. Volume variance:
(Actual quantity of work done − Standard quantity of work done) × Standard fixed overhead
rate = (270 × 24 − 6,000) × £50 = £24,000 favourable.

CHAPTER 20

1. a) £200; b) £210.
2. Invested at 5 per cent half-yearly: £2,000 + 5% = £2,100; £2,100 + 5% = £2,205. Invested at 10 per cent per annum = £2,000 + 10% = £2,200.
3. Compound amount of £1: 1.061; 1.407; 2.159; 3.497; 7.138. Totals: 20.159; 30.954; 92.837; 601.484; 2,469.748.
4. a) To do with the paying and receiving of interest; b) calculating the present value of a future income stream; c) deducting the original cost of a project from the total of its discounted income stream; d) that discount rate which gives an NPV of zero.
5. PV of £1: 0.863; 0.627; 0.422; 0.163; 0.099. PV of amount: 20.712; 42.009; 38.824; 23.798; 31.185.
6. Discount at 6 per cent;

	Net cash flows (£)	Discount factor	PV (£)
Year 0	(20,000)	1.0	(20,000)
1	6,800	0.926	6,296.8
2	8,500	0.857	7,284.5
3	8,100	0.794	6,431.4
NPV			12.7

7.

	EXE Ltd (£)	WYE Ltd (£)
20 per cent return on capital	160,000	160,000
Less debenture interest		36,000
		124,000
Less corporation tax at 30%	48,000	37,200
Available to ordinary shares	112,000	86,600
Rate of return per share	14%	17.36%

8. a) 6.4; b) 7.0; c) 7.2; d) 7.0%.
9.

	L Prop	L Rate	L P×R	M Prop	M Rate	M P×R	N Prop	N Rate	N P×R
Ordy	10	16	160	6	16	96	5	16	80
Pref				4	14	56	1	14	14
Deb							4	6	24
Total			160			152			118
Cost capital			16%			15.2%			11.8%

INDEX